ADVANCED COMPUTER DESIGN

J. K. ILIFFE

Queen Mary College
University of London

Prentice/Hall International

London   Englewood Cliffs, New Jersey   New Delhi
Singapore   Sydney   Tokyo   Toronto   Wellington

Library of Congress Cataloging in Publication Data

Iliffe, J. K.
  Advanced computer design.

  Bibliography: p.
  Includes index.
  1. System design   2. Electronic digital
computers — Programming.   3. Programming languages
(Electronic computers)   I. Title.
QA76.9.S88I47   621.3819'5   81-5877
ISBN 0-13-011254-2   AACR2

British Library Cataloging in Publication Data

Iliffe, J. K.
  Advanced computer design.
  1. Electronic digital computers — Design and
  construction
  I. Title
  621.3819'582   TK7888.3

  ISBN 0-13-011254-2

ISBN 0-13-011254-2

PRENTICE-HALL INTERNATIONAL, INC., *London*
PRENTICE-HALL OF AUSTRALIA PTY., LTD., *Sydney*
PRENTICE-HALL CANADA INC., *Toronto*
PRENTICE-HALL OF INDIA PRIVATE LIMITED, *New Delhi*
PRENTICE-HALL OF JAPAN, INC., *Tokyo*
PRENTICE-HALL OF SOUTHEAST ASIA PTE., LTD., *Singapore*
PRENTICE-HALL, INC., *Englewood Cliffs, New Jersey*
WHITEHALL BOOKS LIMITED, *Wellington, New Zealand*

Printed in the United States of America

10 9 8 7 6 5 4 3 2 1

CONTENTS

Preface   **vii**

1   **BACKGROUND AND NOTATION**   **1**

   1.1   Formal grammars   8
   1.2   Machine states   10
   1.3   Register transfers   11
   1.4   Sequencing rules   13
   1.5   Assignment and addressing rules   15
   1.6   Terminology   18
   1.7   Further reading   19

PART 1   INTERPRETIVE MACHINES   **21**

Foreword to Part 1   22

2   **INTERPRETERS**   **23**

   2.1   Interpreting PDP-11 instructions   24
   2.2   Interpreting ICL 1900 instructions   32
   2.3   Aims of interpretation   35

3   **MICROPROGRAMMABLE MACHINES**   **39**

   3.1   Design principles   40
   3.2   Generalized host machines   54
   3.3   Further reading   62

4   **PREPACKAGED MICROMACHINES**   **63**

   4.1   The ALU slice: AM2901   68
   4.2   The control device: AM2910   71
   4.3   Microinstruction formats   72
   4.4   Microprogramming exercises   79
   4.5   Further reading   81

iii

5 DIRECT EXECUTION OF LANGUAGES 82

5.1 Expression evaluation 85
5.2 Data access paths 90
5.3 Requirements of the SIL 95
5.4 Further reading 97

6 CASE STUDIES: FORTRAN, COBOL AND VCS 98

6.1 Fortran target code 99
6.2 Cobol target code 105
6.3 An example of a SIL: the Variable Computer System 114
6.4 Further reading 121

7 MICROSYSTEM DESIGN 122

7.1 The effect on language parameters 124
7.2 Microsystem problems 126
7.3 Tactical responses 128
7.4 Future developments 131
7.5 Questions and further reading on Part 1 134

PART 2 COMPUTING IN STORE 139

Foreword to Part 2 140

8 HIGH-SPEED DATA 141

8.1 The FPS AP-120B array processor 146
8.2 The CRAY-1 computer 151
8.3 Case study: Illiac-IV 157
8.4 Active Memory Arrays 162
8.5 Theory versus practice 166
8.6 Further reading 170

9 ACTIVE MEMORY OPERATIONS 172

9.1 AMA register transfer notation 174
9.2 Processing element structure 182
9.3 Arithmetic and logic subroutines 182
9.4 Routing subroutines 189
9.5 Counting the cost 194
9.6 Exercises 197

10 PARALLEL PROCEDURES 200

10.1 Bit-serial algorithms 203
10.2 Parallel sorting 207
10.3 Matrix operations 217
10.4 Further reading 222

11   **IMAGE ENHANCEMENT FUNCTIONS   225**

11.1   Area functions   228
11.2   Line functions   232
11.3   Coordinate representation   235
11.4   Image processor design   236
11.5   Further reading   241

12   **ICL DISTRIBUTED ARRAY PROCESSOR   243**

12.1   Basic DAP operations   245
12.2   Parallel Fourier transform   249
12.3   DAP Fortran   254
12.4   Control overheads   263
12.5   DAP developments   266

13   **ACTIVE MEMORY IN COMPUTER DESIGN   267**

13.1   Store management   270
13.2   Index management   276
13.3   External connections   279
13.4   Further developments   281
13.5   Questions and further reading on Part 2   283

PART 3   ABSTRACTION   289
Foreword to Part 3   290

14   **THE IMPORTANCE OF STRUCTURE   291**

14.1   Access lists   295
14.2   Abstraction mechanisms   300
14.3   Compile-time abstraction   302
14.4   Further reading   311

15   **CASE STUDIES: CM*, PP250, CAP   314**

15.1   CM*   316
15.2   Plessey PP250   321
15.3   CAP   334
15.4   Further reading   339

16   **THE BASIC LANGUAGE MACHINE   340**

16.1   Operating environment   344
16.2   Process state vectors   347
16.3   Tag-dependent machine instructions   349
16.4   The end of the experiment   354
16.5   Further reading   360

17 IBM SYSTEM/38   363

17.1 What the user sees   365
17.2 Authorization   370
17.3 Process activity   373
17.4 Micromachine support   374
17.5 Further reading   378

18 POINTER-NUMBER MACHINES   379

18.1 Workspaces   381
18.2 MicroPN: schematic   388
18.3 Microsystem functions   393
18.4 Data abstraction example   400

19 ABSTRACTION IN SYSTEM DESIGN   410

19.1 Physical partitions   413
19.2 Levels of control   415
19.3 Summing up   417
19.4 Questions and further reading on Part 3   420

APPENDICES   425

1 Programming in *P*   427

Outline of a module   428
Expressions   431
Assignment   434
Control statements   436
Procedure and module interfacing   437
Kernel functions   441
Array statements   441
Syntax of control modules   441

2 Solutions to selected exercises   445

3 References   450

Index   465

PREFACE

This book explores three topics that are likely to be dominant in computer design for the foreseeable future, namely: (1) the encoding and execution of problem-oriented or high-level programming languages; (2) the provision of high-speed operations on numeric and non-numeric data; and (3) the reduction and containment of programming costs. The choice of topics is discussed in the introductory chapter, which also explains notations used in all sections.

There follow three sets of chapters in the order given above, each of the same pattern: a statement of requirements and general discussion of the technologies at our disposal; case studies drawn from product line or research laboratory to illustrate practical applications; and further general comment on problems to be solved, possible future developments, and suggestions for study. Where appropriate, "drill" exercises (and solutions) are included in the text.

The sets of chapters are to a large extent independent of one another and can be read in any order. However, in looking to the future it seems that for the preferred techniques to emerge in each area support is needed from the other two. The best way to illustrate such interactions is to give a worked example which takes the form of a computer specification, outlined in the final chapters and bringing together many of the concepts introduced earlier. For some years I have used this machine in simulated form to take the undeserved mystery out of programming for "array", "capability" and "tagged" machines. I hope that studying the examples given will enable the reader first to understand in some depth what is going on and then to see ways of making improvement.

To follow the discussion, knowledge is required of at least one machine at "register" level, of the storage structures commonly used to represent numeric and non-numeric data, and of elementary compiling techniques.

Most students of computer systems or engineering will be so prepared before their final undergraduate year, though perhaps it is fair to draw a distinction between *following the argument* and *seeing the point*: there is only space here to describe what appear to be the most promising engineering techniques and I would strongly recommend the reader who has not already done so to gain experience of operating systems, compiler construction or microprogramming techniques as commonly practised in general-purpose system design. Without such background some of the implied comparisons will have to be taken on trust.

The organization of the text is as follows.

Chapter 1 identifies the objectives of computer design and the major disciplines that contribute to the final product. A notation is introduced for describing elementary state transitions in a programmed machine. The notation is elaborated in later chapters and summarized in the Appendix.

Part 1 (Chapters 2 – 7) describes the principles of *Interpretive Machines*. The characteristics of interpretive control are introduced, and it is shown how specialized machines have evolved to meet the demands of emulation. One of the industry-standard microprogram instruction sets is used to illustrate techniques in common use. The effect of choosing an instruction set to reflect high-level constructs is examined in general and with reference to specific language implementations. The implications of variable instruction sets are examined in terms of system and hardware support. Finally, the problems of microsystem design are reviewed and some feasible system models are outlined.

Part 2 (Chapters 8 – 13) turns attention to high-speed computing, and begins with a summary of some vector and array architectures. The view of memory as an "active" component of a computer is developed, arguing that because one of the tightest bottlenecks in a fast computer is the channel from memory to processing units it is sensible to move some of the computing power into the memory itself — hence the title *Computing in Store*. The concept of an "active memory array" is introduced and it is shown how such an array can be programmed and applied to practical problems. Emphasis is placed on using parallel logic and arithmetic functions in support of conventional workloads, and on developing the ability to "think in parallel".

Part 3 (Chapters 14 – 19) deals with *Abstraction* and the related ideas of protection, authorization, modularity, access lists and "object-oriented" programming. The requirement for a refined protection mechanism is developed from first principles and some criteria for acceptable solutions are suggested. A number of designs offering capability management facilities are examined and assessed. The reasons for using tagged registers and memory cells are discussed. A processor offering protection at the micromachine level of Part 1 is decribed, and it is shown how such a design contributes to the solution of problems encountered in microsystem and array processor design.

For the purpose of graduate teaching, the text can be used selectively as the basis of a one-semester course. The early chapters in each Part cover material often found in undergraduate courses, though the emphasis on goals is vital: the biggest problem of computer design is knowing what to leave out. That has always been the case, and pressures from below to get out of difficulty with an LSI circuit here (and another one there, . . .) are impossible to resist unless there is a clear performance, cost, or end-user objective.

For undergraduate teaching, in which much of the material is probably being encountered for the first time, to cover the ground satisfactorily takes two semesters. For a single-semester course it is recommended to omit one Part entirely.

The course contents have evolved over the last three years of teaching at London University to a mixture of computer systems and electrical engineering students. It is a pleasure to acknowledge my debt to those whose reactions have helped to sharpen the presentation, including students at Syracuse, Rice and Stanford Universities, who saw the text in embryo form. I would particularly like to thank Professor D.J. Howarth for careful review of the entire manuscript. Many others have found time to read sections of the script and point out errors, omissions and obscurities. For the difficulties that remain, I must share the blame with the subject matter.

As far as possible, use is made of realistic examples of machine and program design. Nevertheless, I have had to be extremely selective to bring out the relevant technical points. I take responsibility for any distortion that results, and refer the reader to published material in all cases for fuller descriptions. I wish to thank Advanced Micro Devices, Cray Research, Floating Point Systems, IBM, ICL and Plessey for permission to adapt material from copyright publications. The four drawings by Norman Thelwell appear in *Thelwell Country* and are reproduced with permission of Eyre Methuen on behalf of the author. They appear on pp. 21, 139, 289 and 425.

Last but not least, I would like to record my appreciation of the congenial working environment provided by Professor G.F. Coulouris and colleagues at the Computer Systems Laboratory, Queen Mary College, University of London, during the preparation of the text.

J.K.I.

1 BACKGROUND AND NOTATION

In recent years the electronic component cost of typical computer systems has fallen to under 10% of price, or less than 5% of "lifetime" budget. Why then bring engineering discipline to bear where on good authority we shall soon be using microprocessors "by the bucketful", and where many a data-processing manager can echo the famous cry from the scrummage: "Forget the ball, let's get on with the game"? The truth is that almost all aspects of computing are affected by the underlying engines and although our data-processing manager might wish to be seen as a hardened rugby player a number of more accurate parallels could be drawn, including that of the fairy-tale Princess, unable to rest because of the pea under endless layers of software. In this chapter we shall see how some of those far-reaching effects occur, at the same time outlining a frame of reference and introducing notations to be used later.

The conventional subdivisions of computer design are:

(1) *circuit specification,* which is essentially the province of device manufacturers who offer the familiar ranges of industry-standard packages and, if the inducement is high enough, some non-standard ones as well;
(2) *subsystem* and *mechanical engineering* leading to hardware modules with highly specialized function, electronic or otherwise, e.g. stores, power supplies, switches, cooling systems, arithmetic units, device controllers, etc., some of which might be product-line items;
(3) *sequential machine design* in which the states assumed by an assembly of modules are controlled by program, either implicit in logic design or explicitly stored in "control memory";
(4) *architectural specification* leading firstly to an idealized picture of the computer system and then to a precise characterization of its behavior under all conditions, including start-up, shut-down and error states;
(5) *operating rules* including language, database and job-control functions;
(6) *library* and *application* packages.

The reader will recognize that (1) is the scene of the revolution in large-scale integrated circuits, with excursions into (2) and (3) in the shape of microprocessors; that (2) − (4) are the conventional province of computer system manufacturers; and that the graduation from (4) to (6) is mainly a matter of packaging, though for various technical reasons there is not always complete freedom of choice. In the earliest computers design was considered complete when the workings of processor, store and input − output operations were finalized, roughly corresponding to level (3) or to current microprocessor design. Later it became necessary to provide for the enlargement and interchange of hardware modules, hence the system specification included standard interfaces embodying generalized notions of store, peripheral channel and instruction set (as pioneered, for example, in the IBM 360 architecture in 1964). In recent years it has been common practise to compare computers in terms of the languages and data structures supported, their efficiency in database access, response, reliability and security, so much so that in sophisticated circles the central processor and store themselves are often dismissed, as I have just indicated, as irrelevant "give-away" components. If that is true, the bell tolls for computer design (and designers).

Indeed, the most likely unfolding of events in the next few years is that single-chip devices, currently approaching 100 000 logical devices in context, will reach a point at which processors comparable with mid-range computers of today can be made automatically for, say, one-tenth of present costs. That is a staggering prospect, and one that will have immense impact in situations where hardware costs have hitherto been prohibitive. On the other hand, the design and manufacturing processes involved in producing complex integrated circuits are such as to force the semiconductor manufacturers to follow extremely conservative lines: the devices on offer are likely to be aimed at a mass market slightly off-center of mainframe computer development and some years behind it in architectural refinement. Consequently, where software and operating costs are already high, or when the computer is delivered as part of a substantial applications package, the microprocessor revolution might well be greeted with less than the usual enthusiasm.

In the following chapters we shall be concerned mainly with the design of computers to support advanced system applications in which microprocessors have, literally, only a peripheral part to play. One of the arguments for change is based on restructuring the design activity from levels (2) − (5) with a view to cutting the cost of the final system. The second argument is best conducted at the "user interface" presented at level (6). Investment in Fortran and Cobol code, assembler and job-control macros, file structures and procedures associated with computer operation are often cited as barriers to change. On the other hand the assumptions, variously expressed, that improvements at circuit level will save the day, that the pattern of computer use is static, that the educational process of reducing people to level (5) is permanent and cost-effective, could have equally weighty consequences. In trying to reach a balance between the conflicting forces, one cannot help suggesting that computer design did not reach its peak in the early 1960s. True, there have not been many improvements since then, but the agencies that might have brought them about have been distracted by the silicon chip.

To be brief, it must be assumed that the reader lends an eye to the proposition that computer design is capable of evolving. We shall also assume that he or she recognizes the design activities outlined above and sees the necessity of a carefully organized hierarchy in getting anything to work, and the consequent penalty in performance. For example, a simple addition might take 50 ns at the circuit interface but 5 μs as seen by the user, the 100:1 ratio being accounted for by the series of structural decisions entailed in safely handling the function and its operands. Anyone familiar with the industry will also appreciate the considerable investment in material and personnel at each stage of design and might conclude that a course on "advanced design" should be similarly structured. I have chosen not to do so because of the pressures for change exerted at both ends of the spectrum — one of the suggestions of later chapters is that levels (3) and (4) will coalesce — and because it is impossible to pin the subject down without relying heavily on particular products and manufacturers' styles. That is one example of how low-level decisions show through on the outside. Let us examine some of the others.

In language design it is often remarked that a visitor from space would discern the outline of an IBM 704 from the specification and usage of the main programming languages. Nevertheless, in terms of control and arithmetic primitives many architectural features have been concealed successfully at level (5). A characteristic of most languages is the ability to associate each variable with a particular class of objects, knowing in advance that it will only take values in that class and enabling relevant decisions about storage and operators to be taken at "compile time". The benefit of such a feature is that it "increases efficiency", though how important that is in relation to the ratio just mentioned is an open question. It also recognizes programming errors in advance of computation, though whether it does so at the expense of fluency or clarity is another matter for debate. The point is that early machines' inability to recognize type or to make dynamic adjustments in storage no longer applies to the same extent and might well be overshadowed by other considerations, yet the ability to apply structural checks prior to execution is still regarded as an end in itself by many language designers. In that sense a supposed internal characteristic of the computer has a visible external effect.

One type of datum that cannot conveniently be constrained in advance is the user's job or transaction step. Dealing with such operands requires new types of language and support systems, and our data-processing manager is likely to employ specialists in "job control" or "transaction processing" to fill the gap. Now we cannot expect to make such experts redundant overnight, but it can be argued that the amount of training they need is a direct consequence of the mismatch between computer use and computer design, and that is seen in practical terms as scarcity of trained staff, delay and disappointment in the final product. Perhaps the situation can be summed up by noting that the difficulty of understanding and using computers has deepseated causes, and that the expertise developed to disguise their limitations is unlikely to help in removing them (in fact it has a very conservative influence). To be somewhat cynical, the most one can hope for from expert teams of hardware and software designers is that they will not put too much impediment between those who know what they are doing (the circuit engineers) and those who know what they want (the users).

Some hints on the choice of topics have already been given. They follow from trying to live up to two remote-sounding but extremely important principles:

(1) *that the subject matter of computation is not data in storage cells but various classes of abstract objects which must be consistently and accurately manipulated;*

(2) *that the main performance parameters are to be based not on instruction-execution rates but on time and space taken to carry out the admissible operations on abstract objects in precisely controlled contexts.*

My experience is that (1) subsumes all attempts to reduce and contain programming errors by partitioning, protection mechanisms, language design, segmentation, etc., and it forms the basis of Chapters 14 – 19. Similarly, (2) turns attention to high-level language operations, though the issues are somewhat broader than current languages might suggest. They form the subject of Chapters 2 – 7, which address the problem of how to get from the user interface to the circuit level more economically than with the present design hierarchy. The remaining chapters discuss high-speed data processing from a specialized viewpoint and might seem out of place in the present context. The approach can be dismissed fairly easily as "computing with square words" but I take it for two reasons. Firstly, high performance remains the one currency that can be traded for less tangible benefits, so there is good reason to start the design process with substantial capital in hand. In particular, we shall see how "planar" functions benefit both (1) and (2); moreover, they appear to achieve high performance in a uniquely flexible and economical way, well suited to circuit technology. Secondly, the machine design that is presented offers a fresh approach to problem analysis and description, sufficiently novel to be of educational value in its own right.

Some candidate topics not discussed explicitly are: microprocessors and large-scale integrated circuits, database management, distributed systems, communications. I hope that their essential requirements have been sufficiently recognized in the discussion. For example, databases put a high premium on security, process synchronization, indexing and searching operations, and they are treated individually. The impact of LSI at the circuit level needs no elaboration. The stress on meeting hardware requirements with relatively simple functional units that can be replicated to achieve performance goals is not particularly new. The use of microprocessors to control peripherals, visual displays, telecommunication lines, etc., is implicit in what follows. There is no point in adding to the extensive literature on that subject. With regard to distributed systems, a distinction can be drawn between those with distributed file space, which already exist, and those with distributed programs, which are still at an experimental stage. Both reinforce trends already acknowledged and discussed separately in the text. The computer specification presented in later chapters is of the second type.

One topic that is understated is the assurance of correct function at and below the architectural level. Techniques for fault-avoidance or fault-tolerance are an integral part of the design process that are growing in importance as computers permeate everyday life. In some ways a computer adrift in society is even less accessible for maintenance than one adrift in space, and the need for self-test, diagnosis and reconfiguration is often just as great. It seems probable that many of the disciplines developed to assure spacecraft and satellite reliability will influence the design of earthbound computers, and I regret that they do not figure prominently in the discussion. The best excuse I can offer is that the major contribution a designer can make to reliability is to achieve the required function in as *simple* a way as possible, and that will be a recurring theme in the following chapters. (In contrast, most system manufacturers pride themselves on investment in management disciplines, in the shape of design automation, product testing, quality assurance, project evaluation and review, and appear less concerned by mounting complexity of the final products.)

To explain the choice of topics in more practical terms I shall suggest some models to bear in mind. The primary goal of computer design is to achieve the highest performance at the user interface for a given cost. In talking of languages we shall measure "performance" by counting the operations of an elementary register transfer machine and "cost" by the stored program needed to invoke them. They are, of course, only relative measures, allowing different techniques to be compared. In absolute terms we must add the substantial indirect contribution from design, development, enhancement and other factors mentioned earlier, and however successful our attempts to contain them it will remain the case that indirect costs must be distributed over the broadest possible spectrum of applications. From

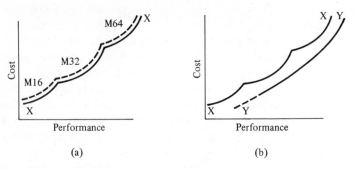

Fig. 1.1 Cost–performance envelopes: (a) multimodel; (b) multicomputer

that point of view we redefine the goal to be to achieve the highest performance across the widest *range* of costs, taking account of direct (operating system) and indirect overheads.

It is unusual to measure performance by counting register transfer operations. In range design as currently practised they are by no means elementary and changing their rate of execution is one of the main techniques used to vary performance. Figure 1.1(a) shows the cost – performance envelope that might result from using hypothetical processors with 16-, 32- and 64-bit data paths. Variations within each model are restricted to add-on functions (e.g. for scientific calculation) and to a limited degree of multi-processing, but, whatever its original merit, recent developments point away from this "multimodel" range concept and the associated idea of centralized system structure. In particular: automation techniques favor the low end of the spectrum; the supposition that elaborate instruction repertoires achieve the highest statement execution rates has been called into question by variable-microprogram machines; and the standardization of software function has made it feasible to detach significant tasks (such as database access and terminal control) from mainstream processing.

Taken together (and it is difficult to take them apart) the above developments appear to suggest a system model consisting of a number of relatively simple semi-autonomous computers, wherein variations in performance (statements/second), capacity (Mbytes of program space) and I – O handling rates will be achieved solely by changing the number of computer modules (Fig. 1.2). They will communicate with one another fairly infrequently, it is hoped, using shared physical connections, but the proof of the pudding will be in the range of performance one can achieve simply by adding "processor-memory" units to the communication system. If successful, one would expect an envelope such as YY in Fig. 1.1(b) to be nearly linear and everywhere better than XX for the same type of work. I hasten to add that I cannot point

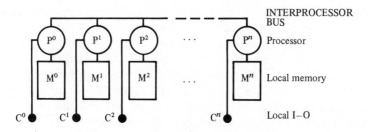

Fig. 1.2　Multicomputer system model

to a general-purpose system with such characteristics, and offer it only as a backdrop to explain why many of the inherited assumptions of system design, such as the level of instruction set, memory and $I - O$ bandwidth, operating system support, compiling technique, etc., need to be re-examined. In particular, it focusses on elementary register transfer operations as measures of machine activity.

Our attention is thus drawn to the design of processor – memory pairs that carry out their own tasks efficiently while contributing to the operation of the assembly. Efficient processing generally means cheaply presenting the right data at the right time, a pursuit which results in the familiar storage hierarchy, that is,

registers (bistable electronic devices with access times comparable with micro-orders of the processor);
control and *scratchpad* memory (semiconductor stores with access times comparable with microinstruction rates);
program space (e.g. main memory); and
database (e.g. mass storage devices with high latency and serial access modes).

The amount of store at each level is inversely proportional to its speed (and cost) so we can think of the store system as a pyramid whose top is being transformed by processing devices (Fig. 1.3). More generally, we can regard

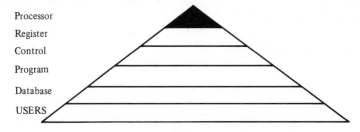

Fig. 1.3　The store hierarchy

each level as being processed by the combination of active devices and stores above it; the hierarchy is then designed to support the highest performance at the base of the pyramid, where it meets the outside world, with the minimum investment in main memory, control, scratchpad, registers and processor logic. Though the problem is unchanged, the new system model (Fig. 1.2) causes us to look for new solutions, particularly when control memory content changes frequently or when programs are distributed across the assembly. In particular, the store hierarchy model serves to emphasize the importance of moving data vertically between levels rather than from side to side, which is the burden of distributed systems. In the context so defined the first set of chapters will be seen to be concerned with encoding control information to minimize the *amount* of data to be transmitted; the second attempts to increase the *rate* at which data are presented to and consumed by the processing units; and the third, though dealing principally with the logical programming environment, can also be used to ensure the *relevance* of information occupying the fastest levels of store, and hence to maximize their effect. However, all attempts to streamline that simple picture of information flow must be conditioned by the overriding system objectives mentioned earlier: a widely applicable architectural definition, precisely engineered software environments, and performance measured in meaningful high-level terms.

In order to explain the principles of machine operation, we make use of a notation expressing elementary arithmetic and logical operations and data transfers. One of the main considerations is that a single operator in the description should approximate to a single operational cycle of a hypothetical processor, which we use with suitable reservations to measure performance. It follows that the notation is low-level in the semantic sense — we cannot follow the conventions of standard high-level programming languages and allow implied address calculation or field selection, for example, or elaborate change of context in calling a procedure. On the other hand we can choose the syntax to help write and understand short sections of program more easily than using an assembly code. The following paragraphs introduce the notation common to all sections. It will be extended and refined as required to describe special machine actions.

1.1 FORMAL GRAMMARS

A formal grammar describes the set of sentences that can be taken to constitute a "language", devoid of any notion of meaning. The method of definition is to give the various forms a sentence might take, inventing new names for the component phrases, then to define the new components, and so on until all possible variants have been described. Many programmers meet such a definition when learning about Algol or one of its relatives, which are described using the "Backus normal form" of syntax (BNF) or a close derivative. In the present context a "sentence" is taken to be a section of program text, or more exactly a *program module* as defined in later chapters.

Most grammars take special precautions to distinguish between *terminal strings*, i.e. identifiers or operator signs that are expected to occur in the source text, and *non-terminals* which are the names of phrases defined elsewhere in the grammar (in corner brackets such as ⟨*term*⟩ in BNF). In the notation we shall use no formal distinction is made: the decision rests simply on whether a defining phrase occurs. The component parts of a phrase definition are joined by the symbol ∘, e.g.

> *relation*:   *simplex* ∘ *relop* ∘ *simplex*

which defines *relation* as a *simplex* followed by a *relop* then a *simplex*. If there are two or more alternative definitions of a phrase they are written out one after the other, separated by spaces or newlines (where BNF uses a vertical bar) thus *relop* might have six forms:

> *relop*:   < =   =   > =   < >   <   >

A grammar can be shortened considerably if optional or repeated occurrences of a term are specially treated. Here as in many other grammars a postfix "?" is used to mark an optional term and "*" to indicate repetition. Thus if Ψ is any terminal or non-terminal:

Ψ?   specifies an optional occurrence of Ψ
Ψ*   specifies (indefinitely) repeated occurrences
Ψ?* and Ψ*?   indicate that zero or more occurrences will be accepted.

It can be seen that the colon, question mark and asterisk play a special part in defining the grammar, consequently a trick has to be played to bring them in as part of terminal strings. For the time being we shall simply name the characters, which usually occur singly, as *colon, query, star*.

For example, *simplex*, which stands for "simple expression" might be defined by:

> *simplex*:   *adop*? ∘ *primary* ∘ *bop**?
> *adop*:   +   −
> *binop*:   +   −   *star*   /
> *primary*:   *number*   (∘ *simplex* ∘)   *ident* ∘ *parlist*?
> *bop*:   *binop* ∘ *primary*

which would include the following instances of *simplex*:

> *number*
> − *number* * (*number* + *ident*)
> *ident parlist* / *number*

Note that *number, ident* and *parlist* are treated as terminals here, but the grammar could be extended later by adding phrase definitions. That is no more than the classic principle of top-down design applied to syntax. In giving examples, comments and display codes will be interpolated when appropriate at points marked by ''○'' in the defining phrases. In computer printout, comments are bracketed as in /* ... */.

1.2 MACHINE STATES

Although high-level languages can disguise the fact, all machine operations center on the manipulation of a small set of (fast) registers. Such registers will be declared in the heading of each program text, indicating by comment how they will be used. Formally:

> *program*:   *heading*○*programsection*
> *heading*:   *REGS*○[○*ident**○]

where each *ident* will henceforth be taken to be an alphanumeric string, the first symbol being alphabetic. In later chapters, *heading* will be expanded to give more information about the program environment.

We shall distinguish two types of register value: numeric and pointer. Initially the distinction will be quite informal, in the sense that it will be implied by the way the registers are used rather than by the coding of their contents. In most examples the type will be indicated by comment in the heading and will be unchanged during the execution of the program. In Chapter 9 onwards the distinction between pointers and numbers will be hardened to achieve special architectural effects and it will be necessary to assume that each register contains a tag indicating the type of value it contains. Numeric values are 16-bit and the arithmetic is 2s complement unless stated otherwise. Pointers refer to **sequences** of values in the program store and therefore contain location numbers. The sequences so addressed are usually *numeric* but may be *control* (i.e. instruction strings) or *mixtures* of pointers and numbers. The type of sequence can vary dynamically, but here again we shall mostly use static structures. Given a pointer to data we can deduce the length of sequence it refers to by enquiring its *limit* value. The length is then 1 + *limit*. In the simplest representation the pointer itself contains type and limit fields, while in very raw machines the limit might be implied by the size of store. There are many intermediate conventions of importance.

Example 1.1   Suppose a section of program is to work on two sequences of integers identified by the pointers *text* and *grammar*, updating a counter c and using three working registers $x, y,$ and z. Then the heading would take the form:

REGS [*text* | Source text pointer
        grammar | Pointer to grammar
        c | Counter
        x y z] | Temporary numerics

Application of the sequencing rules depends on the contents of registers (such as the stack and control pointers) which are concealed from the program simply by being unnamed. They are, however, an 'implied part of the machine state and will need to be described in detail when particular machine organizations are proposed. (In some machines the control registers are named, so a control transfer can result from a register move operation, but such artefacts are avoided here.)

In addition to the registers we assume there exists a set of *condition codes*: a fixed group of status bits implicitly set by arithmetic and logical operations and tested by conditional statements. The result of any such operation sets the conditions as follows:

(a)   zero (*ZE*) or non-zero (*NZ*);
(b)   non-negative (*GE*) or negative (*LT*);
(c)   non-positive (*LE*) or positive (*GT*);
(d)   arithmetic overflow (*OV*) or not (*NV*);
(e)   arithmetic carry (*CA*) or not (*NC*).

In addition, it is often required to know whether the result of operating on a pointer is still a valid address (i.e. within the bounds implied by the original), which leads to the tests:

(f)   valid address (*VA*) or invalid (*IA*).

At any instant the **machine state** is the content of the registers, the condition codes and those regions of memory accessible by operating on pointers using the addressing rule (see below).

1.3 REGISTER TRANSFERS

In general, operations on registers are expressed in the form of an assignment:

    ident° = °*simplex*

where *ident* is a declared register and *simplex* is an expression whose value will be stored in *ident*. Within an expression the operands are either (the contents of) registers or literal values. The operator signs are as shown in

Table 1.1   Register transfer operations

Symbol	Effect
+	Integer add
−	Integer subtract or (unary) negate
|	Logical "or"
&	Logical "and"
≪	Logical left shift
≫	Arithmetic right shift
%	Logical "exclusive or"
mask	Field select (see text)

Table 1.1. Except as dictated by parentheses, expressions are evaluated from left to right, the last operator (if any) setting condition codes. Unary minus is recognized but does not change condition indicators. Literal values are expressed in decimal, hexadecimal (preceded by "$") or octal form (preceded by "0").

Note that in shift operations the right-hand operand must be a literal. In counting machine cycles due to a shift, allowance must be made for the data paths of the arithmetic unit: the operation may, for example, have to be performed as a combination of 1- and 4-bit shifts, but that can always be deduced from the operands.

The effect of *mask* is to select a specified number of low-order bits from the first operand — here again the right operand must be a literal, e.g. z *mask* 4 results in the four low-order bits of z, the remainder being cleared to zero. Conversely, z *mask* − 4 clears the four low-order bits of z, leaving the rest unchanged.

In all arithmetic and logical operations the operands and intermediate results will be numeric (except in Chapter 18).

Implicit assignment

It is known that even in higher-level languages many assignment statements involve only one operator and have in effect the two-address form: *ident∘* = ∘*adop*?∘*ident∘bop**? in which the result of *adop*?∘*ident∘bop**? overwrites the first operand. Such statements will be written in the abbreviated form: *adop*?∘*ident∘bop**? Thus the statement "$x + 1$" is short for "$x = x + 1$", and "$-x$" is short for "$x = -x$". To avoid that interpretation an expression will be written in parentheses: thus "$(y - x$ *mask* 7)" evaluates the expression $y - x$ *mask* 7, sets condition codes, but does not make any assignment.

1.4 SEQUENCING RULES

Register transfer statements written in sequence and separated by semicolons specify a sequence of machine actions. The start of such a sequence can be labelled in the usual way, e.g.:

$$enter3: \quad x = 0; \, y - 1; \, c = z + 7 \gg 3$$

The simplest way of directing control is then to use *goto*, but conditional loop control statements can be used to clarify the flow of control without infringing our broad requirement of maintaining a simple relationship between operators in the text and operations in the register transfer machine.

Accordingly, *programsection* is defined to be a set of labelled statement sequences:

programsection: *def**
def: *label∘colon∘statseq*

where the major statement types are as listed in Table 1.2.

Table 1.2　Basic register transfer statements

stat:	{ ∘*statseq*∘ }	compound statement
	assignment	(see text)
	if∘cond∘stat∘elstat?	conditional
	while∘cond∘do? ∘*stat*	test before
	do∘stat∘while∘cond	test after
	goto∘dest	
	return	
dest:	*ident switch*	
cond:	*ZE NZ GE LT LE LT*	
	OV NV CA NC VA IA	
	(∘*relation*∘)	
elstat:	*else∘stat*	
label:	*ident*	
switch:	[∘*ident**∘] ∘' ∘*simplex*	computed goto
statseq:	*stat∘scstat*	
scstat:	;∘*stat*	

Thus *stat* occurs either as a single statement or a sequence enclosed in curly brackets { ... }. In later chapters *label* is extended to allow a form of procedure declaration. We shall make use of a "parameterless" subroutine call in the early chapters, using an empty *parlist*; e.g., "*sub*4()" can be used as a *statement* or *primary* to effect a subroutine jump to *sub*4. Control is resumed in the calling sequence after executing *return*.

The following examples illustrate the use of loop control statements, assuming the register declaration:

> REGS [x   c]   /*numeric*/

Example 1.2 Form in *c* a count of the number of 1s in *x*, assuming *x* is positive.

> *count*1: $c = 0$; *do* { $c + (x$ *mask* 1); $x \gg 1$ } *while NZ*

Note that the last statement "$x \gg 1$" makes use of the implied assignment convention, returning the result to *x* and setting condition codes which are tested "*NZ*" for loop termination.

Example 1.3 Allowing *x* to be positive or negative, to count the number of 1s in *x* as before.

> *count*2: $c = 0$; $x + 0$; *while NZ do* { *if LT* $c + 1$; $x \ll 1$ }

Here again, use is made of implicit assignment. The effect of "$x + 0$" is simply to set condition codes.

A very common requirement of interpretive code is to take a multi-way branch depending on a small integer value. That will be written as a *switch* destination in which one of a number of destinations is selected by evaluating an expression.

Example 1.4 Suppose it is required to decode the third and fourth bits of *x*, measured from the least-significant end of the word, branching to the defining sequence *error*4, *enter*1 or *exit* according to the values 0, 1 and 2 respectively, but not taking the branch if they have the value 3. Then the control statement would be written as:

> . . . ; *goto* [*error*4   *enter*1   *exit*] '$x \gg 2$; /*continue*/ . . .

Here "$x \gg 2$" is first evaluated (but not assigned), then the branch is taken on the low-order two bits of the result. In general, a *p*-way switch is conditioned by the low-order $\lceil \log_2 p \rceil$ bits of the selector expression.

Within a *programsection* control is assumed to start at the first defined statement sequence and to flow from one statement sequence to the next unless directed otherwise. For the most part, our use of the notation will be to indicate the general nature and complexity of a calculation, and it will be developed as necessary to that end. When the detail is not relevant to the context we shall simply describe in words the intended effect of a statement sequence, e.g.

     ... ; *if OV {sort out overflow}*; ...

Before studying the more complete examples, which are derived from existing library programs, it will be useful to refer to the summary of programming conventions given in the Appendix.

1.5 ASSIGNMENT AND ADDRESSING RULES

At this point Fig. 1.4 may be referred to as a model of the data transfer paths that have been assumed. In a single machine cycle one or two operands (register or literal values) are presented to the ALU inputs, an operation is performed, and the result may be returned to one of the registers. The condition codes are set by the result. If an expression is evaluated it is assumed that there are sufficient implicit working registers to hold temporary results. The implied register manipulations add a small overhead to the measure of

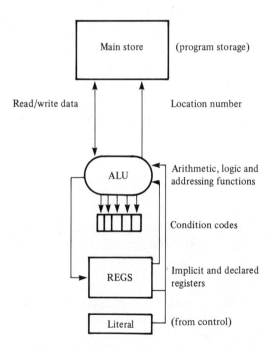

Fig. 1.4   Schematic diagram of data paths in register transfer machines

machine cycles. In a similar way, when compound sequencing statements are used there is a small overhead resulting from the implied control branches. In either case, the overhead can be made explicit by writing out "atomic" register transfer statements and control transfers when necessary.

To complete the data paths it is necessary to provide the means of accessing elements of data sequences, which are held in program storage. We now introduce notations for reading and writing data elements and for manipulating pointers. Each operation is regarded as atomic, though it will be seen that storage functions generally have to be counted separately in measuring machine activity.

The program store can only be accessed by using pointers. If ψ is a pointer, then the value of the first element of the sequence it addresses is denoted by "ψ.". For example, using *text* as declared in Example 1.1, *text.* is the first of the numbers it refers to.

A pointer may be modified by a non-negative integer in order to access successive elements in the sequence it addresses. The operator symbol ' (prime) is used to denote modification. Thus, assuming *text* addresses at least three elements, they can be accessed using the derived pointers *text, text'*1 and *text'*2; the righthand argument of ' may be a literal, a declared register, or an expression in parentheses.

The syntax of expressions is extended to allow the use of addressing operators, which take precedence over arithmetic operators in expression evaluation.

Example 1.5   Suppose *list* is an array of ten integers and it is required to put the largest positive element in x, setting $x = 0$ if they are all negative.

```
REGS [ x y z              working numeric registers
        list ]            list pointer
findmax:   x = 0;
           y = 9;
           do {   z = list' y.;      fetch value
                  if (z > x) x = z;
                  y − 1 } while GE
```

In the last example the assumed array bounds are observed in the construction of the program. Frequently we shall make use of limit information contained in the pointer itself and test explicity for the validity of an address. The next example shows one such application.

Example 1.6   As before, *list* is an array of integers, but the limit is contained in the pointer. It is required to place the largest positive value in the entire array in *x*.

$$REGS \; [\; x \quad z$$

REGS [*x* *z*	working numeric registers
y	working pointer
list]	list pointer
findmax: *x* = 0;	
y = *list*;	
do { *z* = *y*.;	
if (*z* > *x*) *x* = *z*;	
y′ 1 } *while VA*	i.e. *y* = *y*′ 1

At the end of the sequence *y* is an "invalid" pointer.

Not all machines have limit information in pointers, so it will be made clear from the context who takes responsibility for address validation: the programmer, the compiler, or the machine. In later chapters the addressing operations will be extended to allow explicit manipulation of type and limit fields.

Writing a value to store is expressed by the operator symbol " = .". If ψ is a pointer, then assignment to the first position of the sequence addressed by ψ is indicated by the statement form "ψ° = . $^{\circ}simplex$". Normally ψ is a declared register, but it may be represented by any expression which, on evaluation, results in a pointer. For example, to assign zero to the third element of a sequence addressed by *text* one would write simply "*text*′2 = . 0".

We have now introduced three types of assignment statement:

assignment to a register, denoted by " = ";
implicit assignment, also to a register and almost always entailing a simple "updating" operation such as "*x*′ 1" or "*x* − 2";
assignment to storage, denoted by " = .".

There will be many examples of their use in the following chapters. Additional forms of assignment will be introduced when array operations are described. It is often said that most computer operations simply move data from place to place, like the Duke of York's infantry, without seeing much "action" in arithmetic or logical circuits. Much effort, whether in cabling, backplane wiring, printed circuit or mask design, is devoted to providing adequate pathways. Our notation reflects the same preoccupation with interconnection. All store operations are explicitly stated: as mentioned earlier, it is not practical when manipulating pointers at register level to invoke implicit de-referencing actions.

All the addressing operations defined above apply to data pointers. There will be occasion to use *control* pointers, i.e. references to sequences of stored instructions. The "value" of a label can be assigned to a register, where it is recognized as a *control* pointer and a valid destination of *goto*. The addressing operations do not apply to control pointers.

1.6 TERMINOLOGY

I have used technical terms with internationally agreed meanings wherever possible. **Memory** and **store** are interchangeable, as are **task** and **process**. When describing particular products or experiments there is unavoidable conflict between the terms used in the text and those that the reader would find in referring to the original papers. I have aimed to be as consistent as possible, pointing out local variations as they occur.

One set of terms that is notoriously difficult to use with precision is that dealing with reference to data. The reason is that any scheme of reference is relative to a prescribed set of coordinates, while in a computer several coordinate systems co-exist and mapping from one to another takes place frequently. We shall be concerned with the effect of choosing one framework or another, and with asking whether one framework could do the job of two or more. Normally our charts will be drawn in the "system space" which combines all program material. **Pointers** refer to objects in system space. In Parts 1 and 2 we shall mostly be concerned with objects consisting of sequences of elementary values (character, word, plane, instruction) for which pointers take the form of **addresses**. In Part 3 we introduce more abstract forms of object, for which the pointers are **capabilities** and **codewords**. Sets of pointers can be used to define subspaces with reference to which programs or tasks are executed. Those subspaces are termed **operating environments**. The "address" that a programmer might use is transformed into a "system address" by reference to the operating environment. Sometimes an address contains more than just coordinate information: it might say something about the type of data, how it is to be used, etc. The more elaborate form of address is termed a **descriptor**. Descriptors can be relative to the system space, or to an operating environment, and are generally interpreted during program execution to obtain actual data values. At a slightly higher level, the term **qualifier** is used to refer to the encoded form of all the attributes of a particular item of data that might be deduced by a compiler. Usually qualifiers are not seen in running programs, but we shall study one language subsystem in which qualifiers are retained and interpreted during execution. At the opposite extreme, an address is used to generate signals that will activate a store: the relevant part of the "physical address" is normally referred to as a **location number**. It is entirely possible for a location number to be found as part of an address, a descriptor, or even a qualifier, and we shall examine the implications that has for machine design.

Finally, I have used "he" as a stylistic abbreviation for "he or she", "his" for "his or her", etc. The technical term **host** is to be interpreted in the same spirit.

1.7 FURTHER READING

From this introductory chapter it will be clear that although the intention is to explain design principles slightly ahead of current practice the starting point is some distance behind. With so much ground to cover it is impossible to give current architectures the attention they deserve. For broader surveys and quite different organization of material the reader should consult some of the recent texts on computer architecture such as KUC78, TAN76 or STO75. Even where the same ground is being covered contrasting emphasis often helps to reach a thorough understanding of design principles.

How far back is it necessary to go? Modern machines are often said to depart from the principles enunciated by von Neumann and his colleagues at the Institute for Advanced Study in Princeton in a report presented to the United States Army Ordnance Department: see BUR46. It is not surprising to find that fundamental ideas about how calculations may be performed have not changed in the intervening period, or indeed since the time of Babbage. The early pioneers were not concerned by the constraints of product engineering, however, or by the overwhelming costs of software production, and it must be admitted that, historical interest apart, the von Neumann machine will be no more relevant to our discussion than Babbage's Analytical Engine. The IBM 360 has had a widespread influence on design, and we shall have several occasions to refer to the standards it set. The explanations offered by its designers are still worth reading (AMD64). To gain a historical perspective, reference to conference proceedings of the early 1950s is recommended, particularly *Proc. IRE*, **41** (October 1953), which contains a number of survey papers. Hopper and Mauchly on the "Influence of programming techniques on the design of computers" provides one of the earliest accounts of the use of interpreters.

PART 1

Interpretive Machines

(From N. Thelwell, *Thelwell Country,* Eyre Methuen (1959))

FOREWORD TO PART 1

There is an evident need to instruct computers in terms as free as possible from useless detail. ADA, APL, BASIC, COBOL, FORTRAN and the rest outline (in different ways) what a programmer needs to know to get a calculation done. The designer's job is to provide the most economical paths between problem statement and solution. Doing the *arithmetic* is the least contentious part. Computers are notorious for the amount of effort that goes into *finding* the data, and it has often been suggested that modern circuits and subsystems can improve on traditional ways of implementing high-level languages. Chapters 2 – 7 are mainly concerned with examining that proposition. It is not necessary to know the languages mentioned in detail or to stand in judgement on their relative merits. It will be an advantage to know in advance how a program in "source" form is normally translated into machine code ready for execution, and how it is supported by "run-time" or "library" programs. We shall move fairly rapidly from one level of design to the next, bearing in mind the overall system objective of meeting performance goals over a *range* of languages and a *range* of costs.

I am grateful to O.V.D. Evans of ICL, M.J. Flynn of Stanford University, and L.W. Hoevel of IBM for reading and commenting on parts of Chapters 5 and 6 of which they have first-hand knowledge.

2   INTERPRETERS

In the present context an *interpreter* is a program written for one computer, which we shall call a **host**, causing it to imitate the behavior of another, which we shall call the **target** machine. That behavior is characterized by the succession of *states* which the target machine can assume, i.e. the numerical values found in all recognized stores, registers, control flags, condition codes, modes, status words, etc, and by the *transition rules* which determine for any given state what the *next* one should be when the machine is working correctly. The task of the interpreter is thus to set up a data structure representing the target machine state at one instant, then by imitating the transition rules to form the data structure representing the next machine state, and so on repeatedly until either (a) there is no defined "next" state, or (b) by interrupting the host machine the interpreter is told to stop. In this chapter we shall characterize the functions of typical host machines.

For most practical purposes transition rules are embodied in the *instruction set* of the target machine. In other words, using the program counter we can select an instruction from store and decompose it into function and operand fields, then select the operands, perform the function, store the result, update the program counter and prepare to obey the next instruction. An instruction determines the size of step from one state to the next: all sorts of intermediate values might be assumed but they are of no interest provided the final state agrees with that set out in the Manual of Operation. Although the technique of interpreting or decoding individual *words* is commonplace in many programs, we make the point of requiring an interpreter to include a *sequencing rule* so that it operates on strings of instructions or target machine programs. The importance of that step is that it allows the programmer to describe algorithms at "target machine level", and if target states are well chosen that will be easier than thinking out the succession of states in the host machine that would have the same final effect.

There are two main reasons for using interpreters. We have just indicated their value in presenting to the user a "state space" in which he or she can express algorithms easily. The reader might have met "linear algebra" or "job control" packages of that type, in which the target machine state is composed of "matrices" or "tasks" respectively. The interpreter is then acting as an abstraction mechanism in the sense more fully discussed in Chapter 14, and it is generally implicit that host machine instructions are not only less easy to use but much more primitive in effect than those of the target machine.

The second use for interpreters is when target software already exists and is valued highly enough to make imitation worthwhile. Emulators designed specifically to run operating-system, library or application packages of existing computers are a familiar example. In the same category are portable software systems using one of the amorphous target instruction sets intended to be easy to interpret on a wide variety of host machines. Here, commercial or educational interests are overriding and it is difficult to make absolute statements about engineering objectives: it is not unusual to find the host machine more complex in some ways than the target, which seems the wrong way round. Nevertheless, if it can be established in advance of the design stage that a machine will spend much of its time acting as host, it is sensible to ask what features it should have to do that job well.

We shall begin by outlining some interpreters, giving just sufficient detail to see how their effort is spent and suggest what support is needed. In Chapter 3 we shall see how specialized interpretive machines attempt to satisfy the requirements. Subsequent chapters turn to the role of interpreters in the system context, with special regard to meeting high-level language specifications.

2.1 INTERPRETING PDP-11 INSTRUCTIONS

Suppose the problem is to intepret a "PDP-11-like" instruction set using as host the register transfer machine outlined in Chapter 1. (For the sake of this discussion we assume there is only one PDP-11 instruction set, ignoring variations between models.) As far as user programs are concerned, the target machine state is fully described by:

(1) a main store of up to 32 768 words of 16 bits;
(2) a file of eight 16-bit user registers; and
(3) a program status word of 16 bits.

The host data structures are thus two word-sequences and a single word that can conveniently be held as a register value. It will be seen that the interpreter needs extra working variables, so the register declaration appears as:

REGS	[mem	pointer to store image of up to 32 768 words
	usr	pointer to 8 user registers
	instr	target instruction register
	x y	working numeric values
	s t	working pointers
	psw]	program status word

In the PDP-11 six general purpose "target" registers $usr'0, \ldots, usr'5$ are followed by a stack pointer (*SP*) at $usr'6$ and the program counter (*PC*) at $usr'7$. Although the user sees *PC* as a pointer to memory we regard it as a numeric index of the store addressed by *mem*, and similarly for *SP*. Both *SP* and *PC* have special significance in function interpretation (see Fig. 2.1).

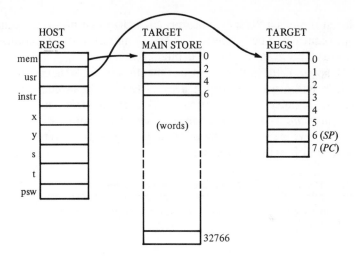

Fig. 2.1   PDP-11 machine state in host data space

The format of instructions is variable, but the principal fields are as shown in the following diagram, where $b = 1$ normally indicates byte operands, *f* is the primary function code, and *v* contains auxiliary function codes, operand specifiers, etc., as required by *f*.

PDP-11 Instruction format:

1	3	12
b	f	v

In *psw* there are three fields. The *mode* bits distinguish user and other states in the sense that the meaning of certain instructions depends on whether they are executed by user, kernel or supervisor programs (there are very few such instructions and we shall ignore them). The current priority level *p* is used to determine whether to service external interrupts: a device will only be attended to if its assigned priority is greater than p, and if $p = 7$ the program is interrupt-free. One machine instruction is provided (in supervisor mode) to set a new value of p.

	4		4		3		5
program status word:	mode				p		TNZVC

The remainder of *psw* is set as a side-effect of arithmetic and logical operations:

N negative sign
Z zero result
V overflow
C carry
     Target condition codes

In addition there is a "trap" indicator T which, when non-zero, causes an interrupt sequence to be entered at the end of almost any instruction. It can then be set by program for use in debugging.

All traps and interrupts make use of the stack index SP to save the current value of PC and *psw* in memory: other registers will be saved as required by the interrupt handler, whose starting location is taken from one of the lower positions in *mem*. The complications of interrupt handling will not concern us here, but we need to be aware that they give the interpreter special conditions and functions to recognize.

Table 2.1   Decoding the PDP-11 operand specification

This table gives the register transfer operations that leave a pointer to the operand word in host register t

2	1	3	
e	i	r	Operand specification

Register value $i = 0$, $e = 0$
     $t = usr'r$
Address in register, index forwards $i = 0$, $e = 1$
     $s = usr'r$; $x = s.$; $s = . x + 2 - b$; $t = mem'x$
Index backwards, address in register $i = 0$, $e = 2$
     $s = usr'r$; $x = s. - 2 + b$; $s = . x$; $t = mem'x$
Address follows instruction, modified by register $i = 0$, $e = 3$
     $s = usr'7$; $x = mem'(s). + usr'r.$; $s = . s. + 2$; $t = mem'x$
Address in register, no indexing $i = 1$, $e = 0$
     $t = mem'(usr'r.)$
Register points to address vector (index forwards) $i = 1$, $e = 1$
     $s = usr'r$; $x = s.$; $s = . x + 2$; $t = mem'(mem'x.)$
Index backwards, register points to address vector $i = 1$, $e = 2$
     $s = usr'r$; $x = s. - 2$; $s = . x$; $t = mem'(mem'x.)$
Address (modified by register) of address vector follows instr. $i = 1$, $e = 3$
     $s = usr'7$; $x = mem'(s). + usr'r.$; $s = . s. + 2$; $t = mem'(mem'x.)$

Returning to the instructions themselves, many operations make use of a general form of operand specification encoded as a six-bit field (v can contain one or two such codes). The specification comprises a register number r, an indirection bit i, and an addressing mode e which selects one of four ways of finding the operand. The interpretation of the operand field is summarized in Table 2.1, giving for each of the eight combinations of e and i the sequence of register transfer operations that leaves in t a pointer to the operand in the host data space. It should be noted that memory is indexed by byte on the PDP-11, so that in mapping onto our 16-bit store the low-order bit of the address is ignored, but used later to select an even or odd byte (if $b=1$). In Table 2.1, r and b are used as if they were host registers: in programming, the corresponding fields must be extracted from *instr*. (If $r = 6$ or $r = 7$, it is implicit that $b = 0$.)

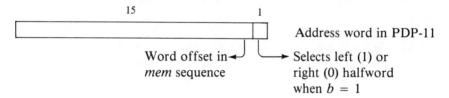

We shall see that while a target instruction is being decoded the program counter PC gives the target address of the next word in memory. When that word is used as part of the operand selection rule ($e = 3$), PC is incremented accordingly.

We are now in a position to sketch the sequence of actions needed to interpret a commonly occurring type of target instruction, which is to form the logical "or" (function $f = 5$) of a word from memory (at location 1048 indexed by $usr'2$) and one of the target registers ($usr'3$), leaving the result in the register. The operation involves words, so $b = 0$. The PDP-11 instruction occupies two words:

	b	f	source	dest
PC:	0	5	302	003
PC + 2:				1048
(bits):	1	3	6	6

The main program loop fetches the first word of the instruction to *instr,* increments PC, then branches on the primary function code f. The instruction is obeyed, and finally certain end effects are dealt with before repeating the loop.

> *mainloop:* $x = usr'7.$; $usr'7 = . x + 2$; $instr = mem'x.$;
>   *goto* $[f0f1f2f3f4f5f6f7]$ ' $inst \gg 12$

The next step for $f = 5$ is to find the two operands according to the general addressing rules. In the present case the v field of *instr* contains two 6-bit specifications. Because they are used in other contexts it is convenient to decode them in two subroutines *source* and *dest* which place the operands in x and y respectively; also, *dest* leaves in t a pointer to the destination word, and leaves in s a control pointer to a terminating sequence. The main loop for primary function group 5 can now be completed as:

f5: *source( );dest( );*	Set register contents x, y, t, s
psw&$fff1;	Clear N, Z and V conditions
$y \mid x$;	Go to s with result in y and host conditions
goto s	set.

Because both *source* and *dest* use the selection rules given in Table 2.1 it is again practical to use a subroutine to find the target address or offset in the *mem* sequence, treating register operands ($e = 0$, $i = 0$) as a special case. We continue to use host registers to pass parameters and results between subroutines, and require a subroutine *offset* to decode an address specification placed in y, returning the target address in y.

source( ): $y = instr \gg 6$ *mask* 6; (y *mask* $-$ 3);	Test *ei* zero
if ZE $\{x = usr'y.$;	Operand in register
(*instr mask* $-$ 15);	Test *b*
if NZ $x \ll 8 \gg 8$;	Extend sign
return};	
offset( );	Interpret y
(*instr mask* $-$ 15);	Test *b*
if NZ $\{(y\&1)$;	Byte operand:
if NZ $x = mem'y. \gg 8$	odd
else $x = mem'y. \ll 8 \gg 8$}	even
else $\{(y\&1)$;	Word operand:
if NZ goto ODDADDR	error
else $x = mem'y.$};	
return	End of source

The form of *dest* is similar to *source*, but leaving the result in y and remembering where it came from in t. The action taken to store a result depends on how it was selected—register, word, odd byte or even byte—so there are different terminating sequences for each:

dest( ):	$y = instr\ mask\ 6;\ (y\ mask\ -3);$	Test *ei* zero
	if ZE { $t = usr'\ y; y = t.$;	Register
	{ *select byte if* $b = 1$ };	
	$s = endr; return$ };	
	offset( );	Intrepret *y*
	$(instr\ mask\ -15);$	Test *b*
	{ *select operand as in source* }	
	return	

Here *endr* labels the common terminating sequence for register word destination, required to set the target machine conditions in N and Z according to the result just obtained, clearing V and leaving C unchanged:

endr:	*if LT psw*	8 *else if ZE psw*	4;	
	$t = .\ y;$	*Store result*
	$(psw\ \&\ 16);\ if\ NZ\ goto\ TRAP;$	*Test T*
	goto mainloop	

There are two "abnormal" exits from the interpreter loop:

(1) to *ODDADDR* from *source* (and similarly from *dest*) when a word operation is requested using an odd address (a program error); and

(2) to *TRAP* when the *T* bit is set. There would be a similar escape when an external request of higher priority than *p* was detected. In each case preparation is made to enter the diagnostic routine (resetting *PC* and *psw*) before re-entering the main loop.

Further branches of the interpreter can be completed from knowledge of the instruction set. However, enough has already been done to suggest the following general comments.

(1) Writing down the instructions of the interpreter is not difficult under the assumptions we have made. If constraints are imposed on space or time, however, there are many trade-offs to consider, the most common being to make the best use of host registers and to minimize the path length round the commonest parts of the interpretive loop. We might, for example, seek to reduce store accesses by mapping *PC* into one of the host registers, with the result that on all register references the case $r = 7$ must be detected and treated separately. We might seek to save program space by writing more general subroutines (e.g. combining *source* and *dest*), but that would mean inserting control statements to discriminate between particular instances of application. In weighing up the alternatives it is invaluable to have on hand a measure of how often particular facilities are used. Table 2.2 gives an example of measurements taken for the operand specification field. The table gives static counts, i.e.

Table 2.2   Relative frequency of address options on PDP-11

i	e	%
0	0	32.0
0	1	24.8
0	2	5.0
0	3	28.4
1	0	8.7
1	1	0.4
1	2	0.0
1	3	0.7

From L.J. Shustek, *Analysis and Performance of Computer Instruction Sets,* Stanford University SLAC Report No. 205, May 1978

measures of instruction space rather than dynamic counts of execution frequency, but one would not expect significant differences in the results. Judging whether the sample studied is representative of all the programs to be executed requires sound understanding of application analysis and programming techniques, but assuming the analysis to be correct the key sections are apparent from the figures. A constraint not uncommon in host machines is that part of the store is faster than the rest: such measures can then be used to guide the allocation of program space.

(2) A general observation on programming style is that strict application of "structured programming" rules would be positively harmful in the present context. The frequent use of "*goto*", including the variable form "*goto s*" in the definition of *f*5 is intended to avoid unnecessary register transfer operations; the use of *ODDADDR* in *source* and *dest* implies non-standard "subroutine return" facilities; and we shall find that host registers and other specialized "hard" resources play a prominent part in program design. At or below the architectural level, these drawbacks can be overcome by relatively heavy investment in the few hundred statements of interpretive code; above that level, in the general system context, programmability of interpreters is nevertheless an important issue, which will be discussed in Chapters 7 and 14.

(3) Some important assumptions have been made about host machine functions, particularly in the areas of memory access and arithmetic. Without them almost every code sequence would have to invoke even more steps to make the adjustment from one set of conventions to another,

from	(*host*)	to	(*target*)
e.g.	16-bit words		24-bit words
	byte addresses		word addresses
	binary arithmetic		decimal arithmetic

and so on. The so-called "universal emulators" are machines with provision in the hardware for making such changes with minimal loss of speed.

(4) One particular area of adjustment familiar to users of the PDP-11 is in mapping from "program address" to "system address" as seen on the memory bus. That transformation is model-dependent, but generally involves the use of further address tables (an extension of the target machine state) and extended calculation preceding access to *mem*. Exactly how that is done is a critical part of the host design which often requires hardware assistance.

(5) There are evidently several "grades" of imitation, depending on what action is taken in exceptional circumstances. For example, we might define *ODDADDR* as termination of the interpreter, being prepared to imitate only programs free from error; alternatively, the system-defined trap sequence might be initiated. In order of increasing difficulty we can list the grades as:

> correct non-privileged (user) programs;
> user programs;
> system programs (requiring privileged modes);
> engineering tests;
> engineering diagnostics (probably meaningless).

Care must be taken to select the grade appropriate to application requirements.

(6) A target instruction set with many different formats, exceptions, modes, etc., makes heavy demands on the interpreter or, equivalently, needs a lot of hardware assistance. The PDP-11 is such an example. Conversely, regular decoding of the instruction and operand specifiers makes for a compact and efficient interpreter: the IBM 360 has the best-known instruction set of that sort. It can be evaluated in two ways: (a) whether it is easy to implement using interpretive techniques (as we have just noted), and (b) whether it does its job well in terms of speed, space and other parameters measured in the context of a given language. Neither the PDP-11 nor IBM 360 code is particularly good in the latter respect, and if we take any language there are many better ways of representing its statements and data structures that take less space and time to execute. They will be studied in Chapters 5 and 6.

(7) It will not have passed unnoticed that the example we have used could have been replaced by a single register transfer statement:

$$usr'3 \ =. \ usr'3. \ | \ mem'(1048 + usr'2.).$$

which takes ten operations instead of the 60 or so outlined. Then why use an interpreter? Before trying to answer that question let us take one other example, showing how various specializations in design of the host contribute to a more "realistic" execution path.

2.2 INTERPRETING ICL 1900 INSTRUCTIONS

The ICL 1900 is typical of many systems in which each non-privileged user program works in an area of store that can be positioned anywhere in main memory starting at a particular base or datum point, but always accessed using "program addresses" ranging from zero up to a variable limit. An interpreter can be designed to work either:

(1) in "user mode" only, in which mapping from target to host adress is decided by the interpreter in conjunction with the supporting *host* system; in this case extended interpretations must be supplied for functions such as supervisor calls that go outside the user program space; or
(2) in "system mode", in which all user programs are embedded in a larger storage area within the host, the allocations being made by the *target* system; by imitating every detail of privileged functions it is then possible to run the target operating system or supervisory programs.

The choice has important consequences for the user: whether the target job control functions can be used, for example, or how efficiently the host resources are employed. Here we assume (2), though the choice is not material to the discussion (Fig. 2.2). As before, the system is treated only in outline and we shall not be concerned with privileged or model-dependent features.

     The word size of the target machine is 24 bits, which we assume for the host in this exercise. We also assume a 24-bit word address. There are eight general-purpose registers, mapped onto the first eight locations of the user program space. Unlike the PDP-11, the target program counter is not addressable and therefore it can be held in "pointer" form in a host register. Program registers 1, 2 and 3 can be selected as address modifiers.

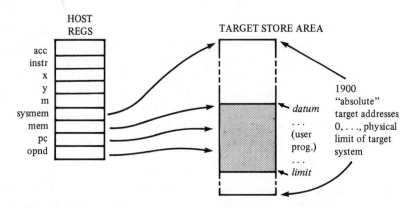

Fig. 2.2   Mapping target system into host data structure

Most instructions are single words (see diagram) containing primary and secondary function codes f, g, a register index X, modifier field M and offset N.

3	4	3	2	12
X	f	g	M	N

ICL 1900 INSTRUCTION

The addressing rule is such that, if $M \neq 0$, the content of the corresponding register is added to N to form an effective address in the target program; otherwise, N gives the address. It should be noted that an address in the range 0, ..., 7 has the effect of selecting one of the registers.

The interpretive sequence can now be followed for a target instruction with the same effect as one used earlier, i.e. logical "or " to a register (index 3) of the word in store location (524 + content of register 2). The instruction takes the form

X	f	g	M	N
3	2	1	2	524

Host registers are declared, followed by the register transfer statements in Fig. 2.3. In studying the program note the following points:

(1) In addition to declared registers we assume the existence of a number of indicator flags, some of which denote target machine states while others are used to mark the state of the interpreter. Apart from *INT*, an interrupt signal, their use is not detailed here.

(2) Attempts to address outside the user-program space are monitored at *resfailcontrol* and *resfaildata*.

(3) At the start of the loop it is assumed that *instr* is already loaded; it is reloaded in the terminating sequence.

(4) The interpretive sequence includes bound checks sufficient for multiprogrammed operation. In the PDP-11 additional interpretive steps (or hardware assistance) would be needed to partition the program address space. We have assumed the facility of the register-transfer machine for indicating pointer validity after modification. To change the program area privileged target instructions must be provided to load *mem* from a sequence of pointers addressed by *sysmem*.

(5) The *INT* flag is examined once in the interpretive loop, i.e. every 20 – 30 instructions. Some interrupts cannot wait that long for service, and some target instructions might take even longer. In general, *INT* must be examined within prescribed intervals whatever else is happening, if necessary saving the current state of the interpreter (some or all of *acc*, *instr*, *x*, *y*, *m*, *opnd*, *pc* and flags) in such a way that the sequence can be resumed later. To do so economically while guaranteeing response to a variety of interrupt conditions is one of the more serious complications of interpreter design.

HOST ENVIRONMENT

REGS	[	*acc*	accumulator/operand
		instr	target instruction
		x y m	working indices
		sysmem	1900 system store ptr
		mem	user program pointer
		pc	program counter
		opnd]	operand pointer

INSTRUCTION FORMAT

X	f	g	M	N
3	2	1	2	524

INTERPRETIVE SEQUENCE

σ	*mainloop:* { *reset flags* };	
δδ	$y = instr\ mask\ 12$;	
δδδ	$x = instr \gg 21\ mask\ 3$;	
δδδ	$m = instr \gg 12\ mask\ 2$;	
φφφμ	*if NZ y + mem' m.*;	Modify
σδδ	*goto* [*f0 f1 f2 ... f15*] *'instr* $\gg$ 17	

... Primary function groups

φφ	*f2: opnd = mem' y;*	
φ	*if IA goto resfaildata;*	
φμ	*acc = opnd.;*	
σδδ	*goto* [*f2g0 f2g1 ... f2g7*]	
	'instr $\gg$ 14	

... Secondary function groups

φαμ	*f2g1: acc*	*mem' x.* ;	Logical "or"
φ	*mem' x = . acc;*	
σ	*goto endlog*	

... Terminating sequence for logical functions

α	*endlog:* { *set target conditions* };	
σ	*if INT goto interrupt;*	
τ	*pc' 1;*	
τ	*if IA goto resfailcontrol;*	
τμ	*instr = pc.;*	
σ	*goto mainloop*	

Figure 2.3   Interpreting an ICL 1900 logical instruction

From Fig. 2.3 it will be seen that approximately 32 elementary transfer operations are required for the function in question, plus 4 accesses to the program area (including modification, but assuming a single cycle for the arithmetic in $f2g1$). To see how they derive, each line is marked with one or more symbols showing the class of operation according to the scheme explained in Table 2.3.

Table 2.3

τ	target machine sequencing	3
σ	host machine sequencing	6
δ	decoding	12
φ	operand access	9
α	arithmetic	2
	Total	32
μ	memory access	+ 4

The distinction is not always easy to make, but the figures do show the major overheads of decoding and operand access when the host is not adapted to the formats of the target machine. We shall see that in practise help is available on specialized machines with provision for field extraction and masking. The arrangement of lines in the interpretive sequence gives an indication of the number of instruction steps taken by a modern general-purpose host machine (about 20). To make further reductions, several actions must somehow be packed into single host instructions, which is not difficult in principle provided they deal with independent parts of the machine state. We could envisage field extraction (y, x and m) in parallel with *reset flags* in *mainloop,* or a combination of operand access and functional branch in $f2$, and that is precisely what happens in more specialized host machines. In the limit, it would not be unusual to find each of the four sequences *mainloop, f2, f2g1* and *endlog* in Fig. 2.3 completed in a single host instruction.

2.3 AIMS OF INTERPRETATION

Before examining specialized machines let us review the cicumstances in which interpretation "pays off". They can be classified as historical, architectural, and electronic.

(a) Historical

As already indicated, one of the commonest uses of interpreters is to emulate existing machines. The examples studied illustrate the types of operation required and have enabled a distinction to be drawn between different grades of interpreter. The choice of "correct single-task programs" rather than "diagnostic tests" represents an order of magnitude difference in the effort involved. One factor working in favor of such design is that a later device technology is always faster or cheaper, consequently on a performance/cost basis interpreters have held their own with the past, even allowing for some mismatch with the host.

A factor weighing against emulation is the increased complexity of modern systems. Despite hardware performance gains it would be impractical to imitate a processor with complex segmentation and paging algorithms without equivalent hard support. Some relief might be gained by downgrading the interpreter, but it seems unlikely that a situation as favorable as the switch from second- to third-generation equipment will recur.

Within a few years it is probable that substantial amounts of good software will exist in portable form, much of it based on "pseudomachine" architectures that can be interpreted fairly directly. If any of these found commercial backing then, as with machine code, they could become targets of emulation irrespective of technical considerations.

(b) Architectural

An interpreted program normally contains tests for dealing with store protection, address translation, illegal functions, traps on exceptions, external interrupts, etc., that are not covered by in-line code, so our notional ratio of 60:10 register transfer operations is misleading. The overhead is substantial but has proved acceptable insofar as it provides a sound basis for multiprogramming activity, store-hierarchy management and error detection.

A closely related observation is that modern systems are expected to support a range of operations on data of many types with very wide variation in performance and cost. That can best be done by moving the architectural definition away from register transfer level in order to leave room for maneuver, and that seems to imply interpretive control (in terms of Fig. 1.1, each of M16, M32, and M64 would require its own interpreter for the defined architecture, but that is better than generating different in-line code for each application).

The above line of reasoning, together with historical precedent, offers the most widely accepted case for interpretive techniques, and leads to secure general-purpose machine range specification. It is a matter of debate whether the result is effective, and many software designers dissent to the point of providing their own specification which is itself interpreted — unfortunately via the system interface. For example APL, an interpreted language, is often implemented by instructions that are themselves interpreted. If security could somehow be separated from architecture we could envisage systematic support for several program interfaces each using a single stage of interpretation. The architectural arguments are thus closely tied in with assumptions about host machines and system organization that are perhaps outdated; at least they need to be reviewed, and we shall do that in Chapter 7.

(c) Electronic

Almost always target code is shorter — much shorter — than the host representation of the same algorithm. If program size is an issue, one can design target formats specifically to minimize the total number of function and address bits in its representation. That has obvious consequences in channel loading and store requirements, and the designer must balance the advantage of needing less store against the disadvantage of needing it for longer periods.

A more common situation is where the processor and store are connected by a relatively low-capacity channel. It is then a design aim to encode the control information, decoding and interpreting it in the processor. The implication is that both the interpreter and a fairly "rich" target machine state should be represented in the processor itself. Such low-capacity channels are not difficult to find in practise; for example,

(1) in microprocessors with physically limited connectivity at the edges (typically 16 instruction bits/major cycle), which incorporate decoding circuits on the chip; and
(2) in minicomputer systems (such as the PDP-11) in which several processors and memories share a common highway.

In neither case can elementary register transfer instructions be delivered to the processor at the required rate, so rather than give up the advantages of single-chip processors or the flexibility of "Unibus" design it is natural to use interpretive techniques.

The circumstances used to justify interpretation lend different emphases to processor structure, though practical systems often combine them. Historical arguments carry great economic weight but have least impact on design. The answer to the earlier question of why we could not simply deliver the register transfer instructions

$$usr'3 = . \; usr'3. \; | \; mem'(1048 + usr'2.).$$

can be found in (b) and (c): what if there is an external interrupt? What if $1048 + usr'2.$ is out of address range? What does the host machine do while waiting for instructions and data to arrive? What if the target program store is too small?

As a broad generalization, modern general-purpose systems have evolved on the assumptions that there is (much) more to be done in obeying a target instruction than meets the eye. Nevertheless, because of the long delays in moving data through the memory hierarchy it is practical to use interpretive techniques to keep pace with program and database activity. However, our simple register transfer operations stretch the interpretive sequence too far, even under the simplifying assumptions made here, and it is necessary to seek specializations that will further reduce the number of host machine cycles needed to interpret given instruction sets. That problem is the subject of the next chapter.

3 MICROPROGRAMMABLE MACHINES

As soon as machine desription moves away from register transfer level (which it did in about 1950) the natural reaction on the part of engineers is to invent rules for building up complex functions from simpler ones, which is, of course, what programming itself is about. Consequently the term "microprogram" came into use for the description of sequences of elementary changes in machine state, whether expressed in terms of logic design diagrams or other symbolic form. The first application of microprogramming as a formal technique based on *stored* instruction steps is attributed to the designers of Edsac-2 at Cambridge University. Its advantage is that transformations of any complexity can be composed by activating a sequence of microinstructions: the limitations imposed by wired interconnection schemes, which are apparent in all phases of machine definition and construction, are thus greatly reduced. At a time when relatively complex target instructions were thought to be the key to greater machine efficiency the regularity of microprogramming had evident attractions.

Microprogram was not widely used in the above sense until methods of manufacturing the stored microprogram had been developed. In the early forms of construction microinstructions could be read but not written under program control. That is sufficient for a well-defined and fixed instruction set, and resulted in heavy use of microprograms from 1964 onwards by many manufacturers in support of "range" architectures, as noted in Chapter 2. The branch of technology that enables a microprogram to interpret a given target instruction set is termed "microsystem design". If one machine is to interpret one order code it is a very localized affair. If several machines must imitate two or three instruction sets the need for standard procedures and documentation arises: in the major application areas that is treated very much as an extension of logic design. The more recent development of microinstruction stores with write capability has been the main stimulus to research in microprogram application, and that brings new problems in microsystem design, as we shall see in later chapters.

Meanwhile, microprocessors have arrived in time to upset the habit of rewriting every technical term with the prefix "micro-" when it resurfaces in the microsystem: a "microprocessor" is clearly not one for executing micro-instructions, and we have to call on "microprogrammable machine" or simply "micromachine" when needing to stress the elementary nature of the control mechanism. At other times "host" is conveniently non-committal, while "emulator" emphasizes the historical justification.

In the present chapter we examine the design of microprogrammable host machines. A very extensive literature has grown up on that subject, but because of rapid changes in logic costs, which force a continual revision in the economics of design, very little in the way of accepted theory has emerged. We begin by reviewing design principles and then discuss some generalizations that have been attempted in recent years. Examples are drawn from various purpose-built host machines to show the type of adaptation that has taken place and which might have relevance to language implementation.

3.1 DESIGN PRINCIPLES

If we regard the state of a processor as that defined by an assembly of registers, control flags, counters, latches, mode indicators, and so on, then a microinstruction determines a simple transition from one state to another. By "simple" it is meant that all the allowed transitions can be completed within a time interval measured in tens rather than hundreds of gate delays, typically transferring a register to a data buffer, or traversing the combinational path through an arithmetic unit. In pursuit of that aim it follows that the decoding circuitry associated with the microinstruction itself must be minimal, and in the simplest practical schemes individual bits of the microinstruction directly control the gates in the processor, i.e. the condition "1" or "0" determines whether a path shall transmit data on the current machine cycle (see diagram). It is fairly easy to evolve a requirement for 100 or more microinstruction bits to control even the simplest processor in that way.

The source of microinstructions is a store, which will be called the **control memory** henceforth. Application of a sequencing rule causes a succession of microinstructions to be fetched from the control memory, each causing a simple transition of the processor state. Again, the sequencing rule must itself be expressible by a short combinational path, a condition met in early

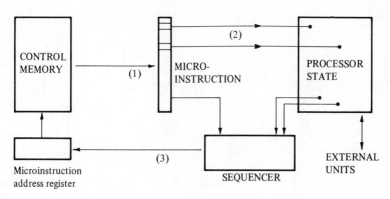

Fig. 3.1   Microprogram control scheme

micromachines by placing the address of the "next" microinstruction in the one currently being obeyed. To achieve conditional branching effects, however, a small amount of calculation is unavoidable.

The elements of the micromachine can be visualized as in Fig. 3.1. The machine operates in three steps, i.e. assuming the microinstruction address has been set:

(1)   access control memory using the microinstruction address;

(2)   use the microinstruction to control one state transition of the processor logic;

(3)   use the microinstruction and processor state to reset the microinstruction address.

The development of microprogrammable machines from the above principle of design leads to great elaboration of detail, the main considerations being (a) to minimize the cost of control memory; (b) to achieve balanced timing of memory access, state transition and sequencing operations; and (c) to organize the registers and data paths of the processor to suit the class of target machines of interest. We shall discuss each aspect of design, giving examples from some of the earlier micromachines.

(a) Minimizing the cost of control memory

As with all memories, the main requirement is to deliver the information required at the right time and as cheaply as possible. That brings us into the rapidly evolving domain of semiconductor devices and some relatively straightforward trading between encoding instructions (to save space) and the consequent delay in presenting control bits to the processor logic. Less

(i)

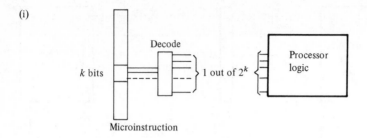

(ii)

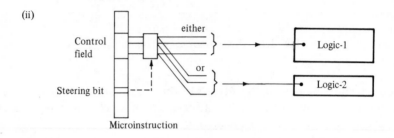

(iii)

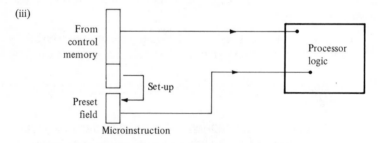

Fig. 3.2   Microinstruction coding schemes: (i) encoded control;
(ii) bit steering; (iii) preset control

easily quantified is the choice between read-only, programmable read-only, and read – write memories, for which the choice depends strongly on operational requirements.

The form of coding in which each microinstruction bit controls a unique gate in the processor is termed *direct* control. It we could find sets of mutually exclusive control signals, such that no more than one is activated in a given cycle, it is possible to encode them: a field of k bits will activate one of 2^k control lines (Fig. 3.2 (i)). That is obviously the case when one of, say, 8 registers can be gated to one input of an adder, where not only is the field *encoded* but the decoded output controls the transfer of a complete data field rather than a single bit. The same technique is used in machine-code design, and it is found in most micromachines from the "first generation" onwards, the individual control fields being referred to as **microorders**.

Three other forms of coding deserve mention. In what is sometimes called *bit steering* the particular data paths controlled by one microorder are determined by another field of the microinstruction (Fig. 3.2 (ii)). The second field directs the first to one or another set of control paths. It is appropriate when the processor logic can be partitioned into sections that do not require activation on every cycle (e.g. control of external units might preclude the use of decimal arithmetic facilities). Carried to the extreme, the entire microinstruction ends up as a primary function group and a number of operand fields, which would be difficult to distinguish at first sight from a conventional machine code.

The second technique derives from the observation that over many sequences of microinstructions the values of certain control lines will remain unchanged, so that they could be set in advance and taken as implicit extensions of the microinstruction. That technique is referred to as *preset* (sometimes *residual*) control. It can be used, for example, if particular carry or shift paths are fixed in advance, or if one of several register sets is being used. A special case of some importance is the use of a "microprogram counter" as part of the sequencing operation. The preset control fields form an extension of the processor state, set by data paths from the microinstruction or registers (Fig. 3.2 (iii)).

Finally, it is easy to see that all 2^{100} versions of a 100-bit microinstruction will not be used, and instead of trying to encode individual fields it would be possible to list all the distinct microinstructions in an application and select those needed from a store containing the list. For example, in a particular application there might be less than 1024 distinct microinstructions. In that case a 2000-word microprogram can be compressed into 20 000 bits, a saving of 90%. All that is required is that the 10-bit microinstruction shall address a store 100 bits wide, containing up to 1024 words, giving a net saving of 40% in space. The second store is sometimes called a *nanostore*.

It is more likely that *some* of the fields of the microinstruction will be fully used, leaving a residue to be handled in the above way. The Nanodata QM-1 machine provides an illustration (Fig. 3.3). The 16-bit microinstruction is fetched to one of the microregisters, from which six bits are used to select a 342-bit **nanoinstruction**. The latter can use the remaining ten microinstruction bits as operand specifiers, so they can be regarded as a form of preset nanocontrol. At this point the designer faces the same set of choices at nano-machine level as we have already introduced in connection with micro-machines. One could use direct control: in fact the QM-1 does not, but obeys a far more elaborate sequence of nanoorders. The reader is referred to the literature for details. The difficulties of evaluating performance in system context are so great, even with two levels of control, that we shall have to

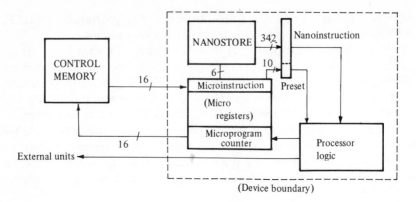

Fig. 3.3   Nanoprogram control

leave nanoprogramming out of consideration. It might be noted, however, that because of its narrow interface with the program store (the dotted boundary in Fig. 3.3) this scheme of control has much in common with that used on microprocessors (reading "target" for "micro" in the above description).

(b) Timing and control considerations

It was seen in Chapter 2 that interpreting one of the common target instructions takes about 20 register transfer operations and from 2 to 4 memory accesses. It follows that if a premium is placed on memory utilization, the effective register transfer rate must be over five times that of main memory access: to achieve that, early machines used a multi-order or **horizontal** instruction that could activate several transfers in parallel. Remembering that each transfer takes at least two microorders (source, destination) it is not surprising to find microinstructions composed of ten or more microorder fields. In such machines the microinstruction is synchronized to the main store, so that a 1.5 μs core memory might be associated with a 500 ns or 750 ns microinstruction cycle. Horizontal coding achieves speed at the expense of generality and ease of programming. The rapid reduction in cost of fast logic and storage devices in recent years has enabled a more "relaxed" form of code to be used, in which each microinstruction contains only 3 or 4 microorders, which is naturally called **vertical** format.

In moving to vertical instructions it is normally the case that the main memory system has a much higher data rate than the micromachine can handle, even with the fastest control memory. The extra capacity is used in direct memory access by I – O devices, in dual processor configurations, and in many instances by using the main memory as a source of microinstructions. The last option is particularly attractive because it affords an escape from the rigid limitation on microprogram size that is imposed by a separate control memory. On the other hand it does impose a control structure that is difficult to rationalize: perhaps the simplest view is to look upon the interpreter as a means of establishing system standards, operating system interfaces, protection bounds, etc., which are not normally present at the microcontrol level.

The elementary steps of the micromachine cycle have already been indicated. If no overlap is attempted, then the major components — control memory and processor — are alternately idle while the other completes its task. To improve performance it is necessary to use faster and therefore more expensive components or to overlap the elementary steps. The options are superficially the same as in machine-code design, the main differences deriving from the fact that microprograms have been for the most part fixed, comparatively small, and tend (as we saw in the last chapter) to make extensive use of multiway decoding or switch instructions. The basic techniques can be illustrated with the help of timing charts which show, starting from "time 0", the activity of the main parts of the micromachine. Assuming equal time for each activity, our original assumption leads to the behavior shown in Fig. 3.4.

Time:	0	1	2	3	4	5	6	7
Activity:								
Instr. fetch:	-----				α.		γ.	
Processor:		-----			α			γ
Sequencer:			$\rightarrow \alpha$			$\rightarrow \gamma$		

Fig. 3.4 Timing chart: non-overlapped micromachine activities

A control memory address is frequently composed from several fields whose values are determined at different points in the machine cycle. The high-order fields are often found as block addresses in preset control, the assumption being that for appreciable intervals the microprogram counter will remain within a restricted region of memory. The address will be completed by a field injected from the microprogram (a *functional branch* in IBM terms), with the possibility of setting low-order bits directly from the processor state. Thus, injecting two condition bits provides an instant four-way switch. In such a micromachine the sequencing operation can take place in parallel with processing (Fig. 3.5); nevertheless, the final address will not be known (in the case of branches) until a late point in the cycle.

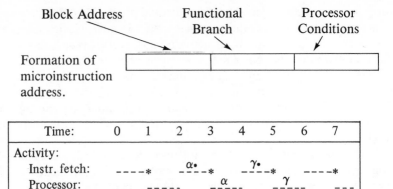

Time:	0	1	2	3	4	5	6	7
Activity:								
Instr. fetch:	- - - -*		$\overset{\alpha\bullet}{- - -}$*		$\overset{\gamma\bullet}{- - -}$*		- - - -*	
Processor:	- - - - -			$- -\overset{\alpha}{- -}-$		$- -\overset{\gamma}{- -}-$	- - -	
Sequencer:	$\overset{\rightarrow\alpha}{- - - -}$		$\overset{\rightarrow\gamma}{- - - -}$		- - - - -		- - -	

Fig. 3.5   Timing chart: overlapped processor and sequencer activity

At the points where the control memory would otherwise be idle (∗ in Fig. 3.5) the designer might decide to speculate on the next address and initiate the next memory cycle. If there is no branch the guess will probably be right (as at α in Fig. 3.6); if there is a branch (as in cycle 3 where the micromachine

Time:	0	1	2	3	4	5	6	7
Activity:								
Instr. fetch:	- - - -	$\overset{\alpha\bullet}{- - -}$	$\overset{\beta\bullet}{- - -}$	$\overset{\gamma\bullet}{- - -}$	- - - -	- - -	- - - -	- - -
Processor:	- - - -	- - -	$- -\overset{\alpha}{-}-$	$- -\overset{\beta\,?}{-}-$	$\overset{\gamma}{- - -}$	- - -	- - - -	- - -
Sequencer:	- - - -	$\overset{\rightarrow\alpha}{- - -}$	$\overset{\rightarrow\gamma}{- - -}$	$\overset{\beta\,?}{- - -}$	- - - -	- - -	- - - -	- - -

Fig. 3.6   Timing chart: overlapped instruction fetch

anticipated β when in fact a branch to γ has taken place) the programmer might be asked to decide what to do with the microinstruction awaiting execution. What that means in practise is that one or two instructions in "normal" sequence after a branch might be obeyed; e.g. in decoding a hypothetical target instruction the microprogram might be written:

> . . . : { *extract function field* }
> α: { *branch to address + function bits (γ)* }
> β: { *increment target program counter* }

Here, although the branch to γ is taken, the instruction at β is still obeyed. In this example the effect is useful, but the programmer might be given the option of dealing with such "run-on" or "pipelining" effects. It is in dealing with such peculiarities and in taking account of critical timing constraints that microprogramming has acquired its distinctive flavor. Figure 3.7 is an

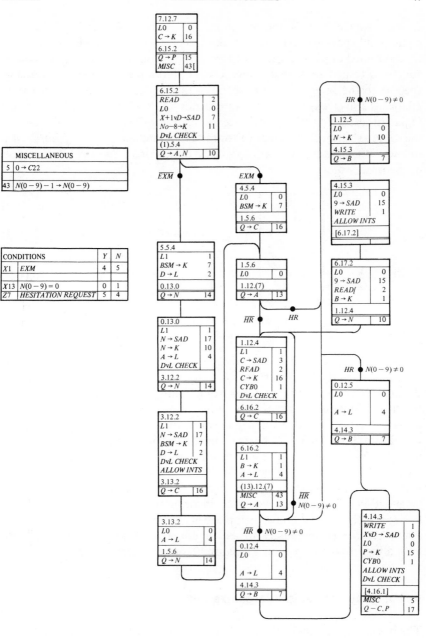

Fig. 3.7 Horizontal microprogram (ICL 1904/5 E & F Microprogram)

excerpt from ICL 1904 microprogram, which must be compared with the equivalent logic diagram to see its true attraction. Here, each microinstruction is represented as a box giving its address, timing (variable, depending on the functions to be carried out), microorders and miscellaneous orders highly specific to the target machine (see inset table). The next microinstruction address is also given, coded as the three fields "$X.Y.Z$": when a field is written in parentheses, e.g. "(7)", reference to the inset CONDITIONS table shows the value to be injected on true (Y) or false (N) outcome of a test. Thus 2-, 4-, or 8-way branches can be generated, based on 1, 2 or 3 independent conditions of the processor.

6.16.2		Location in control mem.
$L1$	1	Timing control
$B{\rightarrow}K$	1	ALU input from B reg
$A{\rightarrow}L$	4	ALU input from A reg
(13).12.(7)		4-way switch on $X13, Z7$
$MISC$	43	Decrement N bits $0, \ldots, 9$
$Q{\rightarrow}A$	13	ALU output to A

Fig. 3.8   1904 microinstruction

Increasing hardware power and the need for more general applicability have promoted the use of vertical microinstructions, perhaps the only way of distinguishing such micromachines from "minis" being in their dedication to the task of modelling processors rather than users' problems. Figure 3.9 shows a vertically coded microprocedure for the same function ("Form-Checksum") as Fig. 3.7. It bears comparison with a conventional program listing except for the primitive nature of the arithmetic, the absence of address modification, and the elaborate field selection and branching operations. Although vertical microprogram appears to be more readily applicable to language interpretation it would be incorrect to think of it as displacing horizontal coding: both have their place in modern systems, and it is possible that when the requirements are better understood horizontal coding will have a bigger part to play in specialized language-oriented design.

(c) Highway and register organization

The basic requirement of the host is to provide space for the target machine state and efficient means of accessing the most commonly used operands. Most of the target machine is represented in main storage, but it is often justified to make special provision for target registers by providing a **scratch-pad** or **local store** closely linked to the micromachine data flow. The scratchpad will contain at least one set of target registers and possibly other

0895		#SEGMENT F127	

0896	0:	SDR ← (0) SHC	SDR ← ZERO (0)
0897	L127	SCXS SET 2	
0898		SHD ← (1) SHD + SDR	USES ALU(1)
0899		SAR ← (0) SCA + GP1	USES ALU(0)
0900		IF GP1.0 MASK 3 = 2 GOTO NACC	IF (EXM & ADTN & DATUMNZ) THEN NOT ACCUMIR
0901		IF CF2=1 GOTO ACUM	
0902	NACC	READ SDR/SAR/0 WORD	
0903	STOR	IF IN1=0 GOTO NOHES	
0904		JSL HES.1	SERVICE HESITATION, PRESERVE ALL
0905	NOHES	GP2 ← (1) GP2 − 1	
0906		SCA ← (0) SCA + 1	
0907		SCXS SET 0	
0908		IF M1S=0 GOTO L127	TESTS ALU(1)
0909		SCX ← SHD	
0910		JUMP TO MVSR.9	
0911			
0912	ACUM	SDR ← SCX	
0913		GOTO STOR	
0914			
0915			
0916	#CHECK	#58A4F4	
0917			
0918			
0919	#END		

SEGMENT F127(0), 10 WORDS MAPPABLE ONTO A 01-WORD BOUNDARY.

Fig. 3.9 An example of microprogram for the E1 emulator performing the ICL 1900 function $f = 127$: form checksum of $N(M)$ words starting at location (X). The micromachine has three register transfer paths, two of which pass through an arithmetic unit. The assignment operator "$←(i)$", $i = 0,1$, discriminates between them.

data such as memory mapping tables or channel status words accessible only through privileged target functions. Further specialization might be justified for target condition codes, program counter, stack address, instruction and operand buffers.

Register transfers are routed through one or more arithmetic and logical units (ALUs) designed to handle sequencing and address calculation as well as arithmetic operations. Study of the target instruction sets and trial coding will show that arbitrary choice of inputs to the ALU is not usually needed, so selective connection to one side or the other can be specified in order to save on microinstruction bits and control lines. External units which might operate asynchronously need special register interfaces: they include main-store data and address registers, peripheral data and status lines, and special function boxes such as shifters or floating-point arithmetic units.

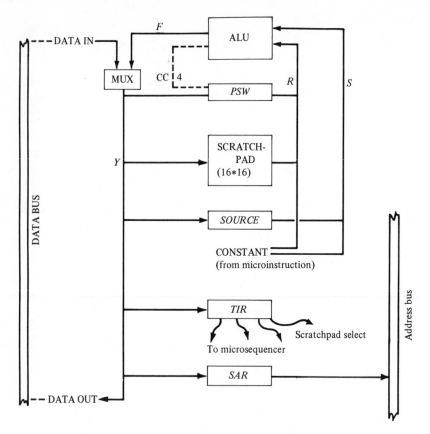

Fig. 3.10   Archetype of PDP-11 micromachine dataflow

A typical data flow for the PDP-11 micromachine is presented in Fig. 3.10 (all data paths are 16 bits unless specified otherwise). Note that the target program counter (*PC*) and stack pointer (*SP*) are held in the scratchpad store. The target instruction register (*TIR*) provides switch addresses for microprogram, and the important decoding statements dealing with primary function, source and destination fields can each be completed in single sequencing steps. Each microinstruction controls ALU input (via *R* and *S* highways), ALU function, ALU output (*F*) and register input (via *Y*); it also controls main store access, and since the main store bus (the Unibus) is asynchronous it has the ability to delay microinstruction sequencing to allow completion of a read or write operation. (On the PDP-11 the addresses on the Unibus are interpreted either as "store" or "device" references, so there is no need for separate channel control functions.)

Many of the time-consuming operand selection and masking operations

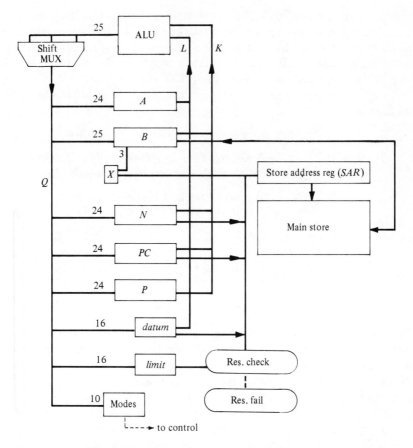

Fig. 3.11   Archetype of ICL 1900 dataflow

that were noted in Chapter 2 are carried out by multiplexors on the ALU input (not shown here) and output (MUX). These provide for byte selection, sign-extension, single-stage left and right shifts and complementation. Such facilities are very commonly used to adapt the micromachine to the target formats: the number of "stages" that can be used is governed by the maximum gate delay allowed in the processor cycle.

A schematic dataflow for our second sample machine (ICL 1904E) is given in Fig. 3.11. There are nine microregisters (*A, B, X,* etc.) each with specialized length and function, and selective input to the arithmetic unit. Remember that the target registers themselves are held in the first eight words of the user program area, starting at *datum*. The *limit* register gives the maximum valid location number, and can be used for reservation check in parallel with other operations. The target program counter is *PC*. Operand locations are formed in N. The register P is used for shifting and byte-extraction operations. B is used as the data register for both store read/write and instruction fetch. In this machine all store accesses, including peripheral transfers, are made via the central processor (single-word or character-transfer requests are referred to as "hesitations" in Figs. 3.7 and 3.9). The steps involved in a simple register-store operation f might be as follows (assuming no indexing):

	Main store access	*Other*
Step 1:	$PC \to SAR$, Res.Check, *READ*; Branch on: Res.Fail $\times$ Modify;	$N = datum + (B$ *mask* 12);
Step 2:	$N \to SAR$, Res.Check, *READ*; Branch on: Res.Fail;	$A = B$
Step 3:	$datum \mid X \to SAR$, *READ-HOLD*; /* destination reg */	$B = f(B,A)$; Set target conditions;
Step 4:	/*result in B*/ *WRITE*; Branch to Step 1 $\times$ Interrupt;	$PC + 1$;

Each step requires one microinstruction of the type illustrated in Fig. 3.7. It will be seen that completion of the micromachine cycle often waits on store-access operation, and that in practise the microorders would be started at different points within the machine cycle. The packaging of microorders into a single instruction word enables the host to activate several transfers in parallel and so match the bandwidth of the main store subsystem.

As a third illustration of the choice of specialized highway and register organization to meet performance/cost objectives, some details of the arithmetic unit of the IBM 360/Model 50 are shown in Fig. 3.12. The ALU is able to perform binary or decimal functions on 32-bit inputs, and in one microinstruction the sources of data to be gated into the adder are specified, together with the function to be performed and the destination of the result. Out of 90 microinstruction bits, 21 are primarily concerned with ALU control:

	bits	function
TR	5	destination of adder latch output
AL	5	shift gating into adder latch
AD	4	adder function (see Table 3.1)
RY	3	right input to adder
LX	3	left input to adder
TC	1	true/complement left input

For example, Table 3.1 shows the actions selected by the AD microorder field. The coding of RY and LX allows for various full or part-register fields

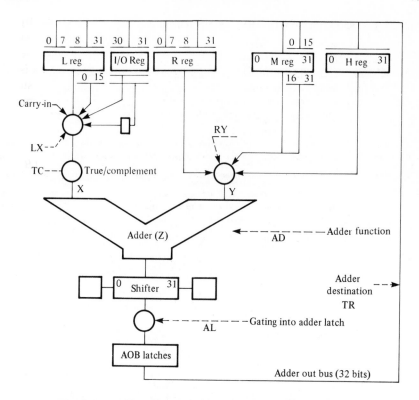

Fig. 3.12 Adder data path for IBM System 360/50 (Samir S. Husson, *Microprogramming: Principles and Practices*, © 1970, p. 229. Reprinted by permission of Prentice-Hall, Inc., Englewood Cliffs, New Jersey)

to be used as inputs, and AL controls a wide range of single- and four-bit shifts to accommodate binary, decimal and floating-point formats.

It should be remembered that although technology has advanced (from capacitor ROM to bipolar control RAM, for example) the algorithmic requirements are little changed. Since the introduction of microprogramming increases in logic speeds have been relatively greater than those of storage systems, with consequent reduction in the need for specialization in the host machine. However, the evolution of single-chip processors is creating conditions not unlike those experienced by early microprogrammers — limited silicon area favoring the use of ROM control, with functions and data paths specialized to the target instruction set and architecture. Hence the techniques used on the first generation of micromachines cannot be entirely relegated to the history books.

Table 3.1   ALU functions on IBM System 360/50

AD FIELD			ROSDR 68-71	ADDER FUNCTION (NULL VALUE: AD1)	
EDGE CHAR	MNEMONIC	BITS	DEC ORDER	FUNCTION	ALU PAGE
		0000	AD0	UNDEFINED	
		0001	AD1	ADD. NO CARRIES ENTERED OR SAVED	
A	BCF0	0010	AD2	ADD. NO CARRY SAVED. IF F REG EQUALS ZERO, INSERT CARRY INTO POSITION 31.	DR031
		0011	AD3	UNDEFINED	
A	BC0	0100	AD4	ADD. SET CARRY STAT TO CARRY OUT OF POSITION 0.	DR032
A	BCVC	0101	AD5	ADD. SET CARRY STAT TO EXCLUSIVE OR OF CARRIES OUT OF POSITIONS 0 AND 1.	DR032
A	BC1B	0110	AD6	ADD. SET CARRY STAT TO CARRY OUT OF POSITION 1. BLOCK CARRY FROM POSITION 8 TO POSITION 7.	DR032
A	BC	0110	AD6	AS ABOVE. USED WITH ORDER AL23.	DR032
A	BC8	0111	AD7	ADD. SET CARRY STAT TO CARRY OUT OF POSITION 8.	DR032
A	DHL	1000	AD8	DECIMAL HALVE (LOW ORDER). BIT 2 OF EACH DIGIT OF THE SUM IS TESTED. IF THE BIT IS ONE, THE NEXT DIGIT POSITION TO THE RIGHT IN THE L REG IS SET TO 0110. IF THE BIT IS ZERO, THE DIGIT IN L REG IS SET TO 0000. THE LEFTMOST DIGIT IN THE L REG IS SET IN THE SAME WAY FROM THE AUXILIARY TRIGGER.	DR031
A	DC0	1001	AD9	DECIMAL ADD. SET STAT 1 TO CARRY OUT OF POSITION 0. INSERT PREVIOUS VALUE OF STAT 1 AS CARRY INTO POSITION 31. TEST CARRY OUT OF EACH DIGIT POSITION. IF CARRY, SET CORRESPONDING DIGIT POSITION IN L REG TO 0000. IF NO CARRY, SET DIGIT IN L REG TO 0110.	DR032
A	DDC0	1010	AD10	DECIMAL DOUBLE. SET STAT 1 TO CARRY OUT OF POSITION 0. INSERT PREVIOUS VALUE OF STAT 1 AS CARRY INTO POSITION 31. TEST EACH DIGIT OF SUM. IF 5 OR GREATER, SET CORRESPONDING DIGIT POSITION IN L REG TO 0110. IF LESS THAN 5, SET DIGIT IN L REG TO 0000.	DR032
A	DHH	1011	AD11	DECIMAL HALVE (HIGH ORDER). BIT 2 OF EACH DIGIT OF THE SUM IS TESTED. IF THE BIT IS ONE, THE NEXT DIGIT POSITION TO THE RIGHT IN THE L REG IS SET TO 0110. IF THE BIT IS ZERO, THE DIGIT IN L REG IS SET TO 0000. THE LEFTMOST DIGIT IN L REG IS SET TO 0000. THE AUXILIARY TRIGGER IS SET TO BIT 2 OF THE RIGHTMOST SUM DIGIT (SUM BIT 30).	DR032
A	DCBS	1100	AD12	DECIMAL ADD. SET STAT 1 TO CARRY OUT OF LEFTMOST BYTE POSITION FOR WHICH A BYTE STAT IS ON. INSERT PREVIOUS VALUE OF STAT 1 AS CARRY INTO POSITION 1. TEST CARRY OUT OF EACH DIGIT POSITION. IF CARRY, SET CORRESPONDING DIGIT POSITION IN L REG TO 0000. IF NO CARRY, SET DIGIT IN L REG TO 0110.	DR032
		1101	AD13	UNDEFINED	
		1110	AD14	UNDEFINED	
		1111	AD15	UNDEFINED	

NOTE: IN ALL CASES ADDITION IS BINARY. THE TERM 'DECIMAL ADD' USED ABOVE REFERS TO THE MANNER OF GENERATING THE CORRECTION FACTOR IN THE L REG.

(Samir S. Husson, *Microprogramming: Principles and Practices,*
© 1970, p. 229. Reprinted by permission of Prentice-Hall, Inc.,
Englewood Cliffs, New Jersey)

3.2 GENERALIZED HOST MACHINES

We have seen some of the ways in which specific features are built into microprogrammable machines to help in modelling particular target instructions. However, our main objective is to consider systems at a level removed from machine code, where the target instruction sets can to some extent be chosen to suit the available host. We therefore examine design generalizations that have been favored in recent years as the result of increased speed of control storage and logical devices. In the latter context regularity of hardware is at least as important as circuit or gate count, which is greatly to the benefit of the microprogrammer.

The design objective of producing a "universal emulator" became feasible with the introduction of writable control memories. It is clear from the outset that machines capable of imitating *any* instruction set at competitive speed could not be produced at competitive cost. Nevertheless, such a machine is invaluable as a vehicle for research into computer architectures, and many of the generalizations aimed at emulation appear equally applicable to language-oriented design. The ICL research emulator E1, the Standard Computer Corporation MLP-900, the Stanford University EMMY, and Nanodata QM-1 have all been fruitful sources of ideas, while in the commercial field Burroughs have been alone in featuring alterable target instruction sets, though many systems currently in production have that capability. All machines in this category lean towards the vertical in microinstruction design.

The basic requirements for imitating a range of target instruction sets are:

(a) arithmetic primitives for constructing the functions of the target machines;
(b) memory mapping and resolution compatible with the data structures of the target systems;
(c) imitation of the internal control states, registers and register access patterns of the target instruction sets; and
(d) peripheral interfaces that reflect the formats, status and timing expected in the target systems.

Within each field the degree of dedication varies with the performance/cost objective. We shall examine each of (a), (b) and (c), drawing examples from the machines mentioned above. In the context of high-level interfaces, recognizing that most languages are non-specific with regard to the means of $I-O$ control, the preferred approach is to match $I-O$ statements using host system procedures. How such supporting software fits into the microsystem will be examined later.

(a) Generalized arithmetic and data paths

One of the obvious ways in which MSI or LSI components affect the arithmetic system is in allowing register lengths to be standardized to a reasonably high value rather than making use of specialized lengths seen in early machines. The effect is to curtail microinstruction sequences, because operations previously performed by iteration can then be carried out in single steps.

The host is still specialized with respect to arithmetic width and shift paths. Two methods have been employed for varying arithmetic precision up to a prescribed field size:

(1) Using a third input to the ALU, which is in fact a mask specifying which fields participate in the operation. The MLP-900 allows the micro-instruction to select one of 32 possible masks which can be used to propagate carry to the normal sign position. A mask might also be used to permit operations on unpacked fields such as decimal characters stored in byte positions. One of the difficulties of working with unpacked data, however, is that they might eventually have to be aligned to an external interface such as the store address bus.

(2) Allowing the ALU width to be variable, i.e. taking sign, carry, overflow and zero-test signals from any position in the ALU. This method is used in the E1 emulator and the B 1700, where the sign position is part of preset control. If more than one arithmetic width is in constant use it is desirable to have more than one preset width, selected by microinstruction.

Variation in ALU width has a counterpart in shift functions. To repro-duce exactly the shift patterns of a word of any length it is necessary to preset the point at which end connections are made (one end can usually be fixed at the end of the host register). The E1 emulator does allow shifts on words of from 2 to 64 bits, but the logic is expensive and most designers have settled for single- or double-length shifts and rotations.

A final area where both the ALU and shifter are affected is in the type of arithmetic carried out. The predominant types are binary integer, decimal and floating point. Generalized facilities for the last are unusually complex and only of interest to emulation. Decimal operations can be built into the ALU in varying degrees from fully signed operations to facilities for detecting carries at the decimal digit positions. The choice rests entirely on the final cost/performance aim. Although an important area of design, it can be factored out in comparative studies of language-oriented and fixed instruc-tion set machines, for which reason we shall not extend the discussion. It is important to remember that if a host has good arithmetic facilities, then any lapse in handling the data access side of a language will be conspicuous, and conversely.

At this point it is useful to refer back to Figs. 3.10 and 3.11 and reflect on the type of generalization that can be offered. Evidently, in place of par-ticular registers (*PSW, SOURCE, TIR,* etc. in Fig. 3.10) there will be a set of general-purpose microregisters. The ALU will be of fixed maximum length with one or more preset sign positions. The multiplexors in the main data paths must be designed to perform the most frequent data selections. The scratchpad must accommodate in size and access mechanism the commonly used registers of the target machine. Where special functions are performed (as *Reservation check* in Fig. 3.11) additional passes through the ALU are needed. Where special decoding is performed (as in *TIR* or *B) mask* and

Table 3.2　Register specialization in E1

Mnemonic	Function	
TIR	Target instruction ⎫	main store data
SDR	Operand ⎭	interface
TCN	Target prog. ctr. ⎫	main store address
SAR	Store address ⎭	interface
SCD ⎫		
SCA ⎬	Shift data and counter	
SHD ⎭		
SCX ⎫		
SCY ⎭	Scratchpad pre-fetch (see text)	
GP1,GP2,GP3	General-purpose registers	
LNA,LNB	I − O multiplexor interfaces	
(Z)	Zero input/output sink	

branching operations will occur in microprogram. There is a clear prospect of generating an excessive amount of microprogram as the result of moving away from the "range archetype". We now examine what more can be expected of the perfect host.

A feature of many micromachines is that the microregisters act both as arithmetic operands and as components of specialized function units. The ALU and the associated bus structure can sometimes be regarded simply as a switch connecting a number of more complex logical units. In "universal" micromachines, the ALU is generalized with respect to registers, but functional dedication is often retained. Table 3.2 shows the assignment of microregisters in E1. One of the effects of specialization is that less control is taken up in register selection. Another effect is that extensive microorder sequences can often be overlapped, provided there is no conflict in register usage, e.g. performing shifts concurrently with store access. The initial choice of function has to be made with careful regard for the class of target machines of interest and, as with any multi-function unit machine, performance is sensitive to the ordering of instructions. The E1 emulator includes the interlocks on register access necessary to force synchronization so that, for example, shifts, ALU and store access operations can be performed in parallel. The overlap so achieved partly compensates for parallelism lost by the vertical mode of issuing microinstructions.

If the path from memory is not selective enough (and it usually is not) facilities are required for extracting fields from microregisters for input to the ALU. Generalized facilities are expensive and might again be confined to limited field selection or to particular registers. Thus the B 1700 provides variable field extraction on one 24-bit register, but defines a range of "microregister addresses" that allows part-words to be extracted. The E1 emulator allows any byte to be extracted for comparison and control purposes. It does not appear that high-level languages demand complete generality, and limitations could be accepted simply on the grounds of coding efficiency.

(b) Memory mapping and address translation

The unstructured nature of machine code, allowing instructions to be used as data, and vice-versa, forces a strict correspondence to be maintained between the target machine and its representation in the host at almost all times. In most machines the target machine word is rounded up when necessary to fit the host, not attempting to make use of every bit in store. The B 1700 goes to the length of resolving addresses to bit level, allowing any string of up to 24 bits to be read or written, starting (or finishing) at a given position. In that case 100% store utilization can always be achieved.

The word selected from memory is made available for analysis in the microregisters. It is an advantage to be able to select from two or more potential data registers to avoid internal transfers. At this point there is also the opportunity to map the data into a more easily managed form. The *cross-points* of the E1 emulator (*language boards* in MLP-900) allow the choice of alternative hardwired data paths to and from memory. They may be used, for example, to prepare target instructions for decoding, to align decimal digits to byte boundaries, or to handle parity conventions on a foreign data bus. The effect of the crosspoint is typically to save 5 or 6 steps in the interpretive loop of 25 − 30 microinstructions. It can be seen as complementing the internal data selection functions: in a machine with powerful field selection orders crosspoints would be less important.

Apart from data, addresses have to be matched to the conventions of the host, and that is a source of serious problems in emulation. For example, if the target machine uses decimal addressing and the host uses binary, then conversion must take place before accessing the store. Similarly, if the target machine operates in virtual program space, then virtual-to-real translation is called for, as we saw in elementary form in the ICL 1900. If page and segment table accesses are implicit in each store reference the conversion could easily exceed the combined steps of instruction decode and execution. The alternative of using hardware assistance — allowing the host to work in virtual space — is expensive and still leads to delay in store access.

In the environment of high-level languages the "address" fields are in fact indices relative to various sequences defined by environmental pointers. Problems of resolution and word alignment remain, but whether the pointers point to real or virtual space is a key question to which we shall return in Chapter 6.

(c) Representing the internal state of the target machine

The primary data of an interpretive program are the registers, the program counter, instruction register, control flags, status and control words of the target machine. A generalized host would expect to have room for the largest machine state of interest, but even so it is unlikely to require more than a few hundred bytes of storage, which can be found by including a scratchpad with flexible addressing facilities.

It is a common requirement to access the scratchpad using an index value. For example, a target machine "register – register" instruction contains two such indices. Microinstructions do not admit the type of address calculation found in target instruction sets, so it is necessary to carry out some preliminary address calculation (remember that in the PDP-11 the source and destination register fields might be used directly for scratchpad addressing, but that is a special case, see Fig. 3.10). To generalize that idea both the field (host register, bit position, size) and scratchpad datum (e.g. start address of register set) must be parameterized, but the problem is how to do that without excessive time penalty.

In the E1 emulator that is done by assigning preset control fields to correspond to tables in scratchpad and arranging that certain host register indices would select the scratchpad words so designated at any instant — a form of indirect addressing, except that it is activated by a change in value of the index field rather than by a microinstruction. The general effect, in conjunction with crosspoint data input, is shown in Fig. 3.13. Here an ICL 1900 instruction is read from store and mapped into a host register with both the accumulator index X and modifier M in the position of predictive indices. Scratchpad access is initiated (by hardware) as soon as X and M are loaded, with the result that the corresponding register contents are available to the next microinstruction by addressing "SCX" or "SCY". Note that here, as in many micromachines, the scratchpad is kept in duplicate, so that two operands can be accessed in the same micromachine cycle. For essentially the same reason control and scratchpad memories are usually separated and the microprogrammer has to handle the problems arising from having two limited resources. That is not the case in EMMY, which has a common store for microprogram and data, as we shall see later.

In the course of interpretation it is often convenient to make use of subroutines for common sequences of microinstructions, as we saw in

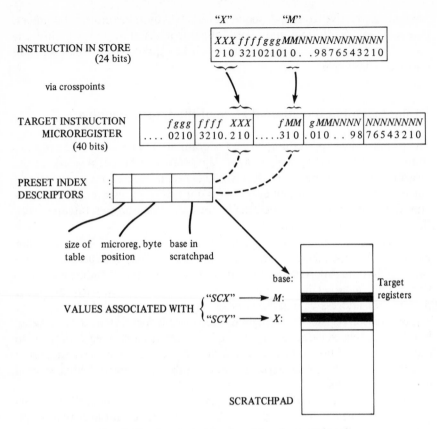

Fig. 3.13   Access to target registers in scratchpad

Chapter 2. In practical terms, *source* and *dest* are realized in two or three microorders with substantial hardware assistance (Fig. 3.10); in other situations, when a subroutine is called from only three or four points and therefore has only three or four points of return, it is possible to discriminate between them using control flags. In general, however, support for subroutine call and return at microprogram level is a valuable aid to interpreter design. It cannot, for reasons of efficiency, have the same generality as in procedural languages. For machines in this category it consists of a hardware stack into which the microprogram counter is pushed on "call" and from which it is popped on "return". The depth of stack is small (typically 4 or 8 levels) and system behavior when the stack is full leaves much to be desired. The stack can only be used with confidence when the depth of subroutine calling is carefully controlled. The placement of parameter and result values is normally decided by software conventions governing the host registers, though some micromachines provide a *complete* change of environment on procedure call for dealing with external interrupts.

The microprogram stack, preset control fields, condition codes and flags are all part of the host but external to the target machine state. In a carefully engineered system it should be possible to make strong assertions about the host at times when the target state is "valid", e.g. at the beginning of the main interpretive loop. For example, one would expect the microcontrol stack to be empty at such times, and if an exception arises (such as *ODDADDR* in *source*) there must be microorders able to unwind the stack without going through the normal return points. At other times it is necessary to *read* all flags and preset control fields and store them temporarily. We shall see that such restarts are not necessarily at the beginning of the main interpretive loop in language-oriented systems, which is the cause of some complication in design.

The primary data of a high-level language machine are the intermediate results, control information, stack and environmental pointers that allow access to contextually relevant data. For the most widely used languages the state can be mapped into host registers and scratchpad quite easily. Moreover, access patterns correspond closely with those of conventional target instruction sets. Hence the scratchpad organization of a universal emulator seems equally applicable to the major programming languages. Whether there are alternative organizations suited to a wider class of languages is an open question: it might be argued that a language is "major" because it happens to fit onto conventional hardware, and that when that constraint is removed more attention can be given to problem-oriented languages.

How much does generality cost in terms of performance? That is impossible to say without detailed analysis of a range of target machines. A slight indication can be given by comparing the vertical encoding of the "or" instruction on the E1 emulator with the horizontal form of the ICL 1904. The actions are classified into five types:

ICL 1900 "or" instruction on:	ICL 1904	E1
Target machine sequencing	2	3
Micromachine sequencing	2	6
Decoding	0	12
Operand access	5	9
Function execution	2	2

It can be seen that the number of elementary steps has doubled. One would expect a greater discrepancy from a simpler host. However, the most startling figure in each column is the ratio of support activity to "useful" function: at least 6:1. Our main concern in later chapters will be to reduce that ratio.

3.3 FURTHER READING

Microprogramming is an enormous subject area embracing many different techniques and applications. For a survey of "classical" principles and an extensive reference list see HUS70. The technical journals survey the field periodically, and RAU80 gives up-to-date references and a review of current activity. See also TUC67 for a discussion of microsystem design for emulation. Specific examples of micromachines are discussed in ECK79 (PDP 11/60), TAN76 (PDP 11/40 and IBM 370/125). AGR76 and AND80 present general discussion of the design of microprogrammable machines and their application.

Generalized host machines are not well documented in open literature, but brief descriptions of the machines mentioned in this chapter can be found in TAN76 (Burroughs B1700), RAK72 (MLP-900), NEU75 (EMMY), ROS72 (QM1) and ILI72b (E1 emulator). For a comparative study of general-purpose micromachines see SAL73.

Undoubtedly, the best way to understand microprogramming is to write an interpreter for a particular target language. Access to manufacturers' operation manuals (see BUR73 or BUR79) is essential, and any practical efforts must be supported by microassembler and diagnostic aids. Users of Pascal might consider how the intermediate P-code which is often used as a target language (see BER78) would be interpreted on a given micromachine.

4 PREPACKAGED MICROMACHINES

The aim of this chapter is to provide practical examples of microprogram design. Without losing the general line of argument readers with prior microprogramming experience might prefer at first reading to skip to Chapter 5. By basing the discussion on one of the industry-standard families of micromachine components we gain immediate access to a realistic set of design options, though it might be added that some of the features mentioned in Chapter 3 are not in such demand that commercial exploitation is justified. On the other hand, language execution makes less stringent demands than universal emulation, hence the generality aimed at by device manufacturers may well provide effective support for the target instruction sets of interest.

The basic requirements of micromachine components are speed and flexibility. The use of fast (bipolar) circuits places limits on the logical complexity of a device which are reinforced by the need to control it at microorder level. Hence, instead of following the path which has put complete but relatively slow microprocessors on a single chip, bipolar LSI devices have reached the stage of presenting complete slices (typically 4 bits wide) of control or arithmetic circuits in a single package. It is important to appreciate the difference: in a microprocessor a target instruction is presented at the chip boundary and is internally broken into function and address fields, which are interpreted by a multistep microprogram within the chip; in a micromachine component a microorder is presented at the chip boundary, then decoded internally and interpreted in a single state transition. Typical microprocessor instructions take about 10 clock cycles (at 5 MHz, say, giving 2.0 µs), whereas micromachine transitions take 100 ns. Of course, the microprocessor does more, but whether it does it in the right direction is the question asked at the end of Chapter 3.

To illustrate the types of component available, two are taken from the Advanced Micro Devices family: the Am2901 arithmetic and logical unit, and the Am2910 microprogram controller. The former is a 4-bit slice that

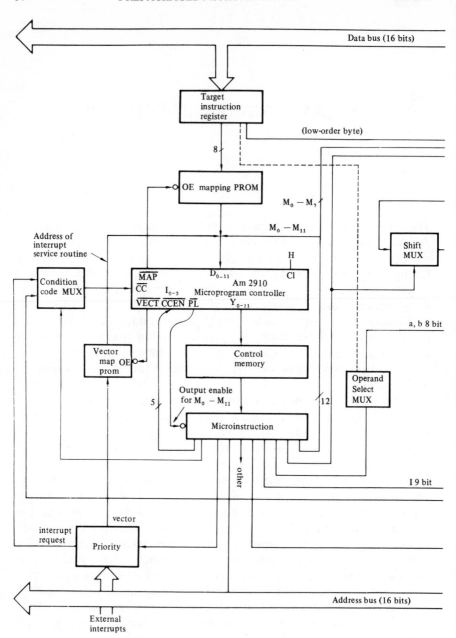

Fig. 4.1 An elementary micromachine using Am2910 and technical description. (Copyright © 1979 Advanced Micro

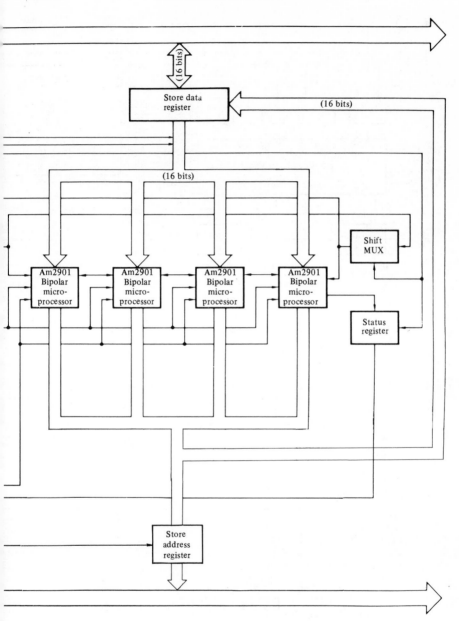

Am2901 devices (adapted from Am2910 Microprogram controller
Devices Inc. Reproduced with permission of copyright owner.)

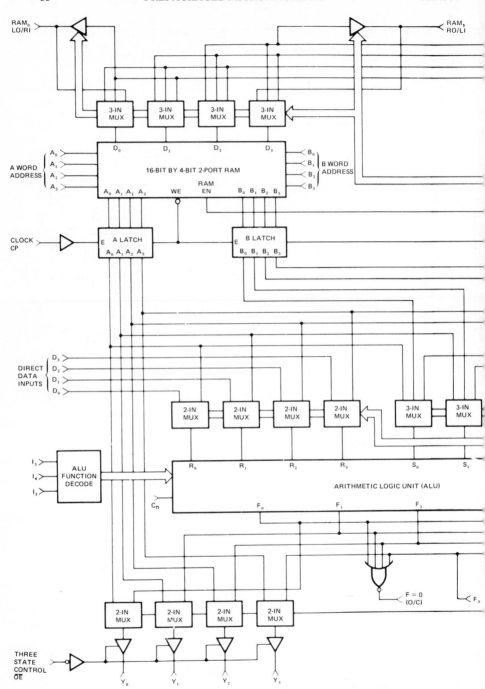

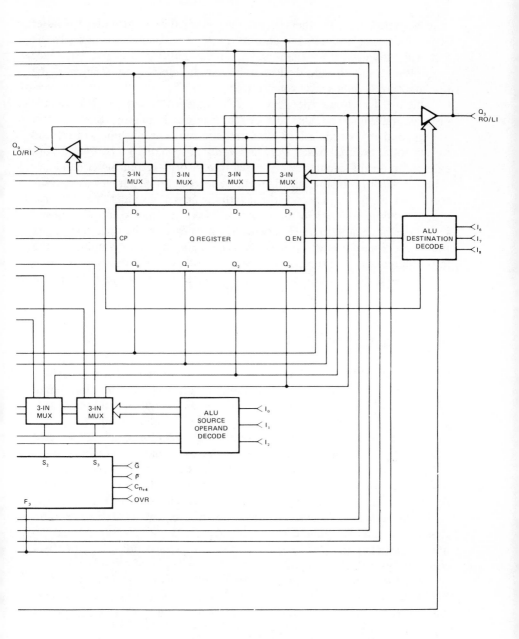

Fig. 4.2 Detailed Am2901 Microprocessor block diagram. (Copyright © 1979 Advanced Micro Devices Inc. Reproduced with permission of copyright owner.)

must be ganged up with others to make the required width of ALU. The latter is a 12-bit device, sufficient to address a 4096-word control memory. In the following discussion we shall make some simplifications and introduce multiplexing and storage devices as required, referring the reader to the manufacturer's data sheets for details.

Figure 4.1 shows the general schematic of a hypothetical micro-programmable machine. On the left of the figure is the microprogram control section, and on the right is a 16-bit arithmetic unit. The machine is interfaced to two 16-bit external buses, *data* and *address*, each of 16 bits. In addition, external interrupt signals are presented to a priority resolution circuit.

The function of the machine will be to read 16-bit target instructions from main memory, to decode them with the help of a small table of micro-program addresses held in the mapping ROM, and to execute the micro-sequences necessary to fetch operands and perform the specified target functions. External interrupts will be serviced by periodic sampling of the interrupt request (*INT*) condition. Target instruction formats are assumed to be fixed, and will be outlined after giving details of the arithmetic unit and controller.

4.1 THE ALU SLICE: AM2901

The internal state of the ALU slice is defined by a random-access file of 16 registers and a separate register (*Q*) used in conjunction with multi-length arithmetic. The external connections include data input (*D*) and three-state output (*Y*). All registers and data paths are 4 bits wide.

In a single state transition the inputs to the arithmetic unit are selected from *Q*, *D* or the RAM, an arithmetic function is applied to them, and the result is returned to one or more of *Y*, *Q* or the RAM. Because the ALU slice is used in association with others, the transition might depend on extra signals received from "left" or "right" neighbors, i.e. carry or shift input to the ALU, shift input to *Q*. Hence, during the microcycle the ALU slice generates signals that can affect one or other neighbor, and it is so arranged that the most significant (left) slice produces status signals indicating the final condition of the ALU output. Figure 4.2 gives details of a single chip.

For the present we assume a 16-bit data word, hence four Am2901s. Figure 4.3 shows the internal data paths which result for this composite device, together with microorder fields and status signals. There are 23 control inputs altogether, and we now summarize their effect.

Register addresses *a, b* (each 4 bits).

In a single cycle any two internal registers can be selected from the RAM for input to the ALU. The *b* address is also used to specify a RAM destination.

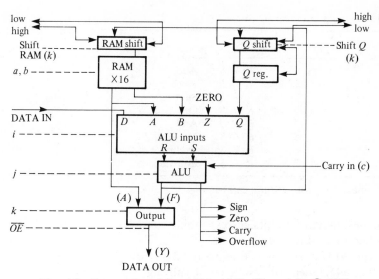

Fig. 4.3 Data paths of the 16-bit ALU. (Copyright © 1979 Advanced Micro Devices Inc. Reproduced with permission of copyright owner.)

ALU sources i (3 bits corresponding to $i_2i_1i_0$ in Fig. 4.2).

Denoting the RAM registers selected by a and b by A,B, there are five possible inputs to the ALU: A,B,D,Q and Z (zero). Eight combinations are selected by the i field (for details, see Table 4.1).

ALU function j (3 bits corresponding to $i_5i_4i_3$ in Fig. 4.2).

The function code selects one of eight operations on R and S, which determines the output (F) of the ALU. In arithmetic (as opposed to logical) functions the carry-in c and *Carry* output are used to propagate carries. See Table 4.2 for details.

Table 4.1   ALU source specification

i	R	S
0	A	Q
1	A	B
2	0	Q
3	0	B
4	0	A
5	D	A
6	D	Q
7	D	0

Table 4.2 ALU function

j		
0	$R + S$	Add*
1	$S - R$	Reverse subtract*
2	$R - S$	Subtract*
3	$R \vee S$	Or
4	$\underline{R} \wedge S$	And
5	$\overline{R} \wedge S$	Not-R and S
6	$\underline{R} \; \underline{\vee} \; \underline{S}$	Exclusive or
7	$R \; \overline{\vee} \; S$	Equivalence

*Arithmetic functions require carry-in c

ALU destination k (3 bits corresponding to $i_8 i_7 i_6$ in Fig. 4.2) and $\overline{OE}$ (1 bit enabling three-state output of Y).

The ALU operation is essentially "2-address" with the option of omitting assignment of result, or of shifting it left or right one position. When shifting, the end connections are determined by external multiplexors set from the microinstruction. Double-length shifts can be carried out in combination with the Q register. The k field also determines the device output (Y): normally F, unshifted, but if $k = 2$ the register A is available. See Table 4.3 for details.

Carry-in c
The input to the low-order bit of the low-order ALU.

Shift connections (4 bits RAM_{low}, RAM_{high}, Q_{low} and Q_{high} in Fig. 4.3).
As required by k, under control of external shift multiplexors.

The external status signals include, besides those shown in Fig. 4.3, two used in conjunction with an optional look-ahead carry generator. Altogether, the 23 control signals, 8 data, 6 status and 3 service connections (clock, power and ground) make a 40-pin integrated-circuit package.

As an aid to understanding the Am2901 it is advisable to ignore the Q

Table 4.3 ALU destination

k	Y	RAM b	Q
0	F		F
1	F		
2	A	F	
3	F	F	
4	F	$F \gg 1$	$Q \gg 1$
5	F	$F \gg 1$	
6	F	$F \ll 1$	$Q \ll 1$
7	F	$F \ll 1$	

register at first (because its main use is in multiplication and division algorithms) and to note that there remain eight binary operations on B and A or on B and D, and three unary operations (identity, negate and not) on A or on D. There are no restrictions on the use of the a and b addresses, so the effect of making them the same and adding is equivalent to a left shift: it could be followed by a RAM shift on the same microcycle.

4.2 THE CONTROL DEVICE: AM2910

A microsequencing unit can be sliced in the same way as the ALU, but because it is not quite as complex, and there is less need for flexibility, the entire sequencing function can also be contained in a single device in conjunction with a condition code multiplexor (Fig. 4.1). Here, all major registers and control paths are 12 bits in width.

The internal state of the Am2910 consists of a microprogram counter μPC, a register/counter R, a 5-word microcontrol stack and a stack pointer. See Fig. 4.4 for details.

State transitions are initiated by external signals consisting of function code I, condition CC and data inputs. In one microcycle a datum output is computed (Y), normally taken to be a microinstruction address. The possible sources of Y are μPC, R, the current top-of-stack value F, an external source D, or zero. The output datum is routed internally to μPC, normally incremented to point to the "next" microinstruction, so the preferred method of sequencing is to obey microinstructions in the order they appear in store.

All functions are nominally conditioned by status signals from, e.g., the ALU, and selected externally. However, there is an enabling control signal $\overline{CCEN}$ which overrides the condition $\overline{CC}$ as follows:

with	$\overline{CCEN}$	= LOW	LOW	HIGH	HIGH
and	$\overline{CC}$	= LOW	HIGH	LOW	HIGH
the test result is		PASS	FAIL	PASS	PASS

Thus, tying $\overline{CCEN}$ to a $HIGH$ state forces the function to a $PASS$ condition.

Table 4.4 details the effect of the 16 control functions I. Here MAP and $VECT$ are to be thought of as two external address sources, possibly ROMs selected by target instruction digits or external interrupt signals, and M is a microinstruction field of 12 bits selected by $\overline{PL}$. Most sequencing functions are close enough to conventional machine code not to need further explanation. Note that three functions ($I = 8,13,15$) use the top value in the stack to provide a destination in iterative loops, without popping it. The register counter R is used ($I = 8,9$) to set an internal condition, independent of $\overline{CC}$, and is combined with $\overline{CC}$ when $I = 15$ to provide a three-way branch to F, D or μPC. Loading R with a value N and counting down to zero using $RFCT$ or $RPCT$ causes $N + 1$ iterations to be performed.

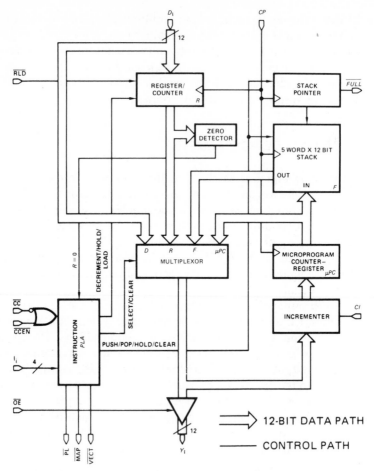

Fig. 4.4   Internal data paths of the Am2901. (Copyright ©
1979 Advanced Micro Devices Inc. Reproduced with permission
of copyright owner.)

When the microprogram stack is empty *POP* functions have no effect;
when full (5 items stacked), the $\overline{FULL}$ status signal is set and further *PUSH*
operations overwrite the top value in the stack: as the manual says, "this
operation is normally avoided". The stack is emptied by the reset function
$I = 0$.

4.3 MICROINSTRUCTION FORMATS

So far we have specified 23 control inputs for the Am2901 and 9 for the
Am2910. Not all are directly supplied from the microinstruction: in the

Table 4.4 Microsequencer control functions

I	Mnemonic	Unconditional		Conditional				Action
					Fail		Pass	
		R	Enable	Y	Stack	Y	Stack	
0	JZ		M	0	clear	0	clear	Jump to address 0
1	CJS		M	PC		D	PUSH	Jump subroutine
2	JMAP		MAP	D		D		Jump to map
3	CJP		M	PC		D		Jump
4	PUSH	LOAD*	M	PC	PUSH	PC	PUSH	Push PC, load R
5	JSRP		M	R	PUSH	D	PUSH	Jump subroutine via R or M
6	CJV		VECT	PC		D		Jump to vector
7	JRP		M	R		D		Jump via R or M
8	RFCT:							
	{ R≠0	DEC	M	F		F	}	Loop control
	{ R=0		M	PC	POP	PC	POP }	using top stack
9	RPCT:							
	{ R≠0	DEC	M	D		D	}	Loop control
	{ R=0		M	PC		PC		using μinstrn.
10	CRTN		M	PC		F	POP	Return
11	CJPP		M	PC		D	POP	Jump via M, pop
12	LDCT	LOAD	M	PC		PC		Load R
13	LOOP		M	F		PC	POP	Jump via F
14	CONT		M	PC		PC		Continue
15	TWB:							
	{ R≠0	DEC	M	F		PC	POP }	Three-way
	{ R=0		M	D	POP	PC	POP }	branch

* Conditional load R if PASS. In all other functions, if $\overline{RLD}$ is LOW, the D input is loaded into R.

Am2901 end connections are provided by external multiplexors under control of a shift microorder, and in the Am2910 the input $\overline{CC}$ is selected by a test field. It is also required to control the data input and output lines associated with the ALU (see Fig. 4.1). That results in the definition of five supplementary microorder fields, as listed in Table 4.5.

For main store control we have assumed the simplest set of functions to read to either of the data buffers (TIR and SDR) and to write from SDR only: the intended use is that TIR will contain a target instruction and SDR a data word. The memory bus operates asynchronously, and the usual methods of control either suspend the micromachine until the bus operation is complete or allow both to work in parallel, providing interlocks on the buffer register concerned. Logically, the options are equivalent and there is no need to be specific in the present context. It is sometimes required to retain control of the bus during a READ – WRITE cycle, and that would imply extra bus control functions. Further controls would be required for, e.g., selective byte accesses.

Table 4.5 Supplementary microorder fields

For Am2901 control

Shift connections $s =$ 0 shift in zero
1 shift in one
2 rotate
3 arithmetic

The direction of shift and single/double length are determined from the ALU destination k (Table 4.3)

Input data $d =$ 0 (none)
1 l.s. byte (M) from microinstruction
2 register TIR (l.s. byte only)
3 register SDR

If $d = 1$ or 2, m.s. byte $= 0$.
If $d \neq 1$, M specifies carry-in to ALU.

Output data $y =$ 0 (none)
1 (not used)
2 register SAR
3 register SDR

If $y \neq 0$, $\overline{OE}$ is enabled

For Am2910 control

Condition selection
PASS condition ($\overline{CC}$ LOW) if:

(constant)	$t =$	0 *TRUE*	8 *FALSE*
ALU zero		1 *ZE*	9 *NZ*
ALU sign $= 1$		2 *LT*	10 *GE*
ALU carry		3 *CA*	11 *NC*
ALU overflow		4 *OV*	12 *NV*
(not used)		5	13
Control stack		6 *FULL*	14 *NFULL*
Interrupts		7 *INT*	15 *NINT*

Memory bus control

$w =$ 0 (no action)
1 *WRITE* from *SDR* to location *SAR*
2 *READ* to *TIR* from location *SAR*
3 *READ* to *SDR* from location *SAR*

The Status Select microorder assumes there are eight status conditions of interest and gives a programmed choice of the pass condition on each. For example, the ALU condition "sign $= 1$" is tested by $t = 2$ and $t = 10$, which respectively set the *PASS* condition in the Am2910 if sign $= 1$ or sign $\neq 1$. It is convenient to give each test a mnemonic as shown in Table 4.5. The constant condition *TRUE* always sets *PASS*, and *FALSE* always sets *FAIL*, irrespective of machine conditions, so that $\overline{CCEN}$ is redundant and can be tied *LOW*.

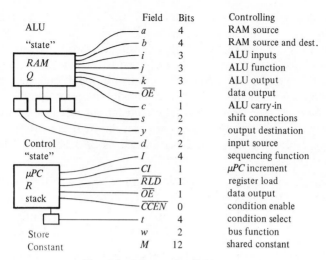

	Field	Bits	Controlling
ALU	a	4	RAM source
"state"	b	4	RAM source and dest.
RAM	i	3	ALU inputs
Q	j	3	ALU function
	k	3	ALU output
	$\overline{OE}$	1	data output
	c	1	ALU carry-in
	s	2	shift connections
	y	2	output destination
Control	d	2	input source
"state"	I	4	sequencing function
μPC	CI	1	μPC increment
R	$\overline{RLD}$	1	register load
stack	$\overline{OE}$	1	data output
	$\overline{CCEN}$	0	condition enable
	t	4	condition select
Store	w	2	bus function
Constant	M	12	shared constant

Fig. 4.5 Microorder fields

The complete list of microorders is given in Fig. 4.5. In horizontal form they would occupy a microinstruction word of 50 bits, though it is assumed that the constant field (M) is shared by ALU and control functions. The action of a single state transition is as follows. At the beginning of a microcycle the output from the control memory is gated into the microinstruction register. The next state transition in the arithmetic section proceeds in parallel with calculation of the next microinstruction address by the Am2910 *and* completion of a control memory read. Thus run-on effects are avoided by assuming a relatively fast control memory, but it must be remembered that the arithmetic conditions refer to the ALU status at the end of the preceding microinstruction.

The Am2910 provides most useful sequencing functions apart from multi-way switches and jumps relative to μPC. The effect of switching can be achieved externally by or-ing a branch into the data input (M) of the sequencer. A faster method is to make use of externally stored tables of switch destinations as suggested by the "*jump MAP*" and "*jump VECTOR*" instructions. Neither is really flexible enough for general-purpose programming and it would be preferable to have a full adder in the sequencer, which is the case in another device of the same family (Am2930).

In the examples that follow we shall make a broad simplification by assuming two microinstruction formats, i.e.

(A) arithmetic, containing a,b,i,j,k,s,y,d and an eight-bit constant field M which includes c; note that $\overline{OE}$ is enabled by $y \neq 0$; and

(C) control, containing I, CI, $\overline{RLD}$, $\overline{OE}$, t,w and a 12-bit constant field M.

Each format, including a single steering bit, fits into a 32-bit microinstruction word. In writing microinstructions we shall give the format followed by numeric or symbolic values of all relevant microorder fields. In microprograms, labels will be used in the usual way to indicate control points. The sequencing rule will be that during arithmetic operations the next microinstruction is fetched and μPC is incremented; but during control operations there is no overlapped arithmetic. This convention violates some of the principles laid down earlier, but should not prevent the reader from seeing their value. The microregisters will be addressed as "$R0, R1, \ldots R15$" unless stated otherwise.

Example 4.1 Shift *R4* arithmetically right 13 places

(*C*) *t = TRUE M* = 12 *I = PUSH*	Initialize counter
(*A*) *s* = 3 *b* = 4 *ijk* = 0305	Shift right 1*
(*C*) *I = RFCT t = TRUE*	Repeat loop

To understand this example, reference should be made to Tables 4.1 – 4.5.

The first instruction is in control (*C*) format, and therefore contains *I*, *CI*, $\overline{RLD}$, $\overline{OE}$, *t*,*w* and *M* fields. The control function *I* is "*PUSH*", which unconditionally pushes μPC onto the control stack and loads the constant field (*M* = 12) into the register/counter *R*. At the end of the instruction cycle the top element of the control stack will be the location of the second instruction, which has also been sent to the control memory via the output (*Y*). Finally, μPC contains the address of the third instruction. The second instruction is placed in the microinstruction register.

The second instruction involves addition (*j* = 0), and specifies a shift-right instruction (*k* = 5) on the RAM output. The inputs *R* and *S* to the ALU (*i* = 3) are zero and *B*, where *B* is the content of register 4 (*b* = 4). The specified shift connection is arithmetic (*s* = 3), the direction and word size (single or double width, the latter involving *Q*) is deduced from *k*. Finally, the RAM shifter output is stored in register 4.

During the arithmetic, the controller is obeying the implicit orders *I = CJP*, *t = FALSE*, *CI* = 1, and finally μPC contains the address of a "fourth" instruction, while the third instruction is placed in the microinstruction register.

The third instruction is again type (*C*), using one of the loop control functions, *RFCT*. Here $R \neq 0$, hence *R* is decremented. The top of stack value (the address of the second instruction) is sent to control memory. Hence the second and third instructions will be repeated until *R* = 0, at which point the stack is popped and the address of the "fourth" instruction is sent to control memory.

---

*   Octal numeric fields have leading zero

In writing microinstructions, inactive microorder fields are ignored (normally contain zero), and control input CI is assumed to be 1.

In control microinstructions $t = TRUE$ will be the default condition.

Example 4.2   Increment $R9$ by 3 and branch to LAB if the result is greater than the content of the Q register.

(A)	$ijk = 0503\ d = 1\ a = 9\ b = 9\ M = 3;$	$R9 + 3$
(A)	$ijk = 0011\ a = 9\ M = 1;$	test $(Q - R9)$
(C)	$I = CJP\ t = LT\ M = LAB$	Branch if sign $= 1$

Example 4.3   Write a subroutine to rotate the bits in $R5$ by the amount given in $R6$ (left if positive, right if negative), using $R4$ as temporary.

Rotate:	(A)	$ijk = 0403\ a = 6\ b = 4;$	$R4 = R6$
	(C)	$I = CJP\ t = LT\ M = RR$	sign?
RL:	(C)	$I = CRTN\ t = ZE;$	Rotate left
	(A)	$ijk = 0307\ b = 5\ s = 2;$	one position
	(A)	$ijk = 0313\ b = 4\ M = 0;$	$R4 - 1$
	(C)	$I = CJP\ M = RL$	repeat
RR:	(A)	$ijk = 0305\ b = 5\ s = 2;$	Right one
	(A)	$ijk = 0303\ b = 4\ M = 1;$	$R4 + 1$
	(C)	$I = CJP\ t = NZ\ M = RR;$	repeat
	(C)	$I = CRTN$	

Example 4.4   Write a subroutine to count the non-zero bits in $R7$ and place the result in $R6$, using $R4$ as temporary.

Count:	(A)	$ijk = 0343\ b = 6;$	$R6 = 0$
	(A)	$ijk = 0403\ a = 7\ b = 4$	$R4 = R7$
bits:	(C)	$I = CRTN\ t = ZE;$	
	(C)	$I = CJP\ t = GE\ M = skip;$	
	(A)	$ijk = 0503\ a = 6\ b = 6\ d = 1\ M = 1$	$R6 + 1$
skip:	(A)	$ijk = 0307\ b = 4\ s = 0;$	$R4 \ll 1$
	(C)	$I = CJP\ M = bits$	

For the next group of examples a simple target machine instruction format is invented. A 16-bit target instruction is divided into an 8-bit function code f and an 8-bit operand specifier n. The interpretation of n will be implied by f. There are no directly addressed target registers, but we assume a number of special-purpose registers. They will be mapped onto the microregisters as follows:

$R0$	Accumulator	AC
$R1$	Program counter	PC

$R2$	Stack pointer	SP
$R3$	Parameter pointer	PP
$R4$	Stack base	SB
$R5$	Program datum	PD
$R6$	Program limit	PL
$R7$	Program status	PS

Henceforth we shall denote $R0, \ldots, R7$ by the mnemonic codes assigned to the target registers. The remaining microregisters will be available for general-purpose use.

$$TIR \quad \boxed{ f \mid n } \quad \text{Target instruction}$$

(It can be seen that if we had wanted to address registers directly provision would have had to be made to substitute fields from TIR for values of the a and b inputs to the Am2901. That decision would be made in the "operand select multiplexor" marked in Fig. 4.1. The microinstruction formats would have to be extended to allow such control.)

A conventional set of single-accumulator load, store, and arithmetic functions is assumed. Source operands are either literal n (unsigned) or $X'n$, where X is one of the pointer registers PC, SP, PP. Destination addresses are $SP'n$ and $PP'n$. Indirection may be specified on certain functions. Addresses contained in the program area are treated as relative to PD and within the limit PL. Addresses contained in the microregisters are in absolute form.

The program counter PC is assumed to contain the location number of the next target instruction to be obeyed. The main interpretive loop might begin by sending the current PC to SAR and replacing it by $PC+1$:

$MAINLOOP$:	(A) $ijk = 0302$ $a = PC$ $M = 1$ $y = 2$ $b = PC$;	
	(C) $w = 2$;	Read to TIR
	(C) $I = JMAP$	Branch via f

It is assumed here that the mapping ROM will present a microprogram address at which the interpretation of f starts. The addresses need not all be distinct: undefined functions, for example, would lead to the same terminating sequence. Sequences will terminate by servicing interrupts and returning to $MAINLOOP$. Some examples of simple target instruction interpretations follow.

Example 4.5 Branch forwards n words.

$BFWD$:	(A) $ijk = 0503$ $a = PC$ $b = PC$ $d = 2$;	$PC + n$
	(C) $I = CJP$ $t = NINT$	Return to $MAINLOOP$
	$M = MAINLOOP$	if no interrupt pending
(Note: if $n = 0$ the content of PC is unchanged.)		

Example 4.6   Load AC with the value in $SP'n$.

$$
\begin{array}{ll}
LDS: & \quad
\begin{array}{l}
(A) \;\; ijk = 0501\; a = SP\; d = 2 \\
\qquad\quad\, y = 2; \\
(C) \;\; w = 3; \\
(A) \;\; ijk = 0733\; b = AC\; d = 3; \\
(C) \;\; I = CJP\; t = NINT \\
\qquad\quad M = MAINLOOP
\end{array}
& \left|
\begin{array}{l}
\\
SAR = SP'n \\
SDR = SAR. \\
AC = SDR
\end{array}
\right.
\end{array}
$$

Example 4.7   Store AC indirect to the program address at $PP'n$. The actual location number required is ($PD + PP'n$.), which must be less than PL, otherwise branch to $STVIOL$.

$$
\begin{array}{ll}
STPI: & \quad
\begin{array}{ll}
(A) & ijk = 0501\; a = PP\; d = 2\; y = 2; \\
(C) & w = 3; \\
(A) & ijk = 0503\; d = 3\; a = PD\; b = 8 \\
& y = 2; \\
(A) & ijk = 0121\; a = 8\; b = PL\; M = 1; \\
(C) & I = CJP\; t = GE\; M = STVIOL; \\
(A) & ijk = 0431\; a = AC\; y = 3; \\
(C) & w = 1\; I = CJP\; t = NINT \\
& M = MAINLOOP
\end{array}
& \left|
\begin{array}{l}
SAR = PP'n \\
SDR = SAR. \\
R8 = SAR = \\
\qquad PD + SDR \\
(R8 - PL) \\
\text{bound check} \\
SDR = AC \\
\\
SAR = .\, SDR
\end{array}
\right.
\end{array}
$$

(Note that each of the sequences given above would be followed by an unconditional branch to the interrupt service routine, e.g.:

$$(C) \quad I = CJV$$

That adds one microinstruction for each function: you can probably devise a way of holding the interrupt address in the microprogram stack and terminating on a three-way branch ($I = TWB$).)

The exercises that follow introduce further facilities to the target machine. The overall aim will be to allow several "programs" of different sizes to share main memory, together with supervisory functions. The latter will be entered by indirectly addressing the first 256 words in memory. The supervisor functions are intended to manage multiprogram activity, to manage service external interrupts, program faults, exceptions, etc.

4.4 MICROPROGRAMMING EXERCISES

In the following exercises use the microinstruction formats and target-machine structure outlined in the last subsection. Solutions to Exercises 1 – 5 and 11 – 15 appear in Appendix 2.

1   Examine the microinstruction loop in Example 4.1 and prepare a timing chart for the first six micromachine cycles, showing for each what is

happening in (a) the ALU; (b) the sequencer; (c) the control memory, and specify the content of (d) the top element of the microprogram stack; (e) the microprogram counter; and (f) the register/counter (R) in the Am2910 at the *end* of the cycle.

2   $R2 = 2 * (R2 + R1 + 1)$

3   If overflow $R8 = R9$ else $R8 = -R9 + 4$

4   Exchange the low and high order bytes in $R4$

5   Treating $R1$ as a byte address in the same way as on PDP-11, load into $R2$ the signed (odd or even) byte to which it points in memory.

6   $SAR = SAR + 2$

7   Multiply $R3$ by 10

8   $R2 = 2 * (R2 + R1) + 1$

9   Form in $R0$ and Q the double-length product of $R1$ and $R2$ (assuming 2s complement integers).

10 What facilities would you add to the micromachine to achieve multi-way branching effects in microcode?

The following exercises refer to the hypothetical target machine described in Section 4.3.

11 Add $PC'n$. to the accumulator AC, i.e. word-modify the current program counter by the 8-bit field n in the target instruction, use the resulting address to access program store, and add the datum at $PC'n$ to AC.

12 Load the stack pointer SP with $SP - n$; if the result is less than SB branch to microinstruction at $STACKVIOL$, otherwise return to $MAINLOOP$.

13 Assume a target stack discipline in which SP is decremented when items are pushed, and incremented when popped. Let SP point to the next "free" position, so that $SP'1$ refers to the last item pushed. At all times ensure that:

$$SB \leqslant SP < PL$$

(branch to $STACKVIOL$ if that condition is not satisfied.).

(a)   write a subroutine to fetch $PC'n$. to SDR;

(b)   Write a target instruction interpretation which pushes $PC'n$. onto the stack, using (a).

14 Let the least-significant bits in the status word PS indicate arithmetic and control conditions as follows:

PS bit 0 = sign of result, after arithmetic or logical operations;

PS bit 1 = 1 if result ZE, otherwise 0;

PS bit 4 = 0 in "user mode", 1 in "system mode".

Assuming that PS bits 0 and 1 are initially zero, write a procedure to set target conditions from the micromachine state. Remember that control (C) microinstructions do not affect conditions, but arithmetic (A) might do so.

15 Branch backwards n instructions if target condition ZE is indicated in PS (no address check is required).

16 Jump to subroutine starting at $PC'n$, pushing the return address onto the target stack. (Remember that "addresses" in program store must be relative to PD to allow relocation of the program area.)

17 Return to the instruction whose address is in $SP'n$, also setting $SP = SP'n$ (i.e. popping the last n items from the stack).

18 Write the microinstruction interpretation of the target instruction AC $mask - n$, i.e. reset to zero the least significant n bits of AC and set conditions in bits 0 and 1 of PS.

19 Suppose that the target machine supervisor state is entered by a supervisor call (SVC) instruction in which n specifies the memory location containing the starting address of a supervisor procedure. At the same time SVC sets bit 4 of PS to denote "supervisor mode". Write an interpretive microprogram for SVC.

20 The target instruction "store AC to absolute location n" is only executable in supervisor mode. Write its interpretive microprogram.

4.5 FURTHER READING

After experience of microcoding at the level described in this chapter it is easy to appreciate the advanced features of more recent products. They are directed towards greater function (as in the Am2903 ALU slice or Am2930 program sequencer) as well as greater integration (the 16-bit Am29116 ALU component). Recent announcements are surveyed in the technical press and detailed data and design manuals are supplied by the manufacturers. Besides the AMD family used in this chapter (see AMD80 and MIC80), refer to the Intel 3000 and Motorola 10800 series.

Current predictions are that the component content of single chips will increase by a factor of four in the next five years and continue to increase, enabling a complete micromachine such as that in Fig. 4.1 to be presented in a single package. As with MOS devices, which have already reached that point, the main design problem is how to configure the circuit to achieve high-volume production runs. If it is seen as part of a control mechanism with limited external vocabulary, the development path will be quite different from that of general-purpose computers. In the latter context emulation is a safer bet (commercially) than adventure into new architecture. By that line of argument it might appear that both MOS and bipolar technologies are converging on VLSI packaged computers with "closed" control systems, and that the opportunities offered by variable control memory will be lost. Is that a cause for regret? In the next two chapters we shall examine the evidence from which a conclusion might be drawn.

5 DIRECT EXECUTION OF LANGUAGES

The existence of writable control memories naturally gives rise to speculation about the likely return from bypassing the conventional instruction set. To do so successfully involves a range of problems concerning definition, security, expansion, maintainability, and so on, whose solution is taken for granted in conventional systems. Before looking at the broader scene it would be reassuring to have some measure of the potential advantage of adapting the target machine to the language, which is the subject of this chapter and the next.

It is easy to find speed improvements in the region of 10:1 or more for a particular algorithm expressed in microprogram and compared with the same in interpreted machine code. In evaluating such figures it must be remembered that they derive from three contributing sources:

(1) the inherent speed of microinstructions, which is the result of the simplicity of the state transitions they control and the use of high-speed control store;
(2) occasional functional advantages of the microorders over target machine functions, particularly in bit manipulation and control sequencing; and
(3) advantages gained from bypassing the architectural framework of the target machine, especially the mechanisms that protect one user from another or that ensure response to external events. The higher the architectural interface the more significant (3) becomes.

It would be meaningless to draw conclusions from isolated algorithms. The minimum basis for comparison is taken to be the combination of hardware and software supporting one of the major programming languages, which provides the syntax and semantics for a class of calculations.

The main parameters of performance are taken to be:

(a)   compile and load time;

(b)   execution time;

(c)   support system size;

(d)   target program size; and

(e)   diagnostic aids in (a) and (b).

The two techniques available for performance comparison are *benchmark* testing, in which space and time measures are obtained for a representative sample of source programs; and *factoring,* in which inferences are made from independent observations of artificially chosen statements. From the design point of view the second is more generally useful, though except in the case of Algol there do not appear to be any widely published sets of reference statements. Needless to say, the object of design is to optimize performance at given system cost over a prescribed (or possibly open-ended) set of languages.

The weights attached to the measured parameters will vary from one mode of use to another and no attempt will be made to determine them here. The aim is to show how variations in processor function — specifically those brought about by microprogramming — affect (a) – (d). At the same time the qualitative effect of diagnostic aids will be assessed. It will be seen that time and space measures depend partly on performance of a second language which will be referred to as the **System Implementation Language** (SIL), generally distinct from any "user" language. Whether the machine is good at compiling Fortran, say, depends on what it has to do to produce executable target code, and how well it does it: as far as possible the second factor will be isolated by measuring the overall performance of the SIL. That observation applies to the compiler, the loader, and to run-time support modules. It also applies to execution of the functions of the language by stored microprogram or hardware, because that does not usually vary from one language implementation to another and it can be measured in basic arithmetic speeds. It would be relevant, however, if one implementation chose to use a decimal radix while another used binary. Most of the language implementations reported in the literature have been rendered useless from a design point of view by not keeping the executive algorithms constant. In other words, if a performance gain is generated it is impossible to tell how much derived from the choice of target code and how much from improved arithmetic or run-time support.

It will be clear that very little can be done about numerical data: the space occupied and the time of access are properties of the main storage system common to all interpreters. Attention is thus turned to the encoding of procedures themselves and to the path which is followed in determining the position, size, and other attributes of the data. It is worth recalling some widely supported measures of instruction frequencies (Table 5.1) showing

Table 5.1   Instruction execution frequencies

(a) Gibson mix, IBM 7090 based, general technical programs

Instruction type	Frequency %
Data movement	
Load/store	31.2
Index register	18
Control	
Branch	16.6
Compare	3.8
Arithmetic	
Fixed point	6.9
Floating point	12.2
Shift/logical	6.0
Other	5.3

(b) IBM 360, general technical programs

Instruction type	Frequency %
Data movement	45.1
Control	27.5
Compare	10.8
Arithmetic	
Fixed point	7.6
Floating point	3.2
Shift/logical	4.5
Other	1.3

(c) PDP-11, running UNIX job mix

Instruction type	Frequency %
Data movement	35.1
Control	26.7
Compare, test	6.5
AND, ADD	5.9
All others (2% or less each)	25.8

the preponderance of data movement actions in conventional instruction sets, many of them incidental to the original expression of the algorithm. It is not clear from such figures how much of the arithmetic is due to address calculation, but it appears that for each "useful" arithmetic operation at least three supporting instructions are needed. That suggests the scope for improvement in space and speed if we stick to interpretive methods, but from what we already know about interpreters there appears to be room for an order-of-magnitude improvement beyond that.

The following subsections draw a broad distinction between source languages making heavy use of formulas and function application, and those using complex data types and structures, i.e. between scientific and commercial usage, though there is obvious overlap in the more ambitious languages. We shall also note the particular requirements of the SIL. In the next chapter there are corresponding subsections offering case studies of experimental systems.

5.1 EXPRESSION EVALUATION

Of course, languages are never *directly* executed in source text form. Well, hardly ever: even in the simplest command language it is usual to clean up the line first, checking on backspace, erase or overprint characters, the result of which is either a character string from an extended alphabet or, going a stage further, a *token* string in which identifiers, numbers, constants and operator symbols have been encoded as single numeric words. At that point we could say the job is done and declare:

(a)   compile and load time: negligible
(b)   execution: whatever it takes to sort out the syntax and perform the operations.

That is not quite as silly as it sounds, particularly if "sorting out the syntax" is much less work than "performing the operations". It is used in a number of APL interpreters and has the advantage that translating from the internal form to original source for diagnostic purposes is relatively easy.

However, the next step in (a) is usually to parse the input string. If we were dealing only with assignment statements with the form defined in Fig. 5.1 a parse tree could be derived for any correct statement, as shown by the example. Here each node corresponds to a matched alternative in one of the phrase definitions: they are numbered upwards from "1" in each production rule, and the parse tree has an integer at each node indicating which alternative first matched the source string. If the matching clause has non-terminal components, they will refer to phrases whose analyses are subtended from the node. Repeated phrases lead to further branches in the tree, terminated by a "0" node. In the example, identifiers and constants are underlined for the moment, though in practice they would be distinctly encoded. Here again we might stop and it is worth mentioning that some language systems have been developed in which the parse tree is directly "executed" (cf. the Vienna Definition Language proposed as a formal mechanism for defining PL/1). An advantage of the tree form is that it can be traversed in various ways and perhaps in parallel by concurrent "evaluators" sensitive to the availability of operands.

The disadvantage of the tree is the amount of space taken by links, but if it is traversed according to a fixed rule (the dotted line in Fig. 5.1) it can be presented in linear form:

/* GRAMMAR */

statement: *ident* ∘ = ∘ *simplex*
simplex: *adop?* ∘ *primary* ∘ *bop?**
adop: + −
binop: + − *star* /
bop: *binop* ∘ *primary*
primary: *number* (∘ *simplex* ∘) *ident* ∘ *parlist?*
parlist.   (∘ *parameters* ∘)
ident: {*analyzed as ident*}
number: {*analyzed as number*}

/* EXAMPLE OF SOURCE TEXT */

$x = -a + b/(-7 * fn \ (parameters))$

/* TREE FORM OF PARSE */

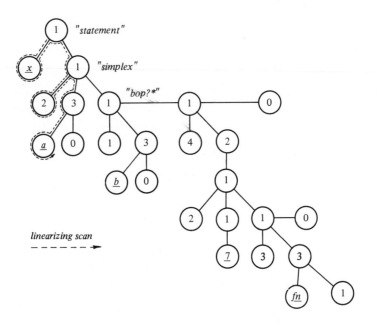

Fig. 5.1   Representing an assignment statement

$$1 \ \underline{x} \ 1 \ 2 \ 3 \ \underline{a} \ 0 \ \overparen{1 \ 1} \ 3 \ \underline{b} \ 0 \ \overparen{1 \ 4} \ 2 \ 1 \ 2 \ 1 \ \underline{7} \ 1 \ 3 \ 3 \ \underline{fn} \ 1 \ 0 \ 0$$

$$x \ - \ a \ \ \ + \ b \ \ \ / \ (\ \ - \ 7 \ \ * \ \ fn(\ ) \ )$$

which begins to look more like executable code: but what is the target machine and what are its states? To abbreviate history, it was soon recognized that there is no advantage in presenting an operator ahead of its operands in the control stream (which is the case for normal infix notation); that the combinations of code found in the linear analysis record (such as "1 1 3" for "add next named operand" or "1 4 2" for "divide by subexpression") are relatively few and can be replaced by simpler format codes; and that the target machine state should include any number of intermediate results from partially evaluated subexpressions. That line of reasoning gave rise to the stack organization that we have already met in connection with microprogram sequencing. In the present context, however, its structure must be such as to allow use for data and control information with no practical restrictions.

Figure 5.2 is a reminder of how an expression would be evaluated using a stack. The target machine instructions or *syllables* are typically short words (12 or 16 bits) with a primary function code distinguishing two sorts of action:

(1)   placing an operand on top of the stack, either

       VALC: a number (value call)
       NAMC: an address (name call)
   or *LTn*:   a constant of *n* words (literal)

(2)   removing one or two operands from the stack, performing an operation, and placing the result (if any) back on top of the stack.

In Fig. 5.2 the stack, which is a sequence of words, is assumed empty initially. The final operator syllable *STOD* (store destructive) requires one operand to be an address, the other to be a number, and after storing the result the stack is once again empty. In the code sequence identifiers are encoded as index pairs (*lexical level, offset*) referring to the target machine state description; on the stack an address can be taken to be a pointer to the corresponding value in store; we denote the index pair corresponding to "Z" by "$\underline{Z}$", the address by "$\#Z$", and the value by "z".

It can be argued that the stack mechanism solves only a minor problem

Expression:		$Z = Y + 2 * (W + V)$							
Target code:	NAMC $\underline{Z}$	VALC $\underline{Y}$	LT1 2	VALC $\underline{W}$	VALC $\underline{V}$	ADD	MULT	ADD	STOD
Stack after operation:	#Z	y #Z	2 y #Z	w 2 y #Z	v w 2 y #Z	w+v 2 y #Z	2*(w+v) y #Z	y+2*(w+v) #Z	

Fig. 5.2   Expression evaluation using syllabic target code

of compilation which can easily be dealt with in the context of a general-purpose register set, but it has firmer advantages in handling control interfaces, particularly when recursive use is contemplated, or when unexpected entries are made to procedures. The stack is then used for linkage data having at least three components:

(1)   program counter (return control pointer);
(2)   dynamic chain (a reference to the immediately preceding linkage information);
(3)   static chain (a reference to the linkage information of the lexically enclosing procedure in source text).

In preparing for procedure entry it is usual to reserve space in the stack by using a *MARK* operator before computing parameter values. The parameters are stored above the linkage data, and finally the *CALL* operator stores the control pointer and transfers control to the next procedure. Within the procedure, parameters, local variables and control information are allocated new positions on top of the stack. On *RETURN* the stack is unwound to the point preceding the last *MARK*, possibly carrying back some results to the top of the stack. Returning to our original example, it would be coded in syllabic form as:

NAMC	VALC	NEG	VALC	LT1	MARK	{ eval. params }	VALC	CALL
x	a		b	-7			fn	

MPY	DIV	ADD	STOD

The target machine state can now be seen to demand at least five registers, i.e.

REGS	[	SB		stack base pointer
		SP		top-of-stack pointer
		LP		local stack frame
		PC		program counter
		PB	]	program base pointer

where *PB* gives access to "global" information, including system procedures, user procedures and data areas. It is in maintaining these registers correctly in relation to the procedure interface that substantial overhead is incurred in many Algol-derived languages. Some factored measurements are given in Table 5.2. It is well known that the Burroughs B 6700 uses a target instruction set tailored to language representation, and its effect can be seen in the times for procedure entry (I have chosen figures for machines with roughly comparable arithmetic times). One would also expect to show up advantageously in array assignment, but in this particular case the compilers spot the indices [1,1] etc. and generate optimized code for the conventional machines. The

Table 5.2 Some Algol statement execution times (*Source*: B.A. Wichman, *Basic Statement Times for Algol 60,* National Physical Laboratory Report NAC 42 (1973).)

Statement	Execution time in microseconds			
	B 6700	PDP-10	IBM 370/165	Univac 1108
$x := y$	3.9	7.5	1.4	1.5
$x := y+z$	5.5	14.8	1.4	3.4
$x := y*z$	11.3	20.1	1.4	4.0
$e1[1] := 1$	5.3	10.6	1.6	2.7
$e2[1,1] := 1$	7.7	14.7	1.7	5.8
$p1(x)$	28.6	368.	60.7	127.
$p2(x,y)$	30.5	455.	83.6	137.

advantage of the language-oriented code is to simplify the compiler rather than to speed up execution.

In comparing target code size, Wichman gives the following figures (normalized with respect to Atlas):

Burroughs B 5500	0.16
Univac 1108	0.31
CDC 6600	0.56

The advantage of the Algol-oriented intermediate form in comparison with some of the best conventional systems is evident. It results from a combination of two effects: the localization of the operator/operand space implied by the source language, and the use of implicit working registers (on the stack) rather than general-purpose accumulators and index registers. It would be possible to compress an operand specification to 3 or 4 bits, for example, provided changes of context, in which the full meaning of the reference is expanded, could be effected without excessive overhead. Unfortunately, very little is known about the consequences of one choice or another; it is not even clear what part procedure boundaries should play in defining context. The use of the stack mechanism may not be optimal: we have seen that some run-time maintenance activity is involved, which a compiler could avoid, and it is known that the majority of expressions found in practise are of very simple forms that do not require the full generality of stack evaluation. Undue attention to block structure certainly draws effort to facilities of little practical value, to the detriment of some of the major programming subsystems. In an interpretive machine one can avoid the issue by defining new target codes, though the point does come up in the interface to the System Implementation Language, which effectively determines the micromachine architecture, as we shall see later.

5.2 DATA ACCESS PATHS

We have seen in principle how to devise compact representations of source text involving expressions and function application. Although not the complete story it would be impractical to go further without taking into account relative statement and operator frequencies in the contexts of particular languages. For long expressions the "overhead" associated with each arithmetic operation is about one operand syllable, which entails about the same number of microsteps as a conventional machine instruction, so there is some hope of speed improvement if the comparison is based on an "unbiased" interpretive microprogram. For more complex functions, for which there is no direct equivalent in a conventional instruction set, there can be more dramatic gains from custom-built target code (as we saw in the case of procedure call).

So far, however, we have ignored the operations involved in retrieving the correct datum of *NAMC* or *VALC,* which can be divided into three phases:

(1) finding the datum in system space, given its indices (such as *lexical level, offset*) in the target instruction stream;
(2) mapping from system space to physical storage;
(3) using type, format and editing information to place the correct interpretation on the datum.

Having mentioned (2), further discussion is deferred until the next subsection while we concentrate on the language subsystem's efforts to say what and where are its data in the frame of reference provided by the host system.

Because Algol provides a common basis for discussion, the operating environment of the Burroughs B 6700 serves as a reminder of what (1) could imply (Figure 5.3). Here the system space is a set of stacks addressed via a *stack vector.* Each stack is a mixture of pointer, numeric and control marks. The pointers refer either to off-stack arrays of data or to sequences of target instructions (the system and user procedures). In the case of arrays the operand found in the stack is a descriptor of an array, or possibly of a vector of further descriptors. The control information consists of the stack marks mentioned earlier, in which the static chain links determine the meaning of the lexical level index when it appears in a *NAMC* or *VALC* syllable: a lexical level l refers to the stack frame l steps from the current one. A peculiarity of Burroughs Algol is that the state of a process is represented by three or more stacks (which can be shared between processes), so the stack chain is shown linking stack areas in Fig. 5.3.

The effect of *VALC,* therefore, is notionally to take l steps along the static chain, then use the given offset as a modifier of the stack address to select the operand. The question naturally arises: how far back, on average?

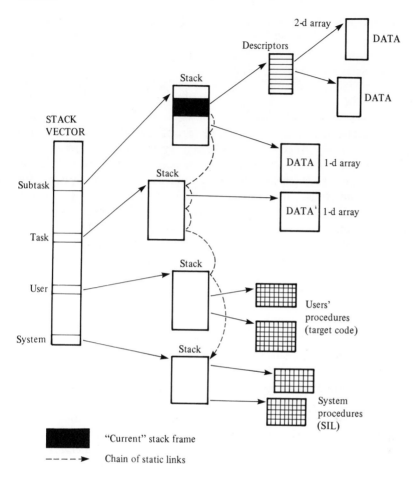

Fig. 5.3 Operating environment in the Burroughs B 6700

It turns out in practice that *l* is most often zero, or whatever it takes to select system or user procedures. Many designs copy the most commonly used stack frame pointers from the static chain into host registers. In the B 6700 there are 32 such *display* registers. It follows that when the current stack frame changes the display must be updated. That is done by *CALL, RETURN* and *GOTO* and in the more esoteric situations in which change of context is implied, including the use of parameters defined by expressions to be evaluated in the context of the *calling* procedure ("call by name").

Scalar values are retrieved by *VALC* directly from the stack. Elements of arrays are accessed by interpreting a succession of descriptors starting in the stack and possibly extending into off-stack descriptor segments. For each dimension an index is required: in the B 6700 the indices are placed on the stack before selecting the descriptor, e.g. the matrix element "$a[i,j-3]$" would be selected by the code syllables:

VALC	LT1	SUB	VALC	VALC
j	3		i	a

where a selects a descriptor which will be modified by i to point to *another* descriptor which, modified by $j-3$, will give a pointer to the operand.

The effect of *NAMC* is substantially the same as *VALC* except that the final operand access is delayed: the result will either be a *reference* to some stack or an *indexed* descriptor. For the reasons already given it is necessary to know the context in which a reference is to be used (it might refer to a procedure, for example, for which display registers will be loaded when it is *CALL*ed). Therefore the reference consists of a mark index together with the offset from that mark to the datum. In the B 6700 such a reference includes a stack index.

So far we have evolved a need for a system space consisting of a number of stacks, one associated with each process. Each will contain numeric data together with pointers to areas of target code, system support (SIL) procedures and array data. Within this fairly simple structure, which is common to many languages, there will be cross-linkages such as the stack marks and references needed to define the state of computation, highly specific to the language and normally expressed as index groups such as (*lexical level, offset*), (*stack, mark, offset*), (*procedure number, program offset*). We have also seen that in the interest of minimizing activity the host can pre-compute the values of commonly used pointers and save them in index or display registers. In principle, the host can keep track of the types of operand in the stacks by following the declarations of the source language. In practice, many language-oriented designs take the approach of tagging the operands on the stack to indicate their type. Thus, on the B 6700 each stack element is a word (or word pair) containing 48 data bits (96 if double length) and 3 (or 6) tag bits (see Table 5.3). The tags are examined and set by machine functions. The superficial effect of this approach is that it simplifies the compiler at the

Table 5.3   Tag interpretations in the B 6700

tag 0:   integer, real or boolean scalar
    1:   reference
    2:   double precision real
    3:   stack mark/link information
    4:   —
    5:   descriptor (data)
    6:   descriptor (program)
    7:   control pointer

expense of the interpreter, but provided the commonest paths can be completed without delaying data access that would be acceptable. More importantly, dynamic tag checking provides a means of dealing with situations where data types are not known in advance, either because the language is not designed in that way (cf. APL) or because parts of the source code (such as the SIL) are written and running before others have been specified.

Figure 5.4 is a summary of what is involved for the *VALC* syllable. Here

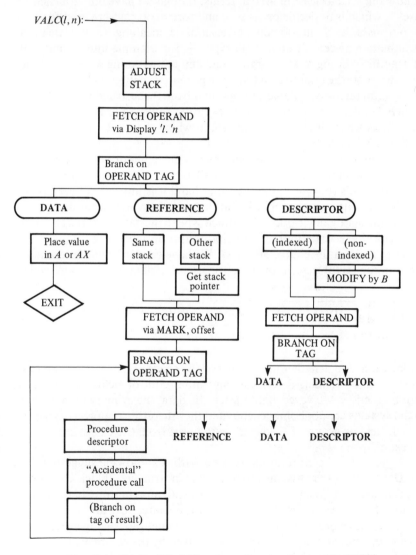

Fig. 5.4 A simplified flowchart for the Burroughs B6700 value call operator

the top two stack elements are held in host registers A (or double length AX) and B (BY) in order to reduce store accesses, and at any time one or both might be "empty". The *ADJUST STACK* operation is needed to make room in A for the result of *VALC*, if necessary by pushing A into B and B into store. Note that references are automatically followed through until a DATA item is produced, and that might involve a procedure call.

At this point the search for a "scientific" datum is over. We know where and how big it is, at least in system terms, though we have only touched on phase (3) which is to decide on its type and format. If tags are used for control purposes it is an obvious extension of meaning to use them to discriminate between different data types − for example integer and real. The benefits of doing so are marginal and amount to taking secondary function codes from the data stream (only the primary function such as *ADD* appearing as an operator syllable), rather than from the instruction (*ADDINT*, *ADDREAL,* etc.). The options were explored fully in the Basic Language Machine, as we shall see in Chapter 16, in which the single *ADD* function had 49 useful variants.

For "commercial" data the options are more important because type has many meanings and to encode them all as part of the instruction stream appreciably adds to its size. On the other hand it is impractical because of remapping features (the ability to treat the same data area according to two or more conflicting descriptions) to attach type to the data in store. The commonest solution is to define data descriptors appropriate to the language and to refer to them in the course of access. We have encountered the technique already in the vector descriptors used for scientific data (see diagram) which

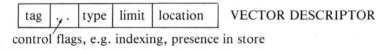

VECTOR DESCRIPTOR

control flags, e.g. indexing, presence in store

give location and length of data in system space, type of element (e.g. character, integer, real, descriptor) and other control fields examined by microinstruction. However, unlike scientific data, the primary data of commercial systems are not homogeneous and they therefore require a descriptor for each field or group of fields, as we shall see from the Cobol example in the next chapter.

A generalized picture of data access paths can now be suggested (Fig. 5.5). Data elements are assumed to be created in structures (block activations, record areas, etc.) which are not necessarily contiguous in store, but selectable by the offset index n. Data identifiers in the source text are mapped into indices m, which are used to refer to a table of **qualifiers** giving lexical level, offset size, type, and other information derived by the compiler. In general, several qualifiers can refer to the same block of store, and one qualifier can

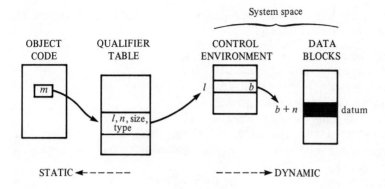

Fig. 5.5 Generalized access path

refer to several blocks (through dynamic adjustment of the control environment).

Languages differ in the amount of descriptive information carried into the execution phase, the method of changing the control environment, the time at which attributes are assigned, and hence in the ways in which components of the access path are stored. In Fortran, for example, almost all attributes are absorbed into object code and acess to data is "direct" as far as the program space is concerned; in APL most attributes are dynamically assigned; in Algol the (l,n) pair and size can be absorbed into the object code while the type is sometimes attached to the data in the form of a tag. In theory, "language-oriented design" should take into account the wide variation in access mechanisms that are invoked by current languages. All too often a design is claimed to be language-oriented on the grounds of superficial attention to stack management or as the result of specific adaptation. Alterable microprogram leaves the options open, but it is still necessary to have a framework in which to describe the action of the interpreter. That is represented by the system space offered by the SIL.

5.3 REQUIREMENTS OF THE SIL

It must be clear that we have been treading a difficult path between sets of ideas that are almost always fused together in practical systems. That is not helped by reference to the B 6700, for which the Burroughs version of Algol *is* the SIL and for which the target instruction set is fixed.

In general, however, the SIL is distinct from any user language, it will use a distinct target instruction set, and it will be chosen without prior knowledge of the subsystems to be supported. Its semantics are a specification of permanent microsystem facilities and we can begin to list some of the requirements it should meet:

(1) no practical limit to the number of language subsystems;
(2) assignment of physical resources to meet modern concepts of store management, program modularity and reliability, input – output, task and multicomputer management;
(3) preferably not heavily dependent on micromachine facilities, but allowing full and effective use of microregisters and microfunctions;
(4) access to common microprogram procedures (such as arithmetic operators);
(5) access to system utilities in the form of text editors, database access, software diagnostics, compiler writing aids, etc.;
(6) no security hazards during language development and maintenance;

and, of course,

(7) language-specific target codes, qualifier formats and control structures.

The inclusion of certain facilities (such as input – output) is clear-cut in principle, but the SIL differs from conventional support systems in two important respects.

Firstly, the interface between user (i.e. language engineer) and host system is defined at both micromachine and target levels. An example from APL should make this clear (Fig. 5.6). Here, the expression to be evaluated (the first line) requires input from the terminal ($\square$) and delivers output ($\square \leftarrow$). (In APL, remember that expressions are evaluated from right to left and that * means "raise to the power".) Both syntax analysis and arithmetic would be carried out by microprogram in language-directed design, but on reaching the first $\square$ it is necessary to call the SIL from microprogram to ask for input (display " $\square$:" and wait). The input could be an expression, which will be evaluated before returning to the original expression for V, and we can see that there are three more system calls to be made. In general, it need not be known in the APL microprogram whether the system function is expressed at micromachine or target level; in some cases the algorithm might even be

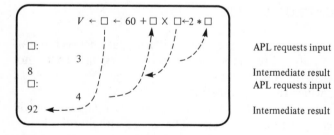

Fig. 5.6   SIL interactions in APL

expressed in APL target code. In that respect language-oriented microprogram is quite different from the emulation systems discussed in earlier chapters.

The second point has already been mentioned. If there are shared resources the SIL must be responsible for managing them, in particular providing functions to define and access physical program storage. However, it would be impractical to call a SIL procedure on every store access, and somehow the language subsystem must take responsibility for mapping from a "system pointer" into physical store locations. How to do that without creating security hazards is discussed in Chapter 7.

5.4 FURTHER READING

Following Weber's account of a microprogrammed implementation of Euler (WEB67) very little can be added to the principle of using language-oriented instruction sets for compilation or execution. What is needed is a measure of how languages are used in practice, which would influence the choice of instruction codes and microinstruction paths. Apart from KNU71 and WIC73 there is a scarcity of published data on commercially important languages. Hence it is very difficult to assess such results as given by Wilner for the Burroughs B 1700 (WIL72). As far as can be judged, space economies claimed for the same language on different micromachines (Cobol on E1 or B 1700, for example) are roughly equivalent. If so, it might be argued that program design compensates for eccentricities of the underlying engine, and that the latter should be designed to offer "speed" rather than "features". Performance comparisons of different machines provide very little input to the design process.

Further accounts of language use will be found in ROB75 (Fortran), ELS76 (PL/1), SAL75 and ALJ79 (Cobol). A more theoretical study, which presents a challenge to designers of instruction sets, is to be found in HEH77.

6 CASE STUDIES: FORTRAN, COBOL AND VCS

In this chapter we shall examine how two major programming languages respond to the treatment outlined in Chapter 5. In any study of language implementation the basic question is: "For a given cost, what method gives the best combination of execution time and space that can be achieved on the available hardware?", and it will be apparent that if the cost or hardware changes, so too might the answer. By its nature, experimental work is confined to low cost levels and generalized micromachine functions, in which context saving in hardware and software design effort is more important than it might be in a major product. Interpretation of the few quantitative results reported is correspondingly difficult, especially in comparing an emergent technology with a mature one. For the present it seems best to concentrate on the available techniques, leaving language engineers to decide which will be most effective, but as a matter of record here are the claimed advantages of the two systems we shall study:

	Fortran	*Cobol*
Basis of comparison	IBM 360	ICL 1900
Emulator	EMMY	E1
Method: Comparison of microprogrammed target instruction sets		
Comparison data	benchmark	factored
Ratio of execution times*	1:5	1:1.8
Ratio of target program sizes	1:5.3	1:3.2

* Language-oriented code: fixed instruction set

It will become evident that the unadorned micromachine is a misleading basis for comparison and that support from the microsystem is crucial in bringing whatever is on the menu to the table in palatable form. The choice of support functions materially affects the cost of language implementation, but as mentioned earlier a well-designed system will benefit from a gearing effect: not only is there less to do, but the SIL benefits from the same factors as any other language. The aim of the SIL is to provide a fixed set of functions that can be used in all language applications to reduce development effort and code duplication at micro- and target machine levels. In doing so it sets standards that can be used also in the variable part. There is no doubt that certain operations such as input – output and frequently used arithmetic procedures are properly part of the SIL. How far one can go depends on the type of system: if the integrity of system data cannot be guaranteed, the amount of support the SIL can give is limited. On the other hand, commitment to support functions that are rarely used complicates the system and wastes resources. The interesting design area is thus the "fringe" of functions just inside or just outside the SIL. There are no widely used systems of that type, but we can illustrate some of the design issues by reference to the Variable Computer System (VCS) developed in the ICL research laboratories in support of several language subsystems.

6.1 FORTRAN TARGET CODE

The following representation of Fortran programs is based on the work of Hoevel and Flynn at Stanford University, using the EMMY microprogrammed host. The intermediate target language is called "DELtran". The main goal has been to interpret the Fortran II subset in a single program environment.

The limitations of the source language are such that all storage allocation can be made on a static basis, i.e. apart from parameters the position in store associated with a variable (or constant) in main program, subroutine or function can be fixed by the compiler. The storage elements themselves are limited to single and double precision (32-, 64-bit) fixed and floating-point scalars and one- or two-dimensional arrays of the same. There is no block structure in the Algol sense, the only limits on scope of locally declared data being at the subroutine or function boundaries. Consequently, it is possible to associate a unique *template* with each subroutine containing as fixed information:

(1)   descriptors giving the store position and word size of each constant or variable (scalar or array) that is addressed;

(2)   a descriptor for each label pointing to an instruction (by bit location in target code).

This template is augmented by a variable component containing:

(3)   control variables;
(4)   parameter descriptors.

Because recursion is disallowed, there will be at most one copy of the variable component for each subroutine, function or main program.

All references to labels, constants or variables in the source code can thus be replaced by their indices in the corresponding template: the size of the index field depends on the program, and is adjusted to its minimum width in each subroutine.

The target machine state comprises in main store the data (local, COMMON, and workspace), code and template areas. In addition there is an evaluation stack for intermediate results, not needed for control because the linkage information is held in the templates. The template of the currently executing subprogram is held in scratchpad, which in EMMY is part of the control memory. In other words, the indices in target code are treated as control memory addresses. Figure 6.1 outlines how the compiled Fortran program maps into EMMY resources.

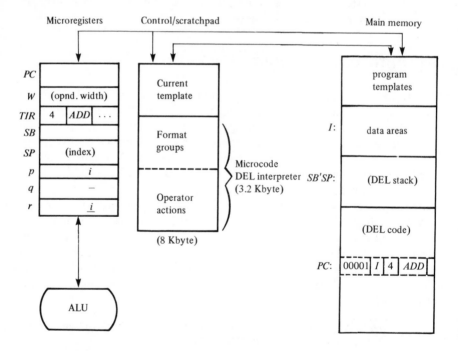

Fig. 6.1 Mapping DELTRAN into EMMY stores (showing register states during interpretation, after preparing the operand *I*)

The microregisters comprise:

REGS	[	SB		stack base pointer
		SP		index of stack top (6 bits)
		W		operand index width (6 bits)
		PC		program counter
		TIR		target instruction (32 bits)
		p q r	]	working registers

The effect of the *CALL* operator in source code is to save *W, PC, TIR* and the variable part of the current environment in the template area of main store; then the template of the called subprogram is loaded to control memory, its parameter descriptors are initialized, and new values obtained for *W* and *PC. RETURN* simply reverses the effect of *CALL*.

Expression evaluation follows a stack discipline with variations to take advantage of the known prevalence of simple forms, notably simple assignment or *MOVE* ("$A = B$") and updating ("$A = A + B$"). Many designers have found it expedient to add stack-manipulating operators (such as "duplicate" or "exchange top items") to improve performance of syllabic code. In the present instance a more systematic treatment has been attempted, starting with the general three-address form "$r = p \omega q$" and enumerating the special cases where one or both of the source operands (p,q) is on the stack, or when an identifier is repeated. A further set of special cases arises when the result (r) is left on top of the evaluation stack. The fifteen possibilities are listed in Table 6.1 for a binary operator $\omega = f2$. A further set of five forms deals with unary operators $f1$.

The instruction coding used in DELtran uses a primary format code to distinguish statement types: a five-bit field is sufficient for the 20 basic forms, leaving 12 for the major control statements. In each case the requisite number of the operand specifiers occurs after the operation code (to the right in the instruction word), followed by the operator $f0$, $f1$ or $f2$. For example, the assignment:

$$I = I + 4$$

corresponds to format 00001, so the encoded instruction is

$$00001 \ \langle I \rangle \ \langle 4 \rangle \ \langle ADD \rangle$$

where $\langle .. \rangle$ is the index of .. in control memory. In some instances further operands or control bits follow the operator code. Instructions are packed into 32-bit words according to the current operand width. They are decoded by shifting *TIR* left (double word) into a working microregister to obtain $00001, \langle I \rangle, \langle 4 \rangle$, and $\langle ADD \rangle$ in the order required. The next instruction word is fetched when either the format or operator code is zero. The reversed bit coding in Table 6.1 is designed to improve the instruction-packing density,

Table 6.1 DELtran instruction formats

Note: $A,B,C,D, \ldots$ etc. denote operand indices in the current template.
$f0, f1, f2$ are operator codes (see Table 6.2)

The argument interface is defined by the content of the three working microregisters p, q and r

$a,b,c, \ldots$	denote the values of $A,B,C, \ldots$
$\underline{a},\underline{b},\underline{c}, \ldots$	denote the addresses of $A,B,C, \ldots$
$t,\underline{t}$	denote the top of stack value (address)
$u,\underline{u}$	denote the next to top value (address)
$s,\underline{s}$	denote a new top stack element (address)

INSTRUCTION UNIT	p	q	r	COMMENT
00000				fetch next instruction
10000 A B				*MOVE* a to $\underline{b}$
01000 $f1$	t		$\underline{t}$	UNARY OPERATIONS
11000 A B $f1$	a		$\underline{b}$	e.g. $b = f1(a)$ etc.
00100 A $f1$	t		$\underline{a}$	see Table 6.2(b)
01100 A $f1$	a		$\underline{s}$	
10100 A $f1$	a		$\underline{a}$	
11100 $f0$				execute $f0$; see Table 6.2(a)
00010 $f2$	u	t	$\underline{u}$	BINARY OPERATIONS
00110 A $f2$	u	t	$\underline{a}$	e.g. $a = f2(u,t)$ etc.
01010 A $f2$	a	t	$\underline{t}$	see Table 6.2(c)
01110 A $f2$	t	a	$\underline{t}$	
10010 A B $f2$	a	b	$\underline{s}$	
10110 A B C $f2$	a	b	$\underline{c}$	
11010 A B $f2$	t	a	$\underline{b}$	
11110 A B $f2$	a	t	$\underline{b}$	
00001 A B $f2$	a	b	$\underline{a}$	
00011 A B $f2$	a	b	$\underline{b}$	
00101 A $f2$	a	t	$\underline{a}$	
00111 A $f2$	t	a	$\underline{a}$	
01001 A $f2$	a	a	$\underline{s}$	
01011 A B $f2$	a	a	$\underline{b}$	
01101 A $f2$	a	a	$\underline{a}$	
01111 n F $A1$ $A2 \ldots$				*CALL* $F(\underline{a}1, \underline{a}2, \ldots)$
10001				*RETURN*
10011 L				*GOTO L*
10101 I L				*GOTO* $(L + i)$
10111 E L				*GOTO* $L,L+1,L+2$ *as e:zero*
11001 L				*GOTO* $L,L+1,L+2$ *as t:zero*
11011 N I M L				$n = n+i$;*GOTO L* if $(n<m)$
11101 N M L				$n = n+1$;*GOTO L* if $(n<m)$
11111				*TRAP*

since trailing zeros do not have to be stored in the last syllable of an instruction word. The full list of operators defined for DELtran is given in Table 6.2; in most cases they are simply related to source-language operators.

The actions of the main interpretive loop should now be clear. Branching on the format code leads to one of 30 microsequences that loads the working microregisters p,q and r with appropriate arguments (values in p and q, address of result in r); for control operations such as *GOTO, DO*, etc., special actions are taken, but for all others there is a branch to the operator microsequence after preparing the argument interface.

To see how DELtran coding works and make comparison with syllabic codes, let us assume that in each case a short operand index of 4 bits is sufficient (i.e. the sample statements will be executed in a context of not more than 16 variables or constants). For syllabic code a 2-bit primary function code is needed to discriminate *NAMC, VALC* and operator syllables. In each case we assume a 4-bit encoding of operators and give (i) the syllabic code for comparison with (ii) DELtran.

Statement		Target code	Bit count
$A = B$	(i)	$NAMC\langle A\rangle; VALC\langle B\rangle; STOD$	18
	(ii)	$10000;\langle A\rangle;\langle B\rangle$	13
$I = J - I$	(i)	$NAMC\langle I\rangle; VALC\langle J\rangle;$	
		$VALC\langle I\rangle; SUB; STOD$	30
	(ii)	$00011;\langle J\rangle;\langle I\rangle; SUB$	17
$I = J * J + I$	(i)	$NAMC\langle I\rangle; VALC\langle J\rangle;$	
		$VALC\langle J\rangle; MULT; VALC\langle I\rangle;$	
		$ADD; STOD$	42
	(ii)	$01001;\langle J\rangle; MULT; 00111;\langle I\rangle;$	
		ADD	26

The above examples show clearly the bias of DELtran coding towards simple forms of statement and subexpression. It is nearly always shorter than syllabic code, even though it is clearly less than optimal in the sense that some of the formats will be rarely used and might be dispensed with, and some will never be used in conjunction with certain operators (for example, look at the subscripting operations). The type of instruction set in which formats and operators are independently encoded is described as *orthogonal*. It is sometimes regarded with favor because it solves a (fairly minor) problem of code generation, whereas correlating formats with operator and literal operand usage almost always gives a more compact representation. In the present context we might even be able to analyze such patterns in a single program or group of programs and hence derive a specification for a tailor-made interpreter. However, that is probably running ahead of what the microsystem can support in the way of variable microprogram.

Table 6.2 DELtran operator codes

Note: the microregisters p, q and r are preset as defined for the format code (Table 6.1)

(a) No formatted operands

$f0$:	000	fetch next instruction word
	100 U F	set IO unit U and format F
	010 n $D1$ $D2..$	input to $\underline{d1}$, $\underline{d2}$,..as per unit/format
	110 n $D1$ $D2..$	output $d1$, $d2$, .. as per unit/format
	001	rewind
	011	backspace
	101	write end-of-file
	111	trap

(b) Unary operators

$f1$:	0000		fetch next instruction word	
	1000 D		d becomes address of $r(p)$	
	0100	r	$float(p)$	
	1100	r	$fix(p)$	
	0010	r	$-p$	/*floating*/
	0110	r	$-p$	/*integer*/
	1010	r	$log(p)$	
	1110	r	$sin(p)$	
	0001 00 D	$r(p)$	d	
	0001 01 D	d	$r(p)$	
	0001 10	$r(p)$	t	
	0001 11	s	$r(p)$	
	0011	r	$cos(p)$	
	0101	r	$tanh(p)$	
	0111	pause with code p		
	1001	stop with code p		
	1011	r	current time $- p$	
	1101	(not used)		
	1111	trap		

(c) Binary operators

$f2$:	0000		fetch next instruction word	
	1000 D		d becomes address of $r(p,q)$	
	0100	r	$p+q$	/*floating*/
	1100	r	$p+q$	/*integer*/
	0010	r	$p-q$	/*floating*/
	0110	r	$p-q$	/*integer*/
	1010	r	$p*q$	/*floating*/
	1110	r	$p*q$	/*integer*/
	0001 00 D	$r(p,q)$	d	
	0001 01 D	d	$r(p,q)$	
	0001 10	$r(p,q)$	t	
	0001 11	s	$r(p,q)$	
	0011	r	p/q	/*floating*/
	0101	r	p/q	/*integer*/
	0111	r	$p**q$	/*floating*/
	1001	r	$p**q$	/*integer*/
	1011	r	$sgn(p)*q$	/*floating*/
	1101	r	$sgn(p)*q$	/*integer*/
	1111	trap		

The fact that a single format code in DELtran usually covers the interpretation of several syllables means there are fewer control branches than in syllabic code. Having fewer instruction words to fetch also means a lower servicing overhead per operand. On an otherwise neutral machine one would therefore expect DELtran to run faster.

To extend the coding to a full version of Fortran, allowance must be made for additional scalar data types, character strings, arrays of higher dimension, together with job control and other standard system functions. As presently conceived, type information is taken from the instruction (Table 6.2) where the four-bit operator code is already bulging at the seams. Rather than extend the operator codes, it would be possible to add descriptive tags to the intermediate operands in the way already discussed. Because the hard support is not available from EMMY, this technique has not been exploited in DELtran. At the machine level all Fortran arrays are, of course, one dimensional, so there is no problem in that connection.

Finally, the reader will have noted that DELtran depends on having a scratchpad store big enough to contain the largest context and capable of switching templates at high speed. In that respect EMMY is helpful in having scratchpad and control memory combined as a single (50 ns) store, and in providing an autonomous channel to main memory. Such features are unusual in micromachines and the strategy of operand encoding would need rethinking on any other host.

6.2 COBOL TARGET CODE

The following description is based on a compiler and support system for a full version of Cobol developed in the ICL research laboratories using the E1 emulator in a multiprogramming environment.

The Cobol source language is a product of many styles and compromises, with the result that it tends to be ignored by language purists despite its great practical importance and the many interesting features it contains. There is some justification for the reputation of being difficult to compile: the source language requires an extensive grammar, many operand types are handled, and elaborate interfaces with the surrounding system must be recognized. Moreover, in many commercial systems the task of compilation is far more complex than the task expressed by the source program, so that compiler designers have had recourse to multi-pass techniques to fit into the available space. The development of language-oriented target codes will have a significant impact on the economics of the compiler itself. In any machine a substantial amount of support code will be written in the SIL, but the features having direct bearing on execution speed and program size are a relatively small subset of the entire language.

A Cobol program is defined by one or more *source modules* that can be compiled independently and later linked to form a *run unit*. In the representation we shall use the linkage is trivial as far as the compiler is concerned —

in fact most of the tables formed by the compiler could carry over without change to the execution phase. For our present purposes the major parts of a source module are the *Data* and *Procedure Divisions*.

The program operates on files presented one record at a time and uses internal records for workspace. The purpose of the Data Division is to declare each possible record format: the same physical record may be mapped according to many different declarations, so there is no question of concealing representation or placing descriptive tags as part of the record. The elementary items of data have a wide variety of representations with a dozen or so basic data types, together with numeric, alphabetic and alphanumeric character strings which figure largely in commercial data processing. The elementary items are named, and may be collected into named groups, which in turn may be grouped, up to the level of the record name itself. With the aid of *PICTURE* descriptions editing characters can be inserted in a field for output, with the result that the "type" code associated with a data item can, in principle, be of any length.

Within a record individual items or groups may be repeated. The number of actual occurrences may vary, depending on a field in a fixed position of the same record. Repeated items may themselves be repeated. They are selected in source programs by following the group or field name by one or more subscripts or by using an implied *Index* value. The Index is a separately declared data item. The rules of allocation within a record are such that the coefficients of any storage-mapping function can be determined by the compiler.

The Procedure Division is composed of a number of *sections*, whose significance derives from the concept of programmed overlays. A section comprises a number of labelled *paragraphs*, each containing one or more *sentences*. A sentence consists of one or more Cobol *statements*.

Individual statements have a fairly simple syntax, typically a "verb" followed by the names of data items, sections or paragraphs, e.g.

ADD P TO Q GIVING DAY _ TOTAL ROUNDED

where *P, Q* and *DAY _ TOTAL* are data names. The definition of Cobol implies strict observation of decimal rounding and truncation rules, taking account of operand types and precision of intermediate results (18 digits maximum). The compiler is required to indicate if results are incompatible, or if any intermediate results are out of range; the fact that the interpreter could give warning at runtime is specified by the reference language to be insufficient. Some indication of verb frequencies is given in Table 6.3. For execution purposes it appears that seven verbs account for over 90% of executed statements, while the same number account for almost 90% of stored statements. In view of physical limitations on control memory size, and practical limitations of generating microprogram, the strategy adopted

Table 6.3 Cobol verb frequencies (benchmark tests)

VERB	DYNAMIC USAGE	STATIC USAGE
MOVE	30%	33%
IF	30%	18%
GOTO	11%	19%
ADD	10%	6%
PERFORM	7%	8%
WRITE	4%	3%
READ	3%	2%
Others	5%	11%

is to commit to microcode just the most frequently used parts of the interpreter, with whatever else comes "for free", providing an escape to supporting SIL code for the remainder. MOVE is one of the wonders of the computing world, and anyone under the impression that it simply picks up data from one spot and puts it down in another would be in for a surprise.

The final form of target code depends on what are regarded as reasonable limits for field sizes in one source module. In the design used here no attempt has been made to compress the target code below a 16-bit instruction unit (Table 6.4), which allows for the following maxima (and up to 256 modules per run-unit):

Variable names: 4096;
Index names: 256;
Files: 256;
Data areas (records): 64;
Procedure variables: 256.

Each Cobol statement is represented by a sequence of instructions with literal values inserted as required.

Cobol control structure is the source of some complexity because of the use of procedure variables and debugging options. Apart from the normal branching determined by GOTO statements it is possible to specify that a particular paragraph or sequence of paragraphs should be PERFORMed one or more times, or until a condition is satisfied (possibly varying some elements on each repetition). A simple compiler cannot tell in advance which paragraphs will be subject to PERFORM, so it will insert a possible branch to a "procedure variable" at the end of each paragraph; if PERFORM does not apply, the branch drops through to the next paragraph in sequence. Further complication derives from the ALTER verb, which can be used to change the destination of GOTO. Rather than change the stored object code,

Table 6.4   A Cobol target instruction set

Format 1

4	12
f	n

f = 0:   Source operand at $DQT'n$
    1:     Destination operand $DQT'n$
    2:     Operand at $DQT'n$
    3:     Integer operand n
 4, 5:   (not used)
    6:     Unconditional branch within code block

Format 2

4	4	8
f	v	n

    7:     n-byte literal operand of type v follows
    8:     scale/round operand, partial result by n or select Index n
    9:     scale first operand by n, then perform arithmetic selected by
        v {*ADD, SUBTRACT, SUBTRACT-GIVING, MULTIPLY,*
        DIVIDE, DIVIDE-REMAINDER}
  10:     unconditional branch to {new code block, procedure variable,
        EXIT AND RESET, BRANCH DEPENDING, SET LINK,
        ALTER}
  11:     conditional branch within code block
        v selects {EQ Flag, LT Flag, LE Flag
              Operand zero, < 0, $\leqslant 0$
              Operand = spaces, *DEBUG ON*,
              Size error,
              Operand is alphabetic/numeric}
  12:     negative conditional versions of 11
  13:     miscellaneous microcode functions
        selected by v {fast *MOVEs*, *COMPAREs*
              CALL, RETURN, set Index, etc.}
        and call run-time system for {*ACCEPT*
              TIME, DATE, DAY, DISPLAY,
              OPEN, CLOSE, READ, WRITE,
              REWRITE, START, DELETE,
              CANCEL, CALL, EXIT}

---

the branch is again directed through the Procedure Variable Table, which has two entries for each PV: one is the normal successor, the other is the "current" successor, which is initialized to the normal value, but can be changed during calculation by *ALTER, PERFORM*, and certain other statement types.

The complication arising from debugging is that any attempt to access a named data item, paragraph, file or Index may be required to enter a Debug Procedure. Whether it does so is decided by the state of the *DEBUG* Flag, which can be set *ON* or *OFF* by Cobol statements, but in addition the name must be declared in advance to be subject to debug rules, and whether on all

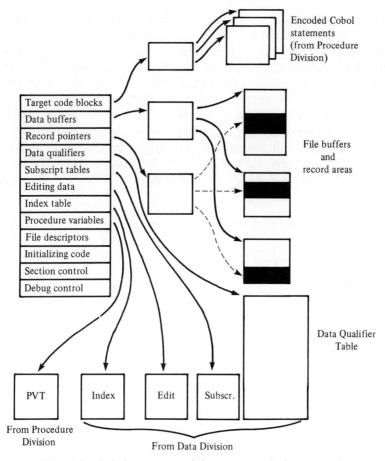

Encoded Cobol
statements
(from Procedure
Division)

Target code blocks
Data buffers
Record pointers
Data qualifiers
Subscript tables
Editing data
Index table
Procedure variables
File descriptors
Initializing code
Section control
Debug control

File buffers
and
record areas

Data Qualifier
Table

PVT   Index   Edit   Subscr.

From Procedure
Division

From Data Division

Fig. 6.2 Cobol source module structure during execution
(showing areas accessed by microprogram)

accesses or just writes. In most compilers that means the code generated for
handling debugged elements is different from (and slower than) normal
code, even when executing with *DEBUG OFF*. In interpretive systems the
same code is generated in all cases and the branch is taken by the interpreter
when inspecting qualifiers.

Cobol target code is assembled into blocks of maximum size 4096 bytes,
taking account of section grouping, and attached to the source module data
structure as a subtree (Fig. 6.2). The Procedure Variable Table is formed and
attached during the processing of the Procedure Division.

In the Data Division all names are mapped unambiguously into indices
of three separate tables: Data Qualifiers (descriptors), filenames and Indices. In most cases information built up during compilation is carried into

the execution phase with no change. Each entry in the DQT is a 64-bit item but supplementary information is given as needed by reference to the editing strings (derived from *PICTURE* declarations), and to subscripting information (derived from *OCCURS* clauses). At run time a data qualifier at DQT $'m$ is accessed to find the index of the record pointer to the area in which the item is stored (and which might change as the result of *READ*, *WRITE*, etc.), and within that area the offset and limit in bytes (or bits) of the data item itself. About 20 microsteps are required to extract the data attributes (from DQT) and place them in microregisters, followed by whatever is needed to extract the datum itself and present it for the next operation. Figure 6.3 shows the breakdown of a DQT entry in greater detail.

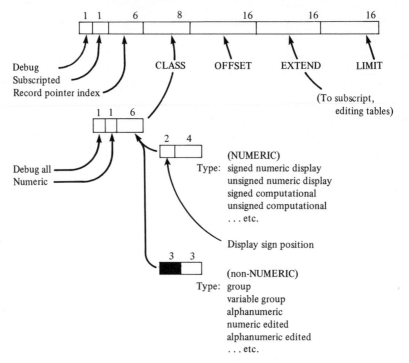

Fig. 6.3   Cobol qualifier format

To see how the Cobol target codes are used let us examine some source statements.

MOVE SPACES TO X

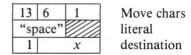

Move chars
literal
destination

13	6	1
"space"	▨	
1		x

Here the first instruction "move characters repeated" prepares to move a literal string of given length (1) to the destination given by the offset x in the Data Qualifier Table — most likely an alphabetic or alphanumeric string.

ADD A, B GIVING D

9	0	sc1		Scale A by $sc1$
0		a		source
0		b		source
8	1	sc2	?	scale $A + B$ $sc2$
1		d		destination

    In Cobol arithmetic there is often a choice between working in decimal or binary, depending on the types of operand. That is important if the host has good decimal facilities, but in E1 all arithmetic is binary and any decimal operands must be converted to binary intermediate form. Note that scaling factors are worked out by the compiler and inserted in target code where necessary. The final result must be converted to the representation of the destination. In working with displayed data the conversion often outweighs the arithmetic and control in terms of microinstruction count. It can be seen that the compiler could detect the common cases where the data are binary and word aligned (*COMP SYNC RIGHT* in Cobol terms), thus avoiding reference to the DQT, but that was not done in this implementation because of its impact on the *DEBUG* mechanism.

ADD 1 TO P

9	0	0	Add, no scale
3		1	literal value
2		p	source/destination

This shows the use of the DQT index for a combined source and destination. Drawing a distinction between usage enables the decoding of the qualifier to be optimized. At the same time it has a functional value in determining the operands of the leading "verb" — in effect, *ADD* applies to a sequence of operands and can deliver a result to a sequence of positions: e.g.

    ADD A1, A2, A3 TO B GIVING D1, D2 (WEEK,DAY) ROUNDED

in which *A1*, *A2* and *A3* appear as sources, *B* is source/destination and *D1*, *D2* are destinations. From this we see that the state of the target machine includes both the intermediate arithmetic result, partially computed addresses and the type of verb in process.

IF X7 IS NUMERIC GOTO P6B

12	14	r	Branch not numeric
	0	x7	source
	10	0	b	branch block/
	3	m	offset

for external block only

Two possibilities will be detected: either the branch is in the same code block, relative position r, or it is in another block b, offset m. In the latter case the inverse function is used for the first branch (12/14: branch if not numeric, with relative address $r=4$), and an unconditional branch to block b,m is inserted as shown. At this point the Cobol interpreter cannot be sure that block b is in memory, and a call to the microsystem will be made to check on availability.

The Cobol run unit support environment defines the structure within which the the interpreter operates. It also contains SIL packages that will be called to execute Cobol verbs which are too complex or too infrequently used to justify their implementation in microcode. The calling sequence is expressed in the target language by a "parameter function", followed by a sequence of parameters, followed by a "call function". The parameter values are stacked in the current stack frame prior to calling the appropriate SIL function. In general, the Cobol microcode relies on the compiler to ensure that correct combinations of target code are presented, but guarantees to terminate and return to the support system without accessing anything outside the support environment or enabling SIL routines to do so.

A Cobol mix

Measurements of Cobol performance were based on a factored set of 20 statements developed to present the verb and data types most frequently encountered in practice. The same set of statements was used for space occupancy (static) and timing (dynamic) measures, but with different weights. Table 6.5 shows the statements used and their weights.

In order to make comparison with conventional architecture measurements were obtained both for the Cobol target language and for the general-purpose instruction set of the ICL 1900, on the same host machine and using comparable microcoding skills in each (an important condition because tuning can easily result in 30% variation in microcode timing).

Space measurements are independent of the host and easier to interpret than timing, which depends on the artificial framework of an isolated loop. The disappointing ratio of 1:1.8 for execution speeds (which can be derived from Table 6.5) is partly accounted for by arithmetic weakness in the host. However, there are two points of significance that can be made from analyzing the results. Firstly, when Cobol use takes account of conventional machine architecture the ICL 1900 statement timings are often *faster* than the generalized Cobol-oriented instructions. Secondly, a significant execution overhead results from interfacing the Cobol subsystem to the SIL, for example in checking operand types and in managing dynamic store assignment. Such functions are unavoidable in practical systems: to understand how they arise it is necessary to look more closely at the SIL itself.

Table 6.5 Cobol statement mix and performance measures

Name:	Statement	Static			Dynamic		
		Weight	Bytes CTL	Bytes 1900	Weight	μs CTL	μs 1900
1A:	MOVE SPACE TO X1	1.30	8	12	1.38	87.5	62.5
1B:	MOVE SPACES TO X7	5.78	8	27	6.15	187.5	162.5
2A:	MOVE S999V9 TO SE5	3.18	6	48	5.46	475.0	1687.5
2B:	MOVE S999V TO S9999V	5.96	6	24	0.5	187.5	125.0
2C:	MOVE TABX4(99V) TO X4	4.87	8	24	3.7	600.0	175.0
2D:	MOVE S999V9 TO E	4.87	6	66	6.17	550.0	1975.0
3:	MOVE 1 TO S999V	4.17	6	24	0.62	137.5	125.0
4A:	MOVE "A" TO X1	1.79	8	15	0.79	150.0	75.0
4B:	MOVE "ABCDE" TO X6	3.01	12	21	1.32	200.0	100.0
5:	PERFORM X	12.03	8	18	8.29	112.5	100.0
6A:	IF X1 = SPACES GOTO 1AX6A	0.35	4	21	0.71	125.0	87.5
6B:	IF X7 IS NUMERIC GOTO 1AX6B	1.91	4	27	3.89	125.0	100.0
7:	IF A4 = X4 GOTO 1AX7	4.21	8	33	8.56	175.0	162.5
8:	IF S999V = 1 GOTO 1AX8	5.05	8	18	10.26	162.5	87.5
9A:	IF X1 = "A" GOTO 1AX9A	2.18	10	33	4.43	175.0	187.5
9B:	IF X6 = "ABCDEF" GOTO 1AX9B	3.07	10	33	6.24	212.5	787.5
A0:	ADD 1 TO S999V	4.51	6	27	6.16	150.0	150.0
A1:	ADD S999V9, S999V GIVING S999V9		10	48	6.16	337.5	325.0
A2:	MULTIPLY S999V9 BY S999V GIVING S999V9	0.30	8	42	0.15	287.5	275.0
A3:	GOTO 1AA3	16.45	2	3	11.39	25.0	12.5 (*)

(*) All times subject to ±12.5 μs absolute error.
Data types are mostly inferred from names,
e.g. X7 has PIC X(7), S999V is signed computational, SE5 has PIC + +9.9,
  E has PIC £££9.9CR

6.3 AN EXAMPLE OF A SIL: THE VARIABLE COMPUTER SYSTEM

The general requirements of the microsystem, which we think of as expressed by the System Implementation Language, were summarized in Section 5.3 and have been illustrated particularly by examination of Cobol. Given the types of program structure that interpreters assume, and the patterns of storage access that they imply, what facilities should the microsystem offer? The answer is in two parts. Firstly there is a kernel of functions available to all language subsystems, including the SIL. Secondly there are particular rules of composition and syntax which lead to a target code specifically for the SIL. It is important to make the distinction because there could be several SILs to suit different tastes, but only one set of kernel functions in a given microsystem. The Variable Computer System includes a system implementation language (VCSL) of which little need be said except that it provides the handles for using all the fixed system functions and components of a standard "VCS machine".

A characteristic of the systems we are dealing with is their hierarchic user-group structure, e.g. starting from the (fixed) SIL functions we expect to add language subsystems, within each of which there will be one or more user groups with different levels of privilege (subsystem maintenance, microprogram development, interactive and batch stream managers, etc). At each level of the hierarchy program structure is dynamic and the extent to which information is shared with other levels is precisely controlled. The requirements cannot be satisfied by the conventional rules of block-structured languages. The most efficient and flexible basis for handling such structures is a capability mechanism such as that of the Basic Language Machine (described more fully in Chapter 16) and in fact VCSL is an adaptation of the system language already to hand for the BLM.

Most of the VCS functions are concerned with creating and manipulating objects in a consistent way. In particular, we find functions for:

(1)   setting up operating environments (*bases*) and defining the objects they contain;
(2)   creating, starting and stopping *tasks*;
(3)   entering and leaving procedures and accessing the task control information (*task vectors*);
(4)   controlling access to storage, including task synchronization;
(5)   interrupt and I − O handling.

In (1) an "object" is a storage segment, task vector, I − O device, or a set of objects represented by a capability segment. The recursive nature of that definition allows each base to be constructed as a tree. A new base is able to share selected information available to its parent at the time of creation (by an indirection mechanism), with the effect that a hierarchy of bases is set up with the "system base" at the apex, and it is this structure that is used in building language subsystems and dependent application environments. Figure 6.4 shows a typical three-level base structure to which an application module such as that shown in Fig. 6.2 might be attached. Clearly, the integrity of any object depends in the end on maintaining the integrity of its representation and of the procedures that are applied to it, including the task-control information.

Superimposed on the program structure is a set of tasks whose purpose is to maintain parts of the operating environment or perform users' jobs. In each base none, one or more tasks can be active. The task structure is also hierarchic in the sense that certain rights and responsibilities are assumed by parents. Tasks are represented by task vectors (TVs) which are protected by the capability mechanism. Each task vector contains registers describing a "current state" of the VCS machine and a historical record of incomplete procedure activations in the same control stream.

VCS functions are implemented for pragmatic reasons at two levels of control: microprogram and the system language VCSL in which (additionally) all compilers and system utilities are written. Procedure calls can be made from either microcode or target-machine level. It follows that if a microprogrammed procedure is called from machine level, or vice versa, some interfacing code must be obeyed to adapt from one level to the other. It is undesirable to impose restrictions at this point because one cannot always predict whether a procedure will be committed to microprogram: the discrimination must be dynamic. For that reason the list of procedure activations associated with any task contains both micro- and target level linkage information. Again, it is undesirable to impose limits on the depth of procedure call, therefore linkage information is stacked in main memory, the host micromachine stack having very limited use.

The VCS machine state is defined by:

> the microprogram counter
> the program counter
> (†) target machine registers (16 $*$ 64 bits plus 16 $*$ 6 bit tags)
> current program base pointer
> (†) current stack and stack base pointers
> target instruction register
> (†) target status and flag words
> micromachine flags.

At *any* target level only(†) the target machine registers, stack and status or flag bits can be used for communication with the SIL; at microprogram level all the elements of the VCS machine can be used. As calculation proceeds it is possible that other host registers will be used, but it is required that all state

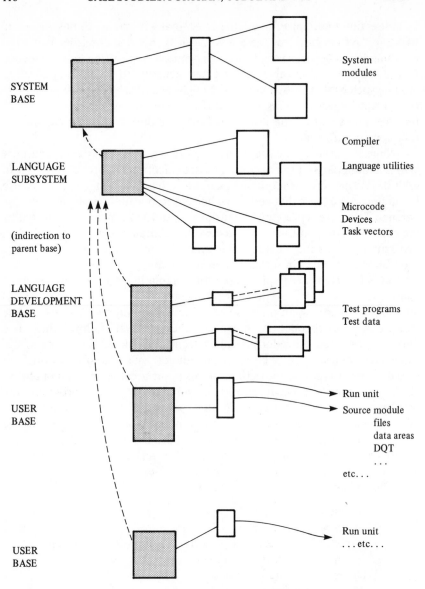

Fig. 6.4 VCS operating environment

information will be contained in the above registers at points where a change of procedure, environment or task might occur. In that way VCS functions can effect procedure and task management without explicit knowledge of the language subsystem, and with a fair degree of independence of the host machine.

Procedure entry and exit are controlled through a dynamic chain of marked links placed in the stack. The purpose of the marks is to distinguish subtask initiation, VCS and user subsystem calls, allowing various types of restart to be employed and giving excellent diagnostics at both control levels.

The interpretation to be placed on a program segment is indicated by a *control type* assigned to each language subsystem. Control type 0 is used for pure data: any attempt to execute it will fail. Control type 1 is for VCS use, type 2 for VCSL target code, and type values for language extensions, e.g. to Cobol, APL, etc., are assigned 3, 4, ... on a global basis. In target level procedure call and return the control type is examined, causing a branch to the appropriate interpreter (in theory at least: in practice, as we shall see later, the control memory content and allocation is a limiting factor).

The most time-critical VCS functions are those concerned with forming physical addresses from system pointers (*codewords*) and using them to access program storage. The root of the problem is the requirement to map the conceptual program space as in Fig. 6.4 into a physical hierarchy with limited capacity at the fastest levels, at the same time resolving contention between tasks for shared resources. At *neither* level of control is it desirable to carry out checks on every store access, but particularly not at microprogram level. Consequently the pointers which establish program structure are subdivided into those which describe the segment structure (cf. Fig. 6.4) and those which, having been checked by the VCS functions, give direct access to physical storage, and they are technically the *addresses* used in VCS. For system reasons a codeword refers indirectly to store via a Global Segment Table (GST):

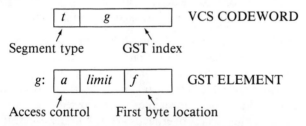

The corresponding address retains the GST index in order to check the accessibility and position of the segment, which happens each time an address is loaded into one of the VCS registers.

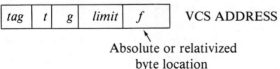

It is a moot point whether addresses should be held in the task vector in absolute or relativized form. It depends on how often store reallocation takes place and how long it takes to scan task vectors to update addresses. In VCS, both possibilities are permitted. The access code in GST is used to control shared (read-only) access by several processes or unique (update) access by individuals. All such control and conversion together with recycling of GST indices and memory is exercised by VCS microprogram, which provides a good example of the application of microcode to system problems.

The "read", "write" and "modify" instructions which should strictly speaking be found in the VCS function list are too often used to be handled by microsubroutine call. Users are therefore allowed to issue them directly for binary data and trusted to observe the protection and limit conventions (the *limit* value is derived during GST access).

In the course of design numerous candidates for position in the SIL function list have to be considered. A fundamental problem in extending the system is to achieve valuable effects without degrading overall performance and security. Sometimes a microcode branch is obtained "for free", while at other times a new facility entails extra tests in a critical path. The available control stores in a range of host machines and the practical limitations on microprogram testing and maintenance have also to be considered, so that the decision to commit to microprogram cannot be taken as lightly as is sometimes suggested. Candidates for inclusion as SIL procedures include:

(1)   selection of data elements by associative key rather than index;
(2)   some form of paging for store management;
(3)   introduction of a third segment type consisting of a set of tagged elements;
(4)   static chaining in the procedure activation list;
(5)   use of semaphore variables for inter-task synchronization.

There are many possible variations of the addressing rule such as (1) and (2), but each entails a loss of space or time that skilled programmers will try to circumvent. The best programming environment appears to be a set of dynamically constructed, variable-sized segments, free from any concept of automatic allocation and deallocation such as a stack discipline: they make optimal use of store and their access overheads are well understood. It is left to language engineers to map programs efficiently into the resulting structures, with the result that the store management implicit in a language such as APL is carried out in part by the language subsystem (which is aware of details of APL usage) and in part by VCS functions which provide the containers for APL workspaces. That is an important division of labor. There is a strong temptation, once committed to microprogram support, to elaborate the system pointer formats to provide the sort of information found in qualifiers, e.g. for Cobol, or to elaborate the tags to distinguish a range of different numeric data types, as in the B 6700. The difficulty is that different languages vary so much in the options they recognize that the final descriptor is too unwieldy to use efficiently. It seems much better to invent qualifiers peculiar to the language, as we have done for the target codes themselves. (In VCS, with the help of the E1 emulator, a group of *user* tags is separated from the tags used by the system.)

The above point is fundamental to microsystem design and can be restated in terms of Fig. 5.5, which shows the general access path from the name index (*m*) to datum value. If the language allows the name to be resolved as a reference, what is required is not the datum itself but a combination of indices which, without further access to qualifier table or control environment, will enable the datum to be retrieved. How should such a variable be represented? The choice is influenced by the rules in the language governing scope and existence of references, which will generally be different from those of the SIL, so it is improbable that reference variables will map directly onto system pointers. The conclusion drawn (in VCS at least) is that allowance must be made for two sorts of access path leading to the same datum: those relative to current qualifiers and control pointers (as in Fig. 5.5); and those relative to an assumed operating environment (such as Fig. 5.3). Microprogram is responsible for evaluating each to obtain system pointers and hence physical addresses, as indicated in Fig. 6.5. The question

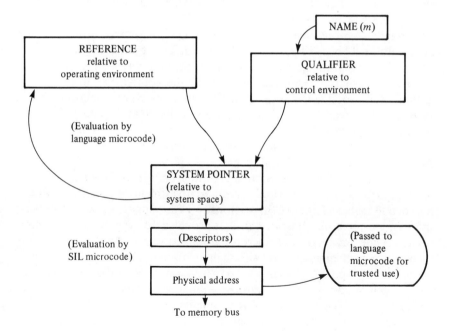

Fig. 6.5   Levels of reference recognized in the microsystem

raised by (2) is whether paging would help in language implementation. The answer appears to be that applied uniformly below the SIL level it would be a hindrance, but in the context of a particular language it could be applied by the microprogram. A similar conclusion is reached for selection by key (1), though we shall see in later chapters that associative selection has important system applications.

The remappings indicated in Fig. 6.5 are carried out by microprogram and must be well optimized. It follows that the most commonly used tables will contain physical addresses: for example, a display as used for the control environment in Algol-derived languages, or the current record pointers referred to in a Cobol qualifier. Hence arises the requirement (3) for a third segment type at micromachine level containing pointers and not limited by the register set or stack structure. We describe such sequences as being of "mixed" type. Maintaining them places some overheads on the microsystem, and might merit hardware support, but their use speeds up data access.

By the same arguments that discourage direct mapping of high-level data structures onto SIL constructs, VCS procedures are not designed to represent the control interfaces of all possible high-level languages. Recognition of static levels (4) involves extra work in procedure management and a variety of actions dealing with special cases that could not be built into a fixed system, so it is intended that such structures will be mapped by the microcode into simulated control stacks.

Finally, various forms of semaphore signalling were considered, but only a minimal "busy" flag was implemented. The argument against greater elaboration is that the access mechanism of the GST already provides direct control over shared resources, associating the control variable with the datum itself, so there is little point in providing more functions to the same end. The release of a segment for rescheduling at the end of a critical section is not automatic: to force it at procedure exit, for example, would again imply unacceptable microprogram overheads, so an explicit VCS *Release* function is provided in its place.

The Variable Computer System provides support for language-oriented microprograms in easily portable form: an investment of about 9 Kbytes of microcode transfers the VCS functions, VCSL support codes, compilers, utilities, etc., to a new host machine. It provides the type of support that is needed if the advantages of microprogrammed interpreters are to be fully realized for each language, and although the function list could be improved in the light of experience it has proved to be a sound method of exploiting the current generation of general-purpose emulators. Many of its key features derive from experience of the Basic Language Machine, and they in turn have evolved into the Pointer Number System described in Chapter 18.

6.4 FURTHER READING

DELtran principles are outlined in FLY77 and HOE77.

The Cobol implementation described in this chapter has not been published elsewhere. The Burroughs Cobol/RPG architecture is outlined in MYE78 and BUR73b. For an implementation of a Cobol "attached processor" see YAM80. A subset known as microCOBOL was marketed in portable form by Computer Analysts and Programmers Ltd., and has been installed on several microcomputer systems. Its internal codes and performance levels have not appeared in open literature, which seems to be the rule for commercial ventures. Further accounts of language implementation and related machine design problems will be found in HAS76 and CHE77.

7 MICROSYSTEM DESIGN

Improving on range-defined architectures without meeting comparable system objectives is no more difficult now than it was 20 years ago. It is worth recalling that the competition for space in the control memory is reflected historically in the argument about "scientific" and "commercial" machines that generated much heat in the early 1960s, to be forcibly cut short in March 1964. The IBM 360 authorized the pattern of a multi-model range using microprogram to support a range-defined instruction set. To present a realistic alternative it must be shown how programming standards can be sustained through a very wide power range (the initial line of IBM 360s aimed at a factor of 50); it must be possible to develop and maintain new languages and subsystems taking full advantage of the architecture without endangering system security; storage and control structures must be designed to suit modern applications rather than those of the early 1960s. As far as I know, no microsystem with the required properties has been put on the commercial market. Even so, it is not sufficient to show that variable microprogram achieves better results than fixed instruction sets: we also need to be convinced that it is the best way of using modern technology. In this chapter we shall draw together the results observed in language-oriented design and consider some system frameworks in which the demonstrated advantages could be retained.

In order to focus attention on design at the architectural level and its immediate support (i.e. levels (3) and (4) in Chapter 1, page 1) we must neutralize two important but nevertheless distracting features of modern technology. As the reader will be well aware, to trump any specific design it is only necessary to wait six months and play the next cards from the circuit dealers; for the same reason, problems never seem to stand still long enough to be solved by analysis, and bad design can be disguised by excess of silicon (which "costs nothing", of course) in the same way that bad cooking can be disguised by excess of seasoning. The point is that the circuit and subsystem levels *are* almost neutral with respect to architecture, and if they have to be used to recover from, for example, a badly designed protection system or instruction set, that achievement should not be confused with using them to make a well-chosen architecture better. For the moment, then, imagine that semiconductor development is suddenly brought to a halt, and that designs will be compared on purely architectural merits.

The second distracting feature is that the pay-off from theoretical gains in speed or space is non-uniform. In the time domain there are limiting paths at all levels which might annul performance improvement: in Cobol, for example, the critical path is often between disk and printer, so it might seem pointless to strive for high rates of statement execution. In space, the various levels of packaging determine, at any point in time, "natural" sizes of scratchpad, control memory and main store against which the sort of economies we have been discussing might seem unimportant. That has always been the case, and the impact of LSI or VLSI is to change the size of the boxes rather than the nature of the problem: since everyone uses the same boxes the real challenge is to pack as much function into them as possible. In that sense extra speed and space that can be traded for better facilities are always worth having and when, occasionally, a box (i.e. cabinet, rack, circuit board, . . .) can be eliminated without loss of function the bonus is plain enough.

The following practical example points out some of the issues. As the examples in Chapter 6 show, many of the measures of language performance are affected strongly by the choice of support system which we suppose to be reflected on the semantics of the SIL. Now suppose the SIL is in fact a copy of the executive package of a conventional machine range, and that a Cobol application is obeyed (1) using the fixed, range-defined instruction set, and (2) using a Cobol target language (CTL) such as that discussed in the last chapter. The observable effects on storage requirements would be as shown in Table 7.1 (using typical figures for a small ICL 1900): in other words, the reward for a great deal of effort and investment in control memory simply does not materialize. Of course, one can present the picture in other ways: larger systems would benefit, and speed gains can be used to advantage if there is sufficient I – O capacity, but the fact remains that unless the support system gains similar advantages from interpretive techniques improvements in language performance will be seriously diluted. Faced with that condition, and with limited budgets, it is not surprising that development engineers have found it simpler to ride on semiconductor developments.

Let us assume, however, that the SIL itself benefits from the use of language-oriented microprogram. The effect might be seen as space reduction and gain in speed; more probably it will surface as improvement in function and flexibility, particularly in moving from low- to high-level language.

Table 7.1

| | Kbytes of program | |
	(1) Fixed instr.	(2) Fixed + CTL
Fixed instruction microcode	6	6
Cobol Target Language microcode	0	9
Executive (kernel) functions	16	16
System management (spooling, job control, terminal system etc.)	20	20
Cobol run-time support	25	25
Application: data (say)	9	9
code (say)	9	3
Total	85	88

In reviewing the parameters listed in Chapter 5 the implied comparison will be with a fixed, general-purpose instruction set implemented by microprogram on a neutral host machine. We shall then look at the microsystem problems to be solved. Finally, we take up the critical question of whether that is the best basis on which to make comparisons.

7.1 THE EFFECT ON LANGUAGE PARAMETERS

What is the effect of varying processor design to meet language characteristics? Throwing caution to the winds, the results of many experiments can be summarized as follows:

(a) Compile and load time

Substantial (say a factor of 5) reduction in CPU time can be made in the portions of a compiler concerned with lexical and syntax analysis, and to a lesser extent in code generation, by microcode interpretation of syntax tables. Where in-line coding has been used in the past the speed gain is smaller but significant saving in space is achieved by table-driven techniques. Compile time is directly affected by the choice of object code under (b), a simple syllabic form being easier to generate than DELtran instruction units. There is scope for optimization at all levels, and no clear advantage for language-oriented codes in that respect.

With regard to the choice of SIL, a number of languages have been devised with facilities appropriate to compiler-writing: list operations, character- and bit-string manipulation are often included, together with syntax and lexical analysis as already mentioned. To the extent that the SIL can incorporate such features it will outclass a fixed target code giving the same type of support (in space or speed: we cannot say which, because the fixed language can use either interpretive or in-line techniques).

Load time is normally determined by the support system. If all programs have to be mapped into a (virtual or real) linear store the time and space overhead in starting a job might be substantial (comparable with the compiler itself in many conventional systems). Moreover, the operating inconvenience can result in such anomalies as separate "batch" and "load-and-go" compilers. There is no reason, however, why the SIL functions should not allow program execution with explicit structure. For example, the operating environments shown in Figs. 6.2 and 6.4 can be maintained with no appreciable overhead on the part of the SIL. In that case, load time is negligible. The structures built by the compiler can be carried over to execution with practically no change.

Compile and load times for a given language directly affect the rate at which applications can be developed and the cost of the final product. By the same token, compile and load time for the SIL contribute to the cost of the language subsystem (compiler, run-time support modules). The quality of the product depends very much on one's ability to detect, control and correct errors, to make enhancements, measure performance, and upgrade existing software. In all these respects the SIL is influential, but it is almost impossible to make quantitative assessment.

(b) Execution time

Excluding arithmetic and $I - O$, execution time is governed by the time of access to variables and the change of control environments, i.e. the subsets of program space immediately available from different points in a program.

The ratio of addressing and control instructions to arithmetic in the output of a conventional compiler is in the region of 4:1, so assuming a 5:1 speed increase from microcoding the former an overall speed gain of 2.8:1 is indicated. One would expect more for the highly structured or "dynamic" languages. Further speed gains can be expected where specialized arithmetic functions are called for, e.g. array, complex, controlled precision or character-string manipulation. A minimum overall gain of 3:1 in speed for a "production" compiler to range standards would be a realistic objective for languages in common use. It should be added, however, that much of the research in this area has been based on control memories in the region of 10 Kbytes for both fixed and variable instruction sets. The economics of semiconductor storage now enable control memories of 32 Kbytes or more to be offered, in which case the fixed and variable parts are not necessarily in competition. In the limit, a "fixed" instruction set containing all the useful addressing paths from Cobol, Fortran, etc. and all the useful instruction formats would run as fast as any we have so far considered. The choice then rests partly on relative speeds of micromachines with different sizes of control memory, which might be negligible for mainstore resident control. Another important factor is whether enough information is available to fix the instruction set in advance, or whether a shorter step towards a microsystem can be taken, leaving the options open to language engineers.

(c) Size of support system

No more need be said about the kernel functions. The SIL and language microprograms tend to expand to fill the available space, but a minimum of 6 Kbytes and preferably 10 Kbytes should be allowed for each target instruction set. The SIL support (system management and kernel functions) is often one of the biggest occupants of main memory, as can be seen from Table 7.1, and benefits from compact representation.

(d) Object program size

It is the localization of environment which allows short addresses to be used, eliminates unnecessary function, register and address bits, and produces the greatest contribution to code compaction. An overall reduction in procedure size of 4:1 for large programs, including qualifier tables, would be a realistic aim. No significant gains in data mapping over a conventional system with word and character addressing can be expected. Gains in space can be seen as gains in main memory and channel capacity and to a less noticeable extent in file space.

(e) Diagnostic aids

As any APL user discovers, interpretive methods can give exceptionally good diagnostic information, sufficient to overcome eccentricities of the language itself. Unfortunately, diagnostic quality is one that cannot be measured and is often overlooked in favor of marginal improvements in the others.

7.2 MICROSYSTEM PROBLEMS

In the system context there are three major obstacles to using interpretive microprogram in the sense just assumed.

(a) Range definition

The microprogram appropriate to a high-performance machine is quite different from that of a slower micromachine. Hence all microprograms have to be reproduced and maintained for each model in the range. There is also an absolute speed limitation: a machine executing target instructions at 10 Mips is obeying microorders at least 10 times as fast, which is beyond the power of vertically encoded (i.e. easily programmed) host machines.

A fixed instruction set overcomes these difficulties firstly by making a closed commitment to microprogram, and secondly by allowing more or less hardware support and parallelism (horizontal microinstructions, multiple micromachines). In other words, optimizing the design to target instruction level recovers some of the losses observed on a neutral micromachine.

(b) Security

Microprogram derives part of its speed advantage by ignoring the security checks inherent in fixed instruction sets. The performance comparisons made in practice give the interpreter responsibility for resources normally regarded as protected. For example, knowing that in a procedure the variables that can be accessed (the immediate working set) are a small subset of the addressable space, a language subsystem can evaluate and retain their physical addresses. Similarly, it can directly access instructions with a guarantee (from the compiler) that valid function and operand fields will be presented. In such cases the security of the system is in the hands of language implementors, either in compiler, interpreter, or both.

A fixed target instruction set prevents unauthorized access to control memory, scratchpad or registers, and usually extends to partitioning the program space to provide protection and controlled sharing of data between independent subsystems.

(c) Flexibility

Microprogram is a static form of code, unwilling to pay the overheads of easy relocation; similarly, scratchpad assignments are bound into micro-instructions. Fast stores have hitherto been relatively small, so the problems of sharing micromachine resources between interpreters and scheduling their use have to be solved. As mentioned earlier, the availability of larger control stores alleviates the problem, but a "solution" based on having all micro-programs in control memory is really little more than a large, fixed instruction set. Perhaps the key requirement is that *any* language should be able to be developed and maintained, enjoying the benefits of language-specific micro-code, without disrupting others. A fixed instruction set makes all languages equal by keeping them above microprogram level.

7.3 TACTICAL RESPONSES

Despite the general arguments against using microprogram, many designers have used it to improve performance or cost. Some common applications are as follows.

(a) Embedded microcode

We have already noted that space and time advantages are diluted in the context of a conventional system, nevertheless those that remain are obtained with minimum investment in redesign. For example, the IBM APL Assist feature running under DOS/VS, OS/VS1 and OS/VS2 has been made available on the System/370 Models 135,138,145 and 148. It consists of an additional 20 Kbytes of microprogram, resident in main store, which interpret APL statements. It carries out virtual−real address translation according to the rules of the host system but returns control to the host to service interrupts and page faults. Hence system integrity depends upon the correct use of addresses in the APL microcode. The advantage gained is that statement analysis and branch to semantic routines is carried out in one interpretive stage instead of two.

In the same context it might also be noted that many systems make use of microprogrammed aids to system and library functions plugged into otherwise undefined function codes. The objective is usually to gain speed, but might also be to get round the architectural rules or to upstage potential imitators. Some interesting problems in range definition are raised, such as how to generate programs that will run on machines in the same family but with different combinations of "assist" functions.

(b) Secure microprogram

The security problem can be tackled at microcode level by introducing the sorts of in-line checks that do not impair performance, and which will be familiar from the early efforts of conventional machines in that direction: key comparison, lockout on fixed-sized blocks of store, etc. For example, the E1 emulator provides protection bits for 16-word frames of scratchpad, 64-word frames of control memory, 16 Kword frames of main storage and all I – O multiplex positions. Their control leads to another familiar branch of design, namely the privileged (micro)system state and functions associated with it. The main drawback to such schemes is the difficulty encountered in handling dynamically changing or moving programs, which occur quite frequently in modern systems. The relation between a language microprogram and the supporting kernel functions which we illustrated in VCS also raises a familiar set of problems in the controlled sharing of information structures, which we shall examine in greater detail in Chapter 14.

An alternative approach to achieving security without loss of performance is to validate addresses when they are formed, and to restrict their use so that further checks are unnecessary. The validation can be made against access control lists or by linguistic means. The kernel functions take responsibility for forming addresses; the language microcodes can modify them within given limits and access the store directly, as we saw in the Variable Computer System. There, addresses were distinguished by tags so that the SIL could find and update them without having specific knowledge of language implementations. For complete security, however, additional hardware support is needed to ensure that addresses are kept within bounds.

(c) Use of dedicated language processors

As a means of overcoming problems of security and flexibility, the use of separate processors for each language is attractive because the technology is available in the form of low-cost microprogrammable machines. The separation is usually physical, in the form of multiple processor-memory pairs, but it could also be achieved by time-slicing. In low-performance systems the individual modules might consist of microprocessors interpreting language-oriented target codes. A typical system model is shown in Fig. 7.1. Each program, together with its interpreter, has unrestricted use of local memory space during execution, but for its own safety it is rolled in and out by the scheduler which forms part of the SIL. The SIL microcode and system procedures can be protected by holding them in read-only storage. Access to shared data or overlays must be through some form of secondary store manager, which checks the declared accessibility of the data, typically maintaining access lists for each active user.

A classification sometimes suggested is that the processors and store management subsystem should be partitioned into a group of one or more "servers" having access to secondary storage and maintaining the database structure by cooperative effort, and "customers" whose main function is to execute high-level language programs. The servers would be enhanced by functions appropriate to database management. The interprocessor connection bus would be designed to reflect the major traffic flows between servers

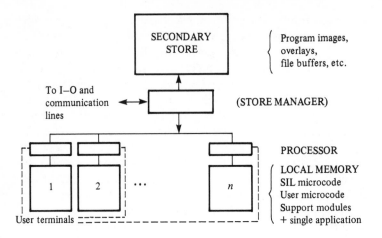

Fig. 7.1 Dedicated language/user application processors

and customers, and might range from specific point-to-point connections down to single bus schemes with ring or broadcast multiplexing conventions.

It can be seen that security and flexibility constraints are overcome in this model simply by replication, and that the severity of physical partitioning has some drawbacks when it comes to fitting a generalized workload onto the system. Nevertheless, the multicomputer model offers a range of performance, it can be tailored to meet specific requirements, it is more tolerant of failure than a centralized system, and it readily lends itself to the "personal computer" mode of working in which a rapid response to users can be guaranteed.

(d) Microprogram overlays

The restricted capacity of fast control memory is relaxed by storing vertically coded microinstructions in main memory, but at the expense of memory cycles. In recently developed microprogrammed machines (including IBM System/38 and Burroughs B 1800) memory traffic is reduced by retaining recently used microinstructions in a slave store in much the same way as in high-speed processors. The access algorithm is simplified by not having to deal with store write operations, and management is assisted by a portion of microprogram permanently resident in the processor. There is no corresponding facility for data. It would be attractive, for example, to "demand" the amount of scratchpad storage necessary for interpretation, and to have it fetched into fast store as the locus of the interpreter changed. At first sight that would be incompatible with the operating speeds expected in micro-program, but the machine outlined in Chapter 18 goes some way towards a solution.

7.4 FUTURE DEVELOPMENTS

Careful choice of words has left the key question unanswered: leaving aside short-term gains, are systems based on multiple micromachines with two levels of writable control the best deployment of modern technology for computer design? The answer appears to lie in strategic considerations rather than unchallenged performance benefits, for the reader will have noticed how often claims have to be hedged by reservations about arithmetic or I – O speeds and "neutral" micromachines. Even store economies, which seem the most clearcut, have to be judged against other methods of reducing the cost of the hierarchy, not the least of which is to do nothing but wait for the arrival of the 64 Kbit (or 256 Kbit . . .) chip.

Perhaps the strongest argument in favor of two-level control is that one never has all the information needed to design the perfect instruction set. In any case, too many people are involved. Designing the computer in two stages, but anticipating the needs of emulation and microsystem support, is a more easily managed proposition. Large-scale integration can be expected to offer room on the chip for control and scratchpad in the foreseeable future, but if the ROM takes one quarter as much space as RAM, should the offer be accepted? History appears to be repeating itself. Assuming that the ambition of processor design is to put the entire IBM 360 or its equivalent on a single chip, the manufacturer will have the option of using two or three such machines, each with its local store, in place of a more adaptable micro-machine. It would be a difficult choice to make on performance grounds, but what one looks for in adaptability is to reduce *total system cost*, including operating system, development and maintenance of software. The unique contributions of an interpreter derive from its ability to retain information about source program structure which can be used during execution to detect errors and improve performance. The need for an interpretive mode of use, fairly close to what we have been calling the micromachine level, is further enhanced by the use of portable languages and operating systems.

A possible conclusion is that future systems will contain processors of both types, with ROM used predominantly for emulation and for "kernel" functions of the microsystem. What rules of combination should be followed to provide effective alternatives to centralized systems? Design choices are most strongly influenced by two considerations: the program addressing mechanism and the control interface. We shall explain the issues, and show how they interact.

One of the drawbacks of the system model in Fig. 7.1 is the under-utilization of program storage: it is much less likely that the mixture of jobs in execution will fit well into the available local stores than in a centralized system with equal memory capacity. There are many areas where a simple "roll-in, roll-out" allocation scheme is unsatisfactory, and user-controlled allocation only leads to a restatement of classic overlay strategies. In modern applications store utilization is so unpredictable that some form of dynamic control is essential. We therefore postulate that program storage is logically and physically subdivided into variable-sized segments, and that a unified or *global* addressing scheme is handled by hardware (micromachine) and kernel (microprogram) functions. Physically, segments are allocated to achieve the best packing of local memories. It follows that if a segment is shared by two or more processors the bus system will allow remote access: otherwise the entire segment would have to be replicated as many times as needed. (Some-times, but not always, it is possible to distribute function so that replication is unnecessary, but the circumstances vary with the application.)

Hence we recognize the need for a remapping mechanism to take account of segment allocation across local memories. To see how that interacts with interpreter design we must look again at the basic control options and develop the idea that interpretation is not an all-or-nothing choice, but subject to degrees of application, depending on the language and compiler technology.

Although there has been a reduction in microsteps obeyed for the "average" high-level language statement there is still room for improvement: in the ICL 1900 a Cobol statement requires about 20 machine instruction steps, which suggests (from our study of the interpretive loop) about 40 "useful" functions rather than the 200 used in Cobol target code (Section 6.2). An interpreter is, after all, simply a means of calling a subroutine from a formalized target instruction. Its weakness is that the interpretive overhead is paid on every instruction unit and qualifier. The options will become clear if we take the model of the access path from an operand specification m in the instruction stream (see Fig. 5.5) via qualifier table *qual* and control environment (display registers) *disp* to the data. In our register transfer nota-tion the path would be described by the expression $disp'l.'offset$ where $(l,offset)$ will be found at $qual'm$. The essential 5 microsteps consist of three "modifications" and two (scratchpad) storage accesses. If we assume no more than two bytes for each microorder, then the whole operation would contribute a "cost" of:

(1) microprogram access: 5 steps @ 2 bytes   = 10 bytes; 5 µsteps

Alternatively, we might use a qualifier-based method requiring only m in the instruction stream (say 1 byte), but costing at least 20 microsteps to decode:

(2) qualifier access: = 1 byte; 20 µsteps

Thirdly, using a fixed target instruction set it is usually found that the addressing rule includes a "modify and fetch" mode, so assuming 3 bytes for each address specification:

(3) fixed addressing rule: 3 modify/fetch   = 9 bytes; 30 µsteps
     (assuming the addressing rule takes 10 µsteps)

Finally, we have noted that under suitable conditions the whole address path can be collapsed to, say, a single modify/fetch combination:

(4) optimized microprogram: 2 steps @ 2 bytes   = 4 bytes; 2 µsteps
(5) optimized addressing rule: 1 modify/fetch   = 3 bytes; 10µsteps

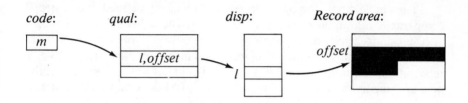

The above figures are intended only to characterize the choices available. In the context of language implementation we have discussed (2), (3) and (5). Evidently there is no absolute "best" method, which is why it is so difficult to design a general-purpose high-level machine, but if "microsteps executed" is the sole issue we must find a way of using (1) and (4). In other words, why not simply generate microprogram when we need to? And why not interpret a qualifier by calling a subroutine when that seems best?

The primary reasons are the security and allocation of microprogram, and it is here that we see the connection with the problem of remapping data and code segments, because accessibility can be checked at the same time as a location is calculated. The interpreter itself uses (1) and (4), but in current systems it does so without security and by fixed allocation of instructions and data. If those limitations could somehow be lifted, not only could micro-programming be offered safely for language interpretation, but it could be used as compiler output as an alternative to DEL representations. In later chapters we shall examine in greater detail how the required properties can be incorporated in processor design.

Achieving security at microinstruction level has an important and potentially dramatic effect in conjunction with the techniques discussed in the preceding chapters: *there is no longer any need for a high-level architectural definition*. In the terms used in Chapter 1, the architectural level (4) dissolves into sequential machine design (3). That might seem a little surprising, but remember that the main objectives in raising the level of architecture were:

(1) to conceal differences in hardware in a multimodel range;

(2)   to establish system interfaces that could not be supported at micromachine level;

(3)   to package the range-defined target instructions into units well matched to high-level languages and compiler technology.

We can now argue that (1) is no longer relevant because range cover is to be achieved with multiple computers; (2) can be achieved at micromachine level, and we shall see in Part 3 how the benefits of abstraction reach the microprogram; and (3) has simply not succeeded as well as intended. The idea that "simplicity is best" is unfortunately the most difficult one for manufacturers to accept.

The above discussion has been based on vaguely defined "microsteps" comparable with simple register transfer orders. The reader might feel concern at reverting to a style of instruction not far removed from that of 20 years ago. Is there a danger of inventing more and more complex microsteps and repeating the evolution of the IBM 360? It would not be surprising to see the host arithmetic functions develop in line with LSI devices, where hardened floating-point and decimal facilities can be expected. However, the lesson to be learned from interpreter design is that the many modes of access that are permanent features of high-level languages benefit very little from complex addressing rules. At the same time, new requirements have been recognized, suggesting hardware support for multicomputer operation, for abstraction, and for parallel operation. In summary, we can expect machine design to evolve from the restart point of interpretive use, but there is no danger of reinventing the wheel in a few years.

7.5 QUESTIONS AND FURTHER READING ON PART 1

1   Explain what is meant by the *state* of a programmable machine. Show how the state of one machine can be mapped into that of another.

2   By means of a flow chart and register transfer statements show how an interpretive program can be used to compute the successor of a target machine state. Use the interpretive program to illustrate actions consequent on:
     (a)   target machine sequencing;
     (b)   host machine sequencing;
     (c)   operand access;
     (d)   decoding;
     (e)   function execution.

3   Give examples of ways in which practical host machines can be designed to minimize the number of separate microorders arising from the actions listed in Question 2 above.

4 Describe the main components of a microprogrammed computer and show how they interact with one another. Outline the engineering constraints that affect the design of such machines and show what steps can be taken to achieve (a) high speed, and (b) low cost.

5 What is a *run-on* effect in microprogramming? Explain how it arises and what its implications are in the design of microprograms.

6 Explain how *data qualifiers* can be used to encode programs written in high-level languages. What features of a language favor such mechanisms? What does the language implementor hope to gain from using them?

7 Discuss the application of microprogram to the problems of accessing multidimensional arrays such as those arising in Algol or Fortran. Suggest primitive target functions and show how they would be invoked.

8 Suppose you were asked to design and implement a subsystem for executing a language such as Pascal using interpretive microprogram. What measurements would you make on existing software to guide the design process?

9 Sometimes interpretive control is an option, while at others it is practically a necessity. Explain why that is (or deny it if you like), giving examples of specific language characteristics to illustrate the points you make.

10 Discuss the difficulties of using variable microprogram in a general system context. If you think they have been exaggerated in Chapter 7, suggest further ways of overcoming them.

11 "Measured in silicon area, the cost of processing is declining in relation to the cost of storage — not vice versa as is widely assumed in the computing industry. A simple processor equates to about 0.5 Kbytes of storage, a PDP-11 to 1 Kbyte, and an IBM 360 to 2 Kbytes. On this basis, it is not very good economics to associate a large storage system with a single processor. Better to find ways of using more processors within the system, if only for trivial functions like address mapping. This size relationship appears intrinsic and in the long term it could lead to radical rethinking about the large and monolithic programs which dominate conventional computing today." (BAR79 pp. 77 – 8). Unravel and argue.

12 The impact of VLSI construction techniques on computer design is examined in PAT80. Discuss the points raised and relate them to the design issues presented in Chapters 7 and 14.

13 Repeat the calculation on p. 125 for any system with which you are familiar, and determine what DEL improvements would be needed to obtain a significant (say 25%) reduction in memory costs.

14 The discussion in Chapters 2 – 7 presupposes that general-purpose facilities are required over a wide range of costs. If those conditions are

relaxed there are many possible avenues for exploiting microprogrammed machines. See the FPS AP-120B (Chapter 8) or HAG80 for application to high-speed numerical calculation. There are innumerable instances of application to individual languages (e.g. see CHU80).

15 Work out the DELtran coding of the Fortran code in Fig. 7.2. Compare its storage requirements with that of the syllabic instructions outlined on p. 88.

```
        DIMENSION A(20), B(20)
        INTEGER I, J, K
        INTEGER C (20)
        J = 20
        K = 0
        DO 150 I = 1, 20
    50  IF (A(I) − B(I)) 100, 150, 150
   100  C(J) = I
        J = J − I
        K = K + (J − I)*(K − 2)
        A(I) = A(I − 1)
        GO TO 50
   150  CONTINUE
```

Fig. 7.2   A sample Fortran code sequence (see Exercise 15)

16 The cost of doing arithmetic has largely been ignored in the examination of language-directed instruction sets. However, it is an important component of the final package. See, for example, HUS70 on the control of arithmetic units, MIC80 and AMD80 for bit-sliced components.

17 It is sometimes suggested that future processors will be supplied with programs in the form of ROM packages. Would that offer any systematic advantages, or is it simply a way of charging for software? Presumably there would be a resident SIL, to which the plug-in packages would look like super-instructions. What functional properties would you expect in the SIL in a practical working environment?

18 Mention has been made of interpretive schemes in which the syntax analysis tree is directly "executed" (p. 86). Architectural proposals along those lines have a long history, but are currently manifested in "data flow", "reduction" or "functional" design. Use your reference library to access papers indexed under those keywords, and estimate how one such design would be measured by the criteria listed at the beginning of Chapter 5. Are the designs justified by other measures? If so, how should DEL techniques be assessed?

19 It was suggested (p. 103) that one might be able to analyze patterns of coding in a limited context and derive improved representations of programs. A target language such as DELtran does that in a minor way by adjusting the size of the "operand index container". If you have access to a flexible syntax analyzer, devise experiments that will detect and exploit frequently occurring constructs in a given sample of source programs.

20 Use your knowledge of microprogramming to develop the model target machine outlined in Section 4.3, defining an addressing rule, basic arithmetic and logical operations, and a sequencing rule that allows for multiprogramming.

PART 2

Computing in store

(From N. Thelwell, *Thelwell Country,* Eyre Methuen (1959))

Foreword to Part 2

Circuits are getting faster all the time, so why is it necessary to buy speed by making architectural changes? They are also getting cheaper, so why not simply buy more? These questions overlook that what is now seen as an "application" is the result of a long process of elimination under algorithmic, linguistic and economic constraints. An untrained person can quite easily pose problems that a computer cannot solve: the distinction between sending a machine to take pictures of Saturn and sending one across the road to buy a box of matches illustrates that point. Amongst the application areas currently being exploited are those which bring people into closest contact with computers, for it is from them that some of the greatest growth in demand is expected: office, factory, home, and school. Undoubtedly the next generation of machines—the office workstation, intelligent robot, home tutor or expert consultant—will call for much greater sophistication than hitherto. There is consequently a need for better algorithms, for languages in which to express them, and in the final analysis for machines to execute them at high speed. Chapters 8 – 13 examine one approach to the design of high-performance machines.

For practical illustrations I have drawn extensively on existing products, and would like to thank M.J.B. Duff of University College, London, J. Marsh of Floating Point Systems, W. Petersen of Cray Research and S.F. Reddaway of ICL for commenting on parts of Chapters 8, 11 and 12 of which they have first-hand knowledge.

8 HIGH-SPEED DATA

In the preceding chapters we have steered lightly round the point at which a location number disappears onto the address bus and the subsequent appearance or discharge of the datum. It is a crucial design issue to achieve a balance between processing and memory-access rates, particularly in high-performance computers where every opportunity is taken to exploit unused capacity on one side or the other. In this chapter we shall introduce by example some of the issues raised by such machines, and prepare to examine in greater detail the design of "active memory" systems.

Recall that the access path from token in the target instruction stream to the high-level datum it addresses is segmented as follows for Read operations (and with obvious variations in Steps 4 and 5 for Write):

(1) acquisition of statically defined attributes such as lexical level, type, offset in activation record, from the instruction stream or qualifier;
(2) ditto for dynamically defined attributes by reference to the control environment, yielding a pointer to the datum;
(3) conversion of the pointer from system space (virtual form) to physical (real) location number if necessary;
(4) submission of the location number to the storage subsystem, merging requests from concurrent operations in the same or other tasks; and
(5) receipt of the datum and conversion where necessary to the radix, word size and character codes of the host.

Note that this path is followed for each scalar quantity in a high-level program, and if explicit structure is imposed by using subscripts the path will be travelled (notionally at least) several times for each datum, e.g. in the Fortran loop:

$$DO\ 100\ I = 1,50$$
$$100 \qquad SUM = SUM + A(I)$$

the access path is covered five times in each iteration, contributing (say) 100 microinstructions in place of the two addressing operations that might be expected from the register transfer form:

$$do \{ \ sum + a. \ ; \ a' 1 \ \} \ while \ VA$$

In these circumstances the ability of the storage subsystem to deliver the goods seems unimportant in comparison with the difficulty of the processor in placing the order.

Consciously or otherwise, language usage has evolved in directions that drastically curtail the sequence described above. With a little effort most of Steps 1, 2 and 3 can appear to be eliminated, which is why Fortran continues to stand in relation to programming as Cheddar does to cheese. We say "appear to be eliminated" because if there is a genuine dynamic or recursive content in an algorithm that has to find rather clumsy expression in Fortran terms. Even Fortran cannot get down to the efficiency of register transfer statements, however, where assembly coding or thinly disguised versions thereof such as BCPL or C have a conspicuous advantage: there is no more economical way of accessing a stream of operands or instructions than by holding a pointer in one of the host registers and modifying it as required to point directly to the data. The idea of checking the pointer against declared program structure or even against task boundaries (Step 3) gets short shrift in the types of machine we are considering, though the assumption that such measures are time-consuming luxuries is incorrect, as will be shown in Part 3.

Having dismantled most of the apparatus of modern programming, our processor is in a position to make instruction and operand requests at speeds comparable with the microinstruction rate. At that point both the storage system and arithmetic unit are under pressure to keep up the flow of data. For example, main storage devices currently in use have access times of $250 - 300$ ns and longer if accessed through a shared highway, whereas quite moderate processor cycle times are in the region of 100 ns. On the other hand, for many jobs normally demanding high data rates the mix of functions is heavily biassed towards multi-step operations such as floating-point arithmetic.

For storage, a preliminary design step is to move the main program memory into local (i.e. non-shared) connection with the processor, which fits in well with our multicomputer model (Fig. 1.2). The next step is to provide fast storage buffers (register files, scratchpad, control memory) within the processor: they might be under program or automatic control. Note that in this type of machine all the register transfer operations are under hardwired control, so that the "control memory" is used to hold target instructions awaiting execution. Finally, the general rule is to place orders on the store in bulk so that even if the storage cycle time is long, say 320 ns, fetching the equivalent of 8 or 16 words at once can give an apparent access time, in favorable circumstances, of 40 or 20 ns.

On the operational side the goal is to present operands to the arithmetic and logical unit at speed comparable with word-access rate to and from main memory. Rather than wait for completion of a multi-step function, the responsibility for computing a result and consigning it to its destination is delegated to the ALU. Moreover, the latter is designed so that it can accept fresh operands on each machine cycle, being organized into two or more stages that each perform part of an arithmetic function (compare the method used in simple micromachines in which partial results are recirculated through the *same* ALU paths). For example, for floating-point addition or subtraction there might be three stages (Fig. 8.1) in which, after loading the two operands, they are first compared and aligned, then added, and finally renormalized.

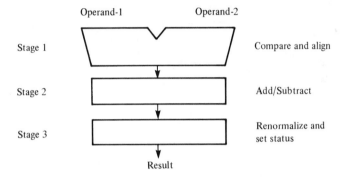

Fig. 8.1   Floating-point add/subtract pipeline

Since each stage latches the intermediate result it is possible for three pairs of operands to be in process at once. Such organization is referred to as a **pipelined** arithmetic unit. To achieve high speed there might be several units in each processor, each specialized to perform a subset of arithmetic or logical functions. To keep them all fully loaded, methods must be found for presenting many operand pairs in a single machine cycle.

Figure 8.2 shows in schematic form the components that have been introduced. In the next subsections we examine two successful commercial designs of that general type, concentrating on their functional properties rather than performance or cost achievements. We shall see that the key to success is the ability of the high-speed data buffers and their associated access mechanisms to switch operands into the pipelines and to route the results back to store. The most favorable circumstances appear to be when the data are distributed uniformly across separate memory banks in main store and subjected to lengthy iterative calculations with few control branches or other exceptional conditions. If that really is the case, then an overall simplification of design can be suggested in which the high-speed buffers are omitted and

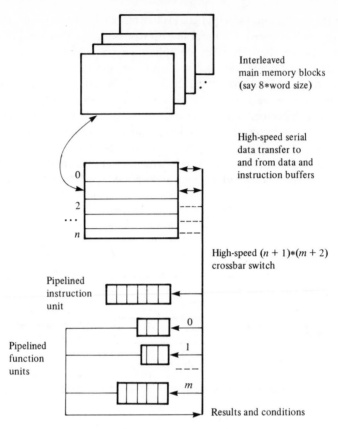

Fig. 8.2 Schematic form of pipelined vector processor

the function units are directly associated with the memory banks. Now the function units are identical to one another and general-purpose in specification. Where the data cannot be found adjacent to the function unit, some means must be found to transfer them "across" the memory banks to the required position, but it is postulated that in many practical situations when repositioning is needed it can be done in parallel for many operands at once by using a **routing network** (Fig. 8.3). The economic advantages of such designs are considerable, and in certain application areas their performance is unchallenged, but there is still genuine uncertainty about the range of problems to which they can be applied. The main incentive to build them derives from the numerical solution of field equations such as those arising in reactor physics, aerodynamics and meteorology. Many important numerical methods are based on a discrete representation of physical space

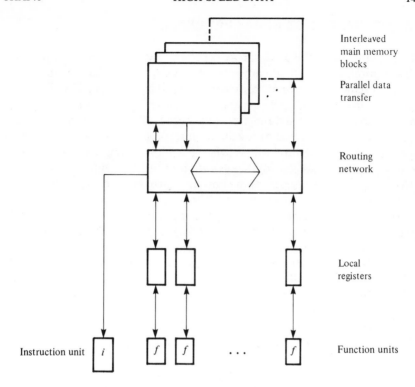

Fig. 8.3 Schematic form of array processor

and time that maps easily onto an array of stores such as Fig. 8.3, and problems of this class create a practically unlimited demand for computing power. The principles of such applications are outlined in the following chapters, but the emphasis of the discussion will be on non-numerical problems, system and language design, which call for careful rethinking of the approach to problem analysis.

In this chapter it will become clear that high data-processing rates will be achieved by the machines under discussion only if certain upsetting situations, which will be identified in the final subsection, can be avoided. How susceptible they are to the "wrong sort of problem" is a matter of great practical concern on which, as in the case of language-oriented design, there is practically no conclusive evidence. What one can be sure of is that judgement based on intuitive understanding of conventional machine design and systems analysis is not a reliable guide. However, we begin this study by outlining the register structure and programming characteristics of some existing machines designed for high-speed computing.

8.1 THE FPS AP-120B ARRAY PROCESSOR

Having introduced the term "array processor" as a description of machine organization, the fact that many other machines and languages also process arrays of data is a source of confusion to guard against. The Floating Point Systems AP-120B follows the general schematic of Fig. 8.2, but provides only the high-speed buffers and function units because it is intended as a device to add to the peripheral bus of a general-purpose host system. The mode of operation is that the host will provide assembly, linkage, I − O and other service functions and control the operation of the AP-120B via a simulated "front panel". Another part of the host interface is a set of registers for controlling direct transfers of data to and from the host memory (or, in some configurations, a dedicated I − O channel), reformatting as required to match the internal 38-bit floating-point format of the AP-120B. There are thus two centers of control: the host system, which is normally driven by a portable library of Fortran programs and subroutines; and the array processor, which executes library programs written in a low-level language and supplied for the most part by the manufacturer. It is possible to generate array programs from high-level (Fortran) source, but because the AP-120B relies for its speed on a form of microprogramming, much of the power is lost. Figure 8.4 indicates the sequence of operations involved in calling for action from the array processor.

The primary aim of the AP-120B is to calculate at high speed and low cost some common vector transforms. The requirement of "programmability" is relatively low, and the internal control scheme is in the form of a microprogrammable machine using a horizontal 64-bit microinstruction of the type discussed in earlier chapters. Figure 8.5 shows the internal stores and data paths. A microinstruction contains 6 groups of microorders, simultaneously controlling the 3-stage floating-point multiplier, 2-stage adder, integer ALU and four fast data buffers. In one machine cycle four floating-point operands can be presented to the function units. An operand from Main Data and Table Memory can be enabled onto both adder and multiplier, and operands from the datapad register banks can be enabled onto any or all of the processor inputs. Note also that the output from adder or multiplier can be gated directly to the input stage. The microinstruction rate is 6 MHz, so if the pipelines are fully loaded the rate of producing floating-point results is 12 Mflops, i.e. 12 million floating-point operations per second (this measure is frequently used to indicate computing power as it discounts any support functions that might be included in a simple "Mips" rate). Table 8.1 gives some examples of the mathematical library functions supplied for the AP-120B, together with the time estimates per vector element. The total time from the host point of view must include the interactions listed in Fig. 8.4.

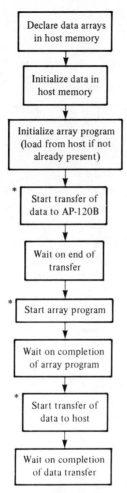

Fig. 8.4 Sequence of operations controlling AP-120B.
*In practice, transfer of input to the array and of results to the host are overlapped with program execution, using DMA transfers to and from a buffer area in the array.

Example 8.1 As an example of AP-120B programming (which incidentally illustrates some aspects of horizontal microprogram control as discussed in Chapter 3), consider the problem of finding the largest element in absolute value in a vector of N floating-point values stored in main data memory, starting at position A and at successive locations $A, A'I, A'(2*I), \ldots A'((N-1)*I)$. The maximum absolute value will be stored at location C, and the pointer to its first occurrence at $C'1$.

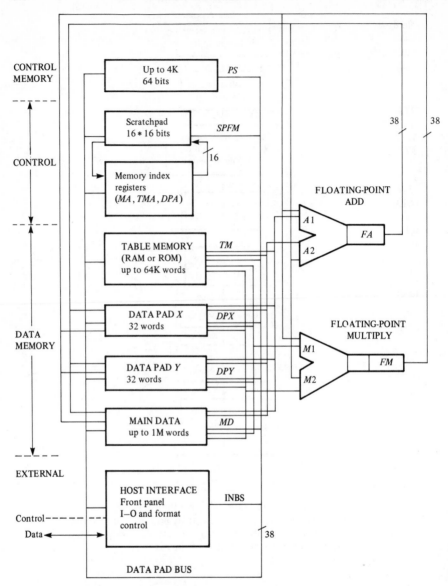

Fig. 8.5 FPS AP-120B Array Processor schematic diagram
(Adapted from data published by Floating Point Systems Inc.)

The vector will be scanned starting at A. Suppose the maximum element
found to date is kept at datapad location addressed by DPX. Then in principle
the search is a straightforward loop:

Table 8.1   Some vector operations in AP-120B

Function name	Operation	Time/element @6 MHz clock (μs)
DOTPR	Dot product	0.8
MAXMGV	Find maximum abs. value	0.3
MMTADD	Vector add (Main Data to Table)	0.7
MTTMUL	Vector multiply (Main × Table to Table)	0.5
RMSQV	Root mean square	0.3
VAND	Vector "and"	0.8
VCLR	Vector clear	0.2
VMAXMG	Vector maximum abs. value	0.8
VLN	Vector natural logarithm	2.7
VSQ	Vector square	0.5
VSQRT	Vector square root	1.8

(Times ignore end-effects)

Adapted from data published by Floating Point Systems Inc. Form 860-7288-005

```
REGS   [   A              Pointer to vector
          DPX             Max. element pointer
           N              Counter
           C  ]           Result pointer
findmax:   DPX =. 0;
           do {(abs(A.) − DPX.);
               if GT { C'1 =. A;
                   DPX =. abs (A)}
               A'I;
               N−1
               } while GT;
           { adjust final index and
           return values in C,C'1 }
```

In practice, the problem arises of making full use of the floating-point adder. Translating the above statements into microorders and mapping them into machine cycles, it is found that forming the absolute value and comparing it with the current maximum takes six machine cycles. That is shown in the first timing chart (which shows only the activity of the adder). It follows that the condition *if GT* is tested on the sixth machine cycle after input of the vector element b, and that during that period the adder is only one-third used. To increase the flow of calculation vector elements must be pipelined through the arithmetic unit.

TIMING CHART showing processing stages for a single element b:

Machine cycle:	0	1	2	3	4	5
ADDER INPUT:	b			b ,DPX		
Stage 1:		b			$fsub$	
Stage 2:			b to datapad (DPY)			set status

If we label successive vector elements a, b, c, d, ... and mark the processing stages of each as b_0, b_1, ..., b_5, etc., then the activity of element b is represented by the second timing chart and the processing sequence a, b, c, d is seen in part fitting together as in the third chart.

TIMING CHART labelling processing stages for the element b:

Machine cycle:	0	1	2	3	4	5
ADDER INPUT:	b_0			b_3		
Stage 1:		b_1			b_4	
Stage 2:			b_2			b_5

TIMING CHART labelling processing stages for elements a, b, c, d:

Machine cycle:	0	1	2	3	4	5
ADDER INPUT:	b_0	a_3	c_0	b_3	d_0	c_3
Stage 1:	·	b_1	a_4	c_1	b_4	d_1
Stage 2:	a_2	·	b_2	a_5	c_2	b_5

Hence, at any one time, assuming no branch is taken, three vector elements are in the pipeline. The main loop consists of two microinstructions. The first (on "even" cycles in the timing chart) starts the absolute-value calculation (c_0 in cycle 2, for example) and takes the adder output (b_2) to datapad DPY. The second microinstruction (cycle 3) starts the floating-point subtraction ($DPY-DPX$) and sets the status a_5 from the preceding comparison. At the same time, microorders are issued to control Main Data memory access, indexing and branching.

If a new maximum is found (for example from the status of a_5 in cycle 3), the branch taken at Step 4 must update the datapad content and save its index. At that point, however, the comparison currently in progress (b_4) is using an out-of-date maximum element. The operation in the pipeline must therefore be repeated before rejoining the main loop. In this example the history of the calculation is recorded by using the datapads DPX and DPY as cyclic buffers, indexed by the scratchpad pointer DPA, which is incremented in the loop. Hence when it is necessary to "back up" the pipeline previous results can be selected by referring to $DPX(-1)$, $DPY(-2)$ etc., which form effective addresses relative to the current value of DPA.

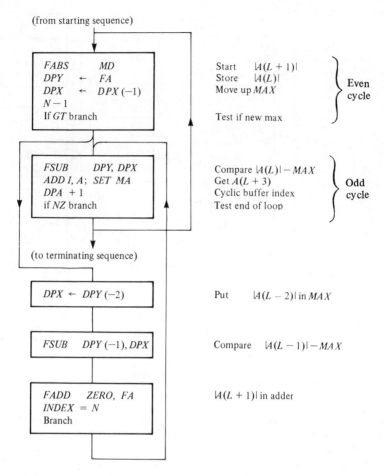

(from starting sequence)

FABS MD DPY ← FA DPX ← DPX (−1) N − 1 If GT branch	Start |A(L + 1)| Store |A(L)| Move up MAX Test if new max

(Even cycle)

FSUB DPY, DPX ADD I, A; SET MA DPA + 1 if NZ branch	Compare |A(L)| − MAX Get A(L + 3) Cyclic buffer index Test end of loop

(Odd cycle)

(to terminating sequence)

DPX ← DPY (−2)	Put |A(L − 2)| in MAX

FSUB DPY (−1), DPX	Compare |A(L − 1)| − MAX

FADD ZERO, FA INDEX = N Branch	|A(L + 1)| in adder

Fig. 8.6 Inner loop of MAXMGV microprogram in FPS AP-120B (Adapted from data published by Floating Point Systems Inc.)

Figure 8.6 shows the resulting loop of two microinstructions and the updating sequence (3 microinstructions). It does not show the starting sequence (10 microinstructions) or the terminating sequence (6 microinstructions).

8.2 THE CRAY-1 COMPUTER

A more powerful, ambitious (and more expensive) example of the same type as the AP-120B is the CRAY-1 computer, Fig.8.7. This system is self-supporting in all phases of computation and is backed by disk controllers

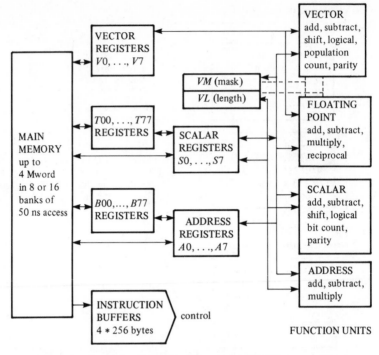

Fig. 8.7 General schematic diagram of CRAY-1 computer (Adapted from CRAY-1 Reference Manual, form no. 224004)

and other $I-O$ channels communicating directly with main storage under control of a resident operating system.

The main memory is organized as 8 or 16 interleaved blocks up to a total of 4M 64-bit words (32 Mbytes). Cycle time of the memory is 50 ns, but by phasing the operation of each block it is possible to transfer a word to the internal registers every ¼ cycle or 12.5 ns, which is the clock rate of the processor. Read and write requests are made either for *scalar,* single word transfers, or *vectors* of up to 64 words each. In the latter case the starting position of the vector and a constant interval between elements is given by the access function: to read or write a vector takes between 64 and 256 processor cycles, depending on the spacing of the data. Numeric data are accessed under program control and transferred to one of eight vector registers *Vi* (Fig. 8.7). Instruction pages are read under automatic control into one of four instruction buffers. Individual instructions are either 16 or 32 bits in length.

The fast data registers are as follows:

Vector registers $V0, \ldots, V7$

Eight 64-word registers that can be used as source or destination of vector arithmetic operators. In each case the order of processing is the same, from index 0 to a limit given by the vector length register VL in the range $1 - 64$. In certain cases (merge operation) the function is controlled by the content of a 64-bit mask register VM, which can be set by program (from a scalar register) or by vector test.

It follows that to process vector operands of arbitrary length N they must be segmented into a vector of length N modulo 64 and a further $N/64$ vectors of length 64. The segmenting operation is under program control and can be carried out in parallel with the arithmetic.

Scalar registers $S0, \ldots , S7, T00, \ldots , T77$

Eight 1-word general-purpose registers backed by a single 64-element vector of temporary storage. The block T of register values can be transferred to or from memory as for a vector register, but in addition single scalar values can be accessed via S.

Address registers $A0, \ldots , A7, B00, \ldots , B77$

Eight 24-bit address and index values backed by a single vector of 64 24-bit words. The block B of address values can be transferred to or from memory as a vector register, but in addition single address values can be accessed via A.

The thirteen function units of CRAY-1 are listed in Table 8.2. Seven

Table 8.2   Function units in CRAY-1

Unit		Number of stages
Vector results to S or V registers:		
1	Floating add/subtract	6
2	Floating multiply	7
3	Floating reciprocal	14
Vector results to V registers:		
4	Integer add/subtract	3
5	Shift	4
6	Logical operators	2
7	Population count/parity	6
Scalar results to S registers:		
8	Logical operations	1
9	Shift	2,3
10	Integer add/subtract	3
11	Bit count/leading zeros	3,4,3
Address calculation (24 bit), result to A registers:		
12	Integer add/subtract	2
13	Integer multiply	6

units are able to carry out vector operations, and once started they autono-
mously fetch their operands from vector of scalar registers and return results
emerging from the pipeline. When a vector instruction is started the required
functional unit and operand registers are reserved for the number of clock
periods determined by the length of vector and number of stages in the pipeline. Hence, using the assignment operator " $\leftarrow$ " to imply term-by-term vector
combination (and assuming floating-point arithmetic):

$$V3 \leftarrow V2 + V5; \quad /* \; add \; vectors \; V2 \; and \; V5 \; */$$
$$V0 \leftarrow V1 + V2$$

causes the second instruction to lock, waiting both for the floating-point adder
and for $V2$. In certain circumstances the output from a pipe can be fed directly
as input to a succeeding instruction. For example, in the operations:

$$V2 \leftarrow V3 * V7;$$
$$V0 \leftarrow V4 + V2$$

the first result of the first operation ($V2'0 =. \; V3'0. * V7'0.$) will appear
after 9 clock periods, at which time (assuming both $V4$ and the adder are free)
the second operation can start. The value of $V0'0$ will be available after a
further 6 clock periods. This facility is known as *chaining*. If the *same* vector
is used as source and destination, as in:

$$V2 \leftarrow V2 * S5$$

(multiplication of vector by scalar), the indexing of source operands does not
start until after the first result emerges from the function unit, at which point
it is chained onto the input of the function unit, and so on for subsequent
results. In the above example the first nine values stored in $V2$ will equal
$V2'0. * S5$, and they in turn are used as input to the multiplier to give
$V2'0.*S5*S5$, repeated eight times, and so to the final three elements with
the values $V2'0.*S5^7$, $V2'0.*S5^7$ and $V2'0.*S5^8$. This rule of iterative use
applies to all pipelines, but the number of iterations depends on the length of
pipe.

The ability of each function unit to retain the vector length, scalar
operand (if any), function code, source and destination addresses at time of
instruction issue enables each to produce a result every clock period, i.e. 80 per
microsecond. In practice, operand unit and register conflicts make it difficult
to approach the theoretical throughput of operands. Further conflicts arise
in traffic to and from main storage, which is limited to one data value (8
bytes) or four instruction words (32 bytes) per clock period. To understand
how to get the best use out of the machine would take long practice, but a
simple example can be used to illustrate some points of programming.

Example 8.2 Suppose it is required to find the index of the maximum
element in absolute value in an array stored at location $A1$ in main memory,

whose elements are separated by constant interval $A2$. For simplicity it is assumed that there are $64 * A3$ elements altogether, where $A3$ is even. The first step is to take the $A3$ vectors and compare them element by element, forming an intermediate result $V1$ consisting of the maximum value (squared) at each element position. A second vector $V2$ is used to remember where the elements of $V1$ came from. The terminating instructions use a scalar comparison subroutine to find the position of the largest element of $V1$, from which the final index is reconstructed by reference to $V2$.

The program is given in register transfer form in Fig. 8.8. We use the identifiers $V0, \ldots, V7$ as pointers to 64-bit word sequences each of 64 elements. The assignment symbol "$\leftarrow$" is used to imply term-by-term expression evaluation and assignment; e.g.,

$$V5 \leftarrow V4 - V1$$

might be re-written as:[†]

  save $[V1 \ V4 \ V5]$;
  do $\{ V5 =. V4. - V1.$;
   $V5'1; \ V4'1; \ V1'1 \}$ *while VA*;
  unsave $[V5 \ V4 \ V1]$

where it assumed that the limit of all vectors is preset to $VL - 1$. In vector $-$ scalar combination the effect is as if a vector of VL elements identical to the scalar value had been used, e.g.

$$V1 \leftarrow 0$$

might be re-written as:

  save $[V1]$;
  do $\{ V1 =. 0; \ V1'1 \}$ *while VA*;
  unsave $[V1]$

Assignment to VM forms a 64-bit Boolean mask according to the outcome of a specified comparison. Finally, in lines /**/ the special notation ? $VM(V4, V1)$ is used to indicate merging under the vector mask VM, giving the value $V4$ at element positions where the corresponding bit of VM is 0, and $V1$ where the mask bit is 1.

It can be judged that under favorable memory access conditions a substantial amount of chaining of vector operations will be achieved; the fact that there is no "compare magnitude" instruction, which forces a multiplication step, is not a major issue. In each loop the vector operations must be completed twice to set the vector mask register so there appear to be a

---

[†] The use of *save* and *unsave* statements will be explained below (p. 181).

On entry $A1$ points to the first element of an array,
              $A2$ gives the element spacing (word count)
              $A3$ gives the array size divided by 64
              VL is implicitly 64
On exit the index of the maximum element is returned

> $maxel$ ( ): $V2'A3 =.-1$;
> $A3 - 1$;
> $V1 \leftarrow 0$;
> $V2 \leftarrow 0$;
> $A1 + (A3 \ll 6)$;

/*   *This loop forms the intermediate vector of maximum elements first in $V3$ then in
        $V1$* */

> do $V0 \leftarrow \{$ *read vector from $A1$, $A1'A2$, ... $\}$
> $V4 \leftarrow V0*V0$;
> $V5 \leftarrow V4 - V1$;
> $VM\leftarrow (V5 < 0)$;   /* *form Boolean mask from sign bits* */
> $S6 = VM$;
> /**/ $V3 \leftarrow ?VM(V4, V1)$;   /* *merge max values* */
> $V2'A3 =. S6$;   /* *save mask* */
> $A1-64; A3-1$;
> $V0 \leftarrow \{$ *read next vector* $\}$;
> $V4 \leftarrow V0*V0$;
> $V5 \leftarrow V4 - V3$;
> $VM\leftarrow (V5<0)$;
> $S6 = VM$;
> /**/ $V1 \leftarrow ?VM(V4, V3)$;
> $V2'A3 =. S6$;
> $A1-64; A3-1$
> $\}$ *while GE*;

/*   *Now find the biggest element in $V1$*   */

> $A3 = VSCAN(V1)$;   /* *returns index of max*   */

/*   *Where did it come from? Look at $A3$' th bit in words of $V2$*   */

> $V0 \leftarrow V2\ll A3$;   /* *shift to sign position*   */
> $VM\leftarrow (V0<0)$;
> $S1 = VM$;
> $A2 = Zerocount (S1)$;   /* *returns no. of leading zeros*   */
> $A2-1$;
> $return (A2 \ll 6 | A3)$

Fig. 8.8   Finding a maximum element in CRAY-1

minimum of 128 machines cycles plus start-up time and relatively slow transfers between scalar and vector registers. The quoted operation times are
given in Table 8.3, which shows the dependence on spacing of elements, the
worst case being when they all fall in the same memory bank ($A2 = 16$).

Table 8.3   Time to find maximum element *maxel*() in CRAY-1

Number of elements (*A*3 * 64)	Spacing (*A*2)		
	1	8	16
256	17.6	24.1	30.1
1024	43.2	68.8	93.8
4096	140.0	241.6	342.0

All times in microseconds
Source: W.P.Petersen, *CRAY-1 Basic Linear Algebra Subprograms for CFT Usage*,
CRAY Research INC, Pub 2240208 (with acknowledgement to T.L.Jordan, Los
Alamos Scientific Laboratory).

It is left as an exercise for the reader to deduce from these figures that the time spent outside the loop is in each case approximately 9 μs, and the number of processor cycles for a single loop varies from approximately 340 to 840.

Figure 8.8 illustrates the main characteristics of vector pipelined machines: use of the main store access mechanism as a serial routing device, "{ *read vector* . . . }"; a small number (relative to vector size) of very high-speed function units; parallel operation on several vectors (the "working set" of the processor) and selective operations conditioned by Boolean masks. What it does not show is the large amount of control circuitry associated with the function units, main store, and switches internal to the processor. In attempting to reduce costs and yet retain high processing rates designers have moved towards identical and simple function units working under control of a single broadcast instruction stream, and have replaced the parallelism that derives from the set of working vectors by strict term-by-term combination of vector elements.

8.3 CASE STUDY: ILLIAC IV

The ninety-degree change of direction between Figs. 8.2 and 8.3 is responsible for the distinct characteristics of array processors: use of main memory as a parallel access channel, the number of function units equal to the main store parallelism, term-by-term operations on vectors, and special provision for program control of routing.

The main engineering stimulus to array processor design comes from the emergence of semiconductor stores as memory components: since they have the same physical and electrical properties as logical devices it is natural to consider closely coupled assemblies of function and memory units. A related factor of extreme importance is that simple and highly repetitive circuits are very suitable for LSI manufacture: some of the processors under consideration require less than 100 logic gates for the function unit and local registers and could eventually represent a negligible cost increase over the main memory itself.

Array processors are of two main types, depending on whether the function units are designed to operate on word or single-bit operands. Illiac IV and the Burroughs BSP are of word type, while Goodyear STARAN, CLIP and ICL DAP are bit organized. The practical choice between them depends on the class of problems tackled as well as circuit components used. As an introduction to architecture and programming, bit organization allows greater flexibility, but because of its importance in the development of parallel computation a glimpse at Illiac IV is in order.

We shall refer to the function unit of an array, together with its local memory and working registers, as a processing element (PE). The Illiac IV contains 64 PEs, each with 2048 words of storage, 4 working registers, an index register and a mode register. The function unit operates on 64-bit words, treated either as single numbers, pairs of 32-bit numbers, or groups of 8 bytes. A comprehensive set of floating-point operations is provided, with times in the submicrosecond range for addition and multiplication (the maximum computing rate achievable is about 40 Mflops).

Operation of the array is directed by a control unit (CU) which obeys two types of instruction: operations local to the CU (such as conditional branches, index manipulations); and PE operations which are partially decoded and broadcast to the array. Figure 8.9 shows the main components of the CU in relation to the PE array. In order to sustain PE activity CU operations are overlapped with PE control, using a queue to buffer instructions prepared for broadcasting. The CU can also broadcast single words of data on a bus common to all PEs, and read or write single words composed of a specified bit from each of the 64 mode registers. Single data words and 8-word blocks can be read to a fast data buffer in the CU.

The CU contains four working registers ($CARi, i = 0, \ldots, 3$) used for address calculation and logical manipulation (more complex scalar operations being delegated to a PE). A store address is generated from three components: an offset specified in the instruction, a base in one of the CU working registers, and a local index added to the address in each PE from its own index register. Hence, unless indexing is disabled or all local index registers have identical contents, the locations finally selected in PE local memories will differ. That facility plays an important part in data mapping on Illiac-IV.

The routing network provides a 64-bit data path from each PE to its neighbors distant ± 1, ± 8 modulo 64. Hence the array can be viewed either as a circular pattern of 64 elements or as an 8 * 8 matrix in which each element

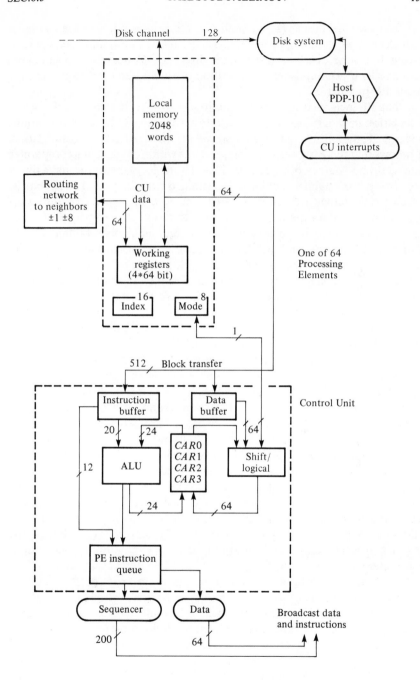

Fig. 8.9   Main components of Illiac IV

has four near-neighbors (as we shall see, the second point of view is more fully developed in bit-organized arrays). In routing operations each operand travels the same distance in the same direction. Communication between distant PEs is accomplished by repetition of single-step operations within a single PE instruction.

The PE local memories each contain 2048 words, so that if we think of a calculation in which each word is used (on average) five times in operations taking 1 μs, the entire memory content will be processed in the order of 10 ms. It follows that there is a need to replace results with fresh data at a comparable rate to keep the array occupied. In Illiac IV the local memories have direct access to a disk channel capable of a sustained transfer rate of $5*10^8$ bits/s, which would reload the entire 1 Mbyte memory in 16 ms. The design of algorithms and data mappings to keep calculation in step with disk $I-O$ rates features largely in Illiac IV programming, and involves taking account of both transfer times and disk latency. Clearly, the seriousness of the $I-O$ problem depends on the amount of calculation that can be supported in PE local memories alone: if the data for a complete interation can be held locally and processed many times before producing a result or requiring new input, then the theoretical computing rate is more likely to be achieved. The timing of the Illiac IV project was unfortunate in anticipating the rapid advance in semiconductor memories that is now apparent.

To run programs on Illiac IV the array is served by a host machine (in this case a DEC PDP-10) which shares access to the disk store. Programs are compiled and data initialized on the disk. The CU is started by the PDP-10. Local memory is loaded from the disk channel and instructions are fetched to a fast buffer in the CU (a block of 8 words contains 16 instructions). Store write action in each PE is enabled by a bit in its mode register: if the operation is conditional, and the bit is set, the operation is performed; otherwise it has no effect. In that way the calculation can be made to depend on preset masks or locally computed results. (A second mask bit is used for 32-bit operations, but there is no mode control on bytes.) Two further mode bits are set as a result of arithmetic exceptions and others can be set by program. Hence, by examining mode bits, the CU can detect general ("all zero") or isolated ("the first negative") conditions of data in the array. Termination of calculation, and requests for $I-O$ transfers, are signalled by interrupting the host.

From the above brief description it can be seen that performance on complete problems depends on the interaction of three processors (the PDP-10, the CU and the PE array) and their interconnecting channels. Isolated pieces of program are therefore not a good guide to performance, but the following example will serve to introduce some common array operations.

Example 8.3   Consider again the problem of finding the index of maximum element in a vector a_i, $i = 0, \ldots, (CAR1 - 1)$, disregarding sign, where the

/* *Word addresses run consecutively through PEs, so that PE_0 contains vector elements a_0, a_{64}, a_{128}, etc., in successive locations of its local memory. Pointers in CU registers are assumed to refer to word sequences; the memory mapping is as follows:* */

	PE_0	PE_1	PE_2	$\cdots$	PE_{63}	
CAR0:	a_0	a_1	a_2	$\cdots$	a_{63}	row 0
	a_{64}	a_{65}	a_{66}	$\cdots$	a_{127}	row 1
	a_{128}	a_{129}	a_{130}	$\cdots$	a_{191}	
	$\cdots$					
$CAR0'(CAR1-64)$:	$\cdots$		(last subvector)			
CAR2:			(column maxima)			
CAR3:			(index values)			

*CAR*1 *initially gives the length of vector (a multiple of 64)* */

Stage 1:   /* *Find column maxima* */

CAR2 ← 0;   CAR3 ← 0;   /* *Clear workspace* */
CAR1−64;
   do   {(CAR2 − abs (CAR0'CAR1)); /* *Vector compare* */
      {let mode bit i = sign from each PE};
      where   (mode i)
          {CAR2 ← abs (CAR0'CAR1);
          CAR3 ← CAR1 /* *broadcast* */};
      CAR1−64 }while GE

Stage 2:   /* *At this point CAR2 points to the column maxima and CAR3 indicates which rows they came from. Now comparisons are made by shifting the elements varying amounts (CAR1) to the left. Finally the index of the maximum element is formed in CAR1 (see text)* */

CAR1 = 32;
   do   {CAR2 − {CAR2 move left CAR1};
      {let mode bit i = sign};
      where   (mode i)
          {CAR2 ← {CAR2 move left CAR1};
          CAR3 ← CAR1 | {CAR3 move left CAR1}};
      CAR1≫1} while NZ;
   CAR1 = CAR3.   /* *result in CAR1* */

Fig. 8.10   Finding a maximum element using array operations

vector elements are stored consecutively starting at address *CAR*0 in PE_0 and occupying successive rows of the array (see Fig. 8.10). Let *CAR*2 and *CAR*3 point to two working rows of 64 elements each.

The method of solution consists of finding the maximum element within each PE memory by parallel comparison of rows, giving a vector of "column maxima" addressed by *CAR*2. The second stage is to compare elements in the vector *CAR*2, which requires routing operations to bring the required elements together. In this example elements distant 32 are compared first, followed by those distant 16, 8, 4, 2 and 1. At each comparison the larger element overwrites the left element of the pair, so that after 6 comparisons the largest element will be in PE_0. At the same time the index of the largest element is formed bit by bit in the vector $CAR3$.

In the example, CU operators are expressed as far as possible by register transfer statements, vector assignments are indicated by the "$\leftarrow$" symbol, and "X" should be read as "the 64-element subvector (row) starting at address X". Conditional array assignments are marked by a "*where*" clause, meaning that only PEs in which the corresponding mode bit is set will be enabled. Note that in Stage 2 $CAR1$ is used both to indicate the routing distance and to form the final index. The sequence of operations can best be illustrated by showing how the index of a maximum element would be formed in an 8-element row, in three steps as follows:

[CU]	[ARRAY]							
$CAR1 = 4$								
$CAR2$: (values)	12	0	17	9	1	4	45	3
$CAR3$: (bits)	000	000	000	000	000	000	000	000
$CAR1 = 2$								
$CAR2$:	12	4	45	9				
$CAR3$:	000	100	100	000				
$CAR1 = 1$								
$CAR2$:	45	9						
$CAR3$:	110	010						
$CAR1 = 0$								
$CAR2$:	45							
$CAR3$:	110							

Thus, at the end of the iteration, the index (110) at $CAR3$ is that of the largest element in the initial row. We shall see much more of that type in algorithm, in which the amount of parallelism is halved at each iteration.

8.4 ACTIVE MEMORY ARRAYS

We now turn to the class of array processors in which each PE operates on single bits of data from its local memory.

Simplicity of design is the consequence of using interconnection paths of single-bit width and providing a primitive instruction set. The complex functions that are needed for arithmetic and data manipulation reside in the form of stored program, and overall speed is achieved not from the speed of the individual function units but from using several thousand of them in parallel. It is possible that improvements in circuit integration will allow us to regard a processor of 1000 or 10 000 gates as "negligible" at some future date, at which time commitment to more powerful functions or wider data paths can be considered as an alternative to closer packing of single-bit processors. The main requirement at present, however, is to understand the trade-offs well enough to make sensible decisions when the time comes, and the study of single-bit processors seems to be the best starting point for that. Accordingly, we shall introduce a new class of machines called **Active Memory Arrays** (AMAs) whose characteristics will be developed in subsequent chapters. Clearly, to keep up with a word-organized array of word length w, there will have to be w times as many PEs in a bit-organized array.

We shall simplify system structure by assuming that the AMA array, together with its control unit, forms a self-contained engine, not requiring external program or I – O support from a host system. Discussion will center on the functions of the controller and PEs, developing the idea that an array processor is an evolutionary step from conventional processor-memory module design rather than an exceptionally demanding peripheral device. Hence the notation used to describe AMA operations is an extension of the register transfer notation introduced in Chapter 1.

Referring to Fig. 8.3, each data path is now 1 bit wide, and each "main-memory block" is simply a $1*m$ Kbit storage device. As in Illiac IV, before being presented to the function units storage bits can be permuted and/or masked in various ways by the routing network. The primitive operations, which determine the geometry of the array, are normally uniform translations with respect to a linear ordering of PEs. The interconnection of Illiac IV (each PE connected to its immediate neighbors and to those distant ± 8) can be seen as one way of providing translations of from 0 up to 63 positions: on average, assuming each is equally likely and allowing end-around connections, just four steps will be required for a 64-element array.

Another way of viewing the routing connections is as a two-dimensional pattern. Many important problems can be mapped in such a natural way that their solutions can be clearly expressed as operations on "planes" of data. The classical problems deriving from the numerical solution of field equations have already been mentioned, and here it is often the case that two coordinate axes (space $*$ space or space $*$ time) can be directly represented in the physical layout of PEs. Another major area is in manipulation of digitized two-dimensional images, as we shall see in Chapter 11, but experienced analysts can often turn apparently unpromising problems into representations with a high degree of planar processing.

For practical purposes only linear and rectangular arrays need be considered. The handling of three-dimensional data is severely limited by the planar form of hardware, which is unlikely to change until radically new methods of manufacture come into use. The form of interconnection within a plane is more open to debate. Many problems find natural expression in polar form, or by using hexagonal cell patterns rather than square; the result of mapping them into a rectangular array is to leave some of the processors and connection patterns unused. However, in the light of experience gained so far, the square array with four near-neighbor connections appears to be the most widely applicable. We shall follow the practice of giving the relative directions the geographical labels N, S, E and W.

Dimensions not mapped directly into the PE geometry will be represented by the layout of data in memory. In the case of bit-oriented array processors there is a choice of word orientation: either in the PE plane, so that each word is stored along a row or column of PEs; or in memory, so that each word occupies consecutive bit positions in the same local store. The second choice gives bit-organized arrays practically unlimited flexibility in the choice of word size and function because each operation from the elementary arithmetic and logic level upwards is constructed from single-bit primitive functions.

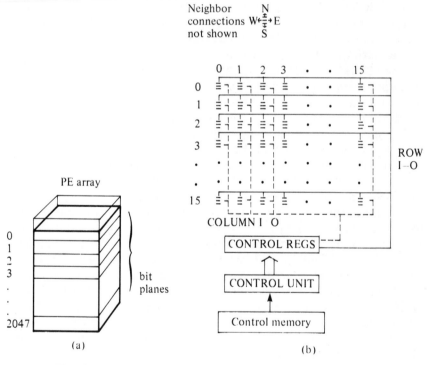

Fig. 8.11 Main components of an Active Memory Array AMA4.2

At this point it is convenient to introduce a model of an Active Memory Array (Fig. 8.11), showing it firstly (a) in perspective and (b) in plan, as seen through the PE plane. We refer to an AMA with sides 2^n elements long as "AMAn", and if it is m Kbits deep it is called "AMA$n.m$". In programming exercises we shall mainly be using AMA4.2, i.e. a 16 * 16 array with 2 Kbits of local storage in each PE. Practical systems with $n = 5$ and $n = 6$ already exist and proposals have been made for $n = 7$. In programming terms we shall see that data are processed by passing them through the PE array, one plane of 2^{2n} bits at a time: there is no possibility of selecting bits from different planes in one operation because the PEs have no local indexing capability.

In all array processors the purpose of the array control unit is to broadcast instructions to the PEs and to do the indexing and scalar operations that cannot be performed in the array. In terms of CRAY-1, the control unit provides the A and S registers, and they must have some means of communicating with the V registers. That is provided either by edge inputs to the array, which are propagated in either E – W or N – S direction, or by broadcast to all elements by means of common row and column data lines. We shall assume that AMAn is driven by a control unit with 2^n-bit numeric registers; any other choice, or the use of non-square PE array, would require part-word or multi-word operations to match the array edge. We shall also assume that when the AMA is used to operate on words stored in the PE plane they extend from N to S in columns, the S containing the sign bit. In other words the last row contains signs of 2^n words and carry is propagated from the N edge to S.

Although the control memory is shown separately in Fig. 8.11, machines of this type often use the array stores to contain instructions. They can be accessed using the row data lines in conjunction with a "column select" signal. In fact the entire AMA can be engineered to act as a conventional passive store if necessary, and it is that viewpoint which is taken in the following chapters. There are very few laboratories or businesses that generate a continuous workload with the high degree of parallelism necessary to keep an array processor fully occupied. In Illiac IV that is overcome by using an extensive communications facility to cover a wide catchment area. The alternative which we shall pursue is to reduce the cost attributable to the array to the extent that it can operate economically at a low duty cycle. One aspect of that design aim is to use the array memory as conventional storage. The other aspect is to use ultimately simple PE designs.

There is no sound way of inferring the characteristics of parallel systems from a knowledge of sequential programming. We have seen already that it is not simply a matter of placing restrictions on well-understood behavior: in some respects parallel machines, and array processors in particular, encourage greater freedom of expression in problem analysis and programming. A broad generalization might be that where high speed is achieved at the cost of high inertia, i.e. heavy investment in registers, cache memory, instruction and data look-ahead or multi-step arithmetic units, speed of response to irregularities in data or control is reduced, but that is also true of sequential machines. In that respect, having practically no inertia, AMA is at a considerable advantage over any other. But to understand such systems there is no alternative to acquiring the practical insight of "thinking in parallel", which we shall induce by example in the next two chapters.

8.5 THEORY VERSUS PRACTICE

"And they try to pretend that nobody cares
Whether you walk on the lines or squares.
But only the sillies believe their talk;
It's ever so portant how you walk."

When we were very young A.A. Milne

There are diverse views on the ways of measuring processor performance: Mips, Mops, Mflops, delivery of results to main memory, delivery of results to user, and so on. Whichever is used there appear to be five main classes of reason for not coming up to expectation. We shall list them and give a simple example of how they arise. All computer structures, including conventional scalar processors, are sensitive to them in different ways, and enthusiasts would claim that the superstructure of modern systems, which includes the educational, operational and analytical procedures, has been so heavily weighted towards sequential data processing that the merits of parallel machines are never fully appreciated. As in the case of micromachines, we have to be cautious in comparing an emergent technology with a mature one: there is certainly no fundamental reason for equating processing speed with inflexibility, unprogrammability or inordinate complexity of design.

Consider a domain that is not square to start with, namely a spherical coordinate system with fewer grid points at the poles than the equator (Fig. 8.12(a)). Suppose also that the spherical surface is layered as it might be in a meteorological problem, where each layer is represented by values of temperature, pressure, humidity, wind velocity, etc. at a different atmospheric level. The discussion assumes we are concerned with following the behavior of the physical variables over a time interval, using equations of motion and gas dynamics to solve for the physical variables after the initial time step. Superficially we might say that if there are, say, 2000 grid points and 10 values to compute at each point involving 50 floating-point operations, then we shall require 100 000 flops per layer, or 1 Mflop for ten layers. Then how is it that a machine running at 20 Mflops will not complete 20 iterations per second of computing time? There are five factors to take into account.

(1)   data *mapping* which prevents a problem from being cast in a form to use all memory banks or all function units at once.

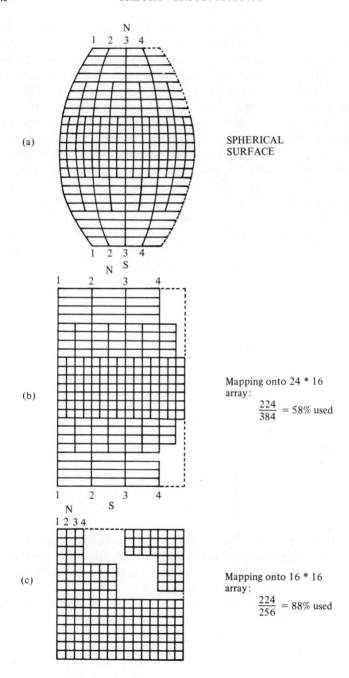

Fig. 8.12   Representing a spherical problem on a rectangular array

The choice of mapping affects the number of physical variables that can be presented to the function units in a computational step. That is obvious in trying to fit the spherical grid points into a rectangular or square array (Fig. 8.12(b) and (c)), leaving a percentage of PEs unused, but it also affects memory utilization and access rates in a machine such as CRAY-1. It might be supposed that data representing different vertical layers will be stacked in local memory banks, which would allow a computing scan to proceed efficiently from surface level upwards or conversely. However, a scan starting in the plane of intersection of longitude zero with the vertical layers and proceeding E or W would have access to only one "column" of data values at a time. Such situations occur often enough for various forms of "skewed" data mapping to be used, which is illustrated in Fig. 8.13 for a two-dimensional problem involving a 4 * 4 matrix presented to a linear array of 4 function units. In the original form only rows of the matrix can be accessed in parallel; in the skewed form both rows and colums can be accessed in parallel with suitable indexing. Of course, trying to access a diagonal is no longer quite so easy.

	ORIGINAL				SKEWED		
PE ARRAY	≡	≡	≡	≡	≡	≡	≡	≡
	00	01	02	03	00	01	02	03
	10	11	12	13	11	12	13	10
	20	21	22	23	22	23	20	21
	30	31	32	33	33	30	31	32

First column:	00	30	20	10
Third row:	33	30	31	32

Fig. 8.13   Accessing a two-dimensional data array in two directions

(2)   data *routing* in which the processor is occupied in unproductive translation operations.

In our sample problem, mapping the grid into a square array distorts the "natural" scheme of connections in which a solution might be expressed, and necessitates extra machine cycles to bring together physically interacting grid points. Again, any sort of convolution or summation that combines operands in the same plane (and therefore in different memory banks) requires movement of data across the array. Such routing problems frequently turn up as indexing overheads in sequential and vector machines.

(3)   control tests and *branching*, in which only a fraction of the mapped stores or function units are active during a particular phase of calculation.

This type of degradation will occur where special calculations are required, e.g. at the N or S poles, or if the physics of the problem demands several different formulas to be used for different physical conditions such as saturated/unsaturated vapor, northern/southern hemisphere, night/day, or supersonic/subsonic flow. Although parts of the formulas might be combined, others will have to be processed in separate branches. In conventional fast processors the same considerations give rise to unwanted tests that break into the instruction and arithmetic pipelines.

(4) *program generation*, in which any parallelism in the program might be lost.

When there are portability requirements or substantial investments in the shape of existing software or trained staff the problem of using on parallel hardware an algorithm written in sequential terms is a major issue. In practical terms, it generates the need to produce effective vector operations from standard Fortran code. As a result a number of "vectorizing" preprocessors or compilers have been marketed, able to recognize some forms of DO loop amenable to parallel expression. Such programs are most effective when their capabilities are known in advance, and ground rules can be given for writing loops that will translate successfully and for avoiding awkward control conditions. It is therefore important to distinguish between amortizing an investment and achieving portability in new programs. In the latter case many designers argue that analyzing problems in terms of parallel functions is easier than writing them out to the last DO loop, given a suitable means of expression. The route to follow is then to start with the parallel algorithm and translate into sequential form for one type of processor and to vector for another.

A separate issue is the ability of the compiler/control unit combination to send instructions to the array or function units at the rate required to keep them fully occupied. Control tests, indexing, scalar arithmetic and system functions are all liable to interrupt the flow of commands to the function units. The basic technique is to achieve concurrent operation by giving the parallel units a degree of autonomy, e.g. issuing vector instruction in CRAY-1, overlapping the control and PE functions in Illiac IV. In AMA design the dual role of the memory (as passive store and processing device) means that a major part of the array is in continuous use, and the relatively low cost of the PE logic means that less than 100% utilization is not a cause for concern. We shall also see that the very fast operations on Boolean variables make an important contribution to indexing functions.

(5) *I – O support* at lower levels of the store hierarchy.

A program generating results at several tens of Mflops requires proportionate support at the lower levels of the store hierarchy (Fig. 1.3). Usually, traffic is scaled down at each stage: registers are used more than scratchpad, scratchpad more than main storage, etc. Nevertheless, very high burst modes of input and output from main memory to secondary storage are sometimes called for. In our example, it might not be possible to store data for all vertical layers in the main memory, so they would be overlayed at twice the rate (old values in, new values out) of computing a new set of results for one layer. Our assumption of 50 arithmetic operations per layer can then be related to the transfer time for 20 variables. In this context the ability to transfer values of no more than the required precision is attractive. Table 8.4 shows some typical data rates into main store for currently announced systems, mostly supported by disk technology. The advent of large semiconductor stores promises to change this picture quite dramatically in two ways: the practical size of main memory will enable more complete models to be held in the store; and the rate of overlaying will be increased by having substantially faster devices in close physical connection with the main storage chips. It might be added that as main store sizes increase it seems almost inevitable that some form of autonomy in organization will have to be introduced to keep them tidy: the AMA structure appears to be well suited to that. Such system requirements will be examined in Chapter 13.

Table 8.4 Transfer rates to main memory

Computer	Size of main memory (max.)	Technology	Size (max.)	Data rate (s)	Latency (max.)
CRAY-1	4 Mword	Disk	96 Gbyte	4 Mbyte*	40 ms
AP-120B	1 Mword	(host)	—	1.5 Mword	—
Illiac IV	128 Kword	F.H. Disk	72 Mbyte	64 Mbyte	20 ms
BSP (Burroughs)	8 Mword	CCD	384 Mbyte	60 Mbyte	0.6 ms

*Per channel: multi-channel transfers possible

8.6 FURTHER READING

Parallel computation is a very active topic of research, and reference must be made to current journals, conference proceedings and review articles to keep abreast of developments (for example, see GOO75, KUC77, INF79 or *ACM Computing Surveys,* **9**(1): Special issue on parallel processors and processing). Historically, the principles of numerical computation using arrays of processing elements trace back to SOLOMON (SLO62, GRE63). Earlier, Unger (UNG58) pointed out the attractions of two-dimensional processor arrays for use in image processing.

Some effects of the convergence of logic and memory technologies are examined in STO70. The reader might notice the resemblance of AMA design to cellular arrays (KAU68, JUM72), whose study is prompted by the same technological projections. The main difference is that the logic and data paths are thought of as fixed in processor arrays but variable (often on a row or column basis) in many cellular designs. There is no intrinsic reason for maintaining the distinction. Further research might show effective ways of combining the two lines of development.

The initial design for Illiac IV is described in KUC68, BAR68 and DAV69. Retrospective comments will be found in an article by Feierbach and Stevenson in INF79. For contemporary products, the manufacturers' literature is the best starting point. Apart from the examples used in this chapter, study of Burroughs Scientific Processor (STO77) and CDC Cyber 205 is recommended. A useful introduction to vector-processing operations in CRAY-1 is given in JOH78, and further details of CRAY-1 are in RUS78.

Array processors such as Illiac IV are referred to as "single-instruction-multiple-data-stream" (SIMD) devices. The classification was suggested by Flynn (FLY66) and is frequently encountered in the literature.

9   ACTIVE MEMORY OPERATIONS

We begin by setting up the apparatus for carrying out arithmetic and logical operations. Recall that the AMA can be thought of as a square prism several thousand bits in length, capped on one end by the PE array. An address cuts the prism in a (bit) plane, and a range of addresses specifies a sequence of adjacent planes. Figure 9.1 shows ten consecutive planes in AMA4, comprising 2560 bits. They can be interpreted in two ways:

(a) as 256 words of ten bits stored *vertically*; or
(b) as 160 words of 16 bits stored *horizontally* in either $N-S$ or $E-W$ direction.

The distinction is clearly that in (a) the length of a word can be varied by adjusting the number of bit planes, while in (b) it is fixed by the array size; and in (a) the level of "operand parallelism" is 256, with the PEs in square form (with near-neighbor connection, as we shall see later), while in (b) the operand parallelism is 16 and the PEs are in linear form. We shall develop programming techniques appropriate to each interpretation. Unless otherwise specified we shall assume in (a) that arithmetic significance increases with the plane index: for example, if the data were signed then the sign bits would be in plane 9; and in (b) the normal orientation is $N-S$, with most significant (or sign) bit in S. Twos complement arithmetic is used for integer representation. The PEs and corresponding elements of bit planes are numbered in row-major order from 0 to 255, starting at the NW corner; the index of a PE can be split into two hexadecimal digits giving its row and column coordinates when viewed from above, as shown in Fig. 9.1.

A fundamental requirement of AMA design is to relate the planes in memory to registers in the control unit. We do that by allowing scalar values (in the case of AMA4, 16-bit words) to be broadcast into a plane in either $N-S$ or $E-W$ direction under program control. Conversely, the content of

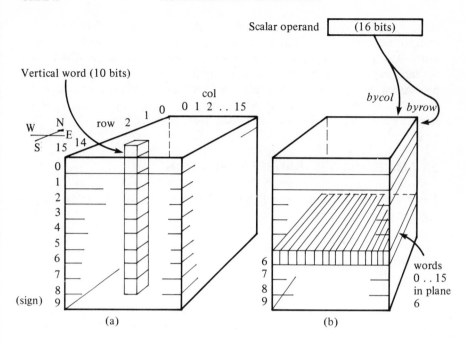

Fig. 9.1 Ten bit-planes in AMA4, viewed in two ways: (a) vertical; (b) horizontal

a plane will be converted to scalar form by ANDing the bits in all words in either direction. Thus, a plane of 1s will yield a scalar value of all 1s when read, and a single zero in the plane will give a single zero in the result, aligned to the row or column in which it occurs. Scalar registers are aligned with most significant bit at the S or W edge as appropriate.

The above operations can be viewed as generalizations of memory read and write functions. The correspondence is completed by arranging that consecutive word addresses, as commonly used for scalar operands, run from W to E and then into the next plane. In Fig. 9.1(b), plane 0 will contain words 0 – 15, plane 1 contains words 16 – 31, ... and plane 9 will contain words with indices 144 – 159. We shall not make use of the orthogonal scheme of word indexing running from N to S.

With the above ways of looking at data, our requirement is to provide elementary functions for manipulating them. They will be presented in the next subsection as an extension of the register transfer notation. We shall then outline the implied physical connections and control signals. The remaining subsections start to build a useful set of active memory operations. In the course of this discussion it will be clear from time to time that the AMA function set could be improved in detail to reduce machine cycles in some critical areas, but that would not affect our understanding of the operations involved. In Chapters 11 and 12 we shall examine such optimizations. It will also be apparent that techniques appropriate to the AMA, particularly in processing horizontal data, might also suit word-organized array processors, and from that viewpoint another set of specializations might be formulated. Thus the study of AMA design is a stepping-stone to understanding a wide class of array-processor organizations.

9.1 AMA REGISTER TRANSFER NOTATION

The following conventions will be used to describe AMA operations in register transfer terms.

(a) Plane pointers

A register value may be defined as a *plane pointer*, which can be used to access a sequence of planes. The operations of modification and limitation,[†] and the address condition indicator operate exactly as for word pointers except that the elementary datum is a plane. In most examples of this chapter the register type will be declared in advance, but for consistency with later use it may be imagined that a pointer contains a *tag* field distinguishing, amongst other things, numbers and plane pointers, as well as a *limit* and *location*, i.e. word or plane index as appropriate relative to the start of memory.

tag	limit	location

4   1 2   1 6   Pointer in AMA4

0: number
9: word pointer
10: plane pointer

Thus in AMA4, pointers formed in the control unit can access up to 2^{16} words or planes, in sequences of up to 2^{12} elements. However, only the first 2^{12} planes are overlapped by word addresses. An operator is supplied to convert from plane to word pointer according to the convention given earlier. It is written as the postfix *word*, so that, e.g. if p is a plane pointer, then $p\,word$ is the pointer to the same data, treated as a word sequence. The limit value is adjusted accordingly. In the example of Fig. 9.1, we might have (a) 10 planes starting at plane location 325, or (b) 160 words starting at 5200.

---

† For use of the limitation operator "^" see Appendix, p. 432.

p	10	9	325	(10 planes)
p word	9	159	5200	(160 words)

There is no "inverse" of *word*, because a word sequence does not in general begin and end on a plane boundary.

There are two further postfix operators useful in the context of pointer manipulation.

To examine the tag value in a given argument, the operator *tag* will deliver it as a number. Similarly, to examine the limit value, the operator *high* may be used, e.g.

p word	9	159	5200	Postfix
p word tag	0	0	9	addressing
p word high	0	0	159	operators
p tag	0	0	10	

(b) Store access operators

We have already introduced the postfix "dot" operator for store read, and " =." for write. When applied using plane pointers these operators are interpreted as if the datum were broadcast by row, i.e. on writing, the datum is written to each word in the plane, and on reading the datum is the AND of all words in the plane. These results can be illustrated using a 4 * 4 plane from AMA2. Let p be a pointer to such a plane. Then:

$$p =. 3$$

writes the value 3 to each word in p:

1	1	1	1	←	1	
1	1	1	1	←	1	Assignment
0	0	0	0	←	0	by row
0	0	0	0	←	0	

Conversely, if the initial content of p is:

0	1	1	0	→	0	
1	1	1	1	→	1	Output by
0	1	0	0	→	0	row
1	1	0	0	→	0	

then "p" has the value "0010", i.e. 2, as a result of ANDing each row. Note also that p word'2. has the value 3 in this example.

To describe the orthogonal broadcast operations two new symbols are introduced:

write: " $= bycol$ " in place of " $=$."

and

read: " $.bycol$ " in place of "."

Thus, again using AMA2:

$$p = bycol\ 5$$

gives the result:

0	1	0	1
↓	↓	↓	↓

0	1	0	1
0	1	0	1
0	1	0	1
0	1	0	1

Assignment
by column

Conversely, if the initial content of the plane p is:

1	0	1	1
↑	↑	↑	↑

1	1	1	1
1	0	1	1
1	1	1	1
1	1	1	1

Output
by column

then $p.bycol$ has the value "1011", i.e. -5 in 2s complement notation.
Application to larger arrays is by direct extension of the above rules.

(c) Planar arithmetic and routing statements

In order to perform arithmetic on planes we shall use three specialized plane registers:

    A: a mask or *activity* plane;
    B: an *accumulator* and shift plane
    C: a *carry* plane.

As we shall see later, one bit of each plane register is assigned to each PE. The array statements are prefixed by the symbol "@" and have the syntax given in Table 9.1. They form two groups: *routing* functions, which apply generalized shift functions to the B plane; and *arithmetic*, which with one exception are applied to every element in the argument planes without dependence on neighbors.

The choice of an accumulator-based set of register transfer statements in contrast to the form of scalar computation statements is deliberate, to make clear what physical data transfers are involved.

Table 9.1   Syntax of array statements $@ \circ arrayop$

arrayop:	$move \circ dirn \circ int \circ geometry?$	/*routing*/
	$pefn \circ min? \circ ident \circ modify?$	/*arithmetic*/
dirn:	W E N S	
geometry:	cyclic	
pefn:	load stm add and or	
	equ mask adw st	
modify:	$' \circ intid?$	
intid:	int ident $(\circ expr \circ)$	

(d) Arithmetic operations

In arithmetic statements the operand is specified by plane pointer *ident*, possibily modified by an index expression. Let P be the first plane of the sequence so addressed. If *ident* is preceded by a minus sign (*min?*) each bit in the plane is complemented before carrying out the planar function. The following interpretations are selected by *pefn*:

load	$B_i = P_i$	
st	$P_i = B_i$	
or	$B_i = B_i \mid P_i$	
equ	$B_i = B_i \equiv P_i$	
and	$B_i = B_i \wedge P_i$	
mask	$A_i = P_i$	$i = 0, \ldots, 255$
stm	where $(A_i = 1)\ P_i = B_i$	(bit index)
add	$B_i = Sum\ (B_i, C_i, P_i)$	
	$C_i = Carry\ (B_i, C_i, P_i)$	
adw	$B_i = B_i + P_i$	$i = 0, \ldots, 15$ (column index)

The first six functions given above are simple generalizations of scalar operations found in most computers. Suppose a plane sequence p is given, to be treated as 256 vertically stored words, and that we require to set up a mask in A, marking all-zero words with "0" and others with "1":

Example 9.1	$REGS$ $[\ p\ q\ r\ ]$	plane pointers
	$save\ [\ p\ ]$;	for later use (see text)
	$@\ load\ -p$;	loads B plane
	$do\ \{\ @\ and\ -p; p'\ 1$	AND successive planes
	$\}\ while\ VA$;	

/* Now the complement of the required mask is in B.
To load A, make use of a temporary plane q */
         $@\ st\ q; @\ mask\ -q; unsave\ [\ p\ ]$

For selective operations, A is used to control store write-enable when *stm* (store masked) is specified in place of *st* (store). The mask might be set up by broadcasting a pattern from scalar registers, or by calculation. For example, suppose we now want to merge *p* into *r* at just the point where the corresponding word in *p* is non-zero, leaving *r* unchanged elsewhere. Assume that the mask plane is set up as the result of Example 9.1 and that the plane sequences are of equal length:

Example 9.2   *save* [*p r*];
                    do { @ *load p*; @ *stm r;p′* 1;*r′* 1 } *while VA*;
                    unsave [*r p*]

The *add* function is designed for vertical (bit-serial) addition and subtraction. It is necessary to preset the carry plane as required, normally "0" for addition, "1" for subtraction. The basic loop for adding a plane sequence *p* to *q* and storing the result in *r* is:

Example 9.3   *save* [*p q r*];
                    do { @ *load p*;@ *add q*;@ *st r;p′* 1;*q′* 1;*r′* 1 } *while VA*;
                    unsave [*r q p*]

where we continue to assume all sequences equal in length.

The exceptional planar function *adw* (add word) carries out horizontal addition or subtraction and therefore propagates carry from *N* to *S* in each word of *B*. Carry-in is determined by *min?*, i.e. zero for add, one for subtract. Exactly the same loop as Example 9.3, but with *adw* in place of *add* will carry out word mode addition. In other words, referring back to Fig. 9.1, we can add 256 10-bit words or 160 16-bit words in the same number of machine cycles.

Figure 9.2 gives further examples of PE functions applied to AMA2.

It will be apparent that most operations on vertically stored words involve modification of the plane pointer(s) by 1 each time round the loop. An abbreviated notation is used in such cases. If the operand plane is denoted by a register identifier, then following the identifier by a modification symbol causes the register to be modified after selecting the operand, e.g. @ *pefn reg′* is equivalent to @ *pefn reg;reg′ 1*, and we may rewrite Example 9.3 as:

Example 9.3′   *save* [*p q r*];
                    do { @ *load p′* ;@ *add q′* ;@ *st r′* } *while VA*;
                    unsave [*r q p*]

This interpretation is not possible when the operand plane is selected by using an index expression.

"store masked" @ *stm P*

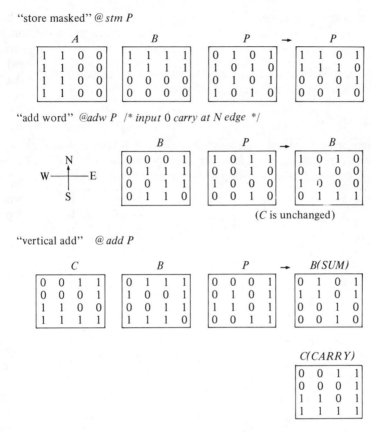

"add word" @*adw P /* input 0 carry at N edge */*

(*C* is unchanged)

"vertical add"   @ *add P*

Fig. 9.2   Some PE functions on planes in AMA2

(e) Routing

All routing operations apply to the accumulator plane *B*. The parameters supplied by the instruction are the *direction, shift count*, and *geometry*. The directions are N, S, E and W, where E – W corresponds to movement across the columns and N – S to movement across the rows. Remember that S is the more significant end of a word and that N – S shifts of *B* effect logical shifts of 16 words in parallel, while E – W movement effects parallel word translation in store. The shift count is always a literal value and will lie in the range 1,...,15 for AMA4.

Geometry is determined by edge inputs, for which we shall recognize:

plane: input zero

cyclic: input the "spill" from the other end of the same row or column.

Other possibilities can be envisaged, but they will be implemented by program. If *cyclic* is not specified, plane is assumed.

Example 9.4

Suppose it is required to move the plane sequence *p* eight places W, with zero input at the edge, and four rows N cyclically. The effect will be as in the following figure, showing 4 * 4 submatrices in the *B* plane of AMA4:

a	b	c	d
e	f	g	h
i	j	k	l
m	n	o	q

$\Longrightarrow$

g	h	0	0
k	l	0	0
o	p	0	0
c	d	0	0

save [*p*];
do { @ load *p*;@ move W 8;@ move N 4 cyclic;
    @ st *p'* } while *VA*;
unsave [*p*]

Finally, remember that store addresses provide yet another form of routing, the simplest way of moving a plane *p* "down" the store 5 positions being via the accumulator, e.g.

...;@ load *p*;@ st *p'* 5;...

If *p* is part of a vertically stored array, then we are in effect doing part of a scaling operation. If *p* is regarded as horizontal data, the net result is part of a vector move.

(f) Subroutine interface

In register transfer terms, most high-level languages offer procedures with only a single parameter, namely a *pointer* to the list of values associated with identifiers appearing in the procedure declaration. In the present context our requirement is to build subroutines more appropriate to micromachine operation, and account must be taken of two circumstances: performance measures are adversely affected by reference to storage for actual parameter values; and most of the functions required can be expressed in terms of zero, one or two formal parameters (as can the functions of a conventional target instruction set).

Accordingly, we shall introduce a form of subroutine which is restricted to no more than two parameters, and in which the parameters are operationally equivalent to declared registers, even to the extent of being used as working variables. For example, we might define an integer addition subroutine as:

Example 9.5

Vertical add under mask, given two plane pointers $a + b$. Assume carry plane is initially zero.

> $addvert(a,b)$:
> > do { @ $load\ a$; @ $add\ b'$; @ $stm\ a'$ } $while\ VA$;
> > $return$

When called, actual parameters of the appropriate type are specified, e.g.:

> $\ldots;addvert(p\char`^7,p'8\char`^7);\ldots$

If in doubt as to the type of parameter, the subroutine will make suitable tests, as it can do by inspecting *tag* and other fields.

Subroutines are assumed to be implemented using a stack mechanism. A subroutine call causes current parameters to be stacked, together with the program counter, and restored on *return*. A pointer or numeric value can be returned if it is intended to make subroutine calls in the course of expression evaluation. Conditions are unaffected by call and by return. It is often useful to set "*IA*" to indicate an error condition, to be detected by the caller.

The context declared by "*REGS*" is unaffected by subroutine definition, and side effects can be caused by altering register contents. To mitigate what some computer scientists would regard as a perverse design decision, we again refer to the use of the micromachine: quite frequently the registers are used to define target machine states (referring to descriptor tables, control environments, etc.) which are preserved across the microprocedure boundaries. In order to provide extra register space, the *save* and *unsave* statements

Table 9.2 Syntax of subroutine definition

---

subroutine: *ident*∘(∘*params*?∘)∘:∘*stat*∘*scstat**?∘*def**?
   params: *ident*∘,∘*ident*
            ident

/* *return statement* */
          return∘*result*?
   result: (∘*expr*∘)

/* *save and unsave statements* */
          save∘[∘*ident**∘]
          unsave∘[∘*ident**∘]

---

are used to transmit register contents to and from the stack in LIFO fashion, as illustrated in earlier examples.

The syntax changes resulting from the use of subroutines are summarized in Table 9.2. In subsequent examples we shall mainly use *subroutine* definitions in place of *programsection*. The interactions between subroutines in wider program context are discussed in Chapter 18.

9.2 PROCESSING ELEMENT STRUCTURE

All the functions of the AMA have now been introduced. It will be helpful to review them at this point by outlining the interconnections and data paths of a single PE. Apart from edge connections (which allow for variations in geometry) all PEs have identical structure and receive identical command signals from the array control unit.

The PE consists of three single-bit registers A, B and C, corresponding to the specialized plane registers defined for the AMA; a local memory organized as $1 * m$ bits, where m is the number of planes in the AMA; and a logical network designed to perform the array operations and to present the output signals required on row and column data lines. Figure 9.3 indicates the general structure.

In a single machine cycle the control unit can broadcast to the PE array either an arithmetic or a routing instruction:

(1)   ALU operations:
        store read: *load, mask, and, or,*
                    equ, add, adw and *invert*
        store write: *st* and *stm*
    For all ALU operations an address is sent to the local memory.
(2)   Routing operations:
        direction: N, S, E or W
    The shift count and geometry are set by the control unit. A routing operation normally requires multiple machine cycles.

In addition to the above instructions, the array also has to service the generalized store access functions, i.e. broadcast read and write by row and column, single-word access with column select for scalar data and instructions.

In practical design it is important to economize on external signals, and many of those shown separately in Fig. 9.3 can in fact be combined.

9.3 ARITHMETIC AND LOGIC SUBROUTINES

In this subsection we shall develop some basic subroutines for parallel arithmetic and outline the construction of others. The general form adopted is a

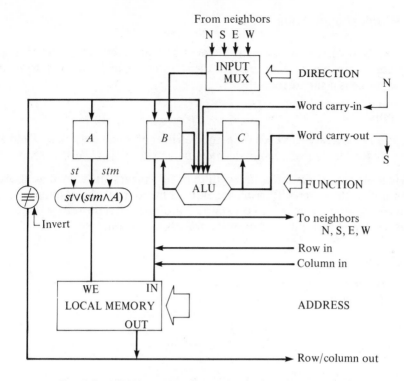

Fig. 9.3   PE schematic diagram for Active Memory Array
single-bit data/signal paths ◄──────
multiple-bit control signals   ⟨═══════

"two address, masked" definition, i.e. the result of a function call $f(a,b)$ will overwrite the first operand in just the "1" positions of the activity plane A: for vertical data a single bit masks each word, while in horizontal mode a column of bits is needed for each word. We shall make the definitions reasonably general with respect to type and precision of argument. The reader will be able to spot shorter or faster special cases as well as useful generalizations.

When workspace is required there is a choice of claiming it from the system manager or using a predefined "common" sequence for all subroutines. For relatively short operations the second method is better, and we shall take the first declared register (wk) to give access to a sufficiently long sequence of workplanes. In some environments it might be controlled as a stack, but that is not necessary in the present context. The following examples assume the register context:

        REGS   [wk | workplane pointer
                       $w\,x\,y\,z\,t$] | temporary and
                                                    | pointer values

(a) Logical operations

There is no need to distinguish horizontal and vertical forms if both operands are plane sequences. If they are equal in length the form of subroutine is a simple loop.

Example 9.6

Form the logical difference (non-equivalence) of plane sequences a and b.

$neq(a,b)$: *do* { @ *load* a;@ *equ* $-b'$;@ *stm* a' } *while VA*; *return*

When the arguments differ in length their first planes are aligned as above, but one or the other will terminate early in the loop. If the destination a is shorter, high-order planes of the source b are ignored; if the source is shorter it is extended with "0" planes in the following version.

Example 9.6′

$neq(a,b)$:   *if*(a *high* > b *high*)
/* b *short* */   {   *do* { @ *load* a;@ *equ* $-b$;
                            @ *stm* a';b' 1 } *while VA*;
                    wk =. 0;   /* *zero plane* */
                    do { @ *load* a;@ *equ* $-wk$;@ *stm* a'
                         } *while VA*
                    }
/* a *short* */ *else*   *do* { @ *load* a;@ *equ* $-b'$;
                            @ *stm* a' } *while VA*;
            return

The definition can be extended easily to the case where the source argument is scalar, but now a distinction must be drawn between vertical and horizontal form, e.g. the integer 1 can be interpreted (vertically) as a plane of "1" followed by successive planes of "0", or (horizontally) as identical planes with "1" in row 0 and "0" elsewhere. Here is the vertical form, which propagates the sign of b:

Example 9.6″

$neq(a,b)$:   *if*(b *tag* = 0)
            { *wk* =. 0;
            do   { b *mask* 1; /**test l.s. bit* */
                    if ZE @ *load* $-wk$ *else* @ *load wk*;
                    @ *equ* a;b ⪢ 1;@ *stm* a'
                    } *while VA*
            }
            else   { *as for* Example 9.6′ };
            return

(b) Integer arithmetic

In arithmetic it is necessary to discriminate between horizontal and vertical forms, but in both cases the higher arithmetic functions have to be built up from elementary addition, subtraction and scaling loops. The choices of argument are essentially the same as for logical operations. For example, Fig. 9.4 gives library procedures for vertical addition and subtraction, catering for operands varying in precision from one bit (i.e. one bit plane) upwards. However, no operation is performed when the second operand (*b*) has greater precision than the first (*a*); if it is shorter, it is assumed to be unsigned. Thus a Boolean plane can be added to or subtracted from a vertical array of integers, with the effect of adding "0" or "1" as appropriate to each element position.

The result of the operation is written over the first operand under a preset mask plane. Overflow is signalled in the *B* plane by a value "0" in all overflow positions and "1" elsewhere. The masked overflow bits are written to *wk*; hence (*wk.* + 1) will return *ZE* after an operation if, and only if, no overflow occurred under the mask.

The second operand can also be an integer (*b tag* = 0), which is treated as defining an array of identical elements.

Uniform scaling can be achieved quite simply by address manipulation, e.g. the matrix operation which might be written as "$a \leftarrow a + 4 * b$" would be invoked by $addv(a'2,b)$, in which the two low-order bits of *a* are ignored. (Exercise 13 illustrates element-by-element scaling.)

In vertical multiplication an integer result of the same precision as the multiplicand is formed. The multiplier digits are used in turn to mask the addition of *a* into the partial product:

Example 9.7

... part of the multiply routine. Here the original mask bits have been saved and the register *w* contains a plane pointer to the partial product planes in the workstore at

```
          wk'2^(a high)...
          wk =. 0; ...                    /* zero workplane */
          do { @ mask b;@ load wk;@ add wk; /* clear C */
               x = w;y = a;
/* add */    do { @ load x;@ add y';@ stm x' } while VA;
             w'1; b'1 } while VA
          /*. finally the product is written under the original mask
          bits to a */
```

A library procedure for integer multiplication, handling various options on the arguments, is given in Fig. 9.5. No overflow indication is given. The multiplier *b* is always treated as positive, truncated if necessary to the same length as *a* because high-order digits will not affect the result.

```
            REGS [wk]
/* wk is expected to point to two workplanes:
    wk is used as a source of ones
    wk'1 is used in computing overflow */

/*          Masked add b to a, returning the address of a
            and leaving '0' in the B plane to mark overflow.
            The masked overflow is written to wk.
            The second argument can be a plane sequence or integer. */

addv(a,b):        if(b tag = 0)return(addint(a,b));
                  wk =. -1;@ load -wk;@ add -wk;  /* clear carry */
            /* Assumes a and b are plane sequences, but ignore if
               b is longer than a */
                  (a high - b high); if LT return(0);
                  save[a]; @ load a'(a high);       /* sign of a    */
                  if ZE {@ equ b'(b high);@ st wk'1;
                          do{@ load a;@ add b';@ stm a'} while VA}
                  else /* extend b with zero sign */
                          {@ equ -wk;@ st wk'1;
                          do{@ load a;@ add b;@ stm a';b'1}while VA;
                          do{@ load a;@ add -wk;@ stm a'}while VA};
            /* wk'1 is 1 where signs were equal.  Set overflow under
               mask in wk and unmasked in B plane */
                  @ add wk;@ or -wk'1;@ stm wk;
                  unsave[a];return(a)

/*          Masked subtract b from a, returning the address of a
            and leaving '0' in the B plane to mark overflow.
            The second argument can be a plane sequence or integer. */
subv(a,b):        if(b tag = 0) return(addint(a,-b));
                  wk =.-1;@ load wk;@ add wk;      /* set carry-in */
            /* Assumes a and b are plane sequences */
                  (a high - b high); if LT return(0);
                  save[a]; @ load a'(a high);       /* sign  of  a */
                  if ZE {@ equ -b'(b high);@ st wk'1;
                          do{@ load a;@ add -b';@ stm a'} while VA}
                  else  {@ equ wk;@ st wk'1;
                          do{@ load a;@ add -b;@ stm a';b'1}while VA;
                          do{@ load a;@ add wk;@ stm a'} while VA};
            /* set overflow indicators */
                  @ add wk;@ or -wk'1;@ stm wk;
                  unsave[a];return(a)

/* integer add, called from addv and subv */
addint(a,n):      wk =. -1;@ load -wk;@ add -wk;  /* clear carry */
                  save[a]; @ load a'(a high);      /* sign of a   */
                  n+0;if LT @ equ wk else @ equ -wk;
                  @ st wk'1;        /* w'1 equals 1 where signs equal */
                  do{@ load a;(n mask 1);if NZ @ add wk else @ add -wk;n>>1;
                  @ stm a'} while VA;
            /* set overflow in B plane */
                  @ add wk;@ or -wk'1;@ stm wk;
                  unsave[a];return(a)
```

Fig. 9.4 Variable-precision vertical add and subtract under mask

```
           REGS [wk w x y]
mulv(a,b):        save[w x y];
                  wk =. 0;
                  wk'1 =. 0;@ load -wk;@ stm wk'1; /* save mask in wk'1 */
           /* Provide workspace for product starting at wk'2 */
                  w = wk'2^(a high);x=w;do{x =. 0;x'1}while VA;
           /* Multiply by adding a into workspace w under control
              of the multiplier b. Here b is truncated to the
              same length as a if it is initially longer */
                  if(b tag = 0) multint()
                  else {x=b^(a high);if VA b=x;
                        do{@ mask b;x=w;y=a;@ load wk;@ add wk;
                                 do{@ load x;@ add y';@ stm x'}while VA;
                        w'1;b'1}while VA };
           /* write back to a under mask */
                  y=a;w = wk'2;@ mask wk'1;do{@ load w';@ stm y'} while VA;
                  unsave[y x w];return (a)

/* Multiply by integer assumes wk and w initialized as in mulv */
multint(a,n):  do{(n mask 1);if NZ {x=w;y=a;@ load wk;@ add wk;
                         do{@ load x;@ add y';@ st x'}while VA';
                  n>>1;w'1} while VA;return
```

Fig. 9.5   Variable-precision vertical multiply under mask

In horizontal multiplication the digits of the multiplier must be projected in turn across each word to mask addition into the partial product. That is done by using column read and write operations, as shown in Example 9.8.

Example 9.8

... part of horizontal multiplication. Here the original mask bits have been saved and the register w contains a plane pointer to a partial product. The multiplicand is held in the plane addressed by z, and scaled by moving S...

Register use: y temporary numeric
                x workplane
                t mask and loop control

```
t = 1;@ load a;@ st z;
do { @ load b;x =. t;@ or -x;
     @ st x; y = x.bycol + 0;
     /* now y contains the multiplier bits */
     if NZ { x = bycol y;@ mask x;
             @ load z;@ adw w;@ stm w} ;
     @ load z;@ move S 1;@ st z;
     t≪1 } while NZ
/*. the above to be repeated for each plane of multiplier and
multiplicand */
```

In both modes of arithmetic the division subroutines develop the quotient by trial subtraction of the divisor from the dividend. It is not necessary to store the result until the sign has been found to be positive, so division algorithms are rather less than double the length of multiplication, depending on the quantity of support code.

(c) Floating point

In floating-point form each number is represented by a pair (M,E) which is taken to have the value $M * r^E$, where r is the base of the representation. The merits of different choices of r and different precisions of M and E are discussed in texts on computer arithmetic (for example, see KUC78). The essential features of floating-point operations are unchanged in moving from scalar to parallel machines, though there is less opportunity to make use of data-dependent optimizing techniques. For example, it is fairly common practice to skip over strings of 1s or 0s in scalar multiplication,

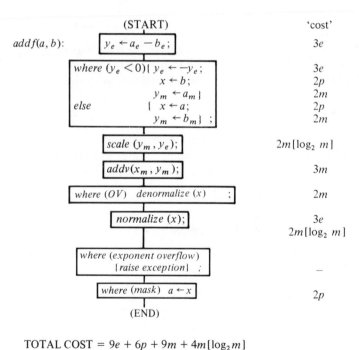

$$\text{TOTAL COST} = 9e + 6p + 9m + 4m\lceil\log_2 m\rceil$$
$$= 15p + 4m\lceil\log_2 m\rceil$$

Fig. 9.6 Floating-point addition of b to a in bit-serial vertical mode, under preset mask

whereas such a condition in each of a parallel array of PEs is so unlikely that it is impractical to make use of it. On the other hand, bit-serial control provides scope for refinement in rounding and truncation rules that is not readily available even in microprogrammed processors.

Much of the "cost" of bit-serial floating-point arises from data movement rather than arithmetic operations, as can be seen from the flowchart for addition of arrays a and b in Fig. 9.6. Alongside each box is written an estimate of the memory references incurred for p-bit operands, with m bits assumed for M and e bits for E. Temporary storage planes are required for x and y. In the figure, suffixes m and e are used to denote subfields M and E respectively. In normalization it has been assumed that $r = 2$, so that $\lceil \log_2 m \rceil$ vertical shifts are required, each involving m bits or less. The "least cost" estimate for $p = 32$ and $m = 24$ works out at 960, of which half is contributed by scaling and renormalization. There is some advantage in choosing higher values of r, e.g. $r = 16$, to reduce the amount of shifting. (We shall see later that the actual cost of floating-point addition on the ICL DAP is about 740 machine cycles, reducing to 380 on the Goodyear MPP; in both machines it is arranged for instructions to be buffered wholly or partly outside the array memory.)

For floating-point multiplication and division the dominant costs arise from multiplication or division of the M components, and less data movement is involved.

9.4 ROUTING SUBROUTINES

The elementary routing functions are provided by the @ *move* statement, using the B register plane, and by store addressing, which deals with vertical translation. Most uniform translations over a given number of rows, columns, or planes can be programmed by simple iterations, but it is useful to have a subroutine form when the distance is variable. To describe shifts, it is convenient to have a unique enumeration of the *bits* in the cuboid defined by a plane pointer. In AMA4 that can be done by calling the NW bit of the first plane "bit 0", counting in row-major order up to bit 255, and continuing from "bit 256" in the NW corner of the next plane. As a result (see diagram) the position of a bit in any of 128 planes can be represented by a 15-bit index.

7	4	4	
t	r	c	Bit index in AMA4

Now we can describe a generalized shift on a plane sequence p by giving the final destination of bit 0 as a bit index n. The interpretation of the function depends partly on the geometry that is assumed. There are two important cases:

(1)   solid geometry, in which the neighboring bits of the cuboid move as if attached in a rigid body;

(2)   linear geometry, in which rows and columns are thought of as a linear sequence (row 1 following row 0).

Furthermore, the treatment of end-effects will vary, and we distinguish two interpretations in each case, namely "shift in zero" and "cyclic". The names of the resulting subroutines, and an example of their effects, are given in Fig. 9.7. More complex routing operations can often be composed by repeated application of these subroutines, or by masking their output.

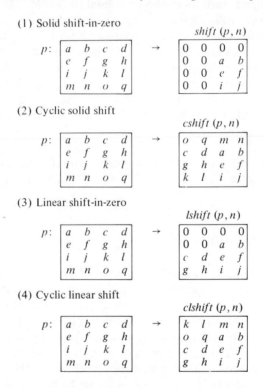

Fig. 9.7   Uniform shifts in AMA4

*In these examples only translation within the PE plane is illustrated. If the shift distance were greater than 255 vertical translation would be carried out, cyclic or zero input as appropriate. The examples are given for an AMA4 plane, showing 4 * 4 submatrices of a plane sequence p, and assuming a shift distance (n) equal to 72 (hexadecimal \$48) in each case.

Many of the higher-level routing functions, including sorting, make use of the set of two-way shifts generated in the following way. First, assume a linear array in which the total number of elements is a power of two (say 2^8) and write out the binary index of the ith element as:

$$i_7 i_6 i_5 i_4 i_3 i_2 i_1 i_0,$$

where each i_j is either 1 or 0. Now take an integer j in the range $0..7$ and examine the corresponding bit of i:

> *if* $i_j = 0$, move the corresponding element "up" by 2^j places;
> *else* $i_j = 1$, move the corresponding element "down" by 2^j places.

In effect, pairs of elements distant 2^j are exchanged. This operation is termed a "power-of-two shift-exchange", *potse(p,j)*. For example, for an eight-element array we have:

p:	a	b	c	d	e	f	g	h
potse(p,0):	b	a	d	c	f	e	h	g
potse(p,1):	c	d	a	b	g	h	e	f
potse(p,2):	e	f	g	h	a	b	c	d

The same operation is defined for both solid and linear geometries, and it extends to bit planes by suitable choice of j, e.g. *potse(p,8)* interchanges even and odd planes in AMA4. An outline of *potse( )* in register transfer terms is given in Fig. 9.8.

The power-of-two shift-exchange can be viewed as the result of *inverting* one of the bits in the index of each bit in the cuboid. A related and equally fundamental permutation derives from *exchanging* the values of a pair of bits in the index: if they are equal nothing happens, but otherwise an exchange takes place. If the weights of the index bits are i and j, the elements exchanged are distant $|2^i - 2^j|$. In the particular case that $i = j + 1$ the distance is 2^j. That results in a power of two shift which will be called *shuff(p,j)* since it generates a crude shuffle of the data. For an eight-element array its effect can be contrasted with that shown earlier for *potse*:

Binary index $i_2 i_1 i_0$:	000	001	010	011	100	101	110	111
p:	a	b	c	d	e	f	g	h
shuff(p,0):	a	c	b	d	e	g	f	h
shuff(p,1):	a	b	e	f	c	d	g	h

A *perfect shuffle* is the effect produced on a vector by splitting it into two halves like a pack of cards and then merging the halves together without any cards sticking together, as for the 8-element vector:

Binary index $i_2 i_1 i_0$:	000	001	010	011	100	101	110	111
p:	a	b	c	d	e	f	g	h
shuffle(p,2):	a	e	b	f	c	g	d	h

```
        REGS [wk]

/* Procedure to permute the bits of a plane sequence p
   by inverting the n'th bit of the index.

   For 0<=n<4, perform column exhanges;
       4<=n<8, perform row exchanges;
       8<=n<15   perform vertical planar exchanges.     */

potse(p,n):      save[p];
                 if(n>3)goto rows;
                 wk =bycol msk'n.;
                 goto[n0 n1 n2 n3]'n

       exit:     unsave[p];return(p)

       n0:       do{@ load p;@ move W 1 cyclic;@ mask wk;
                     @ stm p;@ move E 2 cyclic;@ mask -wk;
                     @ stm p'} while VA; goto exit
       n1:       do{@ load p;@ move W 2 cyclic;@ mask wk;
                     @ stm p;@ move E 4 cyclic;@ mask -wk;
                     @ stm p'} while VA; goto exit
       n2:       do{@ load p;@ move W 4 cyclic;@ mask wk;
                     @ stm p;@ move E 8 cyclic;@ mask -wk;
                     @ stm p'} while VA; goto exit
       n3:       do{@ load p;@ move W 8 cyclic;@ mask wk;
                     @ stm p;@ mask -wk;@stm p'} while VA;goto exit

       rows:     if(n>7) goto planes;
                 n-4; wk =. ims'n.;
                 goto[n4 n5 n6 n7]'n

       n4:       do{@ load p;@ move N 1 cyclic;@ mask wk;
                     @ stm p;@ move S 2 cyclic;@ mask -wk;
                     @ stm p'} while VA; goto exit
       n5:       do{@ load p;@ move N 2 cyclic;@ mask wk;
                     @ stm p;@ move S 4 cyclic;@ mask -wk;
                     @ stm p'} while VA; goto exit
       n6:       do{@ load p;@ move N 4 cyclic;@ mask wk;
                     @ stm p;@ move S 8 cyclic;@ mask -wk;
                     @ stm p'} while VA; goto exit
       n7:       do{@ load p;@ move N 8 cyclic;@ mask wk;
                     @ stm p;@ mask -wk;@ stm p'} while VA; goto exit

       planes: n-8;n = (1,2,4,8,16,32,64,128)'n.;
               do{ex(p^(n-1),p'n);p'(n<<1)} while VA;
               goto exit

/* Procedure to exchange plane sequences a and b */
ex(a,b):         do{@ load b;@ st wk;@ load a;
                     @ st b';@ load wk;@ st a'} while VA;
                 return

msk:     ($aaaa, $cccc, $f0f0, $ff00)
ims:     ($5555, $3333, $0f0f, $00ff)
```

Fig. 9.8 Variable-precision power of two shift exchanges

The reverse permutation is called an *unshuffle*. With only near-neighbor connections it takes $2^n - 1$ exchange steps to shuffle 2^{n+1} elements perfectly (here " $\leftrightarrow$ " joins elements to be exchanged on the next step):

	Initial order:	a	b	c	d$\leftrightarrow$e	f	g	h
After	Step 1	a	b	c$\leftrightarrow$e	d$\leftrightarrow$f	g	h
	2	a	b$\leftrightarrow$e	c$\leftrightarrow$f	d$\leftrightarrow$g	h
	3	a	e	b	f	c	g	d	h

However, for larger arrays with four-neighbor connection the perfect shuffle can be realized more economically in *n* applications of the imperfect shuffle:

shuffle(p,n): *do* { *shuff(p,n − 1);n − 1* } *while GT*;
       return

The individual steps of *shuff* can be seen as row, column or plane inter-changes, except (in AMA4) when $n = 3$ or $n = 7$. (Discussion of this topic is resumed in Section 10.4.)

One of the early decisions in problem analysis is whether to treat the arithmetic data as horizontal or vertical. The decision rests on the degree of parallelism, precision, routing patterns, use of scalar arithmetic in the con-trol unit, I−O and other factors. It might be decided to use both, in different phases of calculation. It is then necessary to convert from one form to the other, which is done by the *rotate (a,b)* subroutine. Its effect is shown in Fig. 9.9. We assume initially that both *a* and *b* are cubes, and imagine *b* being rotated *in situ*, but finally stored in position given by *a*.

In Fig. 9.9 *ABCD* is a word plane. The diagonal plane *IJJ′I′* intersects

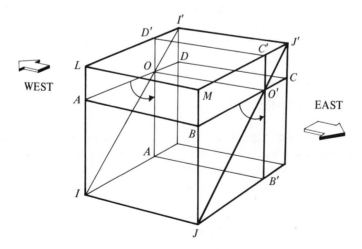

Fig. 9.9 Rotation from horizontal to vertical in AMA*n*

```
                REGS [wk y z]

rotate(a,b):    save[y z];y=a;
                wk =. 1;            /* Write 1 in row 0 of mask, i.e.
                                      I'J' in Figure 9-9 */
                do{ @ load b;z = 16;@ mask wk;
                     do{@ stm y'; if IA y=a;
                     @ move N 1 cyclic;z-1} while NZ;
                y'1;@ load wk;@ move S 1;@ st wk;
                b'1} while VA;
                unsave[z y];return(a)
```

```
/* Here the precision of b is variable, but a must address a
   sequence of 16 planes. Execution time is proportional to
   16*(length of b), or more generally to N squared, N being
   the edge length of the array. A more efficient procedure
   with execution time proportional to N*logN is outlined at
   the end of Chapter 10 */
```

Fig. 9.10   Rotation from horizontal to vertical, and vice versa

ABCD in line *OO'*. Conversion from horizontal to vertical is done by rotating *ABCD* through $\frac{1}{2}\pi$ about *OO'*, ending up as *A'B'C'D'*. That is done for each plane in the cube, so that all the signs end up in the high index plane.

The rotation is such that a matrix of words seen through the sign plane *LMJI* as 2^n rows of 2^n columns (horizontal) has the same form after rotation when viewed from above, the first row being along the North edge of the array. Moreover, the *same* rotation applied to a vertical matrix returns it to the original horizontal form. You will see that this is not the rotation of a solid object. When you have followed the program (Fig. 9.10) for AMA4 you will be well on the way to thinking in parallel. In the next chapter we shall examine some more complex routing functions, but study of the exercises at the end of this chapter is recommended first.

9.5 COUNTING THE COST

The reader might well begin to ask what this has to do with high-speed computation, because the AMA appears to have to work hard to achieve fairly basic effects. Let us postpone further development and tackle that question. As usual, the answer divides into what is theoretically possible and what can be achieved in practice.

On theoretical questions machine activity can be costed in terms of elementary operations such as memory cycles, scalar and planar register transfers and routing operations. The close correspondence between register transfer notation and machine functions enables estimates to be made by inspection of simple programs, but we can go a step further and arrange for a simulator program to count operations in AMA4. In particular, we can measure:

(1) instructions obeyed;
(2) data accesses to local memory;
(3) total planar routing distance

for any section of program. The results can be presented in terms of precision of argument and size of array. There is scope for confusion in deriving performance figures, for the usual reasons of accounting for instruction lookahead, conflict with data accesses, overlapped scalar and array operations. Under one simplifying assumption the total number of machine cycles is the sum of (1), (2), and (3). At the other extreme it might be assumed that all instructions are buffered (or held in control memory) and that execution time is determined primarily by the speed of local memory and planar routing. For example, in the comparison loop:

$$do \ \{ \ @ \ load \ a' \ ; \ @ \ move \ W \ 2 \ cyclic; \ @ \ add \ - b' \ \} \ while \ VA$$

the assumptions give respectively counts of 8 (4 instruction, 2 memory accesses, 2 moves) and 4 for each iteration. Some measurements are given in Table 9.3 for various elementary operations on vertical data.

Table 9.3 Machine Cycles in Vertical Mode

Operation		In terms of precision p		
	(A)	Worst case (Instr.fetch + data access + routing)	(B)	Best case (Data access + routing only)
Integer add		$45 + 7p$		$13 + 3p$
Integer multiply		$56 + 24p + 3.5p^2$		$10 + 8p + 1.5p^2$
copy		$1 + 5p$		$2p$
maxel		$14 + 13p$		$4 + 4p$
rotate		$7 + 144p$		$5 + 54p$
compare – exchange		$50 + 18p$		$34 + 8p$
Batcher sort		$6000 + 972p$		$1800 + 552p$

Let us suppose that execution time is in fact determined by memory speed, but take a fairly moderate cycle time of 200 ns to allow for loading instruction buffers and performing scalar register transfers and tests. Then the "best" estimate (B) for multiplication using 56-bit operands gives approximately 5000 machine cycles, independent of the size of the array. In other words, to produce results at a rate of 4 Mflops we would need to present 4096 operand pairs in parallel, using AMA6. That is the memory-to-memory rate, which will be compared with 26 Mflops in CRAY-1, though in terms of machine cycles the ratio AMA:CRAY is about 5:3. As in other aspects of design, differences at circuit level must somehow be neutralized when making architectural comparisons.

To take one other example, consider the problem of finding the largest elements in absolute value in a vertically stored matrix. We assume a numerical representation using normalized sign-and-magnitude with characteristic form of exponent, for which comparison can be made as for integers.

Example 9.9   This subroutine starts with the activity plane A equal to "1" at points where the maximum value of argument is to be found. It terminates with "1" at just the positions in the activity plane corresponding to maximum values.

The method used is to scan the argument array starting with the most-significant bit plane, continuously adjusting the activity mask.

> $maxel(a)$:   save $[x]$; $x = a \ high \ - \ 1$;   /*most-sig.bit*/
> $wk = . \ - 1$;@ $load \ - wk$;@ $stm \ wk$;
> $do \ \{ @ \ load \ - a'x$;@ $stm \ wk$;
> $(wk. + 1)$; $if \ NZ \ @ \ mask \ - wk$;
> $x - 1 \}$ $while \ GE$;
> $unsave \ [x]$; $return$

In the above example under the "best" assumption 4 memory accesses are required for each iteration, or 256 for a 64-plane array. Reference to Table 8.3 shows that for a 256-element array the number of machine cycles in CRAY-1 is at best about 1400. There are of course many other factors to take into account on both sides, but the conclusion can be drawn that, contrary to first appearances, AMA design can compete with the alternative of switching vectors through multiple function units. It boils down to the fact that in direct memory operations an AMA can present more data to the arithmetic and logical circuits in a single machine cycle than a pipelined machine. Of course, when there is intensive calculation at register level the result of such a comparison would be reversed because of the faster access rates afforded by registers.

With regard to achieving something close to theoretical performance, we have already mentioned the difficulties faced by all high-speed machines. In the short term, unfamiliarity with programming techniques is probably the biggest hurdle, and for some users the ability to obey "standard Fortran" is an overwhelming requirement. To exploit active memory arrays problems must be analyzed so as to achieve a high degree of parallelism and to make maximum use of their flexibility, particularly in choice of precision and data orientation. This is a relatively new subject yielding some surprising and interesting results which we shall present before offering further comment.

In the present context it might have been noted that the difficulty of estimating AMA performance is the result of close coupling between controller and memory. The same would apply even with a passive memory, and we saw in earlier chapters how processor design has evolved to higher-level "architectural" standards in which relatively complex function sets are interpreted by microprogram. We saw in Chapter 8 that the FPS AP120-B is essentially a microprogrammed engine, but from most users' points of view it is a high-level architecture able to support "vector operations". Is it possible that AMA design will evolve in the same direction? That is certainly something to bear in mind, but it is also worth remembering that the variety of operations on vertical arrays is even greater than on scalars or vectors, so it would be correspondingly difficult to define a stable architectural interface. Readers of Part 1 will recall that the *need* for a high-level architectural definition is related to a number of subtle problems in system design. We shall return to them in Chapter 13.

9.6 EXERCISES

The following exercises are roughly graded in order of difficulty. The solutions to odd-numbered exercises that are given in the Appendix assume AMA4 dimensions and use the register declaration:

REGS [		*wk*	plane workspace pointer
	p *q*	*r*	temporary pointers
	x *y*	*z*]	temporary numerics

which will be adapted to the problem as necessary. Where appropriate, solutions will be given in subroutine form.

1　If p points to a Boolean plane sequence (i.e. having only one element, limit zero), how would you detect that the plane contains (a) at least one zero; (b) at least one one?

2　Assuming p refers to a plane sequence, how would you find out if it is entirely zero?

3　Given a Boolean plane p containing exactly one zero, how would you construct its coordinates in register x? (Assume AMA4 dimensions, giving an 8-bit result.)

4 Construct a plane with the following alternating pattern of 0s and 1s:

```
0  1  0  1  0  1  0    . . .        (16 cols)
1  0  1  0  1  0  1    . . .
0  1  0  1  0  1  0    . . .
(16 rows)                . . .
```

Assume cyclic geometry in all directions.

5 A black and white picture can be represented by a Boolean plane with 0s for white cells and 1s for black. If p is a plane representing a $16 * 16$ picture, write a procedure to eliminate any "isolated" white cells, i.e. those having eight black near-neighbors. Assume plane geometry.

6 Given a $16 * 16$ image p, derive a Boolean plane q marking with 1 any "lower left-hand corners" in p, i.e. patterns conforming to the following template:

```
0  1  *
0  1  1
0  0  0
```

where * means "dont't care". Ignore edge elements.

7 Let a point to a sequence of planes containing horizontal data, and let n be a numeric argument. Write a subroutine $assoc(a,n)$ which returns the index of the first element of a that matches n, setting the "VA" condition. If there is none, set "IA" and return n. (*Note*: the result returned, if valid, will be such that $a\ word\ '\ assoc\ (a,n) = n$.)

8 Repeat 7 for vertically stored data, truncating high-order bits of n if necessary, and assuming $a\ high < 16$ (Here the result will be an 8-bit row/column index in AMA4.)

9 Given a sequence a of three planes and a Boolean matrix b, write a subroutine to form vertically in a the sum of the four near-neighbor elements at the corresponding position of b. Assume cyclic geometry.

10 Assuming horizontal data, given two equal-length plane sequences a and b, assign to a the modulus of the data in b. Ignore overflow and assume twos complement arithmetic.

11 Assuming vertical data representation, given two plane sequences a and b of equal length, compare corresponding elements arithmetically and assign the larger in each pair to a and the smaller to b. Ignore overflow and assume 2s complement arithmetic.

12 Given a signed integer n and a vertically stored array of integers a, scale each element of a by n, i.e. multiply by 2^n.

13 Assuming vertical data, given an array of 256 elements a and an array of 256 unsigned integers b, scale each element of a down by the corresponding element of b, i.e. multiply a by 2^{-b} term-by-term.

14 Using the function *shuff* described in the text, write a program to perform the perfect shuffle on columns of the plane sequence p.

15 Show how the *shuff* procedure would be used to obtain a perfect *unshuffle* of rows and columns in AMA4.

16 Given a vertically stored array *a* of four-bit unsigned integers, write a procedure to return their sum as a scalar value, i.e. *sum(a)* returns $\Sigma_i\Sigma_j a_{ij}$.

17 Show how the problem represented by a hexagonal pattern in a plane as in Fig. 9.11(a) could be mapped onto a square array with four nearneighbors as in Fig. 9.11(b). Mark the data paths corresponding to the arrowed lines in (a). Write a procedure to move a plane *p* of data (one bit per cell) three steps in the direction of the arrows, ignoring edge effects.

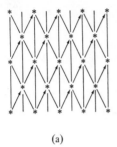

(a)

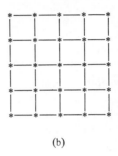

(b)

Fig. 9.11

18 Let *p* be a plane sequence containing positive integers in horizontal form and in ascending order. Let *n* be a positive integer. Write a procedure *ins(p,n)* to insert the value *n* into the sequence so that it remains in ascending order, using plane operations to economize on data movement. (Discard the last element of the original sequence.)

19 Suppose *b* is a set of barometric pressure readings from sites in a 16 * 16 array of observation posts. It would be represented in AMA4 by a plane sequence of vertical data. You are required to obtain a sequence of Boolean matrices *a* which represent the regions of constant pressure. Write a procedure *iso(a,b)* that will put the mask of the highest pressure region in *a'*0, the next in *a'*1, and so on for as many planes as are available in *a*, or as many pressure regions are distinguished. (*Hint*: use *maxel(b)*.)

20 Following from Exercise 19 show how, in principle, you could obtain the isobars, i.e. lines separating regions of constant pressure, by operating on the sequence *a*.

10 PARALLEL PROCEDURES

We now resume the study of programming techniques appropriate to active memory arrays, but at a slightly higher level than in Chapter 9. It is not intended to exhaust the subject (or the reader), but to show by examples which are useful in their own right some of the important themes of problem analysis and presentation. The effectiveness of a machine design is unknown until the complete process of getting an answer to a practical question has been understood.

Most procedures will be presented in terms of the physical size of array offered by the AMA, e.g. 16- or 256-element vectors in AMA4, 32 or 1024 elements in AMA5, and so on. Real problems can be classified as having a dimension that is either (1) equal to, or slightly less than, the AMA size; or (2) rounded up to some multiple of the AMA size. In practice this means that there are discontinuities in solution time that could be serious for relatively small arrays (Fig. 10.1), and when there is a lot of variability in the dimensions of a problem horizontal data might be chosen because it gives a

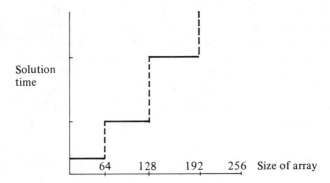

Fig. 10.1 Variation of solution time with problem size

"smoother" response. However, in the following subsections we shall assume vertical data, unless stated otherwise, because that leads to the exploitation of variable-precision and bit-serial operations. Many of the algorithms could be applied to horizontal data with suitable changes in the routing operations (and their timing) and a restricted choice of precision.

Three general approaches to problem analysis can be identified. The first is to decompose the original into subproblems of class (1). For example, many linear-algebra problems can be rewritten as operations on subarrays of fixed size, and solutions to sorting problems can be expressed as merging operations on previously sorted subsequences. A characteristic of such procedures is that the low-level or detailed part of the algorithm might derive from properties of the domain not exploited in the high-level part, and vice versa. Such algorithms are by no means uncommon in conventional systems, and it is even possible that one or other part could be more conveniently expressed in sequential form. A particular set of techniques arises in conjunction with secondary storage devices: e.g. many of the major nuclear codes, and in the commercial field many sort procedures, are written in acute awareness of the size of disk buffer or the performance of the paging mechanism. If this approach is taken, therefore, the programmed solution will be sensitive to array size, and that, though unfortunate, is a situation many programmers have learned to live with.

The second approach is to express the original solution in parametric form, providing automatic means of restructuring in terms of array dimensions, either during compilation (knowing the dimensions of the data) or during execution (as we saw in Example 8.1 for CRAY-1). In AMA design the data must be selected *and aligned* correctly before each arithmetic operation. The idea of "local connectivity" expresses the knowledge that certain realignments, such as translations to relative positions (vector indices) ± 1, ± 16, ± 32, ... are expected to predominate. A given vector is rounded up to the next multiple m of the AMA dimension, but then there is a choice of how to store the vector across the PEs (Fig. 10.2): either (a) putting vector element i in PE number (i modulo 2^n); or (b) in PE number ($i \div m$). The practical difference is that in (a) vector indexing is uniform and coincides with the

PE:	0	1	2	3
	$\equiv$	$\equiv$	$\equiv$	$\equiv$
	v_0	v_1	v_2	v_3
	v_4	v_5	v_6	v_7
	v_8	v_9	v_{10}	v_{11}

PE:	0	1	2	3
	$\equiv$	$\equiv$	$\equiv$	$\equiv$
	v_0	v_3	v_6	v_9
	v_1	v_4	v_7	v_{10}
	v_2	v_5	v_8	v_{11}

Fig. 10.2 Mapping a vector of length 12 in AMA2 ($m = 3$) for vertical data: (a) i modulo 4; (b) $i \div m$

store-addressing scheme in horizontal mode, while (b) tends to "cluster" neighboring vector elements into neighboring PEs. Both methods are used in practice, but (a) is simpler to apply. Matrices can be mapped onto vectors, but many analysts would feel that a valuable perspective is lost in that way, and that it is better to retain the notion of a matrix as a primitive structure in the system. Here again there is a choice of "straight" or "crinkle-cut" overlay into the physical store.

All machines with multiple memory units are sensitive to the layout of data, but whereas vectored memory accesses can deal with a variety of starting positions and intervals between elements, array machines require that each vector element shall be in a distinct local memory. For example, in Fig. 10.2(a), the addressing mechanism of CRAY-1 could select v_1, v_5, v_9 for input to a vector register, which is impossible on an array machine; and Illiac IV could select v_0, v_5, v_{10} and v_7, which would be impossible in AMA design. These differences lead to the third approach to problem analysis which is emphasized in the present context and which can be described as generating parallelism by *merging* and *splitting* techniques. Both exploit the fact that if substantial calculation is involved it is economic to move the data to otherwise "unused" PEs to take advantage of their arithmetic capabilities. For example, if one stage of a calculation entails computing the squares of even-indexed elements in the vector of Fig. 10.2(a), it is best to form a new vector:

$$v_0 \quad v_4 \quad v_2 \quad v_6$$
$$v_8 \qquad\; v_{10}$$

This can be squared in two rather than three parallel stages, restoring the result afterwards. In that case the vector presented for arithmetic is the result of merging two partially active subvectors.

On the other hand, suppose there were two vectors v and w of the same length, stored as in Fig. 10.2(a), and it is required to calculate at each odd index position the value:

$$w_i * v_{i-1} - w_{i-1} * v_i, \qquad i = 1,3, \ldots$$

Then the appropriate preliminary step would be to form an "exchanged copy" of w aligned to v as follows:

$$v_0 \quad v_1 \quad v_2 \quad v_3 \quad \ldots$$
$$w_1 \quad w_0 \quad w_3 \quad w_2 \quad \ldots$$

This allows the multiplication terms of the result to be evaluated in one step, followed by subtraction to produce the final result. Thus a single calculation is "split" to reduce the total calculation time.

With the above tools in mind we can see that although "making the problem fit the array" is a special case, it is an essential part of more general procedures. How much it costs to reduce a general algorithm to AMA dimensions is a matter for continuing research and re-education. As mentioned earlier, the penalties are by no means one-way: some ideas are more easily expressed in parallel form, and in future designers might be faced with the problems of reducing parallel operations to scalar dimension.

10.1 BIT-SERIAL ALGORITHMS

We have seen that the usual arithmetic functions are developed in vertical mode by serial operations on bit planes. In conventional systems the more elaborate arithmetic and transcendental functions are composed by iterative procedures or by polynomial approximation, and therefore take an order of magnitude longer to evaluate. In this subsection economic methods of calculation which develop the results bit by bit will be presented. They have the advantages of taking time comparable with *single* multiplication or division instructions, and of being readily adjusted to the required precision. It is noteworthy that algorithms for some of the most powerful computers have much in common with those of the simplest hand-held calculator.

In each application we are required to find a pair of points (X, Y) on the curve $Y = F(X)$, given one or other coordinate. The basis of the method is:

Step 1:   Scale X and/or Y to bring the range of coordinate values into an interval in which they behave "reasonably", which we take to mean both are monotonic, continuous, and with continuous derivatives. Let the resulting curve be expressed as:

$$y = f(x) \tag{1}$$

Step 2:   Derive an exact difference relation for that interval:

$$y + \delta y = f(x + \delta x) \tag{2}$$

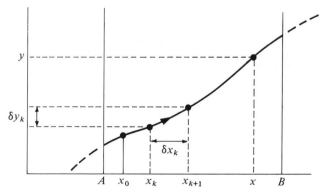

Fig. 10.3   Approximating (x,y) in the interval $A < x < B$

Step 3: Select a starting point (x_0, y_0) on the curve.
Step 4: Advance from the starting point to (x,y) by suitable choice of intervals δx_k from which, using (2):

$$x_{k+1} = x_k + \delta x_k; \quad y_{k+1} = y_k + \delta y_k = f(x_k + \delta x_k) \qquad (3)$$

terminating when the desired approximation has been found.
Step 5: Rescale if necessary to derive the required (X, Y).

The core of the algorithm is Step 4, which has one of two forms, depending on whether the final x or y is given:

Step 4′: x given.
Here successive bits of x can be used to determine δx_k. The corresponding value of δy_k is found from (2) to give successive approximations to y. Typically, x is a fraction, and the increments δx_k are $2^{-1}, 2^{-2}, \ldots, 2^{-p}$.

Step 4″: y given.
Here the successive increments in x are *trial* values used in (3) to see if the approximation is improved. If so, δx_k is accepted and the values of x_k and y_k are updated; otherwise the increment is rejected.

It can easily be seen that, when applied to the equation:

$$y = t * x \qquad (t \text{ constant})$$

the method of Step 4′ corresponds exactly to the multiplication algorithm for binary numbers, and Step 4″ corresponds to division. For that reason the techniques are referred to as *pseudomultiplication* and *pseudodivision* algorithms. Table 10.1 shows how they apply to the equation:

$$y = x^2$$
$$y + \delta y = x^2 + 2 * x * \delta x + (\delta x)^2$$
$$\delta y = 2 * x * \delta x + (\delta x)^2$$

When x is given the effect of using Step 4′ is to evaluate x^2 as in Table 10.1(a). Conversely, if y is given, then Step 4″ is applied as in Table 10.1(b) to give $x = \sqrt{y}$.

In the AMA the approximations are applied in parallel to an entire plane of elements, using the activity register as in multiplication and division to control the formation of the result. The increment δx_k is not necessarily a power of two, nor constant in sign. All that is necessary is that the chosen values should allow convergence in the specified interval. For example, given the exponential function:

$$y = e^x$$

for which: $\quad y + \delta y = y * e^{\delta x} \qquad (4)$

and for small δx: $\quad y + \delta y = y * (1 + \delta x)$

Table 10.1   Serial approximation to the function $y = x^2$
(computed values given in *binary* form)

(a) Pseudomultiplication
Given $x = 0.0101$, to find y

k	x_k	y_k	δx_k	$\delta y_k = 2 * x_k * \delta x_k + (\delta x_k)^2$
0	0	0	0.0	0.0
1	0	0	0.01	0.0001
2	0.01	0.0001	0.000	0.0
3	0.010	0.0001	0.0001	0.00001001
4	0.0101	0.00011001	(*End of iteration*)	

RESULT $y = 0.00011001$

(b) Pseudodivision
Given $y = 0.00110010$, to find x

k	x_k	y_k	Trial δx_k	y_{k+1}	$< y?$	Bits of x
0	0	0	0.1	0.01	no	0.0
1	0	0	0.01	0.0001	yes	0.01
2	0.01	0.0001	0.001	0.001001	yes	0.001
3	0.011	0.001001	0.0001	0.00110001	yes	0.0001
4	0.0111	0.00110001	(*End of iteration*)			

RESULT $x = 0.0111$

the evaluation of δy involves a multiplication at each step. However, starting with $(x_0, y_0) = (0,1)$ and choosing increments such that:

$$e^{\delta x_1} = 1.1 \qquad \text{(binary)}$$
$$e^{\delta x_2} = 1.01 \qquad \text{(binary)}$$
$$e^{\delta x_3} = 1.001 \qquad \text{(binary)}$$
$$\ldots$$

the right-hand side of (4) can be evaluated with one addition. Application of Steps 4′ and 4″ to (4) give exponential and natural logarithm respectively. Some shortcuts are possible for small increments.

For trigonometric functions we have:

$$y = e^{ix}$$

giving: $y + \delta y = (\cos \delta x + i * \sin \delta x) * y$ (5)
and for small δx: $y + \delta y = (1 + i * \delta x) * y$

where x is real and y is the complex number $(\cos x + i * \sin x)$. Initially $x_0 = 0$ and $y_0 = 1$. The problem is to choose values of δx to make (5) computationally simple. For given x, that can be done by writing (5) as:

$$y + \delta y = \cos \delta x * (1 + i * \tan \delta x) * y \qquad (6)$$

and choosing the successive increments $\pm \delta x_k$ such that:

$$\tan \delta x_k = 2^{-k}$$

In this case x is approximated by

$$x_0 \pm \delta x_1 \pm \delta x_2 \pm \delta x_3 \pm \ldots \delta x_{K'}$$

the sign being chosen to improve the approximation at each stage. The product

$$\cos \delta x_1 * \cos \delta x_2 * \cdots * \cos \delta x_K$$

resulting from (6) occurs once only and can be precomputed.

It will be noted that squaring as described above is no improvement on multiplication. It is possible to halve the number of additions by observing that if the K-bit fraction x is expressed in terms of its binary digits as:

$$x = \sum_{i=1}^{K} b_i * 2^{-i} \tag{7}$$

then on writing out the multiplication tableau (Table 10.2) we see that apart from "diagonal" terms ($b_i * b_i$) products occur *twice* in each column, e.g. under 2^{-5} we find $b_1 * b_4$ and $b_4 * b_1$, $b_2 * b_3$ and $b_3 * b_2$. It is sufficient to evaluate such terms once only, doubling the result, as shown in the "reduced" tableau of Table 10.2. As a result, squaring is about twice as fast as multiplication in vertical mode.

The above procedures show the principles of bit-serial approximation. Their practical effects are given for the ICL Distributed Array Processor in Chapter 12.

Table 10.2   Multiplication Tableau for x^2

where $x = \sum\limits_{i=1}^{K} b_i * 2^{-i}$

(Normal)

2^{-1}	2^{-2}	2^{-3}	2^{-4}	2^{-5}		2^{-k}
	$b_1 * b_1$	$b_1 * b_2$	$b_1 * b_3$	$b_1 * b_4$		$b_1 * b_{k-1}$
		$b_2 * b_1$	$b_2 * b_2$	$b_2 * b_3$		$b_2 * b_{k-2}$
			$b_3 * b_1$	$b_3 * b_2$		$b_3 * b_{k-3}$
				$b_4 * b_1$		$b_4 * b_{k-4}$
						$\ldots$

(Reduced)

2^{-1}	2^{-2}	2^{-3}	2^{-4}	2^{-5}		2^{-k}
	$b_1 * b_1$	$\cdot$	$b_2 * b_2$	$\cdot$	$\ldots$	
	$b_1 * b_2$	$b_1 * b_3$	$b_1 * b_4$	$b_1 * b_5$		
			$b_2 * b_3$	$b_2 * b_4$		

10.2 PARALLEL SORTING

Sorting a vector into ascending or descending sequence has been the subject of extensive research for both parallel and sequential machines. In the absence of any more practical standard the basis for assessing different methods is often taken to be the number of comparisons required to complete the procedure for random input data, e.g. for a sequential machine the number of comparisons $B(N)$ required to sort N items by binary insertion is $N * \lceil \log_2 N \rceil - N + 1$, even though the operation of insertion might outweigh comparison. Similarly for parallel machines the *delay* or number of separate comparison – exchange steps is one measure of efficiency. A "minimum delay" parallel sort is shown in Fig. 10.4(a) for $N = 16$. Each horizontal line represents an element of the input vector, each vertical line joins two elements to be compared in a succession of steps going from left to right of the diagram. As a result of comparison, two elements are exchanged if the lower (in the diagram) is lower in value. The resulting values emerge at the right of the diagram, sorted in ascending order from top to bottom. If 8 ALUs were available, several comparisons could be done in parallel; by inspection of the diagram it can be seen that 10 such steps are sufficient (compared with 49 for binary insertion).

No parallel machines have direct routing of the type implied by Fig. 10.4(a), and practical algorithms must take some account of routing overheads. If only two near-neighbor connections are available, then rather than reproduce exactly the minimum delay interchanges it is attractive to use a generalization of bubble sorting in which each element is compared with its immediate neighbor, as in Fig. 10.4(b). For $N = 16$, 8 ALUs allow the procedure to complete in at most 8 stages, each consisting of an "odd" ($1 - 2$, $3 - 4$, $5 - 6$, ...) followed by "even" ($0 - 1$, $2 - 3$, $4 - 5$, ...) comparison. The procedure terminates after the first stage in which no exchange takes place. In the worst case the element initially at index position 0 must propagate to position 15, taking eight odd – even exchange steps or sixteen comparison – exchange steps. In general, odd – even exchange requires at most N steps, given $\frac{1}{2}N$ comparison units.

If the size of vector is greater than the array dimension it can be arranged to present subvectors to the planar ALU. Figure 10.5 shows the register – transfer procedure for sorting a vector r of any number of planes, each regarded as 16 integers (assumed positive, i.e. ignoring overflow on comparison). The main procedure *OEX* sets up some workplanes and then applies the odd – even exchange until no change occurs. Within the loop adjustments are made to the vector to take care of edge effects. The work of scanning the plane sequence and interchanging elements under a given mask m is done by *comp(plane,m)*.

More advanced sorting methods require a means of accelerating

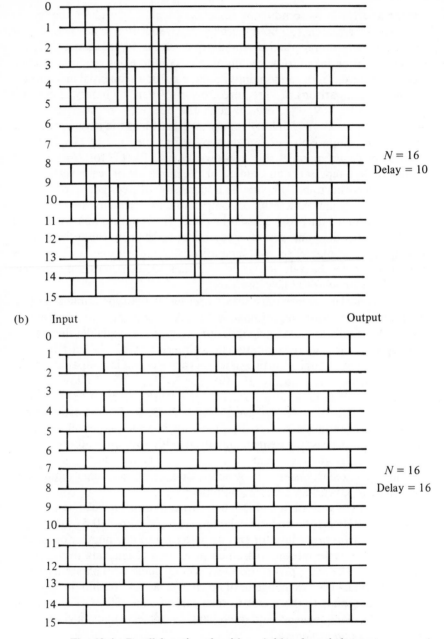

Fig. 10.4 Parallel sorting algorithms (with acknowledgement to KNU73): (a) minimum-delay parallel sort; (b) odd−even exchange sort.

```
            REGS [wk  x  y  z  t]

OEX(r):              save[x  y  z  t];
            /* Assumes wk points to a sequence of three workplanes */
                     wk'2 =. $7fff;
                     do{
            /* Single stage of odd-even exchange, setting y=1 if
               an exchange occurs */

            /* Save first element in z then move up 16 to 0, 32 to 16 etc*/
                     x = r word;z = x.;t = x'16;
                     while VA do {x =. t.;x=t;t'16};x=.$7fff;
            /* Cyclic odd-even exchange in each plane */
                     y = 0;comp(r,$5555);
            /* Move down z to 0, 0 to 16, 16 to 32, etc  */
                     x = r word; do{t = x.;x =.z;z = t;x'16} while VA;
            /* Even-odd exchange in each plane */
                     comp(r,$aaaa)
                     } while (y<>0);
                     unsave[t z y x];
                     return(r)

/* Compare-exchange in each plane under mask m, using 1-place
   shifts and setting y=1 if anything happens */
comp(plane,m):   t = wk'1;
                 do{@ load plane;@ move W 1 cyclic;@ st wk;
                    @ adw -plane;@ or wk'2; @ st t;
                    x = t.bycol & m;
            /* Now x has a 1 where an exchange has to take place */
                    if NZ {y¦1;t =bycol x;@ mask t;@ load wk;
                       @ stm plane;@ load t;@ move E 1 cyclic;
                       @ st t;@ mask t;@ load wk;
                       @ move E 2 cyclic;@ stm plane};
                    plane'1} while VA;
                 return
```

Fig. 10.5 Sorting horizontal data in AMA4 by odd−even exchange

elements to their final positions by using non-local routes. In AMA design with four near-neighbor connections in vertical mode it is possible to consider comparison−exchanges in both N−S and E−W directions: the transport costs are the same for each. Such schemes have also been studied extensively and a number of asymptotic results have been derived, depending on the assumed costs of routing and comparison operations and the final ordering achieved. For horizontal data there are also two routing directions, but transport costs are unequal: routing in the store dimension is independent of distance, whereas it depends linearly on distance when moving E − W (remember that for horizontal data the words run N − S). The best-known algorithms are based either on power-of-two exchange or the perfect shuffle discussed in Chapter 9. However, the former are better served by AMA functions, and provide the basis for Batcher's bitonic sort, surely one of the

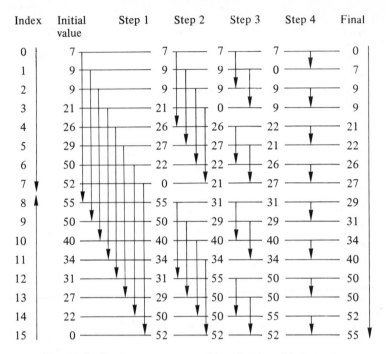

Fig. 10.6 Sorting two vectors of length 8 into 16 elements

wonders of computing: not only difficult to explain but intuitively upsetting to sort half the data in the "wrong" direction most of the time.

The core of the Batcher sort is a series of comparisons that will merge two sorted sequences of length n (a power of two, we shall assume) to give a sorted result of length $2 * n$. The initial input presents the two sequences in opposing order (Fig. 10.6). In the example $n = 8$ and it is required to sort into ascending order. The direction of arrows shows that elements $0, \ldots, 7$ are initially ascending and $8, \ldots, 15$ descending. The required result is achieved in $\log_2(2 * n) = 4$ power-of-two comparison – exchange steps, successive routing distances 8, 4, 2 and 1. To obtain the output in descending order it is simply necessary to reverse the polarity of the comparison.

Given an initial vector of N numbers we set $n = 1$ and form alternating sequences of ascending and descending pairs of values in a single comparison – exchange. The procedure continues, doubling n at each stage until $n \geqslant N$. The resulting pattern of comparisons is shown for $N = 16$ in Fig. 10.7. For sixteen elements ten comparisons are required, assuming 8 comparison – exchange units, and for N elements $\frac{1}{2}\log_2 N(\log_2 N + 1)$, again assuming sufficient parallel units. For reasonably sized N, say 64 upwards, that is significantly better than odd – even exchange, allowing for routing overheads.

Index

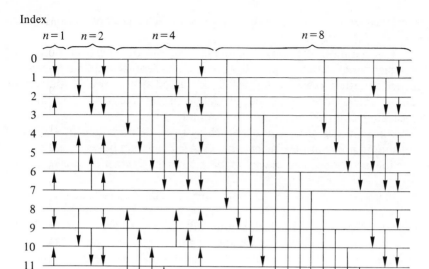

Fig. 10.7   Comparison–interchange for 16-element Batcher sort

The Batcher sort procedure for a sequence p of length some power of two can be expressed as in the recursive schema:

sortup (p):   *if* $(p\ high\ > 0)$
                { *sortup* (p_{LEFT});
                 sortdown (p_{RIGHT});
                 exchup (p) } ;
            return

exchup (p):   *exch* $(p_{LEFT},\ p_{RIGHT})$;
            if $(p\ high\ > 2)$
                { *exchup* (p_{LEFT});
                 exchup (p_{RIGHT}) };
            return

where *sortdown* is similarly defined in terms of *exchdown*. Here the suffixes *LEFT* and *RIGHT* refer to the two halves of the sequence. The actual "sorting" is done in the procedure *exch(a,b)* which compares two equal length sequences a and b term by term and exchanges any pairs in which $a_i > b_i$, $i = 0, \ldots, a$ high.

Translation of the above schema into register transfer operations must take account of data mapping. If we assume horizontal data, p is a plane sequence and the successive "halves" are obtained at first by operating on the plane pointer. Once the number of scalar elements reduces to 16, however, succeeding comparisons imply horizontal routing. At any stage in the algorithm there is an option of switching to another method of sorting, if that should prove more efficient. In AMA4 it is in fact better to use a scalar insertion sort for single planes of data, but the horizontal exchanges are carried out in parallel.

In iterative form, the essential parameters at any stage of calculation are the *distance* between elements and the *polarity* of the exchange. It can be seen from Fig. 10.7 that polarity varies with element index. It can best be expressed by a Boolean mask distinguishing the "up" and "down" exchange. Again, the details depend on the mapping. An iterative procedure for sorting vertical data on AMA4 is given in Fig. 10.8. The argument array is sorted into ascending row-major order. The "polarity" mask indicates either upward (1) or downward (0) sort at each point in the array. A similar iterative procedure for horizontal data will be presented in Chapter 12.

It will be noted that the "shorter" exchanges are repeated most often in the Batcher method, i.e. the succession of routing distances is:

```
1
2  1
4  2  1
8  4  2  1
etc.
```

However, the actual "cost" does not increase in the same way: in vertical mode on AMA4 a difference of 16 index positions is "cheaper" than a difference of 8 because it is realized by $N - S$ translation. It is possible to reduce the total routing overhead by sorting into other than row-major order, e.g. given the element indices in binary form for AMA4:

$$r_3 r_2 r_1 r_0 c_3 c_2 c_1 c_0$$

(here r stands for row digits and c for column), instead of basing the exchanges on the sequence $c_0, c_1, c_2, c_3, r_0, \ldots, r_3$, one could choose $c_0, r_0, c_1, r_1, c_2, \ldots, r_3$, which has the effect of using the shorter translations most often, but leaving the sorted sequence in non-standard form, e.g. for AMA2:

0	1	4	5	*Shuffled-index sorting*
2	3	6	7	
8	9	12	13	
10	11	14	15	

```
                REGS [wk i j q]

BatV(p):              save[i j q];
                      q = Plane(p high +1);
                      i=1; do{j=i-1; do{copy(q,p);potse(q,index'j.);
       /* Compare p with q */  sign(q,p);
       /* Polarity mask    */  setwk(index'i.); @ equ wk;
       /* Shift mask       */  setwk(index'j.); @ equ wk;
                              @ st wk;@ mask wk;
       /* Merge q into p under mask */ merge(p,q);
                              j-1} while GE;
                      i+1} while (i<9);
                      unsave[q j i];return(p)


/* Sort in row major order */
index:   (0,1,2,3,4,5,6,7,8)

/* Sort in shuffled index order

index:   (0,4,1,5,2,6,3,7,8) */

/* Copy b to a */
copy(a,b):       do{@ load b';@ st a'}while VA; return

/* Set mask into wk plane */
setwk(x):        if(x<4) wk =bycol msk'x.
                 else wk =. imsk'x.;
                 return
msk:    ($aaaa, $cccc, $f0f0, $ff00)
imsk:   (0,0,0,0,$5555,$3333,$0f0f,$00ff,$ffff)

/* Compare (a-b) vertically, leaving the sign in the B plane */
sign(a,b):       wk=.0;@ load -wk;@ add -wk;      /* Carry-in */
                 @ load a'(a high);@ equ b'(b high);@ st wk'1;
                 do{@ load a';@ add -b'} while VA;
                 @ load wk;@ add wₙ'1; return

/* Write b to a where mask bit is set */
merge(a,b):      do{@ load b';@ stm a'} while VA; return
```

Fig. 10.8 Variable-precision Batcher sort

Similar considerations for horizontal data indicate that it is better to exchange first in the vertical direction, leaving E – W shifts to the final stages, with the result that the data are sorted in column rather than row order.

It must be asked how parallel sorting methods compare in practice with sequential algorithms. They are clearly better in theory, but asymptotic results are sometimes misleading because low-order terms can easily dominate computing time, and systematic variations such as the influence of source language or compiler might make comparison meaningless. Fig. 10.9 shows the result of comparing sequential and parallel algorithms for horizontal data in AMA4 using the same source language and, as far as possible, the same programming skills. The "time" is taken to be the worst-

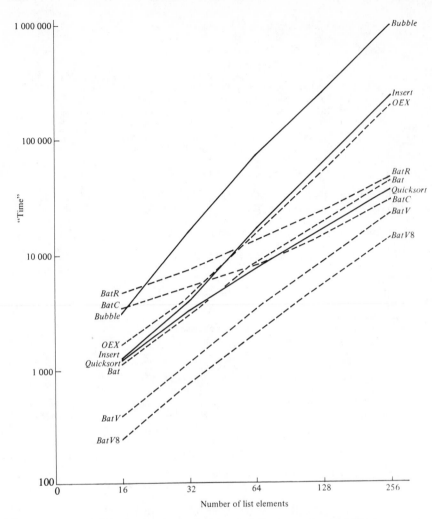

Fig. 10.9   Comparison of scalar and planar sorting in AMA4

case measure of Section 9.4, i.e. instruction count plus store accesses plus total routing distance. In the figure, solid lines are used for scalar algorithms and dashed lines for planar. For visual clarity continuous graphs are used, although in practice, of course, performance is a step function.

Study of Fig. 10.9 reveals some interesting relations between sorting algorithms and, more generally, between serial and parallel methods. The following points should be noted.

(1)   There is a direct comparison between serial and parallel versions of the same algorithm, i.e. *Bubble* and *OEX* respectively. In this example their execution times are in the ratio 5:1 compared with the 8:1 that might be expected in theory. The difference is attributable to the greater probability that an exchange will take place when eight comparisons are made in parallel.

(2)   It can be seen that odd−even exchange just keeps pace with serial insertion, but is always worse than *Quicksort* (here the *Quicksort* algorithm uses *Insert* for lists of 25 elements or less). It seems possible to improve on *Insert* by using parallel comparisons, but there does not appear to be a parallel version of *Quicksort* for this type of machine. (For explanation of the serial algorithms see, for example, D.E. Knuth, *The Art of Computer Programming, Vol 3: Sorting and Searching.*)

(3)   Three sets of results are presented for Batcher algorithms using horizontal data. *Bat* is the procedure expressed on page 211 using recursion. Note that it gets "pulled down" to *Insert* for short arguments, but overheads of recursion are significant for larger lists. *BatR* and *BatC* are iterative procedures sorting in row- and column-major order respectively. They tend to be inefficient for short lists because of the predominance of horizontal routing and control. Overall, sorting by columns reduces machine activity by about one-third.

(4)   Two sets of results are presented for vertical data. *BatV* handles 16-bit operands and *BatV8* handles bytes. Although *BatV* appears to do the same as *BatR* it is about twice as fast for lists of 256 elements, mainly because it deals in 128 comparisons at a time instead of 8, hence the control overheads are lower. The precision of operands can easily be varied in vertical mode. However, there is very little advantage in sorting lists smaller than the array size unless there are several that need sorting at once. For example, four lists of 64 elements can be sorted in the same time as one. In the figure that optimistic assumption is made, so that the "effective" time to sort a list of 64 elements in vertical form is recorded as one quarter of the actual effort, and similarly for other lists of 128 elements or less in vertical form.

(5)   It turns out that the horizontal routing distance is not a major contributor to total time. In greater detail, for lists of 256 elements we have the situation given in Table 10.3. The saving in *BatC* is mainly due to instruction and memory accesses associated with horizontal routing.

(6)   It might be asked how the planar results given in Fig. 10.9 would be affected by using longer lists or a larger PE array. In moving to a list of 1024 elements on AMA5, for example, it can be seen that the number of parallel comparisons goes up from 36 to 55, and in vertical mode the routing distance will quadruple. Applying those ratios to the figures

Table 10.3

	Vertical		Horizontal	
	Bat V	Shuffled index	*BatC*	*BatR*
Instructions	11 100	11 200	19 450	30 150
Memory access	7 012	7 108	8 448	13 550
Distance moved	3 804	3 285	1 261	3 313
Total	21 916	21 593	29 159	47 013
% Move	17	15	4	7

for *Bat V* in Table 10.3 gives a "time" measure of

$$(11\ 100 + 7012) * \frac{55}{36} + 3804 * 4 = 42\ 887 \text{ units.}$$

If the same sort calculation is done on AMA4 the smaller array has to work roughly four times as hard to imitate the larger one, although the routing distance is reduced.

(7) Examination of sorting illustrates the wide variation in performance due to choice of algorithm. Careless analysis would have enabled claims to be made of "performance improvement" due to array functions of anything from 2.5:1 to 75:1. Such effects occur in many problems and might suggest that attempting to translate the *same* algorithm from serial to parallel form is far from being the most effective strategy.

Evidently there are many applications of the AMA to sorting both large and small data sets, and as for sequential machines the eventual choice of algorithm depends on the characteristics of the data and the way they are used. Before leaving this topic it is as well to recall that the need for sorting must be reviewed at the system analysis level. It has been stressed in the past because of the limitations of sequential search methods, but given that an AMA can search N items in parallel there may be no point in retaining data sets of less than N items in sorted form: they can be accessed in any order using the *maxel()* function or some variation thereof. The last comment is particularly relevant where there are multiple keys and the retrieval criterion is a logical or arithmetic function of the keys. An AMA6 would carry out useful searching operations at a rate exceeding 10^{10} bits/second, which is probably one of its most cost-effective application areas.

10.3 MATRIX OPERATIONS

Matrices are stored in either horizontal or vertical mode: AMA4 can process an integer matrix of 16 columns in horizontal form, the local store providing the second dimension; it can process a 16*16 matrix in vertical form, of variable precision. Larger matrices can be handled by partitioning, but as the resulting algorithm is often expressed in terms of operations on submatrices that it usually best done by creating structures of three or more dimensions, the local memory providing the third and higher dimensions. AMA4.2 would contain up to 64 matrices of 16*16 elements in single-precision (32-bit) form. The procedures for combining matrices and vectors term-by-term were outlined in Section 9.3. In this subsection we present some common techniques involving both routing and arithmetic operations. As for sorting techniques, the algorithms are applicable to both horizontal and vertical data with suitable interpretation of routing procedures. In general, horizontal form is attractive in "vectorial" problems of fairly low precision (up to 2^n elements in AMAn) or where frequent scalar operations are implied. Although the processing rate in either mode is theoretically about the same (with suitable arrangements for carry), vertical mode offers variable precision and indexing flexibility that has no counterpart for horizontal data.

One of the disadvantages of single-bit PEs in comparison with array processors such as Illiac IV is that it is uneconomical to provide local store indexing, but that can be offset by use of masking and projection operations, as explained below. We are accustomed to thinking of subsets of matrix or vector elements as defined by lists of indices. For example, if V is a vector of numerical data and I is a list of indices, the typical processing loop in register transfer form would be:

$$\ldots; do \quad \{ \ function \ (V'(I.) \ ); \ I' 1 \ \} \ while \ VA; \ldots$$

where *function* is the transformation applied to each element of V that is specified by I. Literally translating such statements into parallel form is generally unattractive, and the so-called "vectorizing" compilers can only recognize special cases of I (typically equal-spaced indices generated in "*DO*" loops). In the present context we attempt to avoid that line of analysis completely by adopting a decoded representation of I which takes the form of a Boolean matrix or mask. Let i be the mask with a 1 in positions corresponding to the indices in I, and 0 elsewhere. Then the above statement would take the form:

$$\ldots; @ \ mask \ i; \ parfunction \ (V); \ldots$$

where *parfunction* performs the required transformation on each element of the argument vector in parallel, writing the result to store only under the preset mask. The "art" of problem analysis consists in part of controlling the flow of calculation with the help of computed masks: enthusiasts would argue that far from making programming more difficult, the direct correspondence between the masks and the data is an aid to analysis, avoiding somewhat artifical mapping in terms of indices. Here, and in the next two chapters, we shall give examples that should help the reader to form an opinion on that fairly controversial topic.

A *projection* operation is one in which an array of dimension $D+1$ is created by reiterating the elements of an array of dimension D. Thus a matrix can be created by projecting a vector either "by row" or "by column". We have already met operations in which a scalar value is projected (from the control unit) to form a vector of identical elements. An important special case is encountered when the source array is itself a "section" of an array of higher dimension: for example, an element of a vector which is projected to form a new vector, or a row (column) of a matrix projected to form a new matrix. In the latter case it is possible to select the source vector by a mask, which allows not only a row or column to be projected, but *any* selection which specifies just one element from each row (column). In the following example a vector from the source matrix b, stored in vertical form, is projected by row into the destination a, assuming the planar mask register is preset.

Example 10.1 Project by row from matrix b to a, assuming the mask register selects one element in each row: if none, a "1" is projected in each plane; if more than one, the "and" of the corresponding bits of b is projected

```
rowp (a,b): /* register wk assumed to point to workplanes */
    save [x];
    do { wk =. −1; @ load b'; @ stm wk; x = wk.;
         a =. x; a' 1
       } while VA;
    unsave [x];return(a)
```

Analogous procedures can be defined for column projection ($colp(a,b)$), and an "orthogonal" pair in which the vector is selected by row and projected by column or vice versa.

Using the above operations it is possible to express matrix multiplication in "outer-product" form. Recall that for two matrices a and b the (i,j)th element of the product c is:

$$c_{i,j} = \sum_k a_{i,k} * b_{k,j}$$

and that each term of the sum can be obtained by term-by-term multiplication of the two matrices:

$$\begin{bmatrix} a_{0,k} & a_{0,k} & a_{0,k} & \cdots \\ a_{1,k} & a_{1,k} & a_{1,k} & \cdots \\ a_{2,k} & a_{2,k} & a_{2,k} & \cdots \\ \cdots & & & \end{bmatrix} \quad \text{and} \quad \begin{bmatrix} b_{k,0} & b_{k,1} & b_{k,2} & \cdots \\ b_{k,0} & b_{k,1} & b_{k,2} & \cdots \\ b_{k,0} & b_{k,1} & b_{k,2} & \cdots \\ \cdots & & & \end{bmatrix}$$

The first matrix is the row projection of the kth column of a, and the second is the column projection of the kth row of b. For square matrices conforming to the dimension of the AMA the result is formed in a single loop as shown in the next example for integer elements. Using the generalized addition procedure $addv()$ allows the two arguments to be of unequal precision.

Example 10.2   Matrix multiplication a times b. Assume the following register declaration:

```
        REGS  [  wk                    | workplanes
                 c                      | result matrix, same
                                        | precision as a
                 x                      | temporary matrix, same
                                        | precision as a
                 y                      | temporary matrix, same
                                        | precision as b
                 z   t   ]              | numeric mask-generators
matmul(a,b):             z = 1; t = $8000;  /* masks aligned for
                                        column and row selection */
                   do   {
                        wk = bycol t; @ mask wk; rowp(x,a);
                        wk = . z; @ mask wk; colp(y,b);
        /* Add the product of x and y into c */
                        save [y c];
                        do   { @ mask y; addv(c,x);
                               c' 1; y' 1
                             } while VA;
                        unsave [c y];
                        t ≫ 1 mask 15; z ≪ 1
                        } while NZ;
                   return
```

For matrix inversion and the solution of simultaneous sets of equations there are a number of efficient parallel algorithms, one of which is given in Chapter 12. The standard pivoting operation provides another example of projection.

If the equations satisfy suitable convergence criteria, iterative methods of solution are amongst the easiest to apply. We shall consider the important special case of tridiagonal sets of equations, showing how the algorithm might be expressed to make the best use of PEs in an active memory array. The problem is to solve for x the set of equations:

$$A \times x = y \tag{1}$$

where A is an $N * N$ matrix, x and y are N-element vectors, and the only non-zero elements of A are in its leading diagonal and subdiagonals. We shall assume for simplicity that the diagonal elements are all 1 (and in practice the subdiagonals are usually less than 1). Then the complete set of equations can be represented by three vectors, L, U and y, where L and U are defined by the sub-and superdiagonals respectively in Fig. 10.10.

$$
A = \begin{bmatrix}
1 & u_0 & 0 & 0 & \cdot & \cdot & \cdot & \cdot \\
l_1 & 1 & u_1 & 0 & \cdot & \cdot & \cdot & \cdot \\
0 & l_2 & 1 & u_2 & \cdot & \cdot & \cdot & \cdot \\
0 & 0 & l_3 & 1 & \cdot & \cdot & \cdot & \cdot \\
\cdot & \cdot & \cdot & \cdot & \cdot & \cdot & \cdot & \cdot \\
\cdot & \cdot & \cdot & \cdot & l_{N-3} & 1 & u_{N-3} & 0 \\
\cdot & \cdot & \cdot & \cdot & 0 & l_{N-2} & 1 & u_{N-2} \\
\cdot & \cdot & \cdot & \cdot & 0 & 0 & l_{N-1} & 1
\end{bmatrix}
$$

$$l_0 = u_{N-1} = 0$$

Fig. 10.10

A sequential method of solution might start by eliminating x_0 using the first equation, continue by eliminating x_1, x_2 and so on until x_{N-1} is found, from which the remaining elements of x can be found by back-substitution. It can readily be seen that the start of any step in the calculation has to be delayed until completion of the previous one, so it is not suitable for parallel or even vector application in which multistage pipelines are used. Parallel solutions depend on simultaneous operation on several sets of equations, which can be seen by considering three consecutive equations from (1):

$$
\begin{aligned}
l_{i-1} * x_{i-2} + x_{i-1} + u_{i-1} * x_i &= y_{i-1} \\
l_i * x_{i-1} + x_i + u_i * x_{i+1} &= y_i \\
l_{i+1} * x_i + x_{i+1} + u_{i+1} * x_{i+2} &= y_{i+1}
\end{aligned} \tag{2}
$$

By multiplying the first by l_i and subtracting from the second, and multiplying the third by u_i and subtracting from the second it is possible to eliminate x_{i-1} and x_{i+1} from the second equation to give:

$$\hat{l}_i * x_{i-2} + x_i + \hat{u}_i * x_{i+2} = \hat{y}_i \tag{3}$$

where

$$\hat{d}_i = 1 - l_i * u_{i-1} - u_i * l_{i+1}$$
$$\hat{l}_i = -l_i * l_{i-1}/\hat{d}_i$$
$$\hat{u}_i = -u_i * u_{i+1}/\hat{d}_i$$
$$\hat{y}_i = (y_i - l_i * y_{i-1} - u_i * y_{i+1})/\hat{d}_i$$

The reduction from (2) to (3) is exploited in either of two ways, depending on the routing ability of the computer system:

(a)   In *cyclic reduction* the "even" equations are used to eliminate even components of x from the "odd" equations, giving a new tridiagonal system involving only x_1, x_3, x_5, etc., so that, starting with 255 equations, successive systems of 127, 63, ..., 3 and 1 equation would be formed. Solving the last equation enables the preceding 3, 5, 7, ..., 255 equations to be solved by back-substitution.

(b)   In *iterative* solution the reduction is applied simultaneously to all equations (with suitable adjustment for the first and last equations) to give a new system of the *same* dimension but with coefficients of $\hat{A}$ one removed from the diagonal (Fig. 10.11). A reduction similar to (3) is then applied to all equations distant 2, then 4, etc., until after at most $\log_2 N$ steps all off-diagonal elements have been eliminated or reduced to negligible size, and the final $\hat{y}$ gives the required solution.

$$\hat{A} = \begin{bmatrix} 1 & 0 & \hat{u}_1 & 0 & 0 & . & & . \\ 0 & 1 & 0 & \hat{u}_2 & 0 & . & & . \\ \hat{l}_3 & 0 & 1 & 0 & \hat{u}_3 & . & & . \\ 0 & \hat{l}_4 & 0 & 1 & 0 & . & & . \\ . & . & . & . & . & . & & . \end{bmatrix}$$

Fig. 10.11

Which is the better method for array computers? In terms of arithmetic operations (M = multiply; D = divide; A = add/subtract);

(a)   requires $6M$ + $3D$ + $4A$ for reduction from (2) to (3)
             plus $\underline{2M \hspace{3em} + \hspace{1em} 2A}$ for back-substitution
            giving $8M$ + $3D$ + $6A$ for each stage.

But because the number of equations in the system is halved at each stage the total arithmetic is approximately:

$$2N * (8M + 3D + 6A)$$

(b)   requires $6M + 3D + 3A$ for reduction, and at each stage N equations are reduced, giving approximately:

$$N * \log_2 N * (6M + 3D + 4A)$$

arithmetic operations.

In a vector machine such as AP-120B or CRAY-1 one would probably choose (a), depending on storage requirements, but it can be seen that for an array processor the amount of parallelism is reduced at each stage, and the number of computing steps for N PEs and N equations is $\log_2 N$ for both reduction *and* back-substitution. For that reason (b) is in general a more efficient method.

Is there a compromise between (a) and (b)? As usual, the answer depends on the number of equations, the number of PEs, and overhead factors we have not taken into account. If there are more equations than PEs then reduction is worthwhile — in fact it is worth reducing the number of equations to half the number of PEs, then shortening the calculation time by splitting four between two PEs for each equation.

10.4 FURTHER READING

Generalized multiplication and division algorithms are described in CHE72 and MEG62.

For discussion of sorting in general see KNU73, which deals in part with parallel algorithms. The key paper, from which many algorithms derive, is BAT68. Batcher describes sorting applications in terms of *comparison elements* which are devices with two inputs and two outputs, for which one of the outputs is the minimum of the inputs, and the other is the maximum (see diagram). When operating in serial mode, if inputs are presented most-significant digit first, the element can determine the maximum and transmit

input A ⟶ ▭ ⟶ MIN(A,B)
input B ⟶ ▭ ⟶ MAX(A,B)   Comparison element

the digits either directly or interchanged with a single-bit delay. Such a comparator is essentially a three-state device ("don't know", "A is max", "B is max"), and cannot be imitated exactly by the PEs used in AMA design, for which the input values have to be compared and then exchanged in a separate operation. Of course, if it is known in advance what the outcome of comparison will be, then the "state" can be set (by loading the activity plane, for example). In other words, a *particular* permutation can be thought of as the result of tagging the elements of a list with index values marking their final destination and then sorting using the tags as keys. But if we remember the results of the comparisons (as Boolean planes), the next time the *same* permutation is required it is only necessary to reload the planes. It might be possible to find shortcuts by examining the planes associated with a particular permutation.

Much attention has been given to the basic routing algorithms which are critical in sorting and other applications. In Chapter 9 it was seen that some important permutations (power-of-two exchange, shuffle) can be thought of as the results of operating on the binary index of each element in the array. Inversion of single bits, and exchange of pairs of bits were used as examples. The perfect shuffle was expressed as a sequence of adjacent bit exchanges which had the effect of rotating the index of each element in a vector to find its final destination. For example, if the elements of a 16-element vector have binary indices *ijkl*, the application of *shuff* produces the final result *jkli* in three steps:

$$\begin{array}{ccccccc} & shuff(p,2) & & shuff(p,1) & & shuff(p,0) & \\ ijkl & \longrightarrow & jikl & \longrightarrow & jkil & \longrightarrow & jkli \end{array}$$

Treating permutations as functions of the binary digits of the index provides a way of thinking about routing in which similarities and optimizations can easily be visualized. That point of view is clearly expressed by Stone in STO71, in which the application of perfect shuffle as a primitive routing operation in sorting, matrix transposition and Fourier transformation is pointed out.

The *rotate* function (p. 194) can also be expressed as an index transformation. Recall that the position of any bit in a cuboid is represented by the three coordinates t (plane), r (row) and c (column) forming in AMA4 the 15-bit index (t,r,c). Denoting the inversion of bits in a field by underlining, the transformation of index:

$$(t,r,c) \longrightarrow (t,\underline{r},c)$$

can be seen to reverse the rows of the array seen in matrix form from above. Similarly, transposition in the bit plane (row and column interchange) is expressed as:

$$(t,r,c) \longrightarrow (t,c,r)$$

Note that in these examples the plane coordinate is unaffected and the same transformation takes place in each plane.

Now suppose that t is a 4-bit field (so the cuboid has 16 planes). The effect of:

$$(t,r,c) \longrightarrow (r,t,c) \qquad\qquad \text{"}rotate()\text{"}$$

is to transpose the cube (Fig. 9.9) about the diagonal plane $IJJ'I'$. A "solid" rotation through angle $\pi/2$ would be derived from:

$$(t,r,c) \longrightarrow (r,\underline{t},c)$$

From the above discussion it follows that we may define a procedure *rot(t,n)* which has the effect (in AMA4) of interchanging the nth and $(n+4)$th bits in the index of each element in the plane sequence t. By analogy with shuffle operations, *rot* might be called an "imperfect rotation". Then the perfect rotation of Fig. 9.10 can be expressed as:

> *rotate* (*a,b*):   *copy* (*a,b*); *save* [z]; $z = 7$;
> *do* { *rot*(*a,z*); $z - 1$ } *while* ($z > 3$);
> *unsave* [z]; *return* (*a*)

which is generally faster than the method given in Chapter 9, being proportional to the logarithm of the side of the array rather than its length.

Implementation of the basic operations of bit inversion and exchange on a rectangular array is presented in NAS80. Exchange of index bits in different "dimensions" gives rise to some interesting programming problems, and the "cost" of a particular transformation depends on the sequence of exchanges or inversions chosen. Flanders (FLA80) has developed a macrogenerator for the ICL DAP that produces code for any sequence of exchanges and inversions in three dimensions with some optimization of pairs of operations.

For further references on sorting, see NAS79, THO77, LAN76 and BAU75. But take care! From the computer design point of view the critical questions are how often sorting takes place, in what context, and how the data are to be used.

Parallel solution of tridiagonal systems is presented in JOR75 and STO73. The method described in this chapter is numerically unstable. A detailed discussion of parallel techniques for solving linear systems of equations will be found in SAM78.

11 IMAGE ENHANCEMENT FUNCTIONS

A class of applications which can be mapped readily into an active memory array is that arising from manipulation of two-dimensional images. The low precision of data, close correspondence between picture geometry and PEs, and frequent use of Boolean matrices to select fields of interest in the image positively suggest the vertical data structures already described, and the importance attaching to the application area has inspired some of the earliest experiments in array-processor design. In this chapter we examine some typical algorithms for manipulating digitized images and see how PE functions can evolve to give them specialized support.

The process of digitizing a picture usually involves sampling its brightness and perhaps color over a regularly spaced set of points referred to as *pixels* (short for "picture elements"). The scale of measurement depends on the application and will range from simple black and white up to 30 or more intensity levels, coded as 5- or 6-bit integers. Thus the store requirement for a pixel ranges from 1 bit to about 20 for good-quality color representation. The number of elements is also widely variable, from about 20 * 20 for low resolution, which might suit a small repertoire of objects such as single characters of low print quality, to 1000 * 1000 or more for graphic display purposes.

It is attractive to map pixels directly onto PEs, but there are two problems to overcome. Firstly, the AMA will often be smaller in both dimensions than practical picture sizes, but from earlier discussion it will be recalled that the methods of partitioning into subarrays by straight cuts or by crimping are applicable. An alternative approach is to treat the AMA as a linear structure with store providing the second dimension. The options are illustrated in Fig. 11.1 for a picture size of 16 * 16 pixels mapped onto a 4 * 4 array, and the mappings extend directly to larger arrays. Note that AMA4.2 would have storage capacity for just one 256 * 256 image allowing 8 bits for each pixel, or eight black-and-white images of that size. Whichever method is

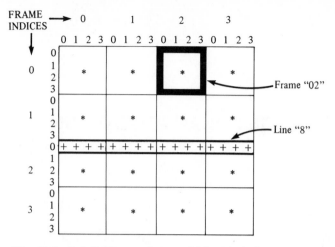

Fig. 11.1 Subdividing an image of 16 * 16 pixels on AMA2: (a) 16 frames of 4 * 4 pixels; (b) 16 grids spaced 4 pixels apart (marked as *); or (c) 16 lines of 16 pixels (marked as +)

chosen leads to some complication in programming and loss of performance in dealing with edge effects, though quantifying the loss depends on the type of algorithm and connectivity of interest. For simplicity, we shall begin by assuming that the PE array is in fact large enough to accommodate the entire image.

The second problem in mapping is that the sample points are often in hexagonal rather than square pattern (Fig. 11.2) and therefore have six equidistant near-neighbors (marked with suffices 1 2 3 4 5 6 in Fig. 11.2(a)). In mapping onto a rectangular array of PEs the neighbors are as shown in Fig. 11.2(b), which indicates that the routing paths are different for even and odd rows, i.e.:

	even	odd
1 becomes	E	E
2	N	NE
3	NW	N
4	W	W
5	SW	S
6	S	SE

It follows that any interactions with neighbors 2, 3, 5, 6 must be programmed separately for even and odd rows. Here again, anticipating the more specialized image processor designs, we shall simplify the examples by assuming a square raster pattern.

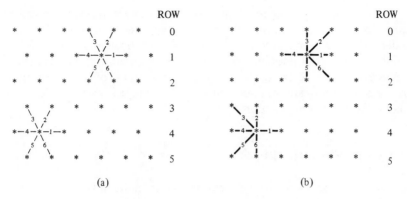

Fig. 11.2 Mapping a hexagonal pattern onto a rectangular grid: (a) hexagonal array of pixels; (b) square array of processing elements

Image-processing applications can be subdivided under two main headings:

(1) *digital picture coding*, in which the main concern is with the transmission of images in the most economical way consistent with the quality expected at the receiving end. The search for correlations between pixels, either in space or time (in dealing with moving pictures) leads to two-dimensional variants of a range of vector transforms, one of which (the Fourier transform) we shall return to in the next chapter.

(2) *image enhancement*, in which "visually improved" images are derived, making use of prior knowledge of the subject matter and the imaging process.

Both areas are of immense practical importance, but the form of computation implied by (1) is less distinctive than (2), which is the main subject of this chapter. We shall see that in certain situations very high processing rates can be achieved by array computers, but it is well to be reminded that cost and other factors play a larger part than usual in the acceptability of solutions. That is most obvious when peripheral constraints are taken into account: installing an image processor in an orbiting satellite, in a domestic television receiver, or on a production line is not the same as solving the same problem in a few milliseconds in AMA6. It can also be seen that image enhancement, if viewed as a preliminary step in feature extraction, scene analysis and recognition, is part of a much more difficult problem that might not be amenable to parallel solution. However, the primitive level of functions and the ability to switch between planar and scalar processing without time penalty make the AMA a suitable starting point for experimental work.

In the next three subsections some basic image transformations are introduced, broadly classified by type of computation involved. It will be understood that practical source data can derive from a huge range of applications, from aerial photographs to biological specimens, physical events, mechanical components, signatures, fingerprints, and so on, and the examples are chosen to illustrate common computing techniques which would require adaptation in each application area.

11.1 AREA FUNCTIONS

In this subsection we consider functions that are uniformly applicable to an entire image, and which consequently achieve a very high degree of parallelism. They arise in two ways:

(a)   As data-independent transformations of the image, to make allowance for irregularities in the process of forming it. These would include correction for distortion due to angle of view, curvature of object, relative motion of object and image during exposure. Also in this category are operations on the intensity levels to correct for non-uniform quantization, irregular illumination across the scene, and attempts to produce better visual effects by artificial recalibration of the intensity scale. Thirdly, there are calculations resulting from change of grid, e.g. in changing from square to hexagonal sampling points, or in aligning repeated exposures of the same scene. By no means all of the above operations lead to highly parallel algorithms. In particular, if a coordinate transformation is involved, for example from "true" sampling points (x,y) to "measured" (X, Y) given by:

$$\begin{aligned} X &= H(x,y) \\ Y &= G(x,y) \end{aligned} \tag{1}$$

then finding the intensity at a given $(x,y) = (\hat{x},\hat{y})$ entails finding the square of the measured grid in which $(\hat{x},\hat{y})$ falls (Fig. 11.3) and

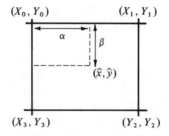

Fig. 11.3

interpolating the measured values $f(X, Y)$ (assuming unit measured square):

$$f(\hat{x},\hat{y}) = (1 - \alpha - \beta + \alpha\beta)f_0 + \alpha(1 - \beta)f_1 + \beta(1 - \alpha)f_3 + \alpha\beta f_2 \quad (2)$$

where $\alpha = \hat{x} - X_0$
$\beta = \hat{y} - Y_0$
and $f_i = f(X_i, Y_i)$, $i = 0,1,2,3$

The evaluation of (2) is not difficult, particularly if H and G are linear in x and y, enabling α and β to be found fairly easily. However, the general problem of finding X_0 and Y_0 is not always straightforward. An alternative approach would be to process the image with reference to the measured grid and to apply corrections when coordinates are extracted (see Section 11.3).

(b) As data-dependent functions based on the supposition that the field of view is composed mainly from a few areas of uniform color and intensity with a uniform "background". The requirement is then to identify the main areas for later analysis. The results of such operations are sets of characteristic or Boolean images, masking pixels belonging to the separated areas. We shall examine the computing procedures involved.

Let $f(i,j)$ measure the gray level intensity at the point (i,j) of an image. The commonest way of detecting areas of uniform intensity is by *thresholding*, i.e. deriving the mask M given two intensity levels t and u, where

$$M(i,j) \quad = \quad \begin{cases} 1 \text{ where } t < f(i,j) < u \\ 0 \text{ elsewhere} \end{cases} \quad (3)$$

M can be found with two parallel comparisons and a logical "and" over the image, with no edge degradation.

However, it might be desirable first to *smooth* the image to eliminate unwanted noise. That is relatively easy when noise appears as isolated points or (in the case of TV-type images) lines. For example, we might compare $f(i,j)$ with each of its neighbors and if it differs substantially from most of them conclude that it is a noise point and replace it by the average:

$$f(i,j) = \tfrac{1}{4}(f(i-1, j) + f(i+1, j) \\ + f(i,j-1) + f(i,j+1)) \quad (4)$$

(Remember that only two parallel additions are required, but extra processing time must be allowed at the edges of the AMA array!). In both line and point smoothing several parameters must be adjusted experimentally to produce the best effect: the extent of the neighborhood set, the threshold at which "substantial" difference of intensity is recognized, the number of points constituting "most". In black-and-white pictures averaging is inappropriate and we would attempt to find isolate black or white pixels and invert them.

An undesirable effect of smoothing is to blur genuine discontinuities such as lines or edges in the picture, and it might be preferred to look for such features initially, then to restrict averaging or gap-filling to supposed interior or background regions. *Edge-detection* functions are examined in the next subsection.

In general, the threshold limits t and u are not known in advance, and without specific knowledge of the scene it is difficult to make guesses. An empirical approach is to form the histogram of $f(i,j)$, i.e. to plot the number of pixels in the entire image at each intensity level, and to take the "peaks" as indicators of major background or object areas (Fig. 11.4). Forming a mask showing pixels at a given intensity level is trivial. Summing the bits in a mask to give frequency is one of the logarithmic procedures already encountered (Chapter 9, Exercise 16). In the AMA4 plane a direct approach is to add neighbors distant 8E, then add the partial results 8S, 4E, 4S, ... E, S, ending up with the sum in PE_0: at each stage the number of usefully active PEs is halved, while the precision of the intermediate result increases from 2 to 9 bits. Various methods have been derived for merging the summation for several planes, and for returning the results in horizontal rather than vertical form. Analysis of the histogram involves forming in parallel a numerical estimate of its first and second derivatives, in which maxima and thresholds can be detected. Application of (3) then gives masks identifying major clusters of pixels in the original image. One would hope, as a result of the smoothing procedure, that they would be contiguous, but the histogram method does not guarantee that.

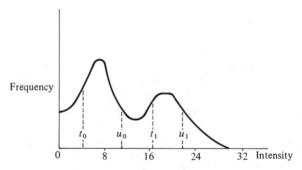

Fig. 11.4   Intensity histogram

Picking out separate clusters from a given mask M involves finding one marked pixel (how would you do that?) and forcing it to "grow" one pixel at a time in each direction provided it intersects the masked region (Fig. 11.5). This is an important type of operation, applicable to both areas and lines, which we refer to as *seeding*. The final result depends on whether the growth occurs in four or eight directions — it would affect whether a 1 at a point

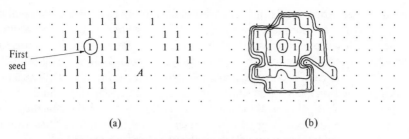

Fig. 11.5 Detecting contiguous regions by seeding: (a) initial mask; (b) successive seeded masks

such as *A* in Fig. 11.5(a) was included in the final mask or not (we have assumed 8-way growth; a complementary procedure for finding the background mask might use 4-way growth). Note that the second cluster in the diagram is eliminated entirely unless the growth procedure has some way of jumping across gaps: that is unusual in detecting areas, but quite common in tracking lines.

Example 11.1   The following procedure can be used to grow a Boolean mask *p* one step in each of the four near-neighbor directions, under control of a preset mask in the AMA activity plane. The return condition *NZ* is used to signal positive growth.

```
grow4(p):    /∗ assume p is a plane pointer and wk is a predeclared
                plane workspace pointer ∗/
    wk = . 0;
    @ load p; @ move N 1;@ stm wk;
    @ move S 2;@ or wk; @ stm wk;
    @ load p;@ move E 1; @ or wk;@ stm wk;
    @ load p;@ move W 1;@ or wk;@ stm wk;
/∗ Now wk contains the grown mask. Is it bigger than p? ∗/
    @ load p;@ equ wk; @ st wk;
/∗ Now wk contains the growth points (0) and 1 elsewhere ∗/
    @ load p;@ or − wk; @ st p; return(wk. + 1)
```

The application of a seeding procedure is illustrated by Example 11.1 for four-way growth. It is assumed that the initial seed is sown in *p*, after which the growth is controlled as in:

$$...;@ \ mask \ M; \ do \ grow4(p) \ while \ NZ; ...$$

where *M* is the image mask. Having found a cluster such as *p* it can be weighed (bit count again, throw away if not significant) and removed from *M*, repeating the procedure until all separate areas have been detected. Remember that growth can take place "inwards" as well as "outwards": one way of detecting closed boundaries, which we shall use in later examples, is to seed the edge of the picture and then grow the background mask.

Note that each step of the growth procedure takes about 25 register transfer functions, and that the number of steps is roughly equal to the radius of a cluster. If typical radii are in the region of 50−100 pixels the computing time required to segment the image begins to be appreciable: that is one of the applications in which specialized help is sought.

11.2 LINE FUNCTIONS

We now turn attention to "lines" in the image, either closed contours such as the boundaries of areas already detected or tracks with distinct endpoints and intersections. In this context the scope for parallelism is less obvious than for area detection, though the fact that the end product is linear does not preclude the use of parallel operations in eliminating false trails.

One simple way of marking a closed boundary is to grow an area mask by one step and form the logical difference of the result with the original. That would give an "outer" bound. To form the boundary of edge points, one would start with the background mask, grow it one step inwards, forming the logical "and" of the result with the area mask. The length of a boundary, together with the area it encloses, is one measure of shape which might be significant. Both are obtained by applying bit-counting procedures to the appropriate masks.

A more general approach to line detection is to look for abrupt changes in gray level or coloration in the original image, which leads to the identification of edges. The essential feature of such algorithms is enhancement of edge points by computing the derivative of intensity, or some approximation to it, then marking the edges by the thresholding techniques already discussed. A difficulty with edge detection is that spurious discontinuities might arise from the presence of noise and, conversely, true edges might have gaps where the gradient is not high enough to meet the threshold. Consequently the initial masking must be supplemented by *tracking* programs to fill in the gaps, and by *thinning* programs to reduce lines, once detected, to minimal width. We shall give two simple examples of such algorithms.

As before, let $f(x,y)$ be the measured intensity of the image at the point (x,y). Then the derivative of f with respect to x and y is $\sqrt{\{(\partial f/\partial x)^2 + (\partial f/\partial y)^2\}}$, which can be approximated in finite difference terms to varying degrees of accuracy by the formulas:

1	2	3
8	*	4
7	6	5

$$\sqrt{\{(f-f_8)^2 + (f-f_2)^2\}} \qquad (5.1)$$

$$\sqrt{\{((f_1 + 2f_2 + f_3) - (f_7 + 2f_6 + f_5))^2 + ((f_3 + 2f_4 + f_5) - (f_1 + 2f_8 + f_7))^2\}} \qquad (5.2)$$

$$|f-f_8| + |f-f_2| \qquad (5.3)$$

$$\max(|f-f_8|, |f-f_2|) \qquad (5.4)$$

where f denotes the value of the intensity measured at (x,y), and f_i, $i = 1, \ldots, 8$ denote corresponding values at neighboring points as shown in the diagram. The choice of formula depends amongst other things on the computing power available. In all cases the gradient can be evaluated in parallel over the entire image. At the same time it is possible to compute a value at each point for the angle of steepest descent, for which

$$\theta = \tan^{-1}\left\{\frac{\partial f}{\partial y} \div \frac{\partial f}{\partial x}\right\}$$

Under ideal conditions the edge, if any, will run at right angles to θ, and if straight lines are being sought an enhancement technique might be based on the histogram for θ.

If sequential tracking techniques are used the next step will be to identify possible edges by thresholding the derivative, then to find a seed that can be used to identify a line segment. The growth procedure should now be governed by knowledge of θ, or perhaps by prior knowledge of the scene, e.g. in looking for vertical or horizontal lines. It is usual to build in some momentum to carry the tracking procedure across short gaps in the line. In looking for parallel line-tracking procedures, one cannot take advantage of momentum but must look instead for elements within some prescribed distance of one another which can be joined by marking intermediate points in the mask.

The following example of a tracking algorithm can easily be implemented in parallel on a Boolean image M. Intuitively, it can be seen to attempt to fill in gaps in horizontal or vertical line segments, and to 4-connect diagonal segments. It therefore looks for four types of pattern (Fig. 11.6) in which two small neighborhoods are partly occupied, and sufficiently close together to be joined. In the figure, the neigborhoods are marked as A_i, B_i and the rule of transformation is that if at some point C the marked neighborhoods are both partly occupied for some value of i, then a 1 is written into the mask at C. As usual, there is scope for variation in what is meant by "partly occupied", but if that is taken to mean "having at least one bit of the mask" it can be implemented economically by planar "or" operations.

The operation of thinning might be undertaken on a black-and-white image or on edges detected by the above procedures. The intention is to

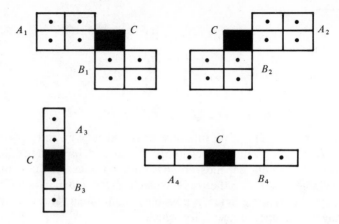

Fig. 11.6 Mask configuration for gap filling

reduce any contiguous region to an 8-way connected figure of the same maximum length as the original, but zero width. Here again, algorithms exist that make use of parallel pattern searches, followed by removal of superfluous mask bits. A set of patterns is given in Fig. 11.7. They are applied in turn to the Boolean mask, each time replacing the central value with zero if the neighbors have the values shown (* means "don't care"). The replacement is carried out in parallel for each mask, and having run through A_1 to B_4 the complete cycle is repeated until there is no change. The register transfer operations for a single mask are illustrated in the next example.

Example 11.2 Apply the thinning mask A_1 to the plane p. Assume that wk is predeclared as a workplane.

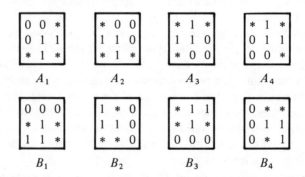

Fig. 11.7 Mask configuration for thinning (From C. Arcelli, L. Cordella and S. Levialdi, "Parallel thinning of binary pictures." *Electronic Letters* **11**, 7 (1975))

*thinA*1(*p*):   @ *load p*;@ *move S* 1;@ *and p*;
                @ *move N* 2;@ *and* −*p*;@ *move W* 1;@ *and* −*p*;
                @ *move S* 1;@ *and* −*p*;@ *move E* 2;@ *and p*;@ *move W* 1;
        /∗ *Now the plane accumulator is* 1 *where the pattern matches, so*
        overwrite p at those points . . . ∗/
                @ *st wk*;@ *mask wk*;@ *load* − *wk*;@ *stm p*;
                return

Here about 20 register transfer operations are required for each mask, 150 for a complete iteration, and the number of iterations will depend on the original width of the lines. Figure 11.8 illustrates the effect of applying the Arcelli−Cordella thinning algorithm to a digitized image.

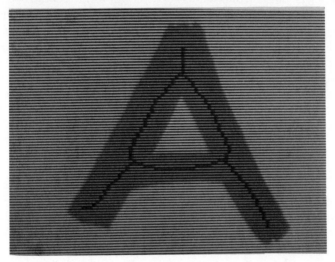

Fig. 11.8   Effect of applying the Arcelli−Cordella thinning algorithm to a digitized image (With acknowledgement to M.J.B. Duff)

11.3 COORDINATE REPRESENTATION

If, as is often the case, segmented Boolean images are insufficient for identification purposes, further algorithms dependent on shape or relative position might be called upon. In some situations it is better to work with the image points in coordinate form rather than using the mask representation. For example, in seeking a "best fit" to a straight line, or in approximating a curve by a series of line segments, or in fitting higher-order curves to experimental edges, the mathematical constraints are most easily expressed in terms of the Euclidean distance from a point to a line or between given points. Conversion from mask to coordinates is a logarithmic procedure for each point, i.e. proportional to the number of bits in the two coordinate values. The output from the conversion will be a vector with a pair of elements for each point: in terms of AMA4 with 256*256 image mask, we can think of the output as a plane sequence with 16 coordinate pairs per plane (frequent use of scalar arithmetic, and relatively low parallelism favor the horizontal form). At that stage, computing requirements fall under the general heading of "vector processing".

So far it has been implicit that procedures under discussion are contributing to the general aim of refining an image presented as input to the computer system. It should also be noted that there is a class of converse problems, of generating an image from an internal description of a scene in two or three dimensions. The resulting procedures are also computation-intensive, particularly if associated with a real-time constraint of generating an image in the refresh time of a television picture — about 20 ms. A number of special-purpose processors and function-boxes have been devised to add power in the right place, but they have not so far taken a form suggesting AMA functions. The extent to which the latter can help in such procedures as clipping, shading, hidden line and area removal, and manipulation of bit-map displays is an open research question.

11.4 IMAGE PROCESSOR DESIGN

In the preceding subsections we have outlined a range of problems likely to be encountered in one branch of digitized picture processing. Some are already well served by AMA functions. Others are inherently unsuitable for parallel solution. There remains an important subset of operations which, within practical cost and time constraints, seems to benefit from special adaptation of the processing elements. We now describe such adaptations, with special reference to the Cellular Logic Information Processors developed at University College, London University.

To begin with technology-driven common features, we still assume a simple PE design with 1-bit data paths and registers, able to execute elementary arithmetic and logical functions. Each PE has local storage sufficient for one or more pixels and characteristic workplanes, the method of addressing being such that a complete plane can be presented to the function unit, or stored, in one parallel machine cycle. There is a single control processor broadcasting instructions to the array, with limited conditional and scalar capabilities, and able to read or write data along common data lines.

Image processor design begins to specialize when taking account of:

(1)   the need for a relatively large number of processors to achieve adequate

resolution over images of practical interest without being degraded by edge effects;

(2)   the frequent use of "seeding" operations in line and area detection, which are fairly laborious to execute on the AMA, as we have seen;

(3)   thresholding operations in which the action of a PE depends on a combination of values in a subset of neighbors;

(4)   experimental or operational requirements for interaction with I–O devices and response to advice or query from users.

The design objective is to reach a satisfactory balance between these special requirements and the performance/cost offered by current technology.

CLIP-3 was an early experimental array of $16 * 12$ PEs, specialized to the type of transformation just described. Each PE has two single-bit working registers A and B, an output N and 16 bits of local storage, D (Fig. 11.9(a)). The array interconnection pattern is either square (8-way) or hexagonal (6-way connection) at internal points. The edge inputs can be set to 1 or 0 as required. There are three types of array instructions:

LOAD: Initialize A and B, using the local store or "zero" as input.

PROCESS: Apply a transformation rule using the inputs N until there is no change in N throughout the array. Any of the neighbor connections can be selected and summed, then compared with a threshold value t supplied in the instruction. The PE input T is set to 1 if the sum exceeds the threshold, else zero. The value of N is $\Phi_1 (B \vee T, A)$ where Φ_1 is one of the 16 Boolean functions of two variables. The PROCESS instruction also selects edge inputs and specifies the neighbor connections.

STORE: A second Boolean function $\Phi_2 (B \vee T, A)$ is evaluated and the result written to a local store plane D_i or combined with the current value of D_i by "and" or "or" operation.

In addition to the above instructions the array controller can execute basic control instructions, including conditional branch on the "and" of all N outputs taken over the 192 PEs. The control memory is separate from the PE local stores. Provision is made to display the A and B planes on a CRT so that the effect of different algorithms can be observed experimentally. The essential difference between CLIP and AMA functions is the arrangement for signals to propagate through the array in all directions during the PROCESS instruction. The propagation delay is data-dependent and termination is sensed by the controller. The following example shows how that property can be used to detect segments in a Boolean mask, and should be compared with the AMA procedure for the growth function (Example 11.1). The notation has been chosen to give the style of operation rather than detailed instruction formats (in practice the STORE instruction is combined with

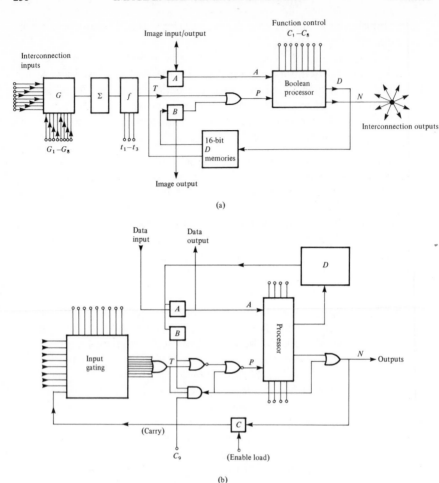

Fig. 11.9   Processing element schematics for CLIP designs: (a) CLIP-3; (b) CLIP-4 (With acknowledgement to M.J.B. Duff)

PROCESS). Figure 11.10 shows the working result obtained after each STORE operation.

Example 11.3   Given an image mask from a biological cell pattern, it is required to select the outlines of all cells wholly within the picture and containing nuclei. Hexagonal connection is assumed throughout, with all six inputs active and threshold zero. In the symbolic description IMAGE, OUTPUT, etc. refer to bit planes in the local store D.

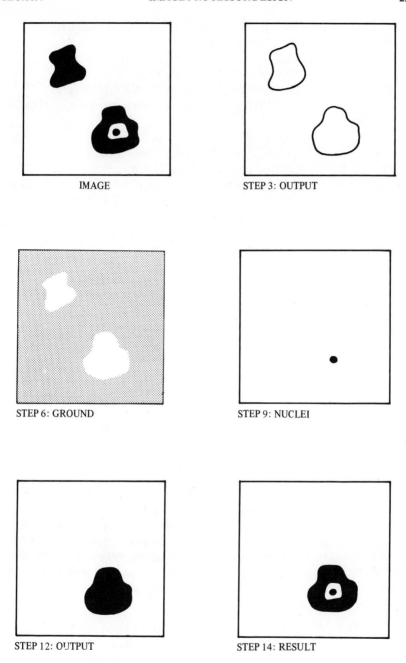

IMAGE

STEP 3: OUTPUT

STEP 6: GROUND

STEP 9: NUCLEI

STEP 12: OUTPUT

STEP 14: RESULT

Fig. 11.10 Working masks formed during Example 11.3

/* Form in OUTPUT the outer edges of the objects in IMAGE */
STEP 1: LOAD A = IMAGE; B = 0;
    2: PROCESS N = (B ∨ T) ∧ $\overline{A}$; Edge input 1;
    3: STORE OUTPUT = (B ∨ T) ∧ A;
/* (refer to Fig. 11.10 for the form of OUTPUT after Step 3)
Now form in GROUND the background mask surrounding IMAGE
objects */
    4: LOAD A = IMAGE; B = 0;
    5: PROCESS N = (B ∨ T) ∧ $\overline{A}$; Edge input 1;
    6: STORE GROUND = (B ∨ T) ∧ $\overline{A}$;
/* Form in NUCLEI the cell nuclei. Propagation starts from the outer
edge in OUTPUT, through 1-valued cells in IMAGE */
    7: LOAD A = IMAGE; B = OUTPUT;
    8: PROCESS N = (B ∨ T) ∧ A; Edge input 0;
    9: STORE NUCLEI = $(\overline{B ∨ T})$ ∧ A;
/* Form in OUTPUT the masks of cells with a nucleus */
    10: LOAD A = GROUND; B = NUCLEI;
    11: PROCESS N = (B ∨ T) ∧ $\overline{A}$; Edge input 0;
    12: STORE OUTPUT = (B ∨ T) ∧ $\overline{A}$;
/* Form in RESULT the nucleated objects */
    13: LOAD A = OUTPUT; B = IMAGE;
    14: STORE RESULT = (B ∨ T) ∧ A

CLIP-4 is an LSI development of CLIP-3 (Fig. 11.9(b)), in which some minor changes have been made to the PE design, including better facilities for vertical arithmetic (carry register C) and replacement of the summation and thresholding logic with a simpler logical "or" of selected inputs. Using NMOS technology eight processors and their local memories (32 bits each) are placed on a single 40-pin integrated-circuit package, and the full array extends to 96*96 elements. The move from TTL circuits in CLIP-3 to MOS in CLIP-4 entails a significant loss of speed, and the time for a LOAD–PROCESS pair is about 25 μs plus 3 μs for cell-to-cell propagation; e.g. growing an area mask of radius 40 cells would take about 150 μs, while the corresponding operation in AMA register transfers would take 40 * 25 = 1000 machine cycles (still ignoring edge effects) or about 200 μs. That shows the clear advantage of the signal propagation. If there is no propagation the comparison is reversed, as the next example shows.

Example 11.4 It is required to apply the thinning mask of A_1 of Fig.
Neighbors: 11.7 to a given Boolean IMAGE plane, as in Example
1 2 3 11.2. Here the neighbor connections are selected by the
8 * 4 PROCESS instruction, e.g. "(128)" means input from
7 6 5 neighbors 1, 2 and 8 as identified in the diagram.

Mask A_1:

0	0	*
0	1	1
*	1	*

$thinA1(IMAGE)$: $LOAD\ A\ =\ IMAGE$; $B\ =\ 0$;
$PROCESS$ (128); $N\ =\ A$; $Square$;
$STORE\ TEMP\ =\ (B \lor T) \land \overline{A}$;
$LOAD\ A\ =\ IMAGE$; $B\ =\ TEMP$;
$PROCESS$ (46); $N\ =\ \overline{A}$; $Square$;
$STORE\ IMAGE\ =\ (B \lor T) \land A$

In Example 11.4 no propagation is involved and the instruction time (about 50 μs) for each mask is rather longer than the time for 20 register transfer operations. Hence any assessment of the effectiveness of the CLIP design must take into account some estimate of the proportion of time spent in mask generation as opposed to arithmetic and logic.

11.5 FURTHER READING

Most proposals for digital image processing derive from original suggestions of S.H. Unger for an array of bit-organized PEs with four near-neighbor connections and (typically) six bits of local storage each. The original publication (UNG58) gives details of an instruction set that includes propagation functions, and develops some worked examples. It is worth reading and quoting:

> (*after showing that such a machine would have tens of thousands of gates*) "... These are alarming figures, and it would probably be difficult to find applications that would justify the costs involved if individual devices had to be employed for each element. However, ... progress in the components field is such that it is reasonable to hope that within a few years we may have available manufacturing processes whereby entire blocks of logical circuitry could be constructed in one unit."

That time has come but, it must be admitted, the problems of knowing how best to process the data during and after enhancement are still with us. In that connection, the best computer design policy seems to be to aim for the greatest generality of function on both scalar and planar data. Apart from the CLIP machines (DUF**), the Illiac III pattern-recognition computer (MCC63) followed a similar line of development before its sudden end.

Basic algorithms for image enhancement are described in HAL79, GON77 and ROS76, and at a more detailed mathematical level in AND77, which also contains an extensive bibliography. Surveys of current literature appear from time to time in specialized journals, for example see *Computer Graphics and Image Processing* (Academic Press), **13**(1) (May 1980).

The serial nature of data produced by raster-scan techniques has resulted in proposals for serially organized processors which carry out a subset of the image enhancement and recognition functions at low cost. Indeed, the sensitivity of many applications to cost suggests that effective designs will only emerge when the PE development can be shared over a wide user population. It is possible that designers will make use of the "frame stores" developed in conjunction with TV image-processing systems. They provide suitable starting points for more elaborate transformations, but it is improbable that an entire image could be processed in parallel, and the problem remains of extracting subframes and returning them quickly enough to the image store. The choice between generality and speed in the processing device is critical.

The design of a computer not particularly sensitive to cost is described in BAT80, and referred to again at the end of Chapter 13.

12 ICL DISTRIBUTED ARRAY PROCESSOR

The ICL Distributed Array Processor (DAP) will easily be recognized as the experimental model from which the principles of the AMA have been extracted. It differs from the latter in two important respects.

Firstly, in details of PE design DAP incorporates data paths and functions that overcome some of the coding inefficiencies apparent from trial programming, as we shall see in Section 12.1. In any practical design the final product attempts to balance perceived operational requirements against engineering constraints, which are quite severe when it is considered that a single connection or register added to a PE will be multiplied by 1024 or 4096 in the final product, with proportional effect on reliability, cost, power and other support functions. The machines currently operational (a pilot array corresponding to AMA5.2 and a production version of AMA6.4) are both based on standard high-speed MSI TTL components and require approximately four integrated-circuit packages for each PE (excluding local storage). Looking to the future, multi-PE chips are predictable, and their constraints have been taken into account in the specification of DAP PEs and their interconnections at local level.

The second difference is more fundamental and concerns the position of the array in the computer system. At the time of DAP design the predominant system structures were based on a central switch connecting processor-like devices (order-code interpreters, channel controllers) with essentially passive memory modules. In order to place the array in this framework and take advantage of the storage capacity it offered, the best approach seemed to be to substitute it for one (or more) of the memory modules. In that way all support services, including program generation and data conversion, could be handled by the host, but unlike vector processors (such as AP-120B, which attaches to the I−O channel) there is no need to export programs and data

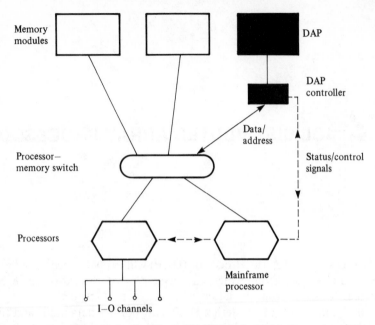

Fig. 12.1 Position of DAP in a host system

for processing, or to import the results: the array store is shared and accessible as conventional word- and byte-aligned units via the DAP controller (Fig. 12.1). However, the DAP remains subordinate to the host architecture in terms of both storage and control structures, with far-reaching effects on program and language design.

That means, for example, that the DAP must fit in with the store partitions of the host, using a special type of segment which is locked in position while executing array programs (it would not be practical for the DAP controller to access system segment tables or to apply the address conversions implicit in many modern systems). It also means that if we think of control as centered in the mainframe processor, then the DAP is activated by a parallel branch of a program (in the same way as a peripheral transfer), but it is not possible for the DAP to initiate mainframe programs, either as subroutines or as parallel tasks. It follows that the "unit" of DAP activity must be large in comparison with system cost in controlling I–O activity, and that to prevent fragmentation of control the DAP controller should ensure continuity by providing loop management, subroutine entry and exit, address calculation and mask-generating functions. Those requirements effectively determine the type of "array-processing language" that can be supported.

The DAP is driven by constructing a *DAP segment* containing all user programs, library procedures, constants, workspace, stack space and declared data regions required for a particular task as a single "monolithic" program area. That is done by the host, which allocates the DAP segment in the range of addresses assigned to the DAP and issues a *Start* command to the DAP controller. The host can then switch to a new task (or a parallel branch of the same task) until completion is signalled. During DAP activation access to the DAP segment is blocked by segment table control, but other parts of the DAP store can be used for conventional purposes.

In contrast, the assumption made for the AMA is that the scalar and planar ALUs are part of a stand-alone system with a single source of control responsible for all store allocation and scheduling. It could also be a member of a multicomputer assembly (Fig. 1.2), but as an "equal" partner. In programming terms the results are that in AMA design planar functions are used by all tasks as required, without distinction between "scalar" and "parallel" subprograms, and that the program space is structured, with an unspecified number — in fact a dynamically changing set — of plane sequences defined for each task. These ideas will be explored more fully in Chapter 18. In the present context the practical consequence of the system structure is that the emphasis of DAP applications is on large problems with static program mapping.

12.1 BASIC DAP OPERATIONS

In contrast to the 21 planar functions used to describe AMA operations (including inversion), the DAP controller interprets about 200 different operation codes, the majority of which are broadcast to the PE array. Amongst the facilities provided are:[†]

(1) logical operations on the activity register plane, so that setting A to a combination of mask bits, which in register transfer form might require
  ...;@ *load p*;@ *and q*;@ *st wk*;@ *mask wk*;...
  takes just two instructions:
  ...; @ *mask p*; @ *and-mask q*;...
(2) direct broadcast to the PE registers from the control unit, instead of via store, including broadcast of single bits and column or row projection of scalar registers;
(3) incorporation of near-neighbor shifts into arithmetic and logic functions, so that, e.g., averaging over two neighbors, which in register transfer

---

[†]In this presentation functional differences between the 32^2 (Pilot) and 64^2 DAP are ignored. The instruction execution rate is 5MHz on both machines.

form requires a six-instruction loop:

...; *do* { @ *load p*;@ *move E* 2;@ *add p*;
    @ *move W* 1; @ *st p'* } *while VA*;...

takes a four-instruction loop:

...; *do* { @ *load p E*; @ *add p W*;@ *st p'* } *while VA*;...

(4) provision of result-to-store addition, with masking, so that the basic addition loop is just two instructions;

(5) provision of word access "by column with row select" in addition to the conventional "by row with column select";

(6) numerous PE register combinations not available in AMA.

Consequently, algorithms can be expressed in fewer instructions than our register transfer form (to the extent that the code generator can master the repertoire). The DAP instructions themselves are coded as 32-bit units compared with 16 for AMA representation (see Chapter 18).

The DAP PE logic is shown in schematic form in Fig. 12.2. The DAP controller uses a set of 8 general-purpose scalar registers and an integer arithmetic and logic unit (64 bits wide in the 64 * 64 array). Instructions are read from the DAP segment but to save store accesses *single* loops of up to 60 instructions can be buffered under program control. An instruction issued at the start of a loop specifies the number of iterations to be performed and the number of instructions it contains. The loop must be free of control jumps other than "skip" and loop termination. After being obeyed each instruction is modified and written to the buffer, where modification can mean either incrementing or decrementing at bit, word or plane level, depending on the context. It follows that a loop such as that considered earlier (Section 9.5):

$$do \{ \ @ \ load \ a'; @ \ move \ W \ 2 \ cyclic; @ \ add \ -b' \ \} while \ VA$$

requires just one or two store cycles to fetch the 3 instructions plus 4 machine cycles for each iteration. The modified instructions are written to the buffer, of course, and not to the DAP segment. Overall, the effect is an appreciable saving in machine cycles on top of that already achieved by register optimization.

Table 12.1 gives some of the performance figures for basic DAP operations. In simple cases it is possible to estimate the contribution of instruction fetches to the total. Comparison can also be made with AMA operation counts. The algorithms used are mostly those described in earlier chapters. The "effective" time quoted is the store-to-store operation time per array element, assuming dimension 1024 or 32 as appropriate. For larger (or smaller) arrays the parallelism and effective single operation times are changed accordingly. For higher or lower precision rough estimates can be derived from known dependence of the algorithm on word length. For the

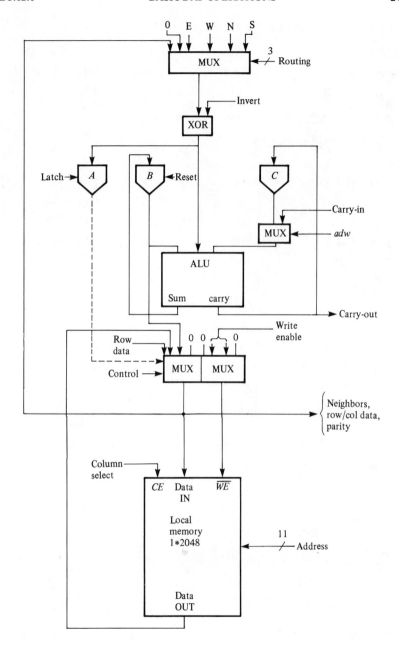

Fig. 12.2 Data paths of 32 * 32 Pilot DAP processing element

Table 12.1 Execution times for 32 * 32 pilot DAP

32-bit FIXED POINT	VERTICAL		HORIZONTAL		SCALAR
Times in µs	Total	Eff	Total	Eff	Total
$R := P + Q$	21	.021	4	0.13	4
$R := P$	14	.014	1	0.03	1
$R := max\,(P,Q)$	34	.034	—	—	—

32-bit FLOATING POINT					
Times in µs					
$T := X + Y$	148	.15	54	1.69	27
$T := X * Y$	305	.3	50	1.56	34
$T := X / Y$	390	.39	100	3.12	100
$T := X ** 2$	155	.15	40	1.25	—
$T := SQRT(X)$	215	.21	—	—	—
$T := LN(X)$	300	.3	—	—	—
$T := SIN(X)$	800	.8	—	—	—

MATRIX OPERATIONS on full DAP plane

Times in ms	(32 * 32)		Precision
$MATMULT(X,Y)$	16	*	⎰ 32-bit
$INVERT(X)$	29	*	⎱ fl.pt
$FFT(X)$ (with reorder)	13.6	*	⎰ complex 32-bit fl.pt
$CONVOLUTION(X)$	4.3	†	16-bit fx.pt
$SORT(X)$ (Batcher)		*	32-bit
no. of elements 1024	7.16		
2048	11.3		
32768	245.0		

SCALAR–MATRIX

Times in µs
scalar S

$X := S * Y$	min	60	
	max	190	
$S := SUM\,(X)$		300	⎱ see p. 257
$S := MAX\,(X)$		50	⎰

---

* DAP Fortran coding   † Assembler coding

64 * 64 array, times are somewhat lower because 4 instructions are fetched on each memory cycle, instead of 1 (the "effective" times are, of course, much lower).

12.2 PARALLEL FOURIER TRANSFORM

The Fourier transform is one of a widely used class of algorithms which, like sorting, provides a yardstick for performance assessment if thoroughly understood. At first sight the amount of routing involved places an array processor at a disadvantage in comparison with vector processing machines, but intuitive judgements should be held in check until quantitative measures have been obtained. In this subsection some practical results from DAP programs will be presented.

Recall that the discrete Fourier transform (DFT) is defined for a vector x of N complex elements to be the vector y such that:

$$y_k = \sum_{n=0}^{N-1} \Phi_{kn}^{(N)} x_n \qquad k = 0,\ldots,N-1 \qquad (1)$$

where $\quad \Phi_{kn}^{(N)} = t_N^{-kn}, \qquad t_N = e^{2\pi i/N}, \qquad i = \sqrt{(-1)} \qquad (2)$

while for the *inverse* DFT, (1) applies with

$$\Phi_{kn}^{(N)} = \frac{1}{N} t_N^{kn} \qquad (3)$$

Formally, application of the inverse DFT to y as computed by (1) would result in the original x. Apparently the calculation entails a complex matrix−vector multiplication, requiring N^2 complex multiplications and N^2 additions, or $4N^2$ real multiplications and $4N^2 - 2N$ real additions. In practical applications vectors of 1000 elements are not uncommon and the transforms are computed many thousands of times, so that finding efficient methods of evaluation is economically important.

Clearly $[\Phi]$ is not an arbitrary complex matrix. The fast Fourier transform algorithms exploit the fact that for suitable choice of N (usually a power of 2) the components of (1) can be factorized so as to express the result as a weighted sum of two Fourier transforms, each of length $\frac{1}{2}N$. Further factorization leads to the calculation of DFTs of length $\frac{1}{4}N, \ldots, 4$ and 2, so that after $\log_2 N$ steps (which will be defined shortly) the calculation is complete. In this discussion we shall assume that an array of N PEs is available, and we shall see that one step involves a single complex multiplication and addition (in parallel), together with a routing operation. The arithmetic ratio of the "direct" to the "fast" method is thus reduced to the order of $N:\log_2 N$, or 10:1 for $N = 1024$.

Returning to (1) and separating the odd and even terms:

$$y_k = \sum_{n \text{ even}} \Phi_{kn}^{(N)} x_n + \sum_{n \text{ odd}} \Phi_{kn}^{(N)} x_n, \quad k = 0,\dots,N-1 \qquad (4)$$

Now for n even, say $n = 2r$, from (2):

$$\Phi_{kn}^{(N)} = t_N^{-kn} = t_N^{-2kr} = t_{N/2}^{-kr} = \Phi_{kr}^{(N/2)}$$

and for n odd, say $n = 2r+1$:

$$\Phi_{kn}^{(N)} = t_N^{-kn} = t_N^{-k} t_N^{-2kr} = t_N^{-k} \Phi_{kr}^{(N/2)}$$

$$\left. \right\} \qquad (5)$$

Hence, in (4):

$$y_k = \sum_{r=0}^{N/2-1} \Phi_{kr}^{(N/2)} x_{2r} + t_N^{-k} \sum_{r=0}^{N/2-1} \Phi_{kr}^{(N/2)} x_{2r+1}, \quad k=0,\dots,N-1 \quad (6)$$

or:

$$y_k = X_k^{\text{even}} + t_N^{-k} X_k^{\text{odd}} \qquad k=0,\dots,\tfrac{1}{2}N-1 \qquad (7)$$

where X^{even} and X^{odd} are vectors of length $\tfrac{1}{2}N$ representing the DFT as defined in (1) for even and odd components of x respectively. Moreover, for $\tfrac{1}{2}N \leqslant k \leqslant N-1$, say $k = \tfrac{1}{2}N+j$:

$$\Phi_{kr}^{(N/2)} = t_{N/2}^{-kr} = e^{-4\pi ikr/N}$$

$$= e^{-2\pi ir} e^{-4\pi ijr/N} = e^{-4\pi ijr/N} = \Phi_{jr}^{(N/2)} \qquad (8)$$

In other words, $\Phi_{kr}^{(N/2)}$ is periodic, repeating after $N/2$ terms, therefore (7) can be extended to apply for $k = \tfrac{1}{2}N,\dots,N-1$, using (8).

Each term of the even and odd transforms contributes to two elements of y, and with suitable ordering of the inputs a single step of the calculation can be represented as in Fig. 12.3 for $N=8$. The connecting arcs flow from input values to output at the end of the step, and a complex multiplier is printed on those arcs in which the input value is multiplied before addition to the convergent arc. Thus y_5 is formed from the sum

$$y_5 = X_1^{\text{even}} + t_8^{-5} X_1^{\text{odd}} \qquad (9)$$

In general, a single step such as Fig. 12.3 involves:

(1) two routing operations (right and left) distance $\tfrac{1}{2}N$ for the complex vectors X^{even} and X^{odd};
(2) a complex multiplication by the factors t_N^{-k}
(3) addition of the result of (2) to the original X^{even} and X^{odd} to give y.

However, the preceding step is to compute X^{even} and X^{odd}, which by an identical line of reasoning with $\tfrac{1}{2}N$ in place of N can be derived from four DFTs

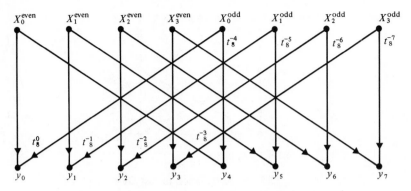

Fig. 12.3 A single step of the fast DFT calculation for $N = 8$

of length $\frac{1}{4}N$. Extending the calculation for $N = 8$ gives the flow of calculation shown in Fig. 12.4.

Note that to present the output in the required order at each stage the initial elements of x must be ordered as shown: the so-called "bit-reversed" index sequence (0, 4, 2, 6, 1, 5, 3, 7) resulting from reversing the binary representation of the indices ($4 = 100_2$ becomes $001_2 = 1$), reordering the vector, and resetting the indices to their original values (so that x_4 ends up at position 1). It should also be noted that because $t_{N/2} = t_N^2$, $t_{N/4} = t_N^4$, and so on, all the multiplying factors can be expressed as powers of t_N: in Fig. 12.4 the exponent value is written on each arc when it is non-zero.

By extending the foregoing analysis to any N, a power of 2, it can be

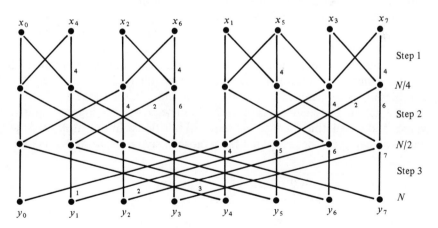

Fig. 12.4 DFT calculation flow for $N = 8$

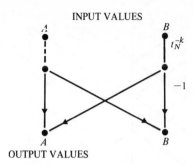

Fig. 12.5 Subcalculation in fast DFT

shown that the complete DFT in its "fast" form requires:

(1) a preliminary sort into bit-reversed order;

(2) $\log_2 N$ computing steps of the form described above.

In sequential algorithms some advantage can be gained by noting that $t_N^{-k} = -t_N^{-k+N/2}$, e.g. in the final stage of Fig. 12.4:

$$y_5 = X_1 + t_8^{-5} X_2^{\text{odd}}$$
$$= X_1 - t_8^{-1} X_2^{\text{odd}} \tag{10}$$

so that the product $t_8^{-1} X_2^{\text{odd}}$, which also occurs in y_1, needs to be formed once only. In an array processor no advantage will be gained unless all PEs are occupied, so there is some interest in trying to split each subcalculation, which takes the form shown in Fig. 12.5 for a pair of PEs distant 2^{p-1} at step p of the calculation. One possible approach is to split each step into real and imaginary components whose evaluation can be shared between the two PEs. At the expense of additional routing the arithmetic can then be reduced to two real multiplications and three addition times. The complex multipliers t_N^{-k} can be either precomputed or calculated as required. In the former case considerations of symmetry show that only values in the range $k = 0, \ldots,$ $\frac{1}{4}N - 1$ need to be retained, and each step will begin by selecting the required values and translating them to the required positions. In the latter case the values at step p can be computed from those at step $p - 1$ from the relation $t_N = \pm \sqrt{(t_{N/2})}$, and since:

$$\sqrt{(t_{N/2})} = \sqrt{(\cos \theta + i \sin \theta)}, \qquad \theta = 4\pi/N$$
$$= \sqrt{[\frac{1}{2}(1 + \cos \theta)]} + i\sqrt{[\frac{1}{2}(1 - \cos \theta)]} \tag{11}$$

the real and imaginary parts of t_N can be found in one parallel application of the square-root procedure.

Table 12.2　Discrete Fourier transform on DAP (1024 elements, complex 32-bit floating-point data in vertical format)

	Count	Time (μs)	Total (ms)
Multiplication	32	305	9.76
Addition	38	148	5.62
Assignment	90	15	1.35
Routing distance	216	7	1.51
Computing r_N^{-k}	16	500	8.
Bit-reversed ordering	268	7	2.18
		Total	28.4 ms

With acknowledgement to D. Parkinson and P.M. Flanders of ICL.

So much for theory. How does it work out in practice? Table 12.2 gives the measured times for a 1024-point DFT calculation on DAP with 32*32 PEs, dividing the time into the phases we have identified. In this algorithm some shortcuts are taken in the early stages, but complex multiplication is not split as suggested earlier.

From Table 12.2 it can be seen that routing (13%) is not a major factor for vectors of size 1024. For arrays of 4096 PEs the routing distance doubles, whereas the computation increases by 8 multiplications and four additions (3 ms) so care must be taken in drawing general conclusions. The time given in Table 12.1 is the consequence of further optimization of the arithmetic and omission of bit-reversal, with the result that routing occupies the DAP for under 10% of the procedure.

There are many versions of the DFT algorithm and the foregoing analysis is intended to give a general feeling for the trade-offs that might be worthwhile, starting from a fairly crude version. Further consideration might suggest the following possibilities:

(1) As precision decreases, or if fixed point arithmetic is used, the routing overheads will increase, but the complete flexibility of the DAP in this area is attractive when dealing with low-precision data such as that arising in digital signal or image processing.

(2) If multiple transforms are required it is advantageous to use the local store dimension for routing. For example, to compute 32 1024 transforms in AMA5 one may store the data as 32 matrices with the ith vector running consecutively through the ith rows of each matrix; in that way the routing overhead is reduced by using the store dimension. It could be further reduced by mapping each 32-element vector into a 4*8

subarray of PEs rather than 1∗32. In all multiple transforms the distribution or calculation of multipliers can be shared.

(3)   Except in low-precision work machines such as DAP are good but not spectacular for DFT computation; where they gain is in using the DFT procedure as part of a larger problem rather than as a peripheral process.

(4)   The inverse transform is identical to the one we have described, with minor changes in coefficients.

Finally, it should be noted that there are various related transforms of importance, such as the Hadamard transform used in image processing and the Fermat number transforms used in signal processing, which are very well suited to the serial nature of DAP functions, and show to advantage in comparison with vector machines without suitably specialized pipelines. It will also be apparent that realizing some of these exciting possibilities will be prohibitively expensive without the help of a programming language in which parallel algorithms can be clearly expressed.

12.3 DAP FORTRAN

With a machine instruction set as extensive as that of DAP, rapid elevation of language is prescribed. The divergence of principle between sticking to a standard language, hoping to extract parallel operations automatically, and providing assistance in the form of an extended grammar and semantics has already been pointed out. The examples given so far should provide ample support for the second approach, and some direct comparisons will be made in this subsection. Purists might think it a retrograde step to base language extension on Fortran, but apart from the obvious preference of the scientific and engineering professions there are sound technical reasons for using such a language: at the present state of machine development and with rather few storage planes it is important to have precise control over store allocation and alignment; moreover, in any system supporting a DAP both the host and DAP controller share a common symbolic description of data areas in the DAP segment, so that the flexibility and explicitness of Fortran with respect to store mapping are decisive advantages. At some future date, when bit planes are more plentiful, it might be possible to be more adventurous. Essentially the same line of reasoning was followed on Illiac IV, and the extended language CFD developed for that machine was influential in the design of DAP Fortran. However, the bit-serial nature of DAP has resulted in a new set of extensions, which we now examine.

All array-processing languages allow element-by-element operations between arrays of similar structure, though the definition of "similar" varies.

The essential linguistic feature is a clear distinction between the names of the entire array and of its components. Once that is provided statements such as:

$$A = B + 3.0 * C$$

can be accepted for three arrays A, B and C in place of the equivalent loop:

$$DO\ 225\ I = 1, IMAX$$
$$225\quad A(I) = B(I) + 3.0 * C(I)$$

where *IMAX* is the length of the arrays. The necessary distinction can be drawn either by the compiler (from data declarations) or by run-time routines (from descriptors). It should be noted in passing that the second method entails dynamic tests of the sort discussed in earlier chapters and it has already been used in a small way in the development of AMA procedures. The customary objection that type checking detracts from arithmetic performance is practically impossible to sustain in the context of array manipulation, which is one of the arguments for using it in languages such as APL. The latter was briefly considered as a basis for high-level DAP programming, but rejected partly because of the difficulty of realizing faithfully the APL functions and data structures with the existing DAP controller and addressing rules.

However, DAP Fortran uses predeclared arrays, and omission of subscripts is sufficient to indicate the use of an entire array as an operand. The extent to which hardware-defined structures, particularly PEs and their interconnections, should be visible at higher language levels arouses lively interest. Portability requirements direct that they should be kept beneath the surface, even though programmers can write better code from knowing what goes on. Conversely, provided the required skills are not outside the range normally expected, efficient use of the PE array is much enhanced by recognizing it in higher-level structures. No doubt this issue will be resolved by advances in hardware and software technology and better understanding of applications, but at present DAP Fortran, like CFD, makes the physical array clearly visible. Two new structures are defined:

(1)   *matrices* of 2 dimensions equal to the PE array edge, whose length is denoted by *DAPSIZE*
(2)   *vectors* of 1 dimension equal to the PE array edge.

Thus, for 64*64 DAP, matrices have 64*64 and vectors have 64 elements. Moreover, matrices are normally stored vertically and vectors horizontally, though conversions are implicit. Higher-level arrays can have matrix and vector elements, e.g.

$$REAL\ M4(,),\ V(),\ MS(,,6),\ HV(,6,4)$$

defines a matrix $M4$ and vector V, and higher-level arrays MS consisting of 6 matrices, and HV consisting of a 6*4 array of vectors. The null indices in the declaration are taken to imply the DAP dimensions.

The elementary data types are integer, real, logical and character. When the corresponding scalar operation is defined matrices and vectors can be combined element-by-element by naming them as operands in the way just illustrated. Certain projections are called implicitly to achieve conformity. For example, in scalar-matrix operations such as:

$$MS(,,4) = 3.0 * M4 + V(5)$$

the scalar value 3.0 is notionally expanded to give a matrix with elements identically equal to 3.0, and the same is true for the scalar value $V(5)$, which is also rotated from horizontal to vertical form. Similar projections are applied in vector expressions. However, for vector–matrix operations the axis of projection is ambiguous, so the operator must be stated explicitly:

Example 12.1   Multiply the first and second matrices of MS, leaving the result in $M4$. (Compare Example 10.2.) The projection operators are $MATR$ for $colp()$ and $MATC$ for $rowp()$.

$$M4 = 0.0$$
$$DO\ 235\ I = 1,\ DAPSIZE$$
$$235\qquad M4 = M4 + MATC(MS(,I,1)) * MATR(MS(I,,2))$$

The omission of a subscript implies the index range 1, ... , $DAPSIZE$, so that, e.g., $MS(,I,1)$ selects a vector consisting of the Ith column of the matrix $MS(,,1)$.

Function definitions are extended to allow vectors and matrices to be returned as results and used in expression evaluation. It is a straightforward linguistic extension to apply standard functions element-by-element to vectors and matrices. They include logarithms, square root, exponential, trigonometric, hyperbolic, fix, float and remainder functions. Less obvious are the standard functions that exploit the connectivity of the PE array in one way or another. Some of them are listed below.

Let S, V, and M denote general operands of type scalar, vector and matrix respectively. Except where noted, the functions are independent of element types, e.g. a matrix M will be transposed by $TRAN(M)$ whether M is integer, real, logical or character. Many of the functions on vectors also apply to matrices listed in column-major order, Fortran style.

Reordering functions TRAN, REV, REVR, REVC

$TRAN(M)$	returns the transpose of M
$REV(V)$	returns V with elements reversed
$REVR(M)$	returns M with rows in reverse order
$REVC(M)$	returns M with columns in reverse order

Translation functions SH**

Shifts apply to matrices in N,S E and W direction and to vectors L (left, spilling low-index elements) and *R* (right). Geometry is specified by the function mnemonic or, if omitted, by a geometry preset for the procedure. The displacement is given by a scalar expression or, in matrix shifts, it may be given by a *vector* of integers specifying a different displacement for each row or column. For example,

SHN(M)	returns *M* shifted N one position
SHN(M,S)	returns *M* shifted N *S* positions
SHN(M, V)	returns *M* with column *i* shifted N *V(i)* positions
SHNP( )	Planar shifts, as above
SHNC( )	Cyclic shifts, as above

Maximum and minimum values MAX, MIN, MAXP, MINP

These functions apply to *V* and *M* operands and return either the scalar value or the position mask of the maximum or minimum element. The floating-point representation is such that integer and real comparisons are almost identical in form.

Row and column selection ROW, ROWS, COL, COLS, ALT, ALTC, ALTR

All these functions generate logical masks used to control PE activity, as we shall see later.

ROW(S)	returns a logical matrix *.TRUE.* in row *S* and *.FALSE.* elsewhere (binary 1 $\Rightarrow$ *.TRUE.*)
ROWS(S1, S2)	returns a logical matrix *.TRUE.* in rows *S1* to *S2* inclusive, and *.FALSE.* elsewhere
ROW(V)	returns a logical matrix *M* in which $$M(I,J) = (V(J) \equiv I)$$

Similarly for *COL()*, *COLS()*

ALT(S)	returns a logical vector with alternating groups of *S .FALSE.* and *.TRUE.* values
ALTC(S)	returns a logical matrix with alternating groups of *S .FALSE.* and *.TRUE.* columns

Similarly for *ALTR. S* is evaluated modulo *DAPSIZE*.

Summation of elements, rows or columns SUM, SUMR, SUMC

SUM(V)	returns the scalar sum of all elements of *V*
SUMR(M)	returns the vector result of adding rows of *M*

Similarly for *SUMC, AND, ANDC, ANDR, OR, ORC, ORR*

The first such that ... ROWN, COLN, FRST

When a conditional test on a matrix or vector yields several elements that satisfy the test, these functions are useful in picking out particular elements.

ROWN(M)   returns an integer vector V whose ith element gives the row in which the first .TRUE. element occurs in column i of the logical matrix M; if none true, the corresponding element of V is returned as zero

Similarly for COLN()

FRST(V)   returns a logical vector containing at most one .TRUE. element, at the position corresponding to the first .TRUE. element in the logical vector V

Element specification EL, ELS, ELL, ELSL

EL(S)   returns a logical vector .FALSE. in all positions except that specified by the index S

ELS(S1,S2)   returns a logical vector .FALSE. in all positions except $S1$ to $S2$ inclusive

ELL and ELSL are similarly defined and return logical matrices with .TRUE. values specified by the column-major indices

Finally, the MERGE function

MERGE(V1,V2,V3)   where $V3$ is a logical vector, returns a vector in which the elements are equal to $V1$ where the corresponding element of $V3$ is .TRUE. and to $V2$ elsewhere.

MERGE is similarly defined for matrix merge under a logical mask.

Logical masks have an important part to play in index specification and conditional tests. Essentially, a set of subscript values can be specified by a mask. That is particularly useful when applied in assignment statements, e.g. if LM is a logical matrix and $M4$ a real matrix as before, then an assignment such as:

$$M4(LM) = 2.5$$

writes the value 2.5 to just the positions of $M4$ at which LM is .TRUE., clearly implemented by evaluating the right-hand expression and assigning the result to $M4$ under control of the activity plane containing LM. In the same way, logical vectors can be used to control vector assignment. Frequently the mask can be generated by evaluating a relational expression with matrix or vector operands, e.g. setting the negative elements of $M4$ to zero would be achieved by:

$$M4 (M4 .LT. 0.0) = 0.0$$

If LV is a logical vector, then

   $M4 (LV,) = V$

sets the rows of $M4$ equal to V at positions corresponding to .$TRUE$. in LV. Orthogonally, for columns:

   $M4 (,LV) = V$

   Logical matrices and vectors may be "summed" by the intrinsic functions ANY and ALL, returning logical scalar values. For example, a test for convergence between two vectors might be formulated by subtracting element-by-element, taking absolute values of the result vector, and comparing it with a constant EPS. If $V1$ and $V2$ were the two vectors this would be written as:

   $IF(ALL(ABS(V1 - V2) .LT. EPS)) GOTO 125$

   The following examples illustrate the use of DAP Fortran to express parallel vector and matrix operations.

Batcher sort for horizontal data (cf. Fig. 10.8)

Remember that a power-of-two exchange is used to prepare for parallel comparison, and that the polarity of the comparison is controlled to form the required ascending and descending sequences. In the example a vector V of $DAPSIZE$ elements is to be sorted. The exchange is carried out by merging left- and right-shifted copies of V under a mask of alternating 1s and 0s:

e.g. for $DAPSIZE = 8$ and $K = 2$:

V:	A	B	C	D	E	F	G	H	
$SHRC(V,2)$:	G	H	A	B	C	D	E	F	
$SHLC(V,2)$:	C	D	E	F	G	H	A	B	
$ALT(2)$:	0	0	1	1	0	0	1	1	
$MERGE(\dots)$:	C	D	A	B	G	H	E	F	(which is *potse* $(V,1)$)

Then if $L = 4$ the derived pattern:

   $ALT(4)$: 0   0   0   0   1   1   1   1

determines whether an ascending (0) or descending (1) sequence is formed. The relational expression:

$$(V.GT.T) .LEQ. ALT(K) .LEQ. ALT(L)$$

in which .LEQ. denotes logical equivalence has the following truth table:

$$
V \leqslant T \begin{cases}
0 & \equiv & 0 & \equiv & 0 & .FALSE. \\
0 & \equiv & 0 & \equiv & 1 & .TRUE. \\
0 & \equiv & 1 & \equiv & 0 & .TRUE. \\
0 & \equiv & 1 & \equiv & 1 & .FALSE.
\end{cases}
$$

$$
V > T \begin{cases}
1 & \equiv & 0 & \equiv & 0 & .TRUE. \\
1 & \equiv & 0 & \equiv & 1 & .FALSE. \\
1 & \equiv & 1 & \equiv & 0 & .FALSE. \\
1 & \equiv & 1 & \equiv & 1 & .TRUE.
\end{cases}
$$

Example 12.2 Batcher sort for a single vector V of length $DAPSIZE$. The vector T is temporary and L, K are integer scalars.

```
          L = 2
100       K = L/2
200       T = MERGE(SHRC(V,K),SHLC(V,K),ALT(K))
          V((V.GT.T).LEQ.ALT(K).LEQ.ALT(L)) = T
          K = K/2
          IF(K.GE.1) GOTO 200
          L = 2 * L
          IF(L.LE.DAPSIZE) GOTO 100
```

Matrix inversion

A complete DAP Fortran subroutine for vertical mode matrix inversion is illustrated in Fig. 12.6. The effect of $INVP(A)$ is to overwrite a given matrix A with its inverse. The declarative part of the program identifies a number of local arrays and masks that will be used as temporary storage. To conserve storage space it is possible to EQUIVALENCE areas used in different parts of the program; alternatively, COMMON areas can be shared with other programs (neither facility is used in this example). The inverse is derived by the Gauss–Jordan method of elimination, which notionally extends A with a unit matrix I and then finds a matrix J such that:

$$J \times [A \quad I] = [I \quad J]$$

which ensures that J is the inverse of A. In practice, I is not stored explicitly and the columns of J, which are found one at a time, gradually overwrite the columns of A in store. The elimination (which reduces one column of A to a unit vector) depends on finding a "pivot" element in A and performing the following assignments (where the pivot is at (p,q)):

```
01  C   DECLARATIONS
02      SUBROUTINE INVP (A)
03      REAL A(,), B(,)
04      LOGICAL PROW (,), PCOL (,), PMASK (,)
05      LOGICAL PIVOT (,), MASK (,), PIVOTS (,)
06      INTEGER RN()
07  C   NOTE THAT THE ARRAY DIMENSIONS ARE IMPLICITLY
08  C   GIVEN BY THE DAPSIZE. A AND B ARE REAL SINGLE
09  C   PRECISION MATRICES IN VERTICAL FORM, RN IS A
10  C   VECTOR AND PROW, PCOL, ETC ARE BOOLEAN MASKS
11
12  C   INITIALIZE MASK TO CONTROL SEARCH FOR PIVOT
13  C   AND LET PIVOTS MARK .TRUE. THOSE ALREADY USED
14      MASK = .TRUE.
15      PIVOTS = .FALSE.
16
17  C   MAIN LOOP
18  C   FRST, MAXP, MATC, MATR ARE STANDARD MATRIX
19  C   FUNCTIONS DEFINED IN THE TEXT. HERE MAXP
20  C   FINDS MAXIMUM ELEMENTS UNDER A GIVEN MASK,
21  C   RETURNING A LOGICAL MATRIX WITH ONE OR MORE
22  C   .TRUE. ELEMENTS
23      DO 1, K = 1, DAPSIZE
24      PIVOT = FRST(MAXP(ABS(A),MASK))
25      S = A(PIVOT)
26      PIVOTS = PIVOTS.OR.PIVOT
27      PROW = MATR(ORR(PIVOT))
28      PCOL = MATC(ORC(PIVOT))
29      PMASK = .NOT.(PROW.OR.PCOL)
30
31      A(PIVOT) = 1.0
32      A = MERGE(A, 0.0,PMASK) − A(,PCOL)*MATC(A(PROW,))/S)
33      PROW = −A
34  1   MASK = MASK.AND.PMASK
35
36  C   THE FINAL STATEMENTS RESHUFFLE ROWS AND COLUMNS
37      RN = ROWN(PIVOTS)
38      DO 2, K = 1, DAPSIZE
39  2   B(K,) = A(RN(K), )
40      DO 3, K = 1,DAPSIZE
41  3   A(,RN(K)) = B(,K)
42      RETURN
43      END
44
```

Fig. 12.6 DAP-Fortran subroutine for matrix inversion by Gauss–Jordan elimination. (With acknowledgement to P.M. Flanders of ICL)

$$
\begin{aligned}
\text{For } i \neq p \text{ and } j \neq q: \quad & A(i,j) = A(i,j) - A(i,q)*A(p,j)/A(p,q) \\
i = p \text{ and } j \neq q: \quad & A(p,j) = A(p,j)/A(p,q) \\
i \neq p \text{ and } j = q: \quad & A(i,q) = - A(i,q)/A(p,q) \\
i = p \text{ and } j = q: \quad & A(p,q) = 1.0/A(p,q)
\end{aligned}
$$

The reduction is carried out for a succession of pivots in distinct rows and columns. For ease of programming the leading diagonal would provide the

```
   DO 10 I = 1, IMAX
   OLDM = M                                /*  save initial values */
   M(R) = 0.25*(M(+,)+M(,+) +M(−,) +M(,−))
10 IF (ALL(ABS(M−OLDM).LT.EPS)) GOTO 20
   CONVERGE = .FALSE.
   RETURN
20 CONVERGE = .TRUE.
   RETURN
```

Fig. 12.7   Iterative solution of Laplace's equation

pivot elements. For numerical accuracy it is better to choose the *largest* remaining pivot at each stage. The effect is then to find a *J* for which:

$$J \times [A \quad I] = [PIVOTS \quad J]$$

and therefore a final reordering is applied to turn the *PIVOTS* matrix into *I*. Study of Fig. 12.7 is recommended at this point to see many of the standard DAP Fortran functions in action. The reader might also find it useful to compare the parallel form of inversion with a sequential program (applied to horizontal data).

Solution of Laplace's equation

A useful facility in parallel programming languages is the ability to combine near-neighbor elements of an array in arithmetic expressions without using the more general shift functions. In DAP Fortran, use of plus or minus sign in a subscript position has the effect of translating a complete matrix or vector one position left, right, N, S, E or W as appropriate. Edge inputs are determined by geometry declared for the function or subroutine, using zero, .FALSE. or null character input, depending on the declared data type, when plane geometry is used. The use of such indices is illustrated by a simple iterative solution of Laplace's equation (Fig. 12.7). At each step the elements of a matrix *M* are replaced by the average of four near-neighbors over a region defined by the logical matrix *R*. Convergence is achieved when the change in value of each element is everywhere less than a preset value *EPS*. A scalar logical value *CONVERGE* is set to indicate whether convergence occurred after *IMAX* iterations.

Tridiagonal equations

As a final example, Fig. 12.8 shows a DAP Fortran function for solving the tridiagonal system of equations discussed on p. 220. The arguments are the lower, diagonal and upper bands of the matrix (*L, D,* and *U* respectively),

```
REAL MATRIX FUNCTION TRIDSOLVE (L, D, U, Y, N)
REAL L(,), D(,), U(,), Y(,)
INTEGER N, ISTEP, K

DO K = 1
DO 10 ISTEP = 1, N
L = L/D
U = U/D
Y = Y/D
D = 1.0 − L*SHRP(U,K) − U*SHLP(L,K)
Y = Y − L*SHRP(Y,L) − U*SHLP(Y,K)
L = − L*SHRP(L,K)
U = − U*SHLP(U,K)
K = K*2
10   CONTINUE
TRIDSOLVE Y/D
RETURN
END
```

Fig. 12.8 Solution of tridiagonal equations. (With acknowledgement to J. Whiteway, DAP Support Unit, Queen Mary College)

the right-hand side Y, and an iteration count N. Each of the arrays is declared as a matrix, though the shift functions treat the elements in linear (column-major) order. There is no test for early convergence, and after N iterations the solution vector is returned as the value of the function.

12.4 CONTROL OVERHEADS

Choosing examples to illustrate features of DAP Fortran gives undue prominence to familiar algorithms that are readily adapted to a wider class of vector and array machines. One of the features of bit-organized array processors is that standard floating-point operations are relatively slow, but that attribute can be put in a more favorable light by saying that control overheads are lower than on sequential machines. It was seen in Part 1 that in scalar computation three or four support functions might be required for each arithmetic operation generated from high-level source code. To reduce that ratio one must use assembly code or optimizing compilers. In high-speed machines the explicit support needed from the instruction stream is minimized by issuing vector or matrix operations, and provided they are recognized at source level it is possible to execute arithmetic functions at high speed without recourse to low-level coding or optimization. It is calculated that the time for matrix inversion (Fig. 12.7) could be improved only from 29 ms to 25 ms by assembly language coding.

The above comments hold generally for machines with built-in functions on multiple data items or with heavily overlapped instruction pipelines. However, "real" calculations have to handle many exceptional conditions, and it is in decision-making capability that bit-organized arrays show disproportionate gains. For example, it is found that DAP is about four times faster than the CDC 7600 on matrix multiply, but seven times faster on matrix inversion: the manipulations involved in pivoting have a more serious effect on the flow of calculation in a conventional processor than on the DAP.

Although the programming language is meant to be helpful, selecting control algorithms depends on acquired skills in parallel program design and, to some extent, on "unlearning" habits formed over years of scalar computation. To take a very elementary example, given a pointer p to a circular buffer b, it is easily seen that indexing the pointer $(p' 1)$ is equivalent to cycling the buffer one position (if the size fits the array) and (@ *move W* 1 *cyclic*) takes about as long. In general, moving data in memory is a "cheap" operation, whereas intuitively one might aim to set up pointer structures with the object of avoiding physical movement.

Consider a vector V of integers from which a new vector W is to be formed by replacing each element by reference to a smaller table T:

$$DO\ 10\ J\ =\ 1,N$$
$$10\quad W(J)\ =\ T(V(J))$$

At first sight that is an essentially serial operation, using unrelated values $V(J)$ to access T. However, the problem can be "turned round" by taking each value of T and broadcasting it to V:

$$DO\ 20\ I\ =\ 1,M$$
$$20\quad W(V.EQ.I)\ =\ T(I)$$

Here the language provides just what is required to express selective assignment efficiently, provided T is much shorter than V.

As a final example, suppose it is required to compute the mutual forces exerted on a large number of particles by gravitational or electromagnetic interaction. The physical attributes (mass, charge, position, velocity, etc.) are given for each particle. An indexing scheme is assumed which allows the attributes of any particle to be accessed, knowing its index I. Then in sequential form the set of resultant forces F might be found according to the schema:

$$DO\ 30\ I\ =\ 2,N$$
$$DO\ 30\ J\ =\ 1,\ I-1$$
$$F(I)\ =\ F(I)\ +\ \Phi(I,J)$$
$$30\quad F(J)\ =\ F(J)\ -\ \Phi(I,J)$$

where $\Phi(I,J)$ evaluates the interaction between particles I and J. Here there is no obvious physical relation that can guide the mapping of particle attributes into store. In a vector processor the above schema might be processed directly, using increasing vector length at each step. How can the resultant forces be calculated using N processing elements in an array?

One possible method is shown in Fig. 12.9 for $N=8$. It is supposed that two sets of attributes are held in store, one being moved cyclically relatively to the other. After each step eight values of $\Phi(I,J)$ can be calculated in parallel, and all the required interactions can be calculated in $N/2$ steps. The resultant forces are summed in two parts, one of which is cycled with the moving attributes. A final cyclic shift at the end of the iteration brings the partial sums into position for addition. In effect, therefore, a problem with apparently variable vector length has been turned into one of fixed length which can be matched to the array.

Although there have been some surprisingly successful problem analyses

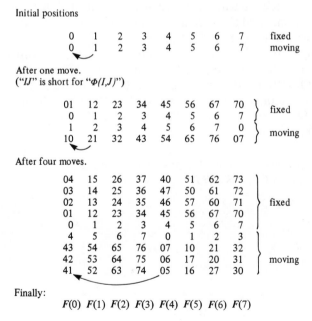

Fig. 12.9 Data routing in many-body problem ($N = 8$)

yielding high degrees of parallelism, other areas seem to be untouchable by definition. One is list processing, which has no analog in array terms (though other types of network, which can be represented in matrix form, have yielded good results). Another is sparse matrix manipulation. Attempts to apply the simplex method of linear programming on bit-organized arrays have been hampered by the lack of indexing facilities in the PEs. Whether new algorithms appropriate to the machine organization can be devised remains to be seen.

12.5 DAP DEVELOPMENTS

In the final analysis, performance is a function of hardware, support system, language, library and human effort. Understanding how such components interact is more important at the present stage of array processor design than striving for ultimate speed. The position of the DAP array relative to other hardware components has enabled greater program support to be offered than on other machines of the same type. At the same time, the use of the array as a passive store partially offsets the initial cost. To evaluate the machine in a realistic environment a 64*64 DAP has been placed at London University by the Science Research Council. Other machines are being installed for specific scientific and engineering calculations. The work now under way should add significantly to knowledge of parallel numerical and combinatorial techniques and language design.

Unfortunately, DAP documentation is not readily accessible. The basic PE design aims are described in RED73 and some performance estimates are given in FLA77. DAP Fortran is described in manufacturer's manuals DAP79. A wealth of material on parallel-processing techniques for DAP and other high-speed machines will be found in INF79.

For further discussion of Fourier and other transforms see OPP65.

A number of languages or language-extensions for array computation have been proposed in recent years. Apart from DAP Fortran, reference may be found to CFD (STE75).

13 ACTIVE MEMORY IN COMPUTER DESIGN

In this chapter we examine the potential contribution of active memory arrays to general-purpose computer design. It is necessarily speculative, but it will provide a framework other than the usual "supercomputer" context in which the developments already outlined can be evaluated. The basic proposition is that AMA functions (or some more refined version of them) could sensibly be assimilated into the instruction set of any micromachine intended for general use. The implied context is one in which main store sizes are upwards of ½ Mbyte, e.g. AMA5.4 or AMA4.16 and larger. Below that level it would be less practical to engineer a PE array, although AMA functions could be implemented in serial form for compatibility purposes.

As usual, we are looking to make an investment T in design and construction and to recover substantially more than T in gross performance. The latter will be measured in part by application to problems with substantial parallel content. The reader might not have been convinced by the examples offered, and could object that the applications so far identified call for extreme specialization of interest and skills. On the other hand, success in some of the newer areas such as image processing and display or data management could have widespread effect on even the most banal interactions. Conventional computer design has managed to span those extreme points of view, and somehow we must do the same.

The second contribution from performance is expected to come from organizing programs to achieve high utilization of resources — "putting the right information in the right place at the right time". Here we distinguish two requirements: to decide on the "right" information, and to move it quickly into position. Planar translations have obvious potential in the latter respect. Some of the problems arising in the context of microsystem design were noted in Chapter 7, but solutions directed specifically at microcode or scratchpad usage are strategically unattractive. We return to that subject in Section 13.1. Planar scanning functions also make an important contribution to deciding what is right and, conversely, what is wrongly placed in program storage, with consequent effect on *allocation* and *ejection* strategies. The techniques available are closely related to the store addressing mechanism, but they will be discussed in the broader context of *index management* (which is elaborated in later chapters) in Section 13.2. One encouraging sign that might be noted at this point is that whereas problem mapping is often imperfect, resulting in loss of parallelism, system data structures can very often be chosen to match the PE array exactly. The remaining subsections discuss the contribution of an "array module" in an assembly of such devices, and some of the issues raised by I−O, reliability and high-performance requirements.

Before claiming the reward it will be useful to have some idea of what T implies. Consider a main store of ½ Mbyte which, using current devices, would require 256 16-Kbit circuits. The *device* cost, \$0.0002/bit, is \$800, but let us say the *installed price* in the memory system is about \$2 000. The effect of adding the PE array as currently implemented, for example, in the ICL DAP is to add rather more than 4 integrated-circuit packages per bit position and to require bipolar storage devices (e.g. 4 ∗ 4 Kbit) instead of MOS, with the result that the active storage subsystem costs at least eight times as much as equivalent passive store, even when the cost of the controller is discounted. In a complete system main storage costs are typically 10−15% of the total, so at least 50% increase in direct costs would be implied — say from \$30 000 for a medium-sized mainframe to \$50 000 for the same with active memory. Matching such figures implies, as we have seen, choosing the special application areas in which substantially more than 50% increase in performance can be expected.

There are two main approaches to reducing T. One is to follow the original intention of using custom-built LSI circuits for the PEs. The limiting factors are the complexity of circuit that can be manufactured without significant fall-off in speed, and the number of edge connections that can be supplied. For comparison purposes a rate of exchange has to be found between PE logic and conventional memory circuits, which we shall take to be 1 PE = 128 (bipolar) storage bits. Thus a 4 ∗ 4 subarray of PE logic would be equivalent in complexity to 2 Kbits of bipolar storage, which is within range of current technology (compare, for example, the Am2901 ALU slice in Chapter 4). Figure 13.1 illustrates why edge limitations favor "square" rather than "linear" subarrays. The overall effect of such designs is to reduce the component count, and hence the support costs, attributable to the PEs to a fraction of a package per bit of the array.

The second line of development is to use MOS in place of bipolar

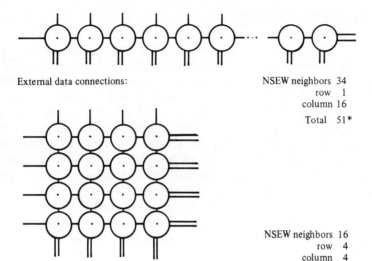

External data connections:

NSEW neighbors 34
row   1
column 16
Total   51*

NSEW neighbors 16
row   4
column   4
Total 24*

* Plus common function, clock, local store data, activity control, power and parity

Fig. 13.1 Subarrays of processing elements: (a) linear 1 * 16;
(b) square 4 * 4

storage circuits, or possibly a combination of the two. The design problem can then be viewed as follows: given the ½ Mbyte MOS store as one level of the hierarchy, how best to organize the flow of information through it to maximize jobs/hour or minimize response time? An irritating feature of conventional design is that although the store array might be capable of delivering 256 bits at once the processor has no way of accepting them. Quite often buffers served by block transfer are introduced for instructions and /or data in order to achieve high effective access rates. A comparison might then be drawn between a conventional processor−memory pair with, say, 32 Kbytes of fast buffers of one sort or another, and AMA4.16 with 1 Kbit of bipolar store attached to each PE. At the prevailing rate of exchange, the PE logic is equivalent to adding another 4 Kbytes of buffer storage: which is the more effective? Clearly there are many architectural questions to be answered before one can pick the "best" configuration, but it is equally clear that, *in the limit*, the cost T attributed to the planar functions would be well below architectural noise levels. Whether the limit is attained depends primarily on finding a widespread application area in which to amortize development costs and on creating the competitive marketing environment necessary to drive down costs in line with conventional storage.

13.1 STORE MANAGEMENT

A circuit configuration of particular interest is one in which the high-speed local store is integrated with planar registers and ALU (Fig. 13.2). The advantage of such an arrangement would be that there is minimal delay in transmission of data from store to PE, and it might be seen as a step towards even closer functional integration of the logic and memory circuits. However, any development of that sort reveals in acute form the competition for space in the function box. How many bits of bipolar storage are required? How would they be allocated to program information? The answers clearly affect the level of integration that might be considered, and hence the influence of active components on system costs and performance. In this subsection we examine combinations of planar operations and address management techniques which might be used in the model suggested by Fig. 13.2. It will be useful to begin with a reminder of general store-management principles.

In order to process information efficiently, it must be made accessible at a rate matching the processor speed. In most calculations the intensity of use of items of information varies immensely in the course of a program, and performance is not seriously impaired if only the most heavily used are supplied at processor speed. To take advantage of that fact arrangements should be made to move information into the store level appropriate to its utilization at any instant. The agency might be the programmer, given facilities for commanding information transfers. Alternatively, one can apply rules that

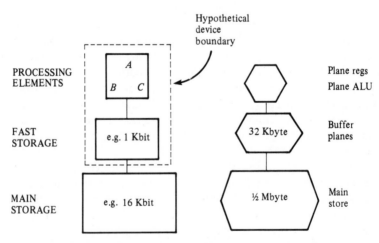

Fig. 13.2 Processing element with local store hierarchy: (a) single bit position; (b) array

are independent of any program. In time-sharing (and therefore space-sharing) systems, some form of automatic control is essential. However, experience shows that abandoning control entirely to a preset algorithm is not entirely satisfactory, and a more useful guideline is to provide the controls appropriate to the programming skills available. For example, in high-level user languages, cushioned to some extent by the compiler subsystem, blissful ignorance might rule, but at the level of design discussed in Chapter 7 a programmer might wish to decide *which* level of the hierarchy contained specific items of data, though not caring *where* they were placed.

In practice, as we saw in Chapter 1, four levels are of prime importance: registers, control and scratchpad (buffers), program space (main store) and auxiliary storage. Let us assume that the units of storage at all levels are measured in bytes, and that they are assigned to sequences of physical locations, identified by their initial location indices $L_0, L_1, \ldots, L_N$. As calculation proceeds, the demand for storage is met by finding blocks of consecutive bytes determined by pairs of numbers (L_i, n_i), $n_i + 1$ being the number of bytes in the sequence, i.e. the last byte occupied is at $L_i + n_i$. The blocks so assigned are said to be *active*. The remainder are *inactive*: they provide at each level a reserve of space from which to satisfy new demands. When that is impossible, a request can only be satisfied by detecting inactive sequences which can be *recycled*, or by ejecting rarely used sequences to another level. The store control subsystem works intimately with the task scheduler in regulating demands for storage.

Placement of sequences is concealed from programs by causing them to use a set of *pointers*, whose meaning is independent of store allocation. In the earliest computers, very little could be done about store management because locations were identified with pointers. Since the acceptance of multiprogramming, crude transformations between pointers and location indices, such as datum-limit registers and paging schemes, have been common. The relation between pointers and locations can be expressed in tabular form. In practice, such a table relates sequences (P_i, n_i) of pointer space to blocks (L_i, n_i) of physical store, with the implication that the jth element of a sequence, $0 \leqslant j \leqslant n_i$, is to be found in the jth position of the corresponding block. The table need only relate P_i to L_i, and give the limit value n_i. There are two methods of using the table:

(a) Unrestricted pointer formation: If the P_i are indistinguishable from numeric data, a table reference will be made on every attempt to access data other than register contents (Fig. 13.3(a)). In the special cases mentioned above, the paging scheme reduces n_i to a constant (a power of 2), and datum register schemes reduce the table to one entry per program.

(b) Controlled pointer formation: If pointers are distinguished from other

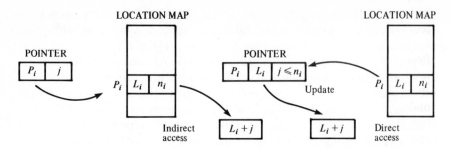

Fig. 13.3 Mapping from pointer to location index: (a) uncontrolled pointer formation; (b) controlled pointer formation

stored items it is possible to retain the tabular entry as part of the pointer itself, only referring to the table to update L_i when P_i changes. (Fig. 13.3(b)).

In general, provided the relevant parts of the location map are held in much faster store than the information required, either method is acceptable. For example, access to a drum can be controlled using a mapping table in main storage. Access to main store requires the table (or at least the most intensely used parts of it) to be in buffer storage. Access to buffer store, on the other hand, is severely penalized by method (a) because the table itself can be accessed no faster that the data to which it refers; moreover it is often so bulky that it must be accessed by associative methods which, by definition, must be *slower* than the data access itself. To accomplish the association in acceptable time a number of special algorithms have been devised, but they all make the assumption that instruction and operand processing are so complex that they can be overlapped with address translation. In the micromachine context that condition is unlikely to hold. The result can be presented as a gain over main store speed or loss of buffer speed, depending on one's point of view.

The advantage of method (b) is that reference to physical store is direct, and a relatively long updating process can be tolerated. It depends, just as a paging system does, on the proposition that pointers are used repeatedly to access the same region of store, though it uses them as *predictors* of future access, which is impossible in method (a). In other words, the existence of a pointer in a register can be taken to imply imminent use of the datum to which it refers. The register set defines a restricted domain or working set D. The construction of processor logic, of compiled code, and of hand-coded programs is normally such that the most urgently required entities, if not in the registers themselves, are in D. A natural way of enhancing performance would therefore be to move D into buffer storage and to adjust pointers accordingly.

The main objections to the above strategy are that D is too volatile, often too large, for effective maintenance. We therefore look for approximations for which the problems of placement, ejection and recycling can be solved. A little thought also shows that at a detailed level of program design pointers can be classified according to usage, e.g. as pointing to buffer, program storage or file areas, and that different maintenance algorithms are appropriate to each. The following examples show what that might imply, using controlled pointer formation in each case (apart from the arguments just given there are sound reasons that will become evident in later chapters for controlling pointer formation). For consistency with later use we call a pointer to program storage a *codeword* (pointers to files are examples of *capabilities;* see Section 13.2).

Example 13.1   One possible approximation to the domain D is to include *all* the recognized buffer blocks, i.e. addressed sequences, of a particular program. The approximation is therefore larger than D (because not all addresses will be in registers), but it is less volatile, and if the total program space can be partitioned, e.g. into task domains, it is accurate enough. It might be applied to the microsystems discussed in Chapter 7, the addressed sequences being microprogram and scratchpad data of an interpretive system, together with pointers to the control environment, the stack, task state vector, etc. In this example the appropriate D would be loaded from main store to buffer when a task was scheduled, using plane transfers, and unloaded at the end of the task time-slot. The mapping table is unnecessary, buffer locations being retained in addresses, exactly as supposed in describing AMA functions. There is no "ejection" algorithm other than that used in scheduling new tasks. However, blocks can be allocated dynamically from a "free plane" list for buffer storage. To recycle disused space it is necessary to identify active plane sequences (effectively reconstructing the mapping table) and, if necessary, to *compact* the active sequences to one end of the location index range. This example is a straightforward application of dynamic memory management within a single task. The contribution of active memory operations is seen mainly in the compaction, loading and ejection phases. They also have an important effect on recycling, as will be shown later.

Example 13.2   Another method of allocating buffer space is to keep addressed sequences in main storage, but temporarily to reassign a subset to buffer planes. A minimal subset would be those planes whose addresses *currently exist in registers.* It would be feasible to use such a rule if the buffers were restricted to a small number, say 64 planes (i.e. 64 bits of fast

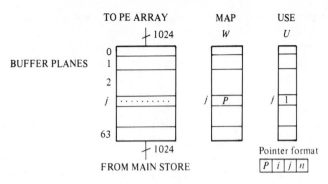

Fig. 13.4   Allocation of buffer planes

memory associated with each PE in Fig. 13.2). A separate mapping table W is required (Fig. 13.4), consisting of 64 words each able to specify the index of the corresponding fast storage plane. A separate 64-bit register U indicates which planes are currently active. The address format is such that, when in a register, the buffer plane index j can be retained together with the plane index P, displacement i, and limit value n. The rules of store maintenance are as follows:

(1) *Allocation*   When an address is formed in a register (e.g. loaded from store) an associative reference is made to W to determine whether the plane it refers to is already in the buffer. If so, the buffer index j is stored in the address. Otherwise, a vacant plane is found by inspecting U, and the required plane fetched from main store. Appropriate entries are made in W and U.

(2) *Ejection*   Planes can be recycled if there is no address referring to them in any register. For example, if a register is overwritten, it is possible that a buffer plane will thereby become inactive. Detection of that condition involves periodic sampling of the register set. If the plane has not been overwritten, it can immediately be re-used. Otherwise it must be returned to main store.

(3) *Access*   Addresses can be used to access buffer storage directly, and continue to be used as long as the plane index is unchanged. For example, in AMA5 a plane contains 128 bytes, so might be accessed 128 times in a scanning operation before needing to load the next plane (or adjust j, since the plane might already be loaded).

(4) *Compaction*   There is no need for compaction, because no assumptions are made about contiguity of buffer planes.

This example is an application of cache memory management techniques, taking advantage of the predictive property of controlled pointer formation, direct access to data in fast store, and adjusting block size to match the planar data paths. It might be expected to minimize storage for a given hit rate, but the net effect needs to be studied by detailed logic design and simulation.

Example 13.3 On descending to the next level of storage, essentially the same two methods as those just described could be used. However, in terms of main program the variability of D is usually much greater than that supposed in Example 13.1, and there is more interest in distributing data sequences, i.e. segments, between main and auxiliary memory. In some instances the main memory is distributed between a number of processor—memory modules, but the problem remains to decide on what is required immediately in the storage planes. The location map is now the *segment table*, and a codeword contains a segment index, g, and an element displacement i. The "unit" element is usually a property of the segment — byte, word, plane, etc. Segments will be allocated to consecutive plane sequences. The segment table can be accessed directly. As in Example 13.2, the physical plane index j and limit n can be retained with the codeword while it is in a register:

		g	i	CODEWORD IN STORE
j	n	g	i	CODEWORD IN REGISTER

Segment table format:

g: | j | n |

Access requests can be made direct to main store, and remain valid as long as $0 \leqslant i \leqslant n$. Loading a segment into main store will be triggered by accessing the segment table and attempting to form the codeword in a register. However, unlike Example 13.2, the loading and ejection rules are determined by a software store manager. In allocation it is often the case that paging techniques are adopted to avoid the need for compaction. They introduce a second level of indirection, call for additional table space, and suffer a further drain on space owing to round-off effects. The use of plane-transfer operations affects the design of the store manager in a number of ways: by providing very fast means of compaction it reduces the need for paging; by using relatively small planes (128 bytes compared with page sizes 1024 bytes or more) it reduces round-off losses. Such factors help the PE array pay for its keep, even though the amount of parallel arithmetic involved might be negligible.

13.2 INDEX MANAGEMENT

"Then you keep moving around, I suppose?" said Alice.
"Exactly so," said the Hatter: "as soon as things get used up."
"But what happens when you come to the beginning again?" Alice
ventured to ask.
"Suppose we change the subject," the March Hare interrupted,
yawning.

Alice in Wonderland Lewis Carroll

This subsection is concerned with the management of "objects of computation", in particular with the problems the AMA creates for itself by having two levels of local storage. The topic is important in the design of any dynamically changing software structure, as will be shown in later chapters. In operating systems, for example, it is recognized that one of the most effective ways of staying in the saddle is to express algorithms in terms of abstract objects such as files, tasks, stacks, and so on, whose integrity is preserved by hardware protection mechanisms. (In static environments much of the security can be enforced in advance by compilers or loader, but in-line mechanisms are necessary for changing or unpredictable program structures.) The two best-known mechanisms are generalizations of those illustrated in Fig. 13.3, i.e.:

(a) Externally applied authorization: Here the program is allowed unrestricted freedom to construct "pointers" to supposed objects of various classes, but before the pointer is used it is checked (by system or microcode) against a "hidden" list of objects currently available to the program. The list is simply a generalization of the location map used in store management.

(b) Pointer control: Here the formation of a new type of elementary datum, distinguished from numeric values, is engineered. The machine instruction set is augmented with functions for pointer manipulation. Pointers include addresses and codewords as already described, but additionally include *capabilities* that are interpreted as references to more general classes of objects.

Comparison of the two mechanisms shows that capability mechanisms are generally more precise and efficient than authorization lists, but that the latter are useful in applying security checks on a macroscopic scale. We shall see how planar operations contribute to each mechanism.

Capability management

With capabilities the general objective is as follows: given a set $\{c\}$ of object types $c = 1, \ldots n$, we need to create instances of objects and to assign attributes to them; to grant and revoke access to different sections of program or different task environments on a selective basis; and to remove objects from the program space when no longer required. A capability identifies an object i of type c by encoding it as a tagged scalar value, e.g. in AMA4:

```
tag    class   id
┌─────┬───────┬─────┐
│  t  │   c   │  i  │     CAPABILITY
└─────┴───────┴─────┘
```

Compare the codeword format:

```
┌─────┬───────┬─────┐
│  t  │   g   │  i  │     CODEWORD
└─────┴───────┴─────┘
```

in which the segment index plays the part of an object identifier. The tag interpretation is such that neither c nor g can be altered without special privilege. Our main concern is with the choice of c, g or i either as a segment table index, a store location (in addresses) or an index in **master object table** M_c associated with the type c. The difficulty is that an index cannot be recycled until all pointers containing it have been found and "annulled". In that sense the management of abstract objects can be seen to imply the management of a small number of "index spaces", where the indices themselves occur in some fraction of the total program space. In the case of codewords, although the mobility of segments is eased by addressing through the segment table, the problem of allocating segment indices remains: if the segment table is to remain small, such indices should be recycled as quickly as possible. For addresses, the same problem arises with location numbers, with the added complication of having to find sequences of indices of prescribed length.

If the occupancy of a master object table is plotted against time its behavior is modelled as shown in Fig. 13.5. Assuming an average rate of consuming indices of r per unit time, and that initially R indices are "free", it will take R/r time units to fill the table. At that point recovery procedures must be invoked to create a new free index list.

The recovery process involves scanning all pointer-bearing regions of program space, starting from known "base" positions. The criterion for recycling an index might be that no pointers to it exist (reference count of zero), or that an explicit deletion operation has been applied. The normal

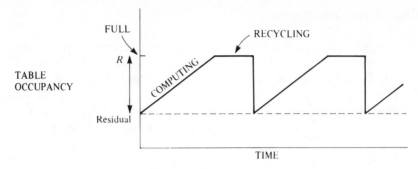

Fig. 13.5 Model of master object table occupancy

action will be in either case to take each capability, refer to the master object table for its class, M_c, and mark the table entry or the capability as appropriate. If the total program space is K bytes and the proportion that has to be scanned is p, then the recovery time is linearly related to pK/T and pKC, where T is the rate of scan and C is the probability of any scanned element being a pointer. The time wasted on index recovery, expressed as a proportion of useful computing time, is:

$$W \simeq \frac{pKr}{R} \left(\frac{1}{T} + C \right)$$

The normal methods used to reduce W might be aimed at eliminating recycling entirely, e.g. by:

(1) enlarging the master object tables to service all foreseeable requests (as the Mad Hatter hoped); or
(2) restricting the use of pointers, e.g. by linguistic devices such as qualifiers, which map higher-level abstractions into system "containers", leaving qualifier management to the language subsystem;

alternatively, one can seek to minimize the actual scanning time by:

(3) limiting the extent of pointer-bearing segments, thus reducing p; or
(4) constraining program structure, e.g. to separate task domains or to a "tree" form.

The effect of planar functions is to reduce the scanning time by a factor 2^n in AMAn, so that the first term of W is correspondingly reduced. It appears that the individual comparisons with M_c have to be done sequentially, so the second term is unchanged. The benefit of AMA will be most marked for operations on individual objects or object classes, for example to find and delete all references to a particular object, or to delete all objects of a given class (recycling the class index c). In most capability-based systems such functions are fairly heavily penalized if not actually forbidden. The effect of the AMA would therefore not be seen in improved performance but in providing new facilities and a relaxation of the rules of program construction.

Authorization lists

A particular application that arises in the context of authorization list management is in binding an encoded control module to its operating environment. Remember that the environment might be both user- and task-dependent, that the control module might be constructed before the form of the environment is known, and that it might be used simultaneously in several different environments. Nevertheless, it is required to bind the "free variables" $\{F_i\}$ in the module correctly to any environment providing definitions of F_i. How can that be done without using inordinately large tables? One answer is simply to use planar functions to offer associative access to the environment. In the system described in Chapter 18 an environment is a list of objects, and the associative key is an encoded form of the free variable name (Fig. 13.6). The dynamic binding takes the place of a program loader.

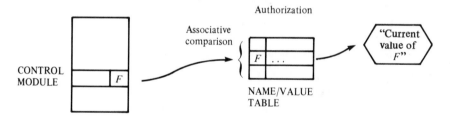

Fig. 13.6   Dynamic binding via authorization list

In that sense the presence of the AMA, which was previously equated with the addition of a small amount of fast store, might in fact reduce overall storage requirements: store can be allocated in smaller units, the resulting structures can be managed effectively in less space, the need for remapping from virtual to real indices is practically eliminated, and a large chunk of system software is dispensed with.

13.3 EXTERNAL CONNECTIONS

The I–O subsystem is a major part of Illiac IV, CLIP, and many other array processors, though it has not featured in our discussion of DAP or Active Memory Arrays. The primary I−O channel for the latter is the interprocessor highway, and the notional transfer rate is of the order of 2^n bits per memory cycle, e.g. 40 Mbytes/s on AMA6 at 5 MHz. Thus, a matrix of 32-bit numbers would be transferred in or out via row data lines in about 2 multiply times. Whether that can be achieved or sustained depends not only on the bus and the method of control, but on the source of data: no single disk would suffice, and most high-speed systems rely on multichannel I−O control. However, the increasing capacity of storage devices widens the range of problems that can be contained wholly in the array. For example, attachment of 64-Kbit stores to each PE in AMA6 would provide internal storage of 32 Mbytes, which covers substantial "complete problems", so it could be that storage of intermediate results will not be such a critical problem in future.

Important questions of connectivity arise in the context of array partitioning. Very briefly, it can be seen that if the size of the array is increased to achieve a certain computing rate, not only does the I−O requirement go up as the square of the dimension but three other problems have to be dealt with:

(1) the failure rate, which increases with the number of components and interconnections;
(2) routing overheads, which increase linearly while compute time stays constant;
(3) applicability is reduced to the specialized class of problems that map into the array dimensions (equally, to the users who can afford to buy one).

A number of proposals have been made for arrays at the AMA7 level, i.e. 128∗128 PEs, with special data paths for reconfiguration. In the context of general-purpose design it would be more attractive in view of (1) and (3) to find a modular solution to a wider class of problems. To take a specific example, suppose it is known that to achieve a certain level of performance 2^{14} PEs must be in action at once. They can be configured in many ways, either as a single AMA7, as four AMA6s, 16 AMA5s, and so on (Fig. 13.7), each array having its own control unit. In terms of processing speed, all three are theoretically equivalent, but they differ when it is required to align data. Taking a single plane in AMA7, to move S one row requires three instructions { @ *load p*; @ *move S* 1; @ *st p*}, whereas both of the other configurations require multiple bus interactions: it is easily seen that the bus traffic increases as the square root of the number of arrays. Sophisticated interprocessor connections have been suggested, which would give fast routing for a wide range of permutations of data, but they need to be investigated in terms of practical effect on known problems. Comparison is not straightforward because of the need for redundant data paths and PEs in large arrays.

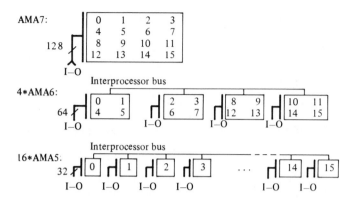

Fig. 13.7 Partitioned array systems

13.4 FURTHER DEVELOPMENTS

In this chapter we have developed the thesis that Active Memory Arays can pay their way in general-purpose system design, and introduced the idea of a multicomputer assembly, each of whose members is a moderate-sized AMA. For system use the most elementary PE functions appear to be sufficient. Moreover, data structures can be adapted to the array dimensions and the SIL can readily incorporate planar functions. It might be asked how such functions should be presented for general use, what advantages there would be in doing so, and whether additional PE or controller functions should be provided for that purpose. Perhaps we should distinguish, as in Part 1, between two types of "general user": those responsible for subsystem development, such as language engineers using a SIL adapted to the machine; and application analysts and programmers concerned with driving the system at higher levels.

The raw facility provided by the AMA is the ability to transform data "in memory" at high speed: in that respect it is always superior to a scalar processor. It is equivalent to (and probably cheaper than) a vector processor *provided only elementary functions are involved*. That can be turned to great advantage in simple transformations (as in image enhancement). It is a dis-advantage for elaborate floating-point calculation. The difference can be illustrated by referring back to Figs. 8.2 and 8.3 (see Fig. 13.8). In AMA design floating-point operations require the partial results to be recycled through the memory, whereas in a vector processor the partial results are staged in the function pipelines and vector registers (comparison is somewhat clouded by entirely new algorithms such as those used for pseudomultiplica-tion and -division). To narrow the performance gap it would be necessary to

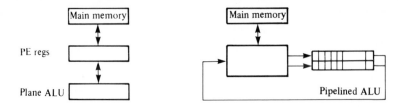

Fig. 13.8   Data paths in array and pipelined vector processors

provide more PE register space and to synchronize the machine to register access times rather than main memory. That approach is illustrated by the proposed Massively Parallel Processor (MPP, Fig. 13.9), which incorporates a shift register in the PE. For example, the shift register might contain the denormalized operand in add or subtract, or the partial product in multiplication. In MPP 32-bit floating-point addition and multiplication are

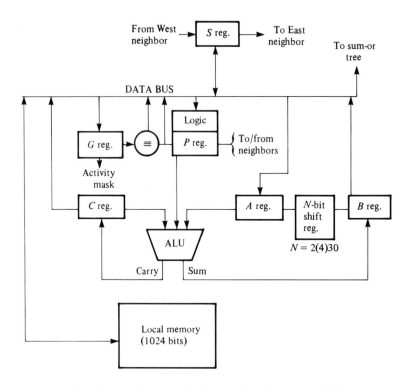

Fig. 13.9   PE schematic diagram for Goodyear MPP

reported to take 380 and 760 machine cycles respectively, compared with 740 and 1525 in DAP code.

The disadvantage of vertical arithmetic is that a relatively large amount of register space has to be provided for intermediate results. An alternative approach is to revert to horizontal arithmetic (as in Illiac IV) and to add floating-point circuits to the planar ALU. To compensate for loss of parallelism they need to deliver results in about 10 machine cycles. Such floating-point units are becoming available in VLSI form and might be considered as optional attachments to basic AMA design. The flexibility of vertical arithmetic would thereby be lost, but so would one of the rigid dimensional limitations of the AMA.

That brings us to one of the most difficult aspects of design: there is much that might be done to improve performance by increasing arithmetic or routing function, but how can it be brought to the surface and widely used? Almost certainly the instruments will be extensions to the existing standard languages, incorporating many of the linguistic devices explored in the machines we have examined. One would certainly expect to remove the limitations on dimensions and alignment that have been apparent, but to retain the expressive power of "thinking in parallel". At that point, goals will be more clearly defined and functions will be assessed in terms of their contribution to high-level interfaces.

However, it would be a mistake to think in terms of "language-oriented" functions supported by "microcode" without taking to heart the lessons of other interpretive systems. New facilities will be required, new algorithms invented, and users will want to control the primitive functions of the array, just as in scalar processing. Hence the concern expressed in Chapter 7 for offering a secure, flexible microsystem applies equally to AMA design. It will be seen in Part 3 that the AMA control and addressing functions have been chosen to meet the essential system requirement.

13.5 QUESTIONS AND FURTHER READING ON PART 2

1   Describe the method of sorting 2^n integers based on *odd−even exchange* as it would be applied on a linear array of 2^n processing elements with near-neighbor connections. How could such an array be applied to larger (or very much larger) lists of integers?

2   In the CRAY-1 Example 8.2, what advantage is gained by writing out the inner loop as a dual iteration, i.e. forming the intermediate vector of maximum elements first in $V3$ and then in $V1$?

3   Distinguish between the horizontal and vertical modes of processing numbers in an Active Memory Array, and state the advantages of each.

Although two solutions appear to process the same amount of data, vertical mode is often faster in execution than horizontal: why is that?

4   Explain how selective operations are performed in an array processor, e.g. to update a vector only where a certain condition holds:

$$where \ (W < 0) \ W \leftarrow W/2$$

Show how the design of PEs reflects that computing requirement.

5   How is the effect of Question 4 obtained in a vector processor such as CRAY-1? How about FPS AP-120B?

6   Show how the shuffle and exchange permutations would be used to achieve (a) matrix transposition, (b) reversal of elements in a vector. Give an example of a simple permutation which cannot be expressed easily by *shuff* and *potse* procedures.

7   What is the purpose of using skewed data mapping in an array processor? Without skewing you might have to rotate or transpose data in memory to achieve the same effect. What are the relative merits of the alternatives?

8   For further revelations on memory mapping, read BAT77. In STARAN, local memories are not directly connected to the PEs, but pass through a routing network which allows both horizontal and vertical access and various intermediate modes.

9   What are the degrading factors that prevent vector and array processors from achieving their theoretical maximum speeds? Give examples of how each arises in specific problems, and compare their effects on the two types of architecture.

10   In an iterative numerical calculation it is required to calculate values at each grid point as functions of values found in neighboring cells. However, for numerical stability it is often necessary to use values from the current iteration in the N and W cells, and from the previous iteration in E and S. The diagram shows the updating scheme for the central cell on the ith iteration, where $\{i\}$ denotes the set of values obtained at the ith iteration. How would you organize the calculation to make maximum use of an array processor?

$$
\begin{array}{ccc}
\bullet & \{i\} & \bullet \\[4pt]
\{i\} & \text{\Large +} & \{i-1\} \\[4pt]
\bullet & \{i-1\} & \bullet
\end{array}
$$

11   What functions would you add to the AMA to improve its effectiveness in comparison–exchange operations? (Start by reading BAT68.)

12   It has been indicated that operations on matrices larger than the AMA dimension can often be partitioned and expressed in terms of sub-operations on matrices that fit the array exactly. Examine the problems

that arise when the matrices are smaller than the AMA. How can calculations be organized to achieve maximum parallelism? Consider as a particular example a set of functions for operating on 4*4 matrices using AMA4.

13 In Example 11.1, the idea of "seeding" was used to mark contiguous regions in a Boolean matrix. Another application of the same technique can be found in the solution to maze problems. Is there a path from A to B (see Fig. 13.10), and if so what is it? The solid lines represent boundary

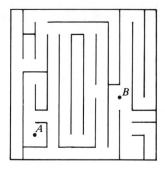

Fig. 13.10

walls which cannot be crossed, so the path must follow the "clear" passages. One method of solution is to grow a path from A, using 4-neighbor connections until either it reaches B or ceases to grow (hence B is inaccessible). However, the problem is still to find the path, knowing that one exists. Suppose a sequence of masks S is formed such that $S'0$ contains just A, $S'1$ contains points one step from A, and $S'i$ contains points accessible from A in exactly i steps and no less. Then if B is accessible in k steps the mask $S'k$ will contain B. Suppose a sequence T is grown from B by the same method as S. Then any point distant i on the path from A to B is in $S'i$ but being distant $(k-i)$ from B it is also in $T'(k-i)$. Hence a third sequence U can be formed containing just points on the path from A to B, and the union of planes in U will represent such a path. Show how you would program such an algorithm for a region mapping onto a single AMA plane. How would you detect and eliminate multiple paths?

This question is a very simple application of the Lee algorithm to a maze. For further discussion see, for example, LEE61 and RUB74.

14 Another type of connectivity arises in problems that can be expressed in terms of directed graphs. For example, the arcs in a graph of N nodes can be represented by an $N*N$ Boolean matrix in which element (I,J) is 1 if there is an arc directed from I to J and 0 otherwise. A sequence of matrices can be derived showing points accessible in $1, 2, \ldots, k$ steps from a given set of starting nodes. Suppose you have to write a segment manager for a program consisting of segments (nodes) containing pointers (arcs) directed from one to another. Given a set of base segments $b_1, \ldots, b_n$, show how to find all the segments that are inaccessible from the bases and therefore available for recycling. How would the algorithm be adapted to spaces of up to (a) 256 or (b) 4096 elements in AMA4?

15   In Question 14 you might find the transitive closure of a graph by logically summing the powers of a Boolean matrix B:

$$C = B \vee B^2 \vee \cdots \vee B^N$$

where matrix product is taken in the logical sense. The calculation of C can be programmed as a simple variation of matrix multiplication (Example 10.2). A more economical solution is given by Warshall (WAR62). Compare the two algorithms for a range of matrix sizes on AMA4.

16   In a chess set there are six different types of piece for each color. Devise a coding scheme that represents the state of play in a single AMA4 plane. Hence show how you would produce Boolean matrices marking:

(a)   all the black pieces;
(b)   all the pieces threatened by a white knight;
(c)   all possible moves open to white.

17   In describing parallel algorithms the effect of exceptional conditions such as overflow cannot be ignored unless there are prior reasons for knowing that they will not occur. Consider the general problem of evaluating expressions involving vectors. Formulate rules that would allow the programmer to detect and act upon exceptions. How would such rules be supported by (a) pipeline and (b) array organizations? (Refer if possible to manufacturers' technical manuals.) In AMA design the possibility exists of using variable precision for vertical-mode data. What rules would you apply in expression evaluation to exploit that feature? What advantages in time or space would be gained thereby?

18   One method of representing a numerical vector is in "block floating point" form, that is with a *single* exponent (of the element largest in magnitude) and a suitably scaled set of fractional values. In a bit-organized array processor how would the use of block floating point affect the timing of matrix operations?

19 Discuss the mapping of DAP Fortran functions onto AMA register transfer operations and procedures. Show for example how the *MERGE* and *ROWN* functions would be represented in AMA terms.

20 From time to time various improvements are suggested for bit-organized array processors, including:

(a) providing 4-bit arithmetic and data paths;

(b) local function control, e.g. add/subtract determined by the activity plane;

(c) extended global geometry and edge connections;

(d) local 8-way or perfect shuffle interconnections;

(e) local "mass storage" such as bubble-memory elements attached to each PE or to each row/column of the array.

Discuss the benefits (or otherwise) or such enhancements, with particular reference to programmability, PE design and interconnection.

PART 3

Abstraction

(From N. Thelwell, *Thelwell Country,* Eyre Methuen (1959))

Foreword to Part 3

Anyone who has taken responsibility for a large software system knows the sinking feeling induced by the news that "a few changes" are needed to meet customer requirements. How many weeks before it gets back to its present state of service? How much machine time for testing? What happened to the people who wrote it? In the life cycles of such systems it is recognized that the major costs derive not from initial programming but from subsequent testing, validation, extension, modification, maintenance and management. Attention is thus turned away from features of individual languages, which can have only marginal effects on the final product, to what might be called the "global" structure of software: how does it all fit together, and how can parts be replaced or upgraded without interfering with the function of the rest of the system? Innovations in both language and machine design are needed to provide satisfactory answers to such questions.

Chapters 14 – 19 examine structuring techniques that have been used in experimental systems and which are beginning to be used in commercial products. Experienced computer engineers will probably find some of the material "difficult" at first reading. In contrast, I have found that new graduates take quite easily to the styles of design and programming that are discussed. The reason for that surprising inversion is that a lot of "experience" is concerned with modelling real-life situations in essentially "dumb" environments, and with realizing just how stupid computers can be. The idea that environments should be created in which the computer recognizes the attributes of the data on which it is told to act seems a natural design objective, but its effect on existing expertise can be shattering.

I am most grateful to A.K. Jones and W.A. Wulf of Carnegie-Mellon University, B.H. Liskov of Massachusetts Institute of Technology and V. Berstis of IBM General Systems Division for reading and commenting on sections describing concepts of which they have first-hand experience.

14 THE IMPORTANCE OF STRUCTURE

In a seat-reservation system the primary user is the clerk dealing with customer enquiries. His working environment (in the case of an airline) is a list of flight numbers distinguished by date. For each there is a list of passengers giving name, origin, destination, class of fare, connecting flights, accounting and other information. The action of the clerk is to interrogate and update such lists, and apart from ergonomic factors his main performance measures are the number of flights the system can handle, the ancillary information it provides, and the distribution of response times, including break-down periods.

It is easy to see that the environment of the reservation clerk is just a fraction of that supported by the application package. Many enquiry stations must be handled simultaneously and without mutual interference, recovery procedures are invoked in the event of breakdown, overall accounting and statistical summaries are provided, flight information is updated, new services are brought on-line, the operating system is modified, mainframe and mass storage devices are upgraded, and so on. At each point engineers, users and programmers view the machine in a different way, and in a well-designed system they are authorized to examine or change only a limited amount of information: the clerk can't alter the tariff structure, the microprogrammer can't book himself a free flight to Rome. In that sense the system is partitioned by its engineering levels, each presenting a formal "interface" to the outside world, and if we ask how it is that a typical transaction viewed on the screen as updating a field in a record can involve (say) 5 file accesses and 10^6 microprogram steps (40 000 instructions) the answer must be found in the long series of structural decisions leading to the display seen at the enquiry desk.

In any complex system it is inevitable that low-level performance parameters (such as instructions per second) will be downgraded in passing to the level of the primary user. The "packaging cost" of an interface depends on the type of engineering involved; whether it is worth paying depends on how widely it is used and how it contributes to reliability, for it is well understood that inability to detect and remove errors quickly enough is a major limiting factor in the development of systems with many interacting components. Thus at one end of the scale the packaging of electronic circuits is relatively expensive, but is practically essential to the design of hardware. The historical growth of physical assemblies from elementary gates to integrated circuits and multilayer boards containing many thousands of components derives from the standardization of circuit families and the precise method of connection provided by electrical conductors. Similarly, the complex instruction codes and channel commands of modern systems follow from what is essentially an extension of hardware interconnection disciplines into microprogram. At the other extreme the mechanisms used to implement clear-cut interfaces between users and their "files" and "jobs" are relatively cheap to implement, even with fairly sophisticated access functions, because the interfacing mechanism (a program) is small in relation to the function performed (a job step, file interrogation, etc.).

The difficult region is the interconnection of programs themselves: the mechanism is neither a wire nor a file identifier but a computed address that cannot always be "fixed" in advance, and in the classic von Neumann machine there is no way to guarantee that such an address will make the intended connection without writing in additional program checks. For that reason software designers have always been faced with the dilemma of choosing between control (as expressed by "high level" implementation tools) and performance, with results that are apparent in the growth of many large operating system and compiler projects.

The lack of secure interfaces in programs can have far-reaching effects on application packages, as we can see by returning to the reservation system. The passage of a single transaction can be visualized as a sequence of phases, each carrying out a clearly defined operation on the input message or the data associated with it. The first phase might handle data input and logging, the second dealing with message analysis, and so on. The programs for each phase will be written by specialist groups, each with different access rights to programs and files. For system integrity it is important to be able to contain errors within each phase, which means, for example, that the program carrying out message analysis in the second phase should only be able to access one input message at a time, together with syntax tables, keywords, and contextual information derived from previous interactions with the same user at the same enquiry desk.

Now consider that 50 transactions are started each second, that each takes 5 s to complete (allowing for file access) and runs through 10 phases. On average, 250 transactions are to be represented at a time, and a change of phase takes place every 2 ms. Such estimates place in perspective the various ways of representing phases: if the "packaging overhead" per phase is 1000 bytes, then ¼ Mbyte of store is committed to protection; a phase change of 1 ms commits 30% of computing power and places a strong constraint on what can be done in a phase — it might be strong enough to prevent the use of high-level programming languages, with consequent loss of control within the phase.

A transaction-processing system presents in acute form the problem that any multiprogramming operating system has to solve: to prevent one section of program from interfering with another, and to allow for controlled sharing of information, at least between user and supervisor programs. The control mechanisms that have been developed all depend on partitioning the program space in some way and providing the "current" program section with a list of the partitions available to it. The list may be very short, e.g. a single base-and-limit pair, or it may contain many segment descriptors as in virtual machine architecture. Unfortunately, architectural rules that seek to preserve the fiction of the "von Neumann address space" never achieve the precision that the application demands (which is understandable because the list is usually designed to keep programs, rather than fragments of programs, apart) and attempts to refine the structure by controlling access to the list have proved to be deficient in both function and performance, as will be seen shortly.

The TP system designer, perceiving the costs associated with strict partitioning, might compromise by mapping either one transaction or one phase to each "program domain" (Fig. 14.1). Neither choice is entirely satisfactory:

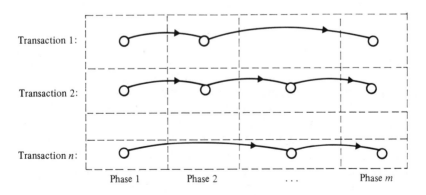

Fig. 14.1 Partitioning in a transaction-processing system

in the former there is no protection between phases; in the latter there is no protection between transactions. What appears to be needed is a very refined method of access control, with low storage and control overheads, which can be applied easily by the user: if that is available we can expect to (1) reduce program development costs, because unexpected interactions between program sections can be eliminated; (2) increase reliability of the final product, for the same reason; and (3) increase performance, because program interfacing is not dependent on the restrictions of a high-level language. In practice such benefits can be traded off in various ways, e.g. by adding more facilities or by using less experienced programmers, but there is no doubt that they have far-reaching effects in all aspects of programming, from planning to maintenance of the final product.

The foregoing line of reasoning has not passed unmarked by the computing profession, and might even be said to underlie most of the effort reported under such headings as "software engineering" and "modular programming". Its importance is that, if correctly understood, the process of constructing programs could be made as predictable as one might expect from the subassemblies and precise tolerances of, e.g., electrical or mechanical design. We shall see that the logical requirements on programs are quite simple. Their implementation must, however, satisfy certain practical constraints to be successful:

(1)   It must be foolproof. In other words, there can be no way of circumventing the control mechanism to establish illicit structures.
(2)   It must be cheap and fast. It will not be used if it degrades price/performance appreciably because there is no tangible compensation in the short term for doing so.
(3)   It must be flexible, i.e. applicable to any size of structural unit and resolving to the byte or statement level.
(4)   It must be easy to use. Most users will not be aware of the control mechanism because it is concealed by language definition. However, it must be easy to map high-level structures into the program space, and to make direct use of access-control facilities within the System Implementation Languages.

Strict application of these constraints leads to rapid thinning, but not complete disappearance, of the list of remedies to the "programming problem". In subsequent chapters we shall examine some of the remnants in detail. Of course, any control mechanism that is not immediately available can be provided by interpretive techniques, and although that runs up against (2) there are many practical situations where interpretive overhead is acceptable. We shall, however, confine attention to designs in which the instruction-execution rate is not drastically affected by the mechanism of program composition.

14.1 ACCESS LISTS

A program is constructed from a number of modules, which the reader will recognize as data areas and subroutines in Cobol, arrays and procedures in Algol, named data sets in a database management system — it is not necessary to be specific on that point, but it is assumed that a pointer uniquely identifies a module and possible an area within it, using offset and limit fields. It has been shown that a key requirement in program partitioning is to be able to make strong assertions about the accessibility of modules at any time during a computation, for which reason the idea of an **access matrix** is introduced.

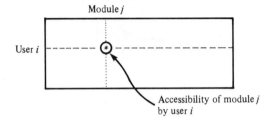

Fig. 14.2 Access matrix

In essence, an access matrix is a statement of which "users" can access which modules. It could be summarized by a matrix (Fig. 14.2) in which rows correspond to users and columns to modules, each element indicating whether access is allowed, and perhaps saying more about the permissible forms of access. In practice, such a matrix is very sparse, and its compression leads to complementary views of accessibility: either listing for each module the users that can access it, or listing for each user the modules that can be accessed. The preferred representation depends on the ratio of users to modules (if lists have to be searched one would like them to be as short as possible), on system dynamics (how often the matrix elements change, and what has to be done to update them), and what exactly is meant by a "user" (is it someone at a terminal, a virtual machine, a task, a procedure, ... ?). The reader is probably familiar with file systems using the "column" representation of the access matrix, listing for each file the registered accounts (or groups) to whom access may be granted.

In the discussion that follows we shall interpret a user as a "locus of control within a task". That will enable precise models to be made of the environments encountered, for example, in the flow of control within a transaction. As a consequence, the access matrix will change principally as the result of instruction sequencing, or creation and deletion of tasks, and therefore the preferred representation is in "row" form. An **access list** is a set of pointers instantly associated with a task indicating which modules can be accessed at any time. It should be stressed that the access list is a property of the control stream and not the user (program or person) who invokes it. For example, in the seat-reservation system a clerk initiates transactions that access files that the clerk would not be allowed to access directly. Let us examine in more detail how such a list might be organized.

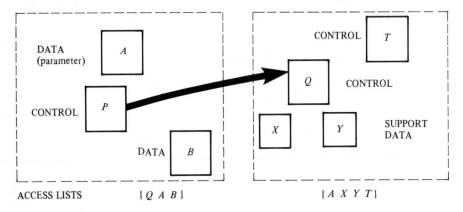

ACCESS LISTS   { Q A B }   { A X Y T }

Fig. 14.3   Change of access list accompanying phase change

We have seen that as calculation proceeds the items that can legitimately be accessed will change, e.g. in moving from one phase to the next in the example given above. Figure 14.3 illustrates in greater detail what happens when control passes from one phase to another. It is supposed that change of phase is accompanied by change of control module, from P to Q, and at the same time the access list is to change from { Q A B } to { A X Y T }. In other, possibly concurrent activations of P and Q the modules accessed might be entirely different, so the list must be associated in some way with the control stream and not with the code segments themselves. There are just two ways in which elements can find their way onto the access list:

(1)   by **inheritance**, i.e. being passed as a parameter such as A in going from P to Q;
(2)   by **construction**, i.e. being "written in" to the definition of the control segment, as "X" and "Y" might be for Q.

The reasons for these restrictions are that (1) is part of the interface specification agreed between designers of P and Q, allowing P to communicate to Q whatever is necessary and sufficient for the next phase of calculation.

However, Q can quite legitimately call on more support data or procedures, thus expanding the list of accessible items. In the example given, it can be said that P is effectively prevented from accessing X and Y except through the agency of Q.

An associated requirement is that "unwanted" pointers should be removed from the access list. In the example, B would be removed: it is not enough to "forget" that it is there, and it must be reinstated if in fact control returns to the previous activation of P as a result of procedural sequencing.

Access-list management therefore devolves into two sets of rules: those concerned with changing a list of pointers, and those concerned with ensuring that it is used correctly. The former must recognize both inherited and constructed elements and will tend to punctuate the control stream at points where the access list is "updated". The second set of rules will be such that all references to program space are *valid*, i.e. limited to the domain specified by the access list. Given a calculated pointer p (in a microregister, for example), there are two ways of ensuring its validity:

(1)   to find that p is within the bounds of *some* element of the access list (we assume that both p and the elements of the access list share the same set of system addresses); or

(2)   to arrange that p includes an index n specifying a *particular* member of the access list which provides a base address and limit, and an *offset* relative to the selected base (see diagram).

p | n | *offset* | Pointer in microregister

| *limit* | *base* | Access list element n
                          ($offset \leqslant limit$)

Evidently (1) implies an associative comparison with all list elements, which is generally uneconomic even with hardware assistance. The second method is more easily applied, but has the unfortunate effect of placing access list indices in program registers, so that the meaning of a pointer might change in moving from one domain to another (refer to Fig. 14.3, where A is the second element in the list in one phase, and first in the other).

At this stage the reader will recognize that the problem could be avoided if access list indices such as n were somehow made invariant or "global", at least in a single control path. There would then be an immediate correspondence between the method (2) just outlined and the methods of addressing based on segmentation. But the problem remains of specifying which segment pointers are in the access list at any instant. One possibility is to enumerate all domains (e.g. phases in the transaction paths of Fig. 14.1) and specify, for each segment, those to which it belonged; if there were 64 domains, a 64-bit mask could be associated with each segment table element s, in which bit $j = 1$

if the segment belonged by construction to access list j, and 0 otherwise. If the index j of the current access list is associated with the control state, validation of access would require checking bit j in all segments referenced. In moving from P to Q the index j would change accordingly.

Access list no:	0	1	2	3	.. j	..	63		
Seg. table entry s:	0	0	1	0	.. 1	..	0	*limit*	*base*

The cost is high, however, and would need to be even higher to take account of more refined controls, for example on "read", "write" or "execute" access. In practical implementations the masks are all presumed to be such that, for some r (depending on s):

$$\text{bit } j = \begin{cases} 0 \text{ if } j \leqslant r \\ 1 \text{ otherwise} \end{cases} \tag{1}$$

so that for each segment table reference it is only necessary to compare j with r to determine whether to permit access. The practical effect of (1) is that within the program space segments are grouped into a series of nested "protection zones" as illustrated in Fig. 14.4, in which the inner zones, with high values of r, require the highest values of j to be associated with the control state. That is interpreted as being "more protected", and the higher the access control index the higher the "privilege" of the code. For example, access to segments in the innermost zone, for which $r = 63$, requires $j = 63$; conversely, for $j = 60$ (say), all segments for which $r \leqslant 60$ would be accessible.

The organization of segments suggested by Fig. 14.4 can be viewed as a generalization of the binary partition between "user" and "system" spaces brought into use in elementary computers to support operating-system actions. Attempting to allocate protection levels to segments has given rise to conjectures about "hierarchical" system organizations. The facts that such structures only vaguely reflect practical programming requirements (in which the same module belongs to many different domains), and that they run into immense complication in dealing with inherited access rights and inter-process communication, have been insufficient to prevent their use.

However, not achieving the stated objectives is incidental to the main criticism of all the methods so far discussed: that they are far from satisfying constraint (2) of being "cheap and fast". In order to circumvent reference to the access list and compete with uncontrolled mechanisms it is necessary to have some prior reasons for believing that a computed pointer is within bounds. How can that be done? In principle, by applying rules of pointer *formation* in the program domain such that from a valid initial state only valid pointers can be derived. In practice, such rules are applied either before program execution, by a compiler/loader subsystem, or during execution, by machine functions. In each case the principal advantage gained is that

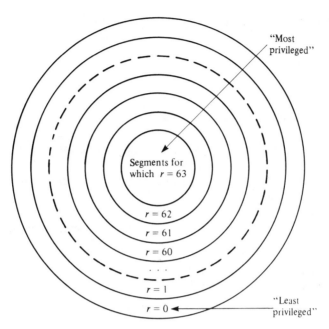

Fig. 14.4 Nested protection zones. Note that in this example high values of r are associated with high privilege. In Multics and other systems the convention is reversed, with $r = 0$ for the most privileged

performance is not degraded by reference to the access list on every data access. Compiler-based rules have the further advantages of being independent of hardware and of adapting relatively easily to current language conventions. They have the disadvantages of demanding fairly static program structures and of greater exposure to malfunction or subversion. However, it is not necessary, as sometimes seems to be suggested, to choose one or the other. The two sets of techniques are complementary in system design, the main interest lying in where to draw the boundary between them. In this and subsequent chapters we shall study examples of each.

Before leaving the topic of access-list management, it should be noted that the mechanisms considered impose both control and data structures on programs, e.g. at the points (in time) when the access list is updated, and in the choice of "granularity" of protection. It is tempting but dangerous to identify them with similar structures occurring in other contexts and serving different purposes. For example, if a clumsy updating mechanism is associated with each procedure call, the programmer will be penalized for using an essential tool. Again, if the unit of physical store management (a segment) invariably defines a protection boundary, then the precision of access control will depend on the competence of the store management system. In general, the design constraint (3) will best be served by decoupling the two sets of ideas as fully as possible.

14.2 ABSTRACTION MECHANISMS

So far we have stressed the need to change the immediate operating environment of a program in a controlled way. To complete the picture we must clarify what is meant by a rule of construction, as applied to access lists. How are they chosen in the first place? There is a suggestion of "to each according to his needs", but the idea of abstraction provides a high-level interface between phases in which the question is answered implicitly. To see how it might arise, consider the earlier example (Fig. 14.3) in which Q, with the help of X and Y and control module T, was seen to be providing a service function for P.

In particular, suppose X and Y are file-control blocks (fcb's) and that Q is a multiple-entry-point module offering procedures to:

(1) *Create* an fcb, returning its pointer (such as X);
(2) *Write* a data area to file, using a specified fcb;
(3) *Delete* a given fcb.

In that sense, Q is seen as manager of a set of fcb's, offering the same level of service to any caller that can access Q in the first place and present an fcb pointer to authorize subsequent interactions. For example, calling for a *Write* operation would require the two parameters A (the data area) and X (fcb pointer).

In practice, the above illustration is not quite adequate because possession of a pointer to X gives P direct access to the fcb, which is generally undesirable. In its place a new type of pointer must be manufactured which uniquely identifies itself as referring to an fcb, but in such a way that only the fcb manager Q can directly access the file attributes (X or Y in the example). In compiler-based systems such references are treated as extensions of the general mechanism for distinguishing data types. In hardware-based systems the fcb pointer is a distinct form of operand usually referred to as a **capability**. In either case the constructed part of the access list is precisely the set of pointers to those data and control modules necessary and sufficient to support the range of functions offered by Q. Knowledge of their existence is unnecessary outside the design group responsible for Q. Note also that inheritance works both ways: at some point P must acquire from Q the pointer to X; later, Q acquires from P the pointer to A. Usually, but by no means invariably, a procedure interface is adopted to formalize such exchanges.

More generally, certain programs will be designated as *class managers*, assuming full responsibility for representing objects of particular types. Such objects will be seen from outside in terms of their *attributes*, which will be examined and updated using procedures offered by the appropriate class manager. Authority to access an object is conferred at the time of its creation by issuing a uniquely coded and unforgeable pointer, sometimes thought of as a "ticket", though unlike most ticketing systems copies of the original remain valid. To the extent that the representation of a class of objects is concealed, while allowing controlled access to all relevant attributes, it is said that a successful **abstraction** has been achieved.

The importance of abstraction in program construction and maintenance cannot be overemphasized. It is the closest one can get to having precisely engineered and tested subassemblies that will continue to work predictably as parts of larger systems. Although it has been introduced here as a generalization of lower-level concepts, it could equally well be derived, as it was historically, by attempting to mechanize the power of expression captured by mathematical notation. Hot pursuit of such an ambition is likely to end up in deep water, but even if we confine ourselves to the simplest constructs some essential facilities can be identified, i.e.:

(1) to *invent* new classes or types of object;
(2) to *create* objects of a specified class with initial attribute values;
(3) to *examine* and *update* attributes;
(4) to *delete* objects;
(5) to delete references to an object in a given context; in particular to *eliminate* all references to, and means of creating, objects of a given class.

In programming terms the need arises for symbolic equivalents of the names one might use in (1) for new types or in (3) for their attributes:

"Let A be a class of objects with attributes $\{a_i\}$ ..."

or in (2) for the objects themselves:

"Let x be a (member of the class) A",

"Let y denote (the same entity as) x",

"Let z be a new A with the same attributes as x" and so on. Internally, capabilities (or equivalent typed values) meet that need, as we shall see later, and it is often convenient to think of the access list as a mixture of capabilities and pointers to program space. Capabilities denote entities of finite but otherwise unconstrained structure, unlimited by the registers, storage organization, or function set of the host computer, and they provide a direct means of mapping the ideas expressed above into register values and register transfer operations.

Mathematical reasoning depends heavily on the axiomatic properties of the objects of discourse, and the same is true of reasoning about programs if suitable abstractions can be found. In other words, proof of correct operation of an application module (such as P in Fig. 14.3) might be established subject to constraints on the service module (Q in the example) which could be shown to be satisfied by independent analysis. Ideally, the demonstration of correctness of a complete program would be subdivided into many such domains, each simple enough to admit conclusive proof of correctness. In practise it would be unusual to follow through a demonstration of correctness on entirely formal lines, but essentially the same principles are followed in the informal process of debugging and maintaining programs, knowing that individual modules can only interact in carefully constrained ways.

Practical implementations tend to highlight issues that are treated lightly in mathematical contexts. They are mentioned briefly here. Their effects will be apparent in subsequent discussion.

Firstly, there are the questions of scope which have been touched on already: when does a class or object come into existence or disappear? In the context of multiple control streams sharing a class definition are the objects they define private or shared? Does an object disappear automatically when the procedure that called it into existence terminates? Is it necessary to declare all data types in advance of calculation? Evidently there are a number of plausible answers to such questions, and an important objective in designing support mechanisms is to preserve as much choice as possible.

Secondly, we are concerned not only with *using* abstractions but also with *implementing* them, in changing from the "user domain" to the "class-manager domain" and back again many times in the course of calculation. An object seen on one hand as a "file-control block" acquires quite different properties when the domain changes. The implementation language (or machine) must reflect such change of type at the same time as the access list is changed. Remember that P (the "user" in our example) might be seen as a "class manager" from some other domain. It is tempting, but fruitless, to expect the separate domains to fall into a hierarchical pattern.

Finally, it will be seen that program space can itself be treated in abstract terms, e.g. by inventing a class of (data) segments consisting of sequences of storage cells and providing operators to read and write values at specified positions. For all practical purposes, however, it is preferable to treat storage as a special case directly dependent on hardware support, and to develop the store management system in advance of other abstractions.

14.3 COMPILE-TIME ABSTRACTION

Abstraction has been compared with extension of the typing convention used in many high-level programming languages. An essential feature of such a mechanism is that all decisions depending on the type of variables can be made before calculation begins, if not during compilation then at the latest when loading control modules into program space. In relatively static programming environments that is not unduly restrictive and we might have expected, in view of the importance attached to the result, to find a number of ready-made languages meeting our requirements. Unfortunately that is not the case. The most troublesome problem is to control access lists with the precision demanded, and in this subsection we shall examine the new forms that might be used to control abstraction during the translation process.

Consider a general form of class definition for a class Q. For most practical purposes we would expect it to occur as a single syntactic unit bracketed by tokens such as:

class Q ...   **end** Q;

Within the defining text there will be procedures to initialize the class representation, to create and delete elements, to manipulate their attributes (Fig. 14.5), all of which are "visible" to external users; in addition there will be local workspace (X, Y) associated with the representation and possibly local procedures (T) assisting in class management.

```
class Q;
var X, Y: array [1. .1000] of integer
procedure create ( );     {returns object index n};
procedure delete (n);     {deletes object representation};
procedure write (n,A);   {writes data A via n};
{. . . and similarly for read ( ), copy ( ) etc.,
allowing access to attributes of objects in Q};
procedure T ( );          {utility procedure};
end Q;
```

Fig. 14.5   A form of definition for the class of objects Q

Implicitly, we expect the class Q to be initialized on entering the block (or program) in which it is declared, and to be erased on leaving that same block. Individual variables can be declared as members of Q, e.g. (Pascal-style):

var x, y, z: Q

and assigned as in:

$x := Q\$create()$;
$y := x$;
$z := Q\$copy(x)$;

where "$Q\$create$" is a compound identifier referring to the *create* function in the class declaration for *Q*, and similarly for "*Q$copy*". Now if we try to regard "**class** ... **end**" as a block definition in the Algol sense the main differences are:

(1) that certain identifiers such as *create* and *copy* are promoted outside the syntactic boundaries of the class declaration and used by procedures having access to *Q*, for which purpose the naming convention is extended;

(2) on the other hand, the workspace defined by *X, Y* and the internal procedure *T* are strictly part of the class implementation, not accessible from outside;

(3) a variable such as *x*, which is declared to be of type "*Q*" in the user domain will be treated differently inside the class definition; for example when presented as a parameter in *Q$copy(x)* it might be used to form a numerical index to one of the arrays *X, Y*.

Consequently, it appears to be necessary to adapt the "scope" and "type" rules of existing languages to meet the requirements of abstraction. Readers who are familiar with Fortran may recall that a fairly good approximation to a class manager can be offered by a subroutine with multiple entry points. The "static" form of storage allocation meets the need for local workspace rather better than "dynamic" allocation of block-structured languages. Even so, the integrity of the representation and the validity of the tickets presented to users are far from secure in Fortran systems.

A number of new languages have been invented in recent years, based on Algol, and providing support for abstraction. We shall examine two of them and point out features that are present as the result of supporting "encapsulated types". The first one, CLU, has been developed in the Programming Methodology Group at M.I.T. An example will be introduced here and used in later chapters for purposes of comparison.

CLU permits the use of abstractions by introducing a new construct known as a **cluster** from which the language derives its name. A cluster implements a data type by defining a representation for objects of that type and by implementing the permissible operations in terms of procedures. Syntactically, a cluster definition has three components (Fig. 14.6):

```
/* Interface */      Q = cluster is create, delete, write, copy

/* Object */         rep = array [ ... ];

/* Operations */     create      ...     end;
                     delete      ...     end;
                       . . .
                     copy        ...     end;

                     end Q;
```

Fig. 14.6 Cluster definition in CLU

(1) the *interface description* which gives a concise summary of the type identifier and the applicable operations seen by external users and defined within the cluster;

(2) the *object description* defines the representation used within the cluster. Externally, objects are regarded as non-decomposable. Internally, the **rep** declaration defines the type interpretation to be used;

(3) *operation definitions* constitute the body of the cluster, and must include definitions of all operations identified in (1). In addition there may be utilities internal to the cluster. All the definitions take the form of normal procedures except for the use of the representation type **rep** and the type conversion operator **cvt**, whose use is explained below.

Before presenting a detailed example it will be useful to understand the environment in which clusters are used. CLU is a modular programming language. Each CLU module supports either a procedure or a cluster. The system maintains a database relating abstractions to their implementations, i.e. for each abstract operation (procedure) there is a specification of the types of all input and output parameters, and for each abstract data type the parameter types are specified for all defined operations. Moreover, for each abstraction there is a list (possibly empty) of modules implementing that abstraction. Abstract specifications can be added to the database at any time and used in the construction of modules before their implementations exist. When a module is submitted for translation a check is made that the declared input and output parameter types agree with those of the abstraction it represents. If the translation is successful information about the module is added to the database.

CLU modules refer to each other via a set of "external names" that are bound to their abstractions during compilation. Complete type checking is therefore possible during translation. Selection of the actual implementation can be deferred to any time prior to execution of the using module. Thus the same procedure can be executed on different occasions with a variety of data representations and without recompiling, which is a good practical illustration of the use of modular programming techniques in conjunction with abstract data definitions. Note, however, that there are no global "data modules", all communication between modules being via parameters.

One abstraction that is important in support of the following example is that handling homogeneous arrays of (theoretically) unbounded size. An array of integers is simply declared as:

array [*int*]

which is treated as a data type. Initially, an array is empty, but a notional "lower bound" is defined, and the array can be extended in either direction one element at a time. The operations defined on arrays include:

create (*i*)	:	returns an **array** [*int*] object *a* with lower bound *i*;
high (*a*)	:	returns the index of the highest defined element of *a*, or *low*(*a*) − 1 if *a* is empty;
low (*a*)	:	returns the index of the lowest defined element of *a*, or the initially defined bound if *a* is empty;
size (*a*)	:	returns *high* (*a*) − *low* (*a*) + 1;
addh(*a*,*v*)	:	extends *a* at the high index position by one element, which is assigned the value *v*.

In all the above examples *a* is required to be of type **array** [*int*]. The meaning of other operations will be clear from the example that follows. Note that external procedure calls are invoked by a compound name consisting of the (external) type name and the operation identifier separated by the "*$*" symbol, so that although the operation *create* might exist in many modules the one required is always made explicit. For internally defined procedures that convention is unnecessary.

Example 14.1 It is required to support a class of integer sets, i.e. finite, unordered collections of integers, without repetition. The following operations will be defined on such sets (*s*) and integers (*v*):

create()	to create an empty set *s*;
insert (*s*,*v*)	to insert an integer *v* in set *s*;
remove(*s*,*v*)	to remove an integer *v* from set *s*;
has (*s*,*v*)	to enquire whether *v*∈*s*;
equal (*s₁*,*s₂*)	to test whether s_1 is identically the same as s_2;
similar (*s₁*,*s₂*)	to test whether two sets contain the same elements, i.e. (∀*v*) (*v*∈s_1 ⟺ *v*∈s_2);
copy (*s*)	to make a copy of *s*.

The cluster for the type *intset* is given in Fig. 14.7. Remember that a user of the integer set abstraction is able to declare and assign variables as in:

> *cards*: *intset*
> *cards* : = *intset$create*()

and to use set operations as in:

> *intset$insert*(*cards*, 12);
> *if intset$has*(*cards*, 1) *then play*();

The following notes highlight points made by the example.

```
intset = cluster is create, insert, remove, is_in, equal, similar, copy
1     rep = array[int]

2     create = proc () returns (cvt)
          return(rep$create(0))
          end create

      insert = proc (s: cvt, v: int)
          if search(s, v) > rep$high(s)
             then rep$addh(s, v) end
          end insert

      remove = proc (s: cvt, v: int)
          i: int := search(s, v)
          if i <= rep$high(s)
             then s[i] := s[rep$high(s)]
                  rep$remh(s)
             end
          end remove

      is_in = proc (s: cvt, v: int) returns (bool)
          return(search(s, v) <= rep$high(s))
          end is_in

4     equal = proc (s1, s2: cvt) returns (bool)
          return(s1 = s2)
          end equal

      similar = proc (s1, s2: cvt) returns (bool)
          if rep$size(s1) ~= rep$size(s2)
             then return(false) end
          for i: int in int$from_to(rep$low(s1), rep$high(s1)) do
             if search(s2, s1[i]) > rep$high(s2)
                then return(false) end
             end
          return(true)
          end similar

      copy = proc (s: cvt) returns (cvt)
          return(rep$copy(s))
          end copy

3     search = proc (s: rep, v: int) returns (int)
          for i: int in int$from_to(rep$low(s), rep$high(s)) do
             if s[i]. = v
                then return(i) end
             end
          return(rep$high(s) + 1)
          end search

5     end intset
```

Fig. 14.7   The *intset* cluster in CLU (with acknowledgement to
Barbara H. Liskov)

Note: *has* is implemented by the procedure *is_in*

¹ The reserved symbol **rep** is defined by the object description; thereafter any occurrence of **rep** can strictly be replaced by its formal definition, e.g. "**rep**$low(s)" is treated as "**array**[int]$low(s)". It follows that the representation could be changed simply be redefining **rep**, provided the implementation chosen had operations corresponding to create, low etc.

² Input parameters of the cluster type are declared as "type" **cvt**, which ensures they are treated internally as **rep** type, in this example **array**[int]. Output parameters of type **cvt** are similarly converted to the cluster type, as can be seen in create, in which the value r is returned, declared as **rep** but presented externally as intset.

³ search is an internal procedure used by remove, is_in and similar, but not offered externally because it discloses too much about the set representation.

⁴ Equality is made to depend on the representation type, but the logical property implied is that in all expressions evaluated subsequently the replacement of one set by its equal will not affect the outcome of calculation. That is only true if the sets in question are constant or physically identical. The weaker condition that they consist of precisely the same integers is expressed by the similar procedure. Notionally, there is an equality procedure for the integer type, "int$equal(i,j)", but that is abbreviated as in "$i = j$".

⁵ For a set representation using a different type of elementary component the form of cluster would be essentially unchanged except for the **rep** definition and treatment of individual elements, e.g. in dealing with character sets, int would be replaced by char as appropriate. The CLU system recognizes such requirements to the extent of supporting parameterized types, so that a single cluster can act as a "type generator". In fact the **array** abstraction is a type generator, **array**[int] being a particular application of the definition. Similarly, a **set** abstraction might be defined as a type generator, intset being defined as **set**[int]. The reader is referred to published papers for details.

Study of the intset example should be sufficient to show how CLU responds to the particular problems associated with abstraction. To understand the consequences of such an approach in a broader context we refer to the constraints listed earlier (p. 294) and try to distinguish limitations imposed by CLU from those inherent in language technology.

(1) It must be foolproof. Assuming the compiler/loader and database are correct at all times there is no way of penetrating the type mechanism. Guaranteeing the implementation of a particular abstraction is a matter for the user. Guaranteeing the correctness of the compiler and database manager are non-trivial matters, both of which benefit from the very

facilities they are intended to support. In a raw machine environment the delicate problems of building up a set of interdependent facilities from scratch are ignored at one's peril: it was a system programmer who first prayed "O Lord, make me secure, *but not yet*". However, in many language environments the support functions, particularly for store and database management, are underwritten by separate microprogram or hardware mechanisms.

(2) It must be cheap and fast. Again, within the framework of the *intset* module that is the case. The example given makes use of a store manager for arrays which is certainly not fast and, in general, compiler-based mechanisms cannot provide a secure abstraction of storage without including run-time checks on computed array indices and consequent loss of speed.

(3) It must be flexible. The language is subject to handling strong type conventions at compile-time, but the structure of abstract objects and operations is unrestricted. The CLU implementation does not take account of modules shared by concurrent control streams, for which synchronizing primitives have to be introduced. It will be noted that there is no *delete* operation for *intset*: in CLU objects exist as long as they are accessible, and no facility is provided for user-defined management. The class manager could make a set "inactive" by marking its representation in some way, for example, using element 0 to indicate whether the set is active. References to such a set would still exist in the user domain, but attempts to *insert* elements or to *copy* sets would lead to monitoring action by the class manager. Treatment of such "dangling references" will be discussed in later chapters. A number of refinements are often associated with abstract objects, for example the right to apply *remove* might be withheld from certain users. As we shall see, that is usually expressed in capability schemes by associating "option bits" with the object identifier:

options	*id*	capability

In CLU it would be necessary to elaborate the meaning of the **cvt** operator to achieve a similar effect.

(4) It must be easy to use. That can be understood in two senses. For application programming the choice of language is a matter of taste; abstraction features should not detract from the style of the language and if properly applied will make a positive contribution to reducing development and maintenance costs. As a "machine-defining" target for compiler output a high-level language such as CLU would not be chosen. One would look for a set of very primitive and very efficient support functions,

and fairly quickly come to the conclusion that hardware support was essential.

We have seen that CLU offers abstraction in the restricted context of procedures communicating only via parameter lists. More generally, procedures within the same task will share an operating environment but provision must still be made for selective concealment of data. Our second example shows how that would be done in ADA, the real-time language developed on the initiative of the US Department of Defense.

The main structural unit of ADA is a **package**, which typically encapsulates data and subprograms providing access to the data. Normally a package is defined in two parts: a **specification** describing the facilities it offers and a **body** in which the facilities are implemented. (In the degenerate case where the specification simply acts as a common pool of data there need be no body. A further special case is provided by more familiar *procedure* and *function* definitions.) The designers of ADA envisage a package as surrounded by a "wall" which separates the enclosed declarations from the rest of the program, penetrated by a "window" through which some or all of the declarations are visible. The shape of the window enables various forms of package to be supported. In the present instance it is required to expose only a type name and the declarations of applicable operations, and that is done by declaring the type to be **private**. By that means a user can create and manipulate variables of the given type, but cannot operate directly on the

```
package INTSET_MANAGER is
         restricted type INTSET is private;
         procedure insert (S: INTSET; I: INTEGER);
         procedure remove (S: INTSET; I: INTEGER);
         procedure has      (S: INTSET; I: INTEGER) return BOOLEAN;
         procedure copy     (S1, S2: INTSET);
    private type INTSET is array [1 .. 1000] of INTEGER;
    end;
```

Fig. 14.8   Specification of an integer-set manager in ADA

type representation. Figure 14.8 outlines the specification part of the integer-set manager as it might appear in ADA. The package body, providing definitions of *insert, remove, has, . . . , copy*, would appear as another compilation unit. Thus CLU and ADA are somewhat similar in supporting the concept of separate compilation with strong type checking by reference to a database containing specification parts. Some notable differences are:

(1) *INTSET_MANAGER* does not take responsibility for storage allocation, whereas the *intset* cluster did so (by calling on the array functions). The type representation is visible to users (Fig. 14.8) even though they cannot exploit their knowledge. In the context of the user package or

program a declaration:

> *x,y : INTSET ; z :* **access** *INTSET*

or assignment:

> *z :* = **new** *INTSET*

creates space on the stack or heap as appropriate. There is no *create* function in *INTSET_MANAGER*.

(2) ADA automatically converts from the (external) package type to the representation array when control passes to one of the implementing procedures, and there is no need for **rep** or **cvt** types.

(3) Assignment and testing for equality of any two objects of identical type are provided by default in ADA, though such operations can be inhibited by declaring the encapsulated type as **restricted**: in the latter case all actions taken on integer sets are obliged to be handled by *INTSET_MANAGER*.

(4) ADA program units (subprograms, packages, blocks) are nested syntactically. Addressability of a package such as *INTSET_MANAGER* is determined in the first place by scope rules almost identical to those of Algol 60. As we have seen, access to elements within a package is decided by the shape of the window. A declaration which takes the form:

> **use** *INTSET_MANAGER*;

promotes the identifiers *INTSET, insert, remove,* etc. into the name space of a user package. A program unit can also be restricted to referencing only a subset of the name space defined by Algol rules. In that way a designer can build up a precise definition of what we have called the constructed part of an access list. Only practical experience will tell whether that is a sufficiently reliable and concise way of making such specifications. (Readers of ADA documentation should note that what we have called constructed access lists are there said to be *inherited* as the result of applying scope rules.)

14.4 FURTHER READING

> *CECILY:*   When I see a spade, I call it a spade.
> *GWENDOLEN:* I am glad to say I have never seen a spade. It is obvious that our social spheres have been widely different.
> The Importance of Being Earnest   Oscar Wilde

Smooth functioning of any large organization demands observances contrary to the inclination of individuals. In social life, the codifications might be seen as rules of etiquette or military discipline. In information systems they appear as restraints on physical access, accountability, privacy of data banks, disclosure of algorithms, responsibility for maintenance, and many other ways, all of which are subsumed by the *security policy* of a system. Implementing a security policy requires a mixture of internal and external control. The latter is seen in the form of verbal directives and disclosures, physical limitations on access to terminals, control keys or communication lines. Internal controls are either programmed, microprogrammed, or hard-wired. Success in subverting internally applied security frequently relies on bypassing the rules by gaining access to programs that implement policy, and altering supposedly privileged code or data. (Hence our concern in Part 1 for who has the authority to write microprograms.) Our intention will be to show how such attacks can be frustrated, even at microprogram level, so that in the absence of hardware failure one can assert that a system does indeed follow a prescribed policy. We shall not propose particular policies, and reference may be made to MAR73, POP79 and TUR75 for discussion of wider issues. While our attention is drawn to highly reliable design, it is well to be reminded that all systems depend ultimately on external controls and on balancing what is at risk against the motivation of users. Thus OS/360 and UNIX (RIT74) have been amongst the most successful operating systems, though both are easily subverted.

Language designers were slow to realize the importance of abstraction, and it was long after the first machine-based mechanisms were in operation that the subject caught the attention of the academic community. It might be thought that Fortran, with its emphasis on modularity, was "close enough" not to need extension. Nevertheless it seems unfortunate that it was not used to put abstraction or type-extension facilities in the hands of professional users. Descriptions of CLU will be found in LIS79 and LIS76. The ADA documentation (ICH79) gives further references to experimental languages. See also *CACM***20**(8) (August 1977): *ACM Conference on Language Design for Reliable Software*. A linguistic treatment of the integer-set manager appears in WUL81.

Obviously, linguistic methods are the only choice when machine design options are closed. What difference does it make? There is no simple answer to that question because the methods used affect function, efficiency, reliability and architectural definition in quite diverse ways. It is dangerous to theorize about this subject since so much depends on the experience of putting programs together and maintaining them in a serviceable state. Abstraction is not an end in itself and it will be a long time before data abstraction rivals procedural decomposition as the principal means of structuring programs. In both machine and language structure there is need for a variety of packaging techniques, and one of the most elusive design problems is to exercise at all times the form of control appropriate to users' requirements. That issue occurs at all levels of design, from high-level language to microprogram, as will be seen in due course.

In this chapter some fundamental requirements of program structure have been argued from first principles and without being drawn into negative aspects of "protection mechanisms". Provided a language or machine is such that only valid data references can be articulated, no further checks are needed. In many existing computers, however, the approach taken is to form an address referring to a virtual program space and then to decide whether it is usable.† Mention has already been made of protection zones and of the problems encountered in dealing with inherited access rights. It is difficult to see a satisfactory outcome to that branch of design. Despite that warning the survey by Salzer and Schroeder (SAL75) is recommended for its tutorial content and reference list. The use of hierarchical decomposition has been advocated by a number of designers. Reference may be made to NEU78 for an introduction to the methodology and its application. An early account of the use of capabilities will be found in DEN66.

When used in filing systems or computer networks capabilities have many of the characteristics ascribed to them here with one major difference: there is no way of assuring the integrity of the capability. In such systems use is made of encryption or other validation techniques that are inappropriate at the design level we are considering, though they do depend on the assurance of program security.

---

† The fortunes of ICL in recent years have rested squarely on the performance and range cover of an architecture of that type.

15 CASE STUDIES: CM*, PP250, CAP

In this chapter we examine three machine designs of recent years whose objectives have included the effective control of access lists and "encapsulated data types" or abstractions. In each case wider considerations affect the choice of mechanism but we allude to them only briefly as the main purpose is to recognize some common threads that run through this branch of computer design. The point of view taken is that of the system or application programmer working at "machine level", and it will be shown how the addresses generated in program registers and in combination with fields from machine instructions yield access to actual data values, and how the parameters of that calculation are varied under program control.

The key requirement, as was seen in Chapter 14, is that certain elements should be distinguished from numerical or control data. To conform with source literature we shall, for the moment, call such elements capabilities. One obvious way to make the distinction is to place an extra tag bit on at least some registers and store locations to describe their contents, and we shall see how that works out in the next chapter. In the present context a simplifying assumption is made: that capabilities can be segregated from other data into a number of distinct regions, whose descriptors indicate the type of elements they contain. It is not then necessary to tag any individual elements.

For storage access the notional path to the ith element of a particular segment involves specifying a cabability c whose id field selects the segment from a "space" associated with the current control stream: the fact that the element so selected can itself be a capability provides the basis for representing precisely delimited but perhaps overlapping storage domains such as those implied by access lists. The selection of a particular data element might entail a sequence of indexing operations: for example (Fig. 15.1) to read an element

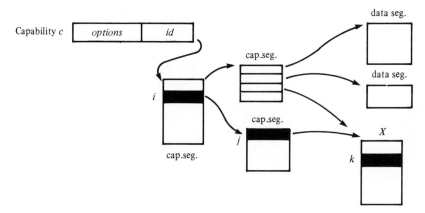

Fig. 15.1 Program structure based on capability and data segments

of segment X requires successive application of the indices i, j, and k to the original capability c. At the machine interface one needs to understand how to compose such operations, and how to select c in the first instance. It is implicit that there is no way of accessing data other than by navigating the program structure, so the choice of c determines at any instant the "visible" part of program space.

   In certain situations the *id* part of a capability can be used as a physical address giving direct access to store, but many designers prefer an indirect reference scheme in which each of the arrowed connections in Fig. 15.1 would be composed by reference to a descriptor (selected by *id*) from which *base, limit, type* and other control information can be extracted, as shown in Fig. 15.2. Combination of *base* with the given offset i completes the first step in the reference chain, in conjunction with a bounds check ($i \leqslant limit$) and perhaps additional checks on access that would be implied by the *control* and *type* codes. The *options* field of the capability and *control* of the descriptor permit various traps that can be deployed by the user (having access to the capability) or by the microsystem and hardware (having access to the descriptor). Their use is elaborated in the case studies that follow. The main advantage gained from using descriptors is that physical store management is simplified: if there are many capabilities containing physical addresses of the same segment, keeping them updated as the segment migrates through storage levels is a headache, but with a unique descriptor that aspect of design is simplified. The principal disadvantage is that access paths, already long, are doubled in length. Each machine takes steps to shortcut the paths in common use. The reader who is familiar with segmentation and paging

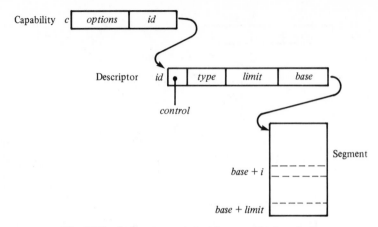

Fig. 15.2   Indirect segment reference via descriptor

schemes as used on more conventional machines might comment on the strong resemblance between the mechanisms involved — in some particulars they might even converge. The main differences to bear in mind are:

(1) that in machines such as the IBM 370 program space, although large, is essentially flat, whereas capability segments can be used to build structures of (theoretically) unlimited depth or connectivity;

(2) that an entire program space (except perhaps for supervisor partitions) is open at all times to user programs in the IBM 370, where in the machines we are considering the accessible region is determined by the choice of capability available to a machine instruction, and the segments that can be reached therefrom by using the defined access paths.

Having said that, the first case for study is one in which capability structure is consciously chosen so that a conventional machine architecture can be imitated if required, for example to import existing software.

15.1 CM*

CM* is an experimental multicomputer system developed at Carnegie-Mellon University. The basic computer module is the standard LSI-11 processor running PDP-11 instructions, hence all access control is carried out by address manipulation external to the processor chip. That is a serious constraint, but one that many VLSI microprocessors are likely to face, so finding practical ways of imposing secure program structures is a matter of wide interest.

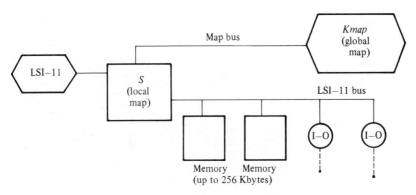

Fig. 15.3 Computer module in CM*

Figure 15.3 shows the essential details of a single computer and its local memory and I – O devices. One of the restrictions of the PDP-11 instruction set is limitation of the address space to 64 Kbytes, but that is relaxed in several models of the range by a remapping facility that constructs from a 16-bit program address an 18-bit bus address, thus allowing use of larger physical memories, though instantaneously the restriction remains. The remapping function is performed here by the device marked S, which has the additional task of mapping from the program address to a system-wide address space of 2^{28} bytes. A reference generated in one processor might be served by any module in the system. A special-purpose mapping processor (marked *Kmap*) is used to carry out the necessary translation and signalling between a group of (up to 14) computer modules of the sort shown in Fig. 15.3. Several such groups can be linked together via their mapping processors. It will be seen shortly that capabilities never reach the LSI-11 processors as such, but the mapping processors can set up tables in the local maps S that effectively control their use. The "hard" feature of the design is that a program address is interpreted by S as being either **local** and therefore served by the LSI-11 bus, or **mapped**. In the latter case it is sent together with function and (for write operations) data to the mapping processor via the *Map bus*, which is shared with other computer modules in the same group. At that point the interpretation falls under microprogram control in *Kmap*, so one can only talk in general terms about the support functions that could be provided. The following notes refer particularly to the STAROS system described by Jones and Gehringer.

The operating environment of a process is seen as a two-level structure (Fig. 15.4). A set of (up to 240) primary capabilities refers to secondary segments that can contain both data and capabilities in separate partitions: the boundary is a fixed attribute of the segment which can be examined in

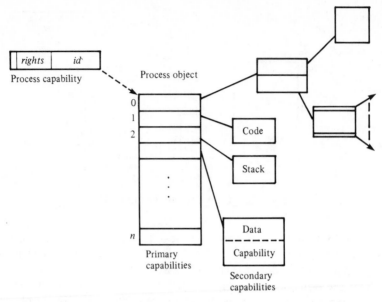

Fig. 15.4 Capability address space in CM*/STAROS

microprogram. The secondary capabilities refer in turn to other objects. There are four types of capability:

(1) Representation capabilities, used to access representation-type objects, i.e. segments. The translation from representation capability to segment location is via descriptors, as in Fig. 15.2, and the *Kmap* contains cached descriptor values for "current" capabilities.

(2) Abstract capabilities identify objects of abstract type, and can be presented to the type (class) manager as tickets.

(3) Data capabilities contain 16-bit data values.

(4) Token capabilities contain unique values and are used to confer authority ("show me your badge") without referring to any object.

Each capability consists of a 3-bit tag (discriminating the primary types), 13-bit capability rights (which indicate, for example, whether the capability itself can be overwritten or copied, or whether the object can be destroyed), and a 16-bit data value or object identifier. The idea behind using a two-level structure for the capability space is that advantage can be taken of associations that might occur between segments belonging to a particular abstraction, or occupying a certain position in the physical store system.

At any instant a process sees the operating environment through a set of 15 *windows*, selected by the most significant 4 bits (w) of a program address (see diagram). Each window contains primary and secondary indices that select a capability in the user environment, and it is the *id* of the capability concatenated with the 12-bit offset in the program address which constitutes the 28-bit global address. It follows that whatever program address is computed by the addressing rule (Table 2.1, p. 26) it cannot lead to a reference outside the domain of 15 segments defined by the window registers. The windows are contained in the local mapping device *S*, and if in fact the evaluation of the capability and descriptor chain leads to a page of 4Kbytes in the local memory the control processor *Kmap* simply writes into the corresponding window of *S* the required base location. Local references of that sort are reported as taking 2 μs, on average, while mapped accesses via *Kmap* within the same group of computer modules take 8.6 μs, not allowing for microcode path and bus contention, and 35 μs outside the group. Hence the importance, at this level of programming, of knowing where things are.

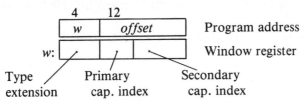

A typical class manager, therefore, might require access to two or three primary capability segments, defining class-specific, task-specific and other resources, using other windows to view lower-level structures, to find workspace, to refer to system utilities, and so on. That would correspond to the constructed part of the domain: a process object is built by defining segments and copying capabilities and data into them to form a structure such as that shown in Fig. 15.4. The (abstract) process capability can only be created by the microsystem at the request of the process manager. The process manager might well be asked to show a token of authority before that function is carried out. Later, a user might ask the process manager to *activate* a given process, at which point the microsystem would be asked to convert the abstract capability back to representation type. That conversion is referred to as **amplification** in STAROS (see diagram).

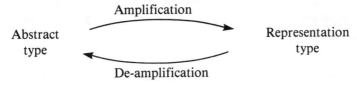

In STAROS each change of access list implies a change of capability address space and, in physical terms, reloading of window registers. The ability to change the immediate environment is provided by making the sixteenth window ($w = 15$) cause a "trap" to a set of functions implemented in *Kmap* microprogram. Thus, writing to a particular program address with $w = 15$ might cause a window register to be loaded with new capability indices. Writing to a different address would invoke a different function. Such functions are implemented by queuing up for service by *Kmap*. For more elaborate actions the communication path is a message channel that can carry capabilities and data between processes: all user abstractions and some system abstractions are implemented as asynchronous and possibly distributed processes. That design decision is a consequence of having no protection boundaries within the process space: to achieve in-process domain changes it is necessary to control *which* capabilities can be loaded into the immediate addressing environment, as illustrated in the next subsection.

The *Kmap* microprogram is substantial: about 22 Kbytes of control memory. The timing of capability functions is given in Table 15.1, assuming

Table 15.1 Timing of Capability Operations in CM*/STAROS microcode

Operation	LSI-11 instr. equivalents	(μs)	Number of refs. to local memory of CMs
Amplify capability	18	133.4	13
Copy capability	13	99.2	10
Create capability			
Representation	16	120.9	12
Data	12	86.2	9
Deamplify capability	18	133.4	13
Load window	9	69.9	8
next mem. ref. (caches window)	+7	+52.0	+5
or, if descr. must be cached too	+13	+94.8	+9
Read capability	11	78.1	8
if descriptor is not in cache	16	120.9	12
Restrict capability	9	67.2	7
Transfer capability	18	130.7	13

Source: Anita K. Jones and Edward F. Gehringer (eds.) "The CM* Multiprocessor Project: a research review" Department of Computer Science, Carnegie-Mellon University Report CMU-CS-80-131 (July 1980)

all references are in-cluster and that there is no *Kmap* or bus contention. The microcode paths are also substantial, and would cause a designer to think twice before using them. At least part of the problem is in having to refer to *Kmap* for capability operations. For user abstractions there is the additional cost of sending and receiving messages. In the next subsection we shall examine a multiprocessor system in which the necessary control is exercised by microprogram within each processor, thereby making reductions in the timing of capability control functions.

15.2 PLESSEY PP250

The PP250 is a multiprocessor system designed by Plessey Telecommunications Research Laboratories, primarily to meet the very stringent reliability requirements of telephone switching systems. Part of that requirement entails carefully engineered software error detection and recovery facilities, which are achieved using a capability mechanism.

In the PP250 the primary requirement of controlling precisely what can be accessed by a program is met by introducing a set of *capability registers* for that purpose. A valid pointer can only be formed by modifying a capability, so in our register machine notation we might denote a pointer by a subexpression of the form:

$$C'E$$

where C is a declared capability register and E is an expression that evaluates to a non-negative integer. For example, suppose we declare:

$$REGS\ [\ x \quad y \quad z\ ] \qquad /* \textit{ integers } */$$
$$CAPS\ [\ A \quad K \quad\quad] \qquad /* \textit{ capabilities } */$$

Then we can express pointers as: $K'3$, $A'y$, $K'(3+z)$, ... where it is assumed that K and A each contain the base and limit addresses of program segments. If the modifier value exceeds the limit, an invalid address condition is detected and causes a program trap.

Now we can ask what the assignment operators mean in the context of capability registers. Evidently we can only assign integers to *REGS* and capabilities to *CAPS* without losing control, so assignments such as:

$$x = 3;\ y = z+1;\ K = A$$

are *valid*, whereas:

$$K = z;\ x = A$$

are *invalid* and can easily be excluded by the program assembler. (In fact we shall see that the last is allowed in a special sense.)

There are two sorts of store segment corresponding to the two sorts of register. Suppose A refers to an integer segment and K to capability. Then we can transfer integers to and from registers, as in:

$$x = A'2. \; ; \; A'z = .y - 4$$

and similarly for capability transfers:

$$K = K'x. \; ; \; K'(z+3) = . A$$

but once again type clashes must be detected and disallowed — otherwise it would be possible to store an integer to a capability segment and read it back to a capability register. For store access, clashes are detected not by the assembler but by microorders invoked during execution.

Loading a capability provides the means of changing environment within a process: starting from K and A it is possible to explore the segment structure to which they give access and set up a new "working environment" comprising any two subordinate segments. One can *never expand* the original structure in that way, and quite often the environment is reduced, as it would be in Fig. 15.5, by

$$K = K'3.$$

which leaves segment (a) inaccessible unless there is some circularity in the data structure, while K delimits (b). In practice one has to think out carefully the structures required in each phase of program and set them up in advance.

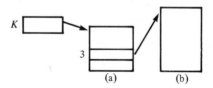

K

3

(a)   (b)

Fig. 15.5   Store access via capability register K

Consider, for example, the requirement (Fig. 14.3) to change the access list from $\{Q\,A\,B\}$ to $\{A\,X\,Y\,T\}$. As the capability registers are limited in number we map each access list into a capability segment that is itself referenced by a capability register, e.g. K (Fig. 15.6). Note that the program segment P is included in the access list. Now how can we attach the environment of Q without giving P access to it? That appears to be impossible without adding extra controls, which appear in the PP250 in the form of options encoded in the capabilities. Apart from the usual read/write/execute options on data the key to access list control is the "enter" right associated with a capability segment, which operates as follows.

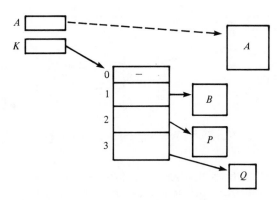

Fig. 15.6   Access via capability registers A, K

Firstly, in making up the data structure Q is replaced (in Fig. 15.6) by a capability segment referring to both the code (Q) and support data (X, Y, T); and that segment's capability is marked with "enter" rights (EC), as in Fig. 15.7. In the absence of any other rights P is thereby restricted only to "enter" $K'3$, which means that the data X, Y, T and code Q is otherwise inaccessible.

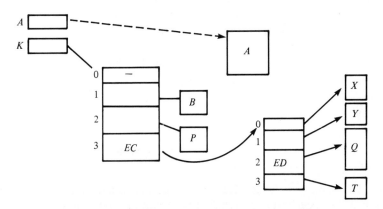

Fig. 15.7   Working environment of P

An effect of the *CALL* instruction is to replace K by the capability (in this case $K'3$.) defining the new access list, at the same time *extending* the rights to include "read capability" (RC), as in Fig. 15.8. In the same *CALL* instruction control is transferred to Q and the previous contents of K and of the program counter are saved. In the new environment it is impossible to refer to the old value of K, hence impossible to refer to B or P. Thus the

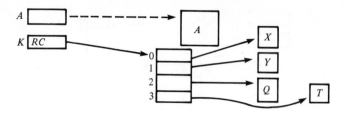

Fig. 15.8 Working environment of Q

accessible store has been changed from $\{P\ A\ B\ Q\}$ to $\{Q\ A\ X\ Y\ T\}$. Conversely, the *RETURN* instruction restores the original $\{P\ B\ Q\}$ and (possibly) A, depending on what has happened to it in Q.

Machine registers and instructions

Turning to the actual mechanisms involved, we find that a PP250 processor has eight 24-bit integer registers ($D0, \ldots , D7$) and eight capability registers ($C0, \ldots , C7$). Because integers and capabilities are always segregated no physical distinction is made in register or store formats. There is only one type of capability, consisting of an access code (8 bits) and object identifier (16 bits). The options expressed in the access field are:

Access bit 0: ⎫
     1: ⎬ Normally 11 (valid capability); 00 = "Null"

2:	Enter	⎫		⎧ EC
3:	Write	⎬ Capability segment		⎨ WC
4:	Read	⎭		⎩ RC
5:	Execute	⎫		⎧ ED
6:	Write	⎬ Data segment		⎨ WD
7:	Read	⎭		⎩ RD

If the access bit = 1 the corresponding right is granted. In theory a segment can be of both capability and data type according to the above encoding; in practice that does not happen except in special situations under system control. The first two access bits are set = 00 when a capability is first created and changed by store-management procedures when a new segment is created.

  Although a capability is notionally a 24-bit element it must be "expanded" before use by obtaining the actual base and limit of the segment to which it refers. That is done by using the segment identifier to select a descriptor table known as the system capability table (SCT) that contains the required information. That happens whenever a capability register is loaded. In all, each capability register needs 64 bits of information ($access(8) + seg.id$ (16) $+ base(24) + limit(16)$) but only 48 are retained in the "real" registers. The remaining 16 are saved in the current *process dump*.

Two capability registers have special status:

C6: Refers to the current access list (as "*K*" in the example just given);

C7: Refers to the current control segment (as "*P*" or "*Q*" in the example).

There are in addition ten special-purpose registers, of which the most relevant to this discussion are:

/* Integer */	*PC* Program counter (offset relative to *C7*);
/* Integer */	*DP* Dump pointer (offset relative to *CD*);
/* Capability */	*CD* Current process dump;
/* Capability */	*SCT* System capability table

The remaining registers are concerned with timing, interrupt and fault management.

The process dump contains fixed slots for the capability register "overflows" from *C0* to *C5*, and for the data registers *D0*, . . . , *D7* when the process is inactive. In addition there is a first-in − last-out list of procedure linkage data, each entry consisting of the saved values of *C6*, *C7* and *PC*. Note that when a capability is saved only the option/segment number is stored, the full information being retrieved from SCT when it is next loaded. Because the capabilities are not modified the "overflow" fields held in the process dump are sufficient to recover the capability register contents at any time.

PROCESS DUMP is a segment formatted as shown in Fig. 15.9.

Instructions appear in data segments with "execute" rights (*ED*). They are always 24 bits and have two formats:

	1	5	3	3		1 2
Direct mode	1	*F*	*D*	*M*		*L*

	1	5	3	3	3	9
Store mode	0	*F*	*D*	*M*	*C*	*A*

Most arithmetic and logical instructions operate on data register *D* and either the store word addressed by $C'(M + A)$ where *M* is one of the modifiers *D*1, . . . , *D7* and *A* is a literal offset, or the integer value $L + M$. Of the 27 functions *F* only 6 are relevant to capability control. They are described in the following paragraphs on the assumption that no exceptions occur, i.e. all capabilities are valid, required access rights are satisfied, etc., and it should also be understood that all the changes necessary in the capabilities in the process dump are made to keep it up to date.

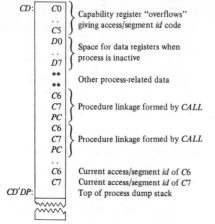

Note also the formats of:

Capability register:	access (8)	limit (16)	base (24)	
SCT element:	use (8)	limit (16)	base (24)	checksum (24)
Capability:	access (8)	SCT index (16)	SCT index is segment id.	

Fig. 15.9   PP250 process dump formats

LOAD CAPABILITY

Here D specifies a *capability* register.

In store mode: $D = C'(M+A)$.
In direct mode: $D = $ Capability M

If $D=7$, reset PC to point to the base of $C7$, i.e. transfer control to a new segment without change of environment.

STORE CAPABILITY

Here D specifies a *capability* register.

In store mode: $C'(M+A) = . D$
In direct mode: invalid instruction

LOAD POINTER

Here D specifies a *data* register.

In store mode: $D = C'(M+A)$.
In direct mode: $D = C$

In either case D receives the access/segment number fields only. It is thereby possible to inspect the access codes and, e.g., use capabilities to contain 22-bit integers (access = 00). Note that the converse assignment is not allowed.

CALL

Here D is ignored

In store mode:	Save PC in process dump $CD'DP$
	Increment DP by 3
	Load capability $C7 = C'(M+A)$.
	Load capability $C6 = C$
	Set RC access right in $C6$
In direct mode:	Invalid instruction

RETURN

In store mode:	Invalid instruction
In direct mode:	Decrement DP by 3
	Load capability $C6 = C6$ ⎤ from process
	Load capability $C7 = C7$ ⎬ dump stack
	Load PC ⎦

CHANGE PROCESS

In store mode:	Dump $PC, DP, D0, \ldots, D7$
	Load capability $CD = C'(M+A)$.
	Load capability $C0 = C0$
	$\ldots$
	$\qquad C7 = C7$
	Load PC
	Load data registers $D0, \ldots, D7$
	from current dump.
	Load special registers
In direct mode:	as above except $CD = $ capability M.

Note that the resulting CD must have RD and WD access as well as RC and WC. One cannot make process dumps generally available without endangering system security. In practice the process-dump capability is part of an abstraction offered to the user by the process manager.

One of the practical requirements of any protection mechanism is that it should be fast, and one measure of speed is the amount of memory activity implied by an operation. Taking account of updating the process dump, Table 15.2 shows the activity implied by the above list of functions.

Table 15.2 Memory references for capability functions in PP250

Function	Memory cycles (24 bit)	
	Store mode	Direct mode
Load capability	5*	2
Store capability	2	n.a.
Load pointer	1	1
Call	8*	n.a.
Return	n.a.	11*
Change process	66*	63*

* References to SCT require 3 cycles because a checksum is stored with each entry. The above counts exclude instruction fetch.

Thus a "round trip" procedure call-and-return involves a minimum overhead of 21 memory cycles, excluding parameter passing, and process change via a process manager procedure entails $66 + 8 + 2 = 76$ references. To access a data item not in a store area addressed by one of the capability registers requires an extra 6 memory cycles for each step through the data structure. Such considerations materially affect the design of programs and the mapping of higher-level languages.

Example 15.1 (The *intset* manager.) To see how the PP250 structures might be used in practice, consider the representation of a class of sets of integers (cf. the *intset* cluster in CLU, p. 304) in which the allowed functions are:

create()	returns an empty set s
insert(s,v)	inserts the integer v into set s
remove(s,v)	removes the integer v from set s
has(s,v)	returns *true* if $v \in s$, else *false*
equal(s_1,s_2)	returns *true* if s_1 is identical to s_2, else *false*
similar(s_1,s_2)	returns *true* if
	$(\forall i)\ (i \in s_1 \Leftrightarrow i \in s_2)$
	else *false*
copy(s)	returns a copy of s

The rules of the game are that *only* the above operations are applicable and that access should be "by ticket only", i.e. no combination of code can affect any integer set except by presenting an authentic capability. In the data structure of one set (see Fig. 15.10) entry to one of the procedures implies access

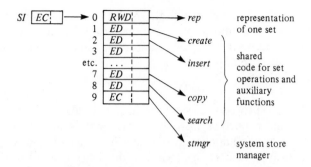

Fig. 15.10   Representation of an integer set in PP250

to a "subject" set, namely that contained in the data area *rep*, so it is
unnecessary to specify *s* or s_2 in the procedure call. The capability *SI* serves as
the ticket for the set: any user acquiring *SI* can issue a *CALL* instruction to
one of the procedures in the capability segment it defines, e.g. to invoke
insert(7) the calling sequence might take the form:

$$C0 = SI;\ D1 = 7;\ CALL\ C0'2;\ \ldots$$

and once *insert* is in control (*C7* = *insert*) the rest of the data structure,
including *rep*, is accessible via *C6*.

The above mechanism is straightforward for *insert, remove* and *has*,
using the auxiliary function *search* to find elements in *rep*. The choice of
structure has some less obvious and potentially serious consequences which
we should consider.

(1) Internal procedures such as *search* are equally accessible from outside
the set representation (*CALL C0'8*) so they are in general a security
hazard — perhaps giving private information about the form or size of
rep. To prevent that, small procedures can be incorporated in the code
segments that use them, but it should be noted that by a design oversight
there is no machine function to jump-to-subroutine-within-segment.
Another possibility is to package the auxiliary functions using an *EC*
capability in the access list addressed by *SI*: that has been done for the
system store management module *stmgr* which contains procedure
entries to create data and capability segments and to set options as
required by *create* and *copy* in forming new set representations.

(2) Two sets *SI*1 and *SI*2 are *equal* if they are the same (according to CLU),
which means they must have the same capability. Using the *LOAD
POINTER* instruction that can simply be determined without calling a
procedure:

$$D1 = SI1;\ D2 = SI2;\ D1 - D2;\ \ldots$$

(3) To test whether two sets are similar both their representations must be accessed, which is impossible using the data structure suggested. One solution would be to introduce a *subset* operation in place of *similar*, leaving the user to apply the rule:

$$s_1 \equiv s_2 \Leftrightarrow (s_1 \subseteq s_2)\&(s_2 \subseteq s_1)$$

The *subset* (s_2) procedure, as applied in s_1, will take each element i from *rep* and enquire whether *has*(i) in s_2, thus establishing whether $s_1 \subseteq s_2$. Similarly *subset* (s_1) applied in s_2 establishes whether $s_2 \subseteq s_1$.

(4) It is not always possible to get round the difficulty as suggested in (3): for logical or physical reasons it may be necessary to scan all objects in the class at once. To share *rep* between all representations is possible (in the same way that *create* and the other procedures are shared), but a way is needed to distinguish one set from another. That could be done by including an "integer" capability (options code 00******) in the structure, where the integer part gives the "set identifier". Set procedures can find their own identifiers by looking in the access list (e.g. $D1 = C6'10$.) but given the capability for another set a function *who*() has to be supplied to return the set identifier (*CALL SI'* 11). Now the data structure is as shown in Fig. 15.11.

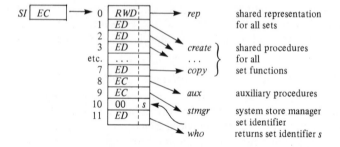

Fig. 15.11 Revised representation of an integer set

(5) Sorry to say our troubles are not over. For suppose we add a procedure *cutout*(*s*) which is intended to eliminate all members of a given set that are not members of *s*. In *cutout* it is necessary to call *who* in *s* (e.g. *CALL s'* 11) to find the set identifier. Using that information it is possible to find the elements of *s* in *rep* and eliminate them from the current set. But we could easily have supplied *any* program package in place of *s* provided it returned an integer from entry point 11: there is no simple way of checking that it really represents a set. And similarly, reverting to the method outlined in (3) we could have supplied a fake "set" with a *has*() entry

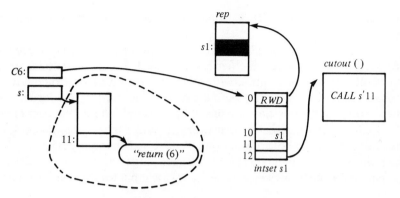

Fig. 15.12 Masquerading in PP250. When *cutout(s)* is applied
in *s*1, it is impossible to be sure that *s* is an integer set

constantly returning the value *true*. In other words there is no simple
way of preventing one type of data structure masquerading as another in
the PP250, which is the result of not having a class identifier in the
capability.

(6) It will be seen that each set carries with it the store and management
overhead of a twelve-element capability segment. Whether that is worth
paying influences the choice of object classes. Some of the problems
mentioned above can be tackled using more elaborate data structures,
but that tends to compound the overhead.

(7) Finally, there are a number of issues not dealt with here (or in CLU) that
deserve attention, e.g.

> how is a set (or other object) deleted?
> how is an object class created and deleted?
> how many objects or object classes can exist (a) at one time, or (b) ever?
> how do the classes of objects that are being introduced relate to the
> user, the operating system, or to the file store?

To answer such questions we have to speculate on the type of system that
might be built around the basic PP250 architecture.

System context

We have seen how the access list is controlled and how "tickets" are acquired
in the course of calculation by inheritance (in the form of parameters passed
in registers $C0, \ldots, C5$) and construction (in the list addressed by $C6$ and the

program segment itself, *C7*). The question remains of how the whole process gets started.

There is a minor paradox in our definition of integer sets: to *create* a new set the capability for another one is needed. It might also be logically undesirable to couple creation with other set operations. In either case the problem could be avoided by defining a new substructure just for creating integer sets. But the question remains of how to establish the first connection.

In the PP250 program structures are initialized by an assembly program that transforms symbolic definitions of data and capability segments into their internal form (the data segments include instructions). In constructing a capability segment such as *SI* (Fig. 15.11) the input text may take the form:

SI: capability segment [*REP(RWD)*, *CREATE(ED)*,
          INSERT(ED), ...
          STMGR(EC), *IDENT*, *WHO(ED)*]

Elsewhere in the text there are definitions of *REP, CREATE,* etc. The access right written into *SI* must, of course, be compatible with the segment definition (e.g. it is illegal to write *REP(EC)* if *REP* is defined as a data segment). In exactly the same way, any capability segment can include *SI* as an element, which has the effect we are looking for if it is (*EC*).

Thus the initial segments of a program are assembled with reference to an environment comprising (a) globally accessible system packages (such as *STMGR*) and (b) all program segments in the same input text (their order is unimportant). Amongst the latter are one or more *process templates* giving amongst other parameters initial values for *C6* and *C7*. The system command "*RUN*", given a template as parameter, is then all that is needed to set up a new process and execute it. To refer back to our transaction processing example (p. 293) each transation entering the system might be the object of a *RUN* command.

Termination of a process causes its representation, which includes the process dump, to be deleted from store. It may be that some segments are thereby made inaccessible (i.e. there are no capabilities anywhere in the system referring to them): they too are deleted. Eventually, all the processes set up to operate on the data structure originally assembled will terminate by one means or another. At that point the data structure itself disappears.

To answer the questions raised above:

A set is deleted by implication when no references to its representation exist.

The "class of sets" is created by the assembly process; whether it initially contains a single element or none is a matter of program design. The class disappears when all its elements and the *create* operation disappear.

The number of objects and object classes at one time is limited by the number of segments the system can support. The segment numbers are re-used, so there is no limit to the total number that can be created.

As far as users are concerned, correctly setting up the initial data structure is a matter of reaching agreement outside the system. If many programmers work on the same project strict control must be exercised over what they include in their data structures. In writing programs each user must take responsibility for the form of data structures he creates.

The operating system takes no responsibility for generalized classes of data, which are all mapped onto storage structures. The objects managed by the system include processes, I−O channels, and user terminals.

The structures used in programs cannot safely be written to detachable media such as tapes and disks, so they are strictly separated from the file store, which only contains data segments. Programs can, however, be allocated dynamically to main memory or auxiliary store as appropriate.

In summary, refer back to the practical constraints on any protection system (p. 294).

(1) *It must be foolproof.* We have seen that the PP250 can be fooled by masquerading. There is another difficulty which arises from the need to provide space for process-specific data such as the working segments that contain the variables of a particular procedure activation. The simplest approach is to attach a "process workspace" through one of the capability registers ($C5$ is used by convention). Such a workspace might be a data or capability segment. In either case it will be controlled as a

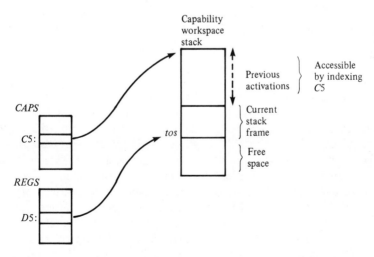

Fig. 15.13 Leakage of protected data via a workspace stack in PP250

stack, growing on procedure entry and shrinking on exit, using a data register as stack pointer. The difficulty here is that there is no way of protecting such a stack: the stack pointer, the capability, or the data themselves might be corrupted by a low-level procedure. The root of the problem is that there is no safe and economical way of dumping capability registers $C0, \ldots, C5$.

(2) *It must be fast.* Most accesses to memory are to data directly addressed by a capability (which includes instructions). The overhead figures given in Table 15.2 are only significant when either the data structures or control structures are "deep", i.e. involving many indirection steps through capability segments or many subroutine entries. All one can say here is that for the class of applications envisaged that was presumably not the case.

(3) *It must be flexible.* The biggest difficulty is that the physical and logical units of protection are the same, i.e. program segments. If a single byte has to be protected it must exist in a segment of its own.

(4) *It must be easy to use.* Managing two small sets of register is always more difficult than one set, especially when there is no simple way of dumping them in store. The PP250 is mostly programmed in a higher-level language (CORAL) which hides the problems, but there are no published figures on its relative performance.

Despite the apparent drawbacks it should be added that the actual systems developed for the PP250 appear to have given good service in the context for which they were intended, i.e. dedicated, multiprocessor, high-reliability applications.

15.3 CAP

CAP is an experimental capability-based machine designed and built at the Cambridge University computer laboratory. Its protection functions are similar to those of the PP250 but, as in CM*, they are applied outside the processor registers. Unlike CM*, however, CAP is a single-processor machine with a comprehensive scientific instruction set implemented by microprogram: the microorders responsible for protection (corresponding to the *Kmap* processor in CM*) occupy about the same volume of control memory as the "normal" instruction set. In this subsection the addressing mechanism of CAP will be summarized before discussing some of the higher-level design problems whose solution has been sought in the CAP operating system.

As before, segments are typed as either data or capability containers. A computed program address provides three indices (see diagram) which select

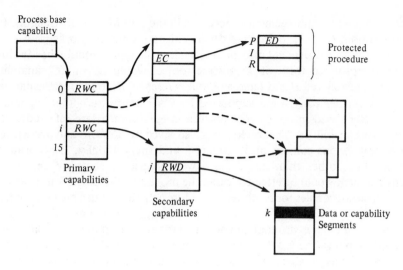

Fig. 15.14   Process environment in CAP

a path through the process environment (Fig. 15.14). Thus *i* selects what in CM* would be a window, and in PP250 a capability register, but the second-level index *j* is calculated by the addressing unit rather than being found in a window register. The offset *k* selects an element (data or capability) of the segment specified by *j*. One obvious result of that interpretation is that by normal indexing rules addresses can range over the first- and second-level capabilities. In comparison, recall that *j* is preset (by the window register) in CM*, and that PP250 would make use of an auxiliary capability register to achieve the same effect. Functions are provided by the CAP system to permit dynamic construction of a process environment, subject to the usual consistency checks. Notice that program addresses are process-dependent and could not meaningfully be transmitted from one process to another.

4	4	8	16
i	0 ¦ *j*	*k*	

CAP program address

In-process protection is established, as in PP250, by forming *EC*-type ("enter") capabilities and implementing an *ENTER* control-transfer function. The protection domain defined by an *EC* capability consists of three capability segments *P*, *I* and *R*, whose defining capabilities are retained during its execution in primary capability registers 4, 5 and 6 respectively. The effect of *ENTER* is to save the current contents of 4, 5 and 6 on the process stack and to replace them with a new set. Conversely, the original environment is restored by *RETURN*. The *P*-capability is expected to refer to executable code, e.g. class-management procedures in the case of data abstraction. By convention, I is used for process-dependent static data and workspace, while R is for object-dependent information such as the representation itself. Thus the encapsulated form of an abstract object would be an EC capability referring to shared P and I and a unique reference, R, to the representation.

A further convention supported by CAP hardware is that capability parameters used in the current protection environment are referred to by primary capability 2. That reference is also saved by $ENTER$, and overwritten by the previous content of 3, leaving 3 undefined initially. If no primary capabilities other than nos 2,...,6 were in use, a complete change of environment would be effected within the process by the $ENTER$ instruction.

The above rules for protected procedure entry and return are independent of programmed subroutine entry and return, which do not affect the protection domain. Thus the control and data structures of a high-level language could map into the CAP process environment without explicit use of CAP structures except where services are required from system- or user-defined protected procedures, for which interfaces are provided in the language-support subsystem (most of the CAP operating system is written in Algol 68).

The program structure illustrated in Fig. 15.14 is maintained through the use of a descriptor mechanism. In CAP the table corresponding to the PP250s SCT is called the Process Resource List (PRL). Unlike the SCT, a PRL is specifically associated with a process, and identifiers found in capabilities provide offsets in their "current" PRL. Consequently, capabilities cannot be used to transmit information from one process to another and each protected procedure has to be bound to a particular PRL. The designer must weight those restrictions against the knowledge that whatever corruption occurs within a process (program error, memory failure in capability segment, incorrect application of access rights, etc.) it cannot spread outside the domain defined by the PRL. The resulting structure can be compared with the multilevel environment implemented in the VCS operating system (Fig. 6.4). The descriptor mechanism, and the microprogram associated with it, is designed to mitigate the effects on performance of having (1) apparently long access paths to frequently used resources such as system procedures; and (2) having a large number of small segments containing capabilities which tend to overload the store management system. The principal technique used in (1) is to load a capability cache memory (64 words) with the result of "evaluating" a chain of references, and to search it using a combination of hash and associative hardware when a capability id has to be interpreted. In (2), the proliferation of small segments representing abstract objects that was noted in PP250 is avoided by packing the P, I and R indices into a single EC capability. At the same time, provision is made to map data capabilities *into* existing segments rather than demanding separate physical segments. In that way CAP can avoid the damage caused by equating *logical* program structures with their *physical* realization.

In CAP, "setting up a process" entails forming a PRL and initial process environment and then obeying the machine function "Enter subprocess". Thereafter, the process is scheduled along with others until it reaches completion: at that point the PRL and all dependent structures effectively disappear. It becomes imperative in such a system to offer a more persistent form of storage in which procedures and data structures can be held from one interaction to the next. In CAP that is provided by a data structure known as the "file system" which mirrors some aspects of the more transient process structure. The main components of the file are data segments, directories, and Procedure Control Blocks (PCBs). Directories are sets of named and typed pointers providing the sort of structure one might find, for example, in the UNIX file system. Pointers are unique identifiers of objects in file space and can be modelled as abstract objects; accessibility is controlled by handing them out in encapsulated form. The "root" directory contains pointers to "user directories" to which access is gained by suitable log-in protocols.

A PCB is the counterpart in file space of a protected procedure in a process environment. It contains a prescription for the *P, I* and *R* capability segments that will be made accessible when it is executed. System functions are provided to move a PCB into a process, converting it into an *EC*-type capability and, conversely, to move a protected procedure into the file space. Analogous functions provide for movement of data segments between file and process spaces. A possible mode of constructing programs, therefore, is as follows: to log into the CAP system; to construct code and data files by editing and compiling operations as appropriate and to store them in a directory; next, to construct PCBs to represent protected procedures; and finally to execute one of the PCBs as a new process.

The mapping of "integer set" procedures from file space to process space is illustrated in Fig. 15.15. Suppose that the program has been compiled and filed as "*ISP*" in the current user's directory *D*. A procedure control block "*IS*" is constructed and placed in the directory using file-management functions, referring to *ISP* and specifying workspace and support functions (e.g. for segment management) required during its execution. Now suppose that a new process is started, and that control enters a protected procedure *DIR* from which reference can be made to the representation of the current file directory *D*. Access to *IS* is gained by presenting the name "*IS*" as a parameter to *DIR*, which is able to search the directory names, find space in the PRL for new *P, I,* and *R* segments, and to return an *EC* capability that can be stored by the user procedure in its own protected domain at *INTOPS*,

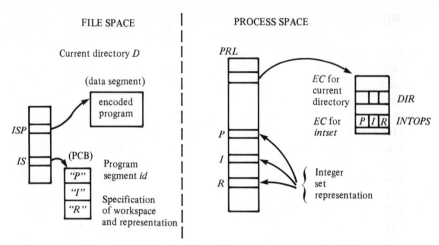

Fig. 15.15 Mapping from file to process space in CAP

say. Thereafter, to call the *create* function, for example, the *EC* capability at *INTOPS* would be used with suitable arguments, and the result returned would be a new *EC* capability with the same *P* and *I* indices and a new *R*. Note that integer sets, when passed as parameters, appear as *EC* capabilities as in PP250.

Meanwhile, what has happened to the idea of an access list? It is instructive to trace its evolution in the PP250 and CAP. In each case the authority to use an object "by construction" derives from a wider definition of what is available. Available files are determined (in CAP) by the log-in protocol and access rights previously assigned by owners (who also determine ability to change rights). Construction of a PCB or protected procedure (or capability segment in PP250) is limited to what is accessible using the current directory, and requests to the file manager during process execution are similarly constrained. On the other hand, there is no restriction on the argument that might be presented to *DIR*, so it must be assumed that any procedure having access to *DIR* might browse or inadvertently use anything it finds in the directory. The examples we have studied illustrate the fact that access lists as seen in register-transfer terms are refinements of the same concept at a higher level. To emphasize the distinction we shall refer to the latter as an **authorization list** in later chapters. In systems in which the file and process (or program) spaces are merged it is not always easy to make a sharp distinction.

15.4 FURTHER READING

Answers to the crucial questions of how to write and run an application program and what overheads of microprogram space and path length are attributable to abstraction are impossible to find in published papers. Hence it is difficult to form an opinion as to whether a particular method of implementation can be recommended. Careful study of current literature will show many interesting variations in features, but the reader should follow through the design as far as possible by thinking of how a particular program (such as a compiler and run-time system) would map onto the structures provided, and how a micromachine might support them.

Further details of CM* will be found in JON80. The PP250 is discussed in ENG74 (the same IRIA publication contains other useful papers, including JON75). The CAP computer is described in NEE77. More general discussion and a useful reference list will be found in FAB74. It was noted at the beginning of this chapter that an obvious way of distinguishing capabilities is to use a tagging mechanism in conjunction with segment partitions. The alternatives are outlined by Fabry, concluding that "... one might expect the tagged approach to dominate in the long run." In succeeding chapters our attention will be turned to computer designs exploiting tagged register and/or memory.

16 THE BASIC LANGUAGE MACHINE

Design of the Basic Language Machine (BLM) started in the ICL Research Laboratories early in 1964 and resulted in the first system to offer precise and flexible control over access to program space. The techniques used remain the most efficient means of achieving abstraction, by virtue of the fact that encoded instructions operate directly on capabilities (in contrast to "external" mechanisms such as CM* and CAP) but, unlike the PP250, the roles of capability register and general address modifier are merged in a simple rule of address formation. As a result it could be claimed that the benefits of abstraction were achievable with no loss of speed (in terms of microinstruction paths or memory cycles) or additional cost (control memory, register or circuitry) compared with conventional designs. An extensive experimental program was set in motion to challenge that claim.

To understand the direction in which the BLM developed we must refer back to the ideas expressed in Chapter 1 (p. 5): that the goal is to achieve the highest performance over the widest *range* of costs, taking account of direct and indirect overheads. Although at some levels of technology an overhead might be concealed, it is very difficult to guarantee to conceal it throughout a range, particularly at the extreme edges: elaborate segmentation and paging schemes, for example, are a hindrance to both high-performance and low-cost design. The BLM minimized the need for address translation, but the problems remained of achieving (1) a wide physical addressing range, and (2) a comprehensive function set that could be tuned to given performance goals or commercial/scientific job ratios. These problems were later solved in the IBM 360 (1) by introducing the base-and-offset rule of addressing, in which a 24-bit program address could be constructed from relatively small fields supplied in the instruction stream; and (2) by adopting a powerful range-defined instruction set implemented for the most part by microprogram.

At the time of BLM design an alternative approach was offered by the abstraction mechanisms themselves: (1) to submerge address formats below the architectural interface, so that addresses were known only in terms of their attributes; and (2) to conceal instruction formats so that options on field size, number of registers, function encoding and interpretation methods could be exercised to meet engineering goals at each point in the performance spectrum. The result was a symbolic definition of the range architecture which became known as the "Basic Language".† The form of symbols could have been anything from a pseudomachine instruction set to an abstract data-structure definition. For various practical reasons a conventional form of assembly program text was adopted and used in the dual role of a machine definition and System Implementation Language.

A further result of self-applied abstraction was the observation that the operation of the computer system, whether at a user's terminal or operator's console, could be viewed in terms of manipulating a number of abstract objects: files, program modules, devices, jobs, other users, and so on. It was therefore possible to include within the architectural definition the operations of job control, and to use the Basic Language in a *third* role, that of Job Control Language (JCL). A separate and high-level JCL, with its tortuous rules of construction, is necessary only when the computer system does not recognize the objects of interest at the architectural level. The mode of use was therefore one in which programs were written in (or compiled into) Basic Language, translated into machine instructions and stored as execute-only program segments. Control commands could be applied directly to running programs or similarly translated for later use. It followed that all machine states of interest to the user must be reported in the symbolic terms originally used, so the system incorporated diagnostic programs to report errors, register contents and storage structures in terms of the architectural interface. Users of interpretive systems such as APL will be familiar with such facilities and their attractions, but it should be noted that in the BLM they applied to the entire system and user population and were achieved without loss of performance.

The above comments explain the "linguistic" aspects of BLM development. For our present purposes the form of language is unimportant, but the control of formation of instructions is crucial to the protection system. In the subsections that follow the action of the machine is explained in terms of register transfer operations.

One aspect of any structured program space that causes apprehension is the proportion of operations involving indirect access to data via capabilities

---

†Not to be confused with the BASIC interactive programming language.

and therefore incurring a visible overhead in store activity. The first point to bear in mind is that indirection, like fragmentation, arises from two sources:

(1) the nature of the *problem*, in demanding explicit structural control;
(2) the nature of the *machine*, by repeatedly mapping program addresses into physical locations using, for example, segment or page tables.

In the BLM (2) was eliminated and so, too, was the need for an address-translation unit or its elaboration as seen for example in CM* or CAP. The question remained as to how much indirection resulted from (1) and what might be done to mitigate its effect on performance.

Fortunately, program structures of the type planned for the BLM had already been investigated on the Rice University computer and it was possible to obtain measures of indirect memory references. It was also possible to postulate a form of cache ("slave store" as it was then called) that could save recently evaluated capabilities and hence avoid re-access to main memory. Figure 16.1 shows some results of simulating cache behavior, from which it

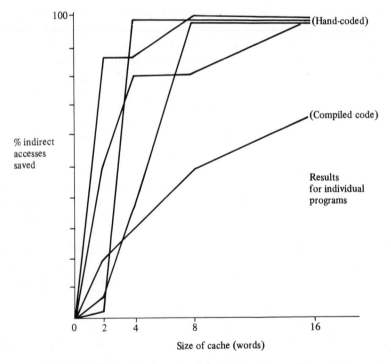

Fig. 16.1   Effect of using a "codeword slave" store (From J.K. Iliffe, *Some Observations on Codeword-based Programming,* Rice University Computer Project (1964))

was concluded that with quite a small store the majority of capability references could be saved. However, the more important result was that indirection accounted for no more than 5–10% of memory accesses on average, and it would be more profitable to apply the cache to data and instruction accesses, as shown in Fig. 16.2.

Since the above measurements were made many improved and larger versions of cache have come into use and it would be impossible to compare one with another on general terms, but two points should be borne in mind. First, in the BLM a cache is an optional performance-enhancement device, whereas in conventional design segment/page translation stores are essential to recover normal operating speeds. When cost or speed considerations inhibit the use of cache techniques the mechanism used on the BLM still achieves its objective, which is important in microsystems (Chapter 7) and array-processor design (Chapter 8). Second, when implemented on a tagged machine, the cache memory is a "look-ahead" device (Section 13.1) giving generally better prediction of performance than the "look-aside" strategies usually employed.

In the following subsections we anticipate a change of terminology to be

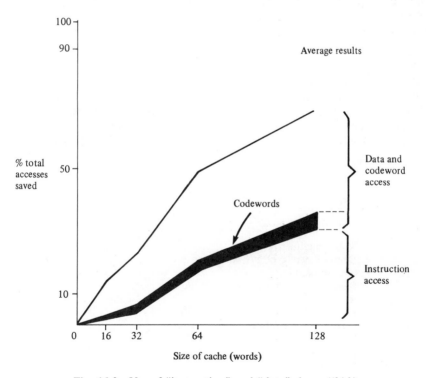

Fig. 16.2   Use of "instruction" and "data" slaves (*ibid.*)

used in Chapter 18. The practical importance of storage as an abstraction has already been mentioned, and we recognize this fact by calling the class of capabilities that point to storage segments **codewords**. A codeword contains a segment identifier and encoded options governing its usage in the way discussed in the preceding chapter. A *pointer* is more generally understood to be any non-numeric quantity that can be construed as referring to data, which would include capabilities, codewords and addresses.

16.1 OPERATING ENVIRONMENT

The program store of the BLM consists of a number of *bases*, each of which can be undergoing transformation by one or more processes. A base consists of a named set of objects, each of which is represented by a capability according to the classification of Table 16.1. Because an object can be a capability segment the base structure is to a first approximation that of a tree. We shall see later that write-access to capability segments is restricted to store-management programs in order to control the type of structure that can be formed (partly in the interest of controlling system overheads but also to make easily intelligible use of the diagnostic facilities). The various types of segment derived from the encoded field *pts* are as shown in Table 16.2. The use of "relative" codewords enables complete subtrees to be packaged as single store segments and is one of the techniques used to avoid overloading the store-management subsystem (Fig. 16.3); they occur only in control segments, which represent Basic Language program modules. "Mixed" segments contain fully tagged elements in the register format of Table 16.3; they are used only in the representation of process states in the BLM.

A base provides a high-level authorization boundary in the system,

Table 16.1   Capabililty classes in BLM

Class	Object represented
0	Null (undefined)
1	Data segment type *pts*; identifier *id*
2	(unassigned)
3	Relative data type *pts*; offset *r*; limit *l*
4	Relative control mode *m*; offset *r*
5	Lock-out (synchronization control)
6	Auxiliary store reference
7	File capability
8	Soft capability
9	Process capability
10	Inter-base reference

Table 16.2   Segment types in BLM

pts	Subtype	Access	Size (bits)
0	Binary word	RW	32
1	Byte	RW	8
2	Binary word	R	32
3	Byte	R	8
4	Floating point	RW	64
5	Floating point	RW	32
6	Floating point	R	64
7	Floating point	R	32
8	Capability	R	32
9	Control module	E	32
10	Mixed	RW	64 + tag
11	Mixed	R	64 + tag

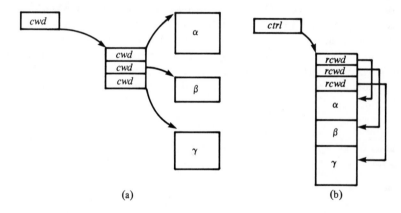

(a)   (b)

Fig. 16.3   A subtree in (a) absolute, and (b) relative form in storage

Table 16.3   Tagged elements in BLM

tag	Register fields
0	32-bit integer
1	Null
2	Data address type pts; limit l; location f
3	Control address mode m; location f
4	64-bit floating point

roughly corresponding to the PRL in CAP, though it is independent of process existence and provides continuity of program storage from one interaction to the next. On logging into the system a user is assigned to work in a pre-determined base, and references to other bases are rare except when setting up hierarchical subsystems (compare Fig. 6.4 (p. 116)). In order to provide a lower-level protection boundary it is necessary to control which base elements can be referenced in a particular context. In the BLM that is done by con-trolling the formation of base *indices* within control segments. Figure 16.4 shows the base structures that might be used to represent the environment of our earlier example (p. 296). The requirement was to establish access control to $\{Q\,A\,B\}$ when in procedure P, and to $\{A\,X\,Y\,T\}$ when in Q. It is supposed, as before, that A is an inherited reference to be communicated through the process registers. The remaining rights are determined solely by the inclusion of the indices t,b,q,x or y as appropriate in the control segments. That mechanism corresponds to the formation of *ENTER*-type capabilities and their associated PRL indices in CAP. Change of access lists is implicit in change of control segment, and can in fact be refined to the level of single statements, because if the external name of X or Y does not occur in a state-ment there is no way it can construct a reference to either of those objects (in contrast to CAP or CM*, which could by chance construct a program address referring to any primary capability or window register).

Control of constructed access rights depends on authorization granted at

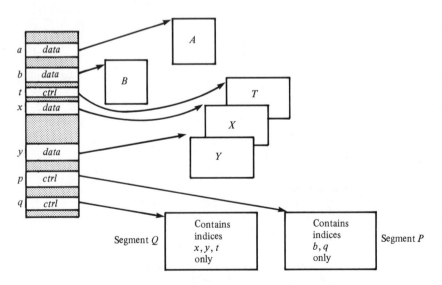

Fig. 16.4 Constructed access rights in BLM

the time of program formation being carried through to the time of execution, and exercise of authority can be subject to more or less formal controls. In the BLM there were just two lists of external names associated with each base: those of protected system objects such as workspace associated with class abstractions, file-control blocks, etc.; and those invented by users with access to the base. Within those broad groupings it was project managers' responsibility to ensure that no unauthorized references were made. That division of authority worked well in practice, though it could have been carried further to provide formal controls.

It will be noted that the BLM used a global addressing scheme and that pointers, once formed, could be passed from one process to another without loss of meaning. The reason for that was to ease communication between asynchronous I−O processes operating in system space. The *lockout* capability provided a simple means of synchronizing access to the same data areas by two or more activities.

16.2 PROCESS STATE VECTORS

The state of a process is defined by a mixed segment known as the Process State Vector (PSV) which is subdivided into a number of *stack frames* containing the working variables of incomplete procedure activations, a *dynamic chain* of control links, sixteen *machine registers* and sundry status indicators, resource and accounting information (Fig. 16.5). Operations on the PSV ensure that a secure protection boundary with respect to inherited access rights can be enforced on procedure change. In effect, the current stack frame is "sealed" by a procedure call and reopened when the procedure terminates according to the normal rules.

The machine register values (Table 16.3) determine the immediate working environment of a process. Each register contains either a number or a pointer, as indicated by its tag. Codewords are found only in store, being converted to addresses when loaded into registers (p. 118). The *Null* value is treated as "undefined" numerically, and barred from taking part in arithmetic or logical operations.

Physically, each tagged element can occupy up to 68 bits, which has led some designers to propose extra tag bits for every word in store. In fact only a small fraction of store is occupied by tagged elements and it is infrequently accessed, so that almost any method of packing the elements is satisfactory. In the experimental BLM three store words of 32 bits were used for each tagged element and for each control link.

Twelve of the machine registers are available for general use and four serve special purposes:

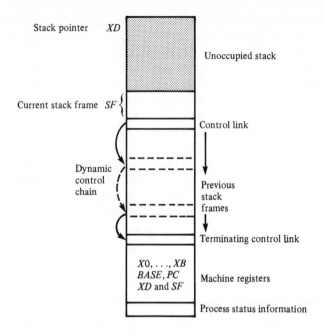

Fig. 16.5 Process state vector in BLM

BASE (*tag* 2) refers to the base on which the process acts;
  PC (*tag* 3) is the program counter;
  XD (*tag* 2) is the PSV address;
  SF (*tag* 2) defines the current stack frame.

It follows that references to the specialized registers must not be generated without special privilege; they are protected by the name-authorization mechanism mentioned earlier in the context of system procedures.

The use of numeric and pointer registers has already been encountered, of course, in our register transfer notation. There is very little to add to the conventions already introduced. However, instead of relying on comments or declarations to distinguish one sort of value from another it is now understood that each register carries its own descriptor and that the partition of registers into numeric and pointer values varies in the course of calculation. The provision of the stack and functions for temporarily storing registers on it avoided the problems of securing privacy of workspace later encountered on the PP250.

16.3 TAG-DEPENDENT MACHINE INSTRUCTIONS

The main objective in detecting tags at hardware level is to ensure that structures set up to preserve the integrity of data are correctly interpreted. Acquisition of a non-numeric tag is normally the result of some authorization procedure carried out earlier in the calculation, and is intended to save having to repeat the authorization at a later time: that applies to elementary rights such as being able to use an address to refer directly to store, and to more complex situations such as pointing to a file for update access. Most operations on capabilities are interpreted by stored program supplied by the system or user, but operations on codewords require hardware or microprogram support.

With regard to arithmetic and logical operations the motivation for using tags is less clearcut. The reader will recognize the close connection between the register formats used in the BLM and those used in certain language implementations (Table 5.3, p. 92) and it was intended that such features would be found in the Basic Language interface. It will be seen in Table 16.3 that floating-point and integer values were distinguished by tag, and from Table 16.2 that the distinction was carried to segment level. The difficulty with that approach is that it is never possible to accommodate all the data types that might be encountered, or to satisfy all the rules of type coercion in a single architectural interface. The benefits to the language subsystem are hardly justified by the complication caused, and in retrospect it seems preferable to concentrate tag interpretation on providing the controls that cannot adequately be offered by linguistic means.

As an illustration of the interpretation applied in the BLM, any arithmetic function applied to two machine registers (say $X1$ and $X2$) was subject to five possible outcomes depending on the tags of the arguments, i.e.:

CONDITION	RESULT in register transfer notation
$X1$ and $X2$ both numeric	$X1 + X2$
$X1$ numeric, $X2$ data address	$X1 + X2.$
$X1$ data address, $X2$ numeric	$X1 =. X1. + X2$
$X1$ and $X2$ both data address	$X1 =. X1. + X2.$
None of the above	Program trap

Further, the operation (*add* in the example) is modulated by the subtype and size of operand. Hence the " + " operator, which occurs as a single machine function, leads to $7*7 = 49$ valid interpretations, the remainder being program traps (there are 5 sorts of numeric data elements in store and two sorts of numeric register).

The remaining functions can be divided into six groups outlined below, where we ignore the actions taken on exceptional conditions (stack overflow, illegal tags, etc.).

Let $X1$ and $X2$ denote general-purpose registers.

(1) Load register from program store, e.g.: $X1 = X2$.
Here $X2$ must be a data pointer. The result in $X1$ depends on the *pts* code in $X2$. If numeric, $X1$ is an integer or floating-point number, extended if necessary. If capability there is a program trap on all but codewords, so that attempts to access Null, Lockout, File and other objects are subject to program interpretation before reaching the registers. Codewords are evaluated into addresses.

(2) Store register value, e.g. $X2 =. X1$
Here $X2$ must be a data pointer. For numeric sequences truncation and coercion to the type of $X2$ is carried out. Non-numeric values can only be stored in the stack, as described in (5) below.

(3) Address manipulation
The register set determines the current protection domain. It can be changed by loading new codewords from store, allowing the programmer to explore the environment and perhaps derive more restricted domains. A second method of changing the environment is by operating on addresses: the basic operations are *modification* ($'$) which has already been encountered in the register transfer notation, and *limitation* ($\hat{\ }$). Both operations have the effect when valid of shortening the sequence of elements addressed originally, and provide a means of delimiting protection domains to the precision of single bytes without adding to the burdens of the store manager. A third operation is needed to change the subtype, as one would in Fortran code when *EQUIVALENCE*ing floating-point and integer data areas. That is provided by an operator to change *pts* (protection, type and size coding), subject to the constraint that capability addresses cannot be changed into numeric or vice versa, and access rights cannot be expanded in any way to endanger program security. Functions are also provided to examine the *limit* and *pts* fields of a register. One of the shortcomings of the original instruction set was the omission of functions allowing mere *enquiry* about the environment without provoking the system into elaborate responses ("No thanks, I'm just browsing").

(4) Stack usage
Functions are required to *save* and *unsave* registers on the current stack frame in the sense already used in our register transfer programs. A separate function is provided to *clear* a register to Null, but that could sensibly have been combined with *save* when preparing for procedure

entry (to prevent unwanted rights being inherited). In the reverse direction, *clear* is used to prevent private access rights of the procedure from being inherited by the caller.

(5) Control transfers

The destination of control must always be a control address. It can be formed by offset relative to the current *PC* or by evaluating a control codeword. In procedure calls the old value of *PC* is stacked, with the *limit* from *SF*, which forms a link in the dynamic chain. Then *PC* is given its new value and the *limit* in *SF* is set to zero. In that way the stack is sealed and the content of previous stack frames is inaccessible to the called procedure. On normal return the previous stack frame is reinstated.

(6) Base access and other privileged instructions.

There are two instructions for making the *BASE* connection described earlier. One forms an address to the object in the base given by an offset index. For example, if the object with external name *Y* is located at position *y*, the effect of the base access instruction is to return the address *BASE'y^0*. The second instruction performs a similar operation for a "fixed" system base, giving access to commonly accessible system service functions.

Certain system procedures need to be able to flout convention by constructing and storing capabilities. The key to all such operations is a tag-forming instruction which by setting the tag field allows arbitrary values to be constructed. Of course, strict authorization is needed to be able to use such a function in program construction.

The following example shows how the conventions established for the BLM would be applied to the problem of integer-set representation tackled in the preceding chapters.

Example 16.1 A feasible solution for the BLM is to package all set-management procedures in a single control segment attached to the program base. Entry to a procedure is via a set of relative codewords in the control segment so that, for example, to call the third operation, *remove*, one might write:

$$\ldots ; \; CALL \; INTOPS.'2(s,v); \; \ldots$$

where *INTOPS* is the external name of the set-management module. The set representations themselves could be packed in the control segment but more freedom is obtained by attaching a separate and dynamically allocated substructure (*SETREP*) to the base. *SETREP* refers to a codeword segment; each integer set is represented by a data segment. To hand over a pointer to the set codeword as an authentic ticket is not quite satisfactory because it

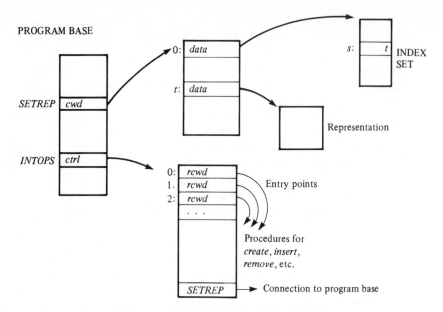

Fig. 16.6   Integer-set representation in BLM

gives the user access to the set itself. It is better to create an "index set" of integers (attaching it at *SETREP.* '0) and hand over a pointer (*s*) with read-only access to the integer *t* which gives the index in *SETREP* of the actual representation. It is that ticket which must be presented in subsequent operations, e.g. *insert(s,v)*, *similar(s₁,s₂)* and so on.

The above mechanism is straightforward for all set operations. The control segment may contain auxiliary procedures (such as *search()*) but they would not be visible from outside. User segments would be authorized as necessary to refer to *INTOPS* but not to *SETREP*. Some consequences of the representation should be noted.

(1)   *INTOPS* needs to be able to create and delete data segments, which it does by calling service functions in the system base.

(2)   Two sets s_1 and s_2 are equal (according to CLU) if and only if they are physically the same. It is not sufficient that two pointers refer to the same index *t* because one or both might be masquerading. A machine function *MEM* was provided in the BLM for comparing pointers. It would be used to establish equality. It would also be used to verify that a supposed ticket did in fact refer to an element of the index set *SETREP.* '0.

(3)   All set representations are visible to *INTOPS*, so there is no problem with operations involving two or more sets, such as *similar(s₁,s₂)*.

(4) System objects such as devices, files, processes and bases are represented exactly as shown except that instead of returning the pointer *s* a special capability is manufactured containing the index *t*. The capability type (Table 16.1) indicates the object class. The advantages gained are mainly in improved efficiency, but there are two logical differences of importance. First, there is room in the capability for various *options*, as seen in other machines. For example, in the case of the integer set we might want to ensure that elements are never removed by a particular user, and would inhibit the application of *remove*() (see diagram). Second, although the representation allows *INTOPS* to detect imitations there is no way for another procedure — for example, in a diagnostic package — to distinguish pointers used as tickets for abstract objects from any other sort. The encoding of capabilities makes that clear.

Soft capability | 8 | *intset* | *options* | *t* |

(Class)   (Object *id*)

(5) The overhead on each integer set amounts to a codeword in *SETREP* and an element of the index set.

(6) Several processes acting on the same base can use *INTOPS* provided the set operations are synchronized to update *SETREP* one at a time. If each process requires its own *SETREP* the simplest method in the BLM is to give each a new base, sharing references to *INTOPS* but arranging for each to define *SETREP*.

(7) With regard to deletion, a separate *delete*(*s*) operation must be provided as the system has no ready way of detecting that all pointers such as *s* have disappeared. After deletion the slot *t* in *SETREP* can immediately be re-used, but the index referred to by *s* cannot. In the scheme described above the size of codeword set *SETREP* is determined by the number of sets defined at any instant, whereas the index set must be large enough to accommodate all sets that might ever be defined. Thus the index set might be very sparsely populated: if so, there are various well-known ways of reducing it in size.

(8) A new object class is created when *SETREP* is initialized. That might be when the base is formed or as the result of calling a special function in *INTOPS*. The object class is deleted when *SETREP* is deleted or redefined. The store management procedures annul all references to undefined segments.

It should be added that in practical terms relatively little use was made of abstraction outside the BLM system itself. That is partly because use of the "soft" capability was restricted (we shall see in Chapter 18 how it can be made generally available). Also, it has to be said that choosing stable abstractions outside the range of obvious examples found in textbooks such as this is quite a difficult art. By far the greatest benefit is obtained from informal management of access lists and the knowledge that many systems can coexist in the same base without risk of damaging one another and with minimal overhead in moving between domains.

16.4 THE END OF THE EXPERIMENT

The essential proposition for the BLM was that inclusion of explicit structural information in programs, and adaptation of function to maintain consistent representations, would be of material benefit to both manufacturer and user. The test material was chosen to be typical of expected data processing loads: scientific and commercial work, multi-access use, file handling, compiler and operating system development. Assessment was based on:

(1) program efficiency;
(2) operating characteristics;
(3) coding and debugging costs;
(4) system overheads.

The implied comparison was with a conventional multiprogrammed system *not* offering in-program structural control: the lessons of OS/360 and other complex systems had yet to be taught, and expert opinion generally held that high-level languages would be entirely adequate tools for the task ahead. As events turned out, the design, development, and maintenance of large software systems did become a topic of importance, and it is perhaps superfluous now to stress the need for hardware support in that area. The problems remained of achieving beneficial effects without cost or performance penalties, and of showing that the benefits have practical significance to computer users.

Before commenting on general aspects of design we review in the context of the BLM the particular requirements of the abstraction mechanism listed earlier (p. 294).

(1) It must be foolproof. It should be clear by now that one must be cautious in making absolute claims in this area. It is certainly possible to hand out tickets and guarantee integrity of data representations without the problems of masquerading and leakage of workspace noted in the PP250.

There is still the problem of carrying private information in the machine registers across procedure boundaries. In either direction it is a matter of programming discipline to clear from the registers any values that are not needed by the caller (or callee). Usually a compiler will exercise such discipline. To close the gap by formalizing the procedure interface still further is counterproductive, and it is preferable to make the next formal interface at the *process* level, implying a complete change of process vectors.

Questions of authorization are also left open. Access to private system data is authorized to "system programmers" somehow identified in the log-in procedure. The same mechanism could be extended to other subsets of users, but how that is done depends on the general security policy of an installation.

(2) It must be fast. Using memory reference counts as a measure of speed the cost of operations involving codewords and addresses can be summarized as in Table 16.4, in which 32-bit memory words are assumed. The figures exclude instruction fetch, which was 2 or 4 byte on the BLM. Hence the round trip to a procedure cost between 7 and 11 memory references and stepping down the program structure cost $1\frac{1}{2} - 4$ references at each level, only slightly more than similar operations on unstructured machines. Perhaps the most important attributes were that a complete change of environment could be achieved in a few tens of microinstructions, compared with hundreds in later systems such as STAROS or CAP; and that the effect could be achieved without excessive storage fragmentation as seen in PP250.

Table 16.4 Memory cycles in BLM

Function	Memory cycles	
	direct	via segment table
Addressing operations	0	0
Address formation:		
from relative codeword	1	1
from absolute codeword	2	3
from stack	3	4
Transfer register to/from stack	3	3/4
Procedure call: in segment	3	3
via codeword	4	5
Procedure return:	3	4

(3) It must be flexible. The idea is not to provide all possible structures, but to support a set of containers into which higher-level structures can conveniently be mapped. By operating on addresses a BLM program can

resolve the immediate working environment to byte precision, partly decoupling the problems of protection from those of physical store management. The least flexible features were the attachment to tree structures and restrictions on storing tagged elements, to which we return below.

(4) It must be easy to use. In most respects the use of tagged registers allows conventional programming practice to be followed. The most important difference is in the detection of programming errors, where because of tag and address limit checks machines of this type can give both an immediate indication of a possible error and sufficient diagnostic information to work out its cause and remedy very quickly.

In more general terms it was to be expected that, because many decisions normally taken at compile or load time were deferred to the execution phase, there would be an adverse effect on performance. Conversely, it was hoped that the power of tag-dependent instructions would lead to more compact code. For the chosen test applications neither effect was significant, nor could cost penalties be deduced from length of microprogram path or size of control memory. It was conceded that for problems of dynamically changing structure the BLM would be at an advantage, but the experimental material did not reflect the growing importance of such problems, nor were there (in 1966) enough programmers sufficiently experienced to take advantage of the opportunities that did arise.

By "operating characteristics" the experiment was intended to assess such matters as system initiation, update, dump and restart, operator and terminal user response, job control, device management, machine test and diagnostic procedures, reconfiguration and the many other practical matters that fall outside the conventional flow of program activity. The main result of the experimental work was to demonstrate that the operating environment could be adapted to such diverse situations. Any positive benefit would follow from application of protection and abstraction to, e.g., job control, operating system structure, or the design of software test environments. Users of the BLM were aware of its economy and safety in such areas, but the results could not be quantified for the benefit of outside observers.

One area in which unanimity was reached was that of program development, in which the ease of debugging surpassed expectations. By logging all test runs it was shown that about half those that failed on execution contained errors detected by tag or type conflict or address modification overflow and undetectable by the compiler. Excellent diagnostics enabled errors to be located and corrected quickly: the structure of the operating environment allowed modules to be individually recompiled and re-bound to the base (Fig. 16.4) in matters of seconds rather than minutes (or hours, as might be the case with operating systems).

In summary, the experimental results were the best that could be expected on ground chosen by the opposition. The main debate, which was to be used to abandon the BLM project, rested on store management techniques and the related topic of reliability in the face of hardware failure. The same issues recur in any tagged architecture and it is important to understand the design options. The characteristic property of such systems is that structural information is fragmented and diffused through program space. That is the source of their flexibility, but it also means that:

(1) store management procedures have an open-ended commitment to managing data structures at all levels of the physical store hierarchy;
(2) failure in any part of storage can endanger total system security by generating illegal pointers;
(3) the physical transport mechanism must be secure and able to handle non-numeric (tagged) data without loss of performance.

In practice, the total information structure within a system can be partitioned into *database, program,* and *process workspace* (Fig. 16.7). Each is structured, but is subject to separate logical and physical control. Whether to present the database as a continuation of program storage is optional, but almost certainly one would do so by temporarily mapping parts of it into program storage rather than by propagating codewords into the database. In the BLM, pointers in process workspace could refer to program storage, but not vice versa, and pointers in program storage could refer to the database, but not vice versa. Each of the lower levels can use "master object tables" to assist physical management (for example, system internal names for data sets, descriptor tables for segments). If such a strategy is followed the database is no more vulnerable on a tagged machine than any other, and

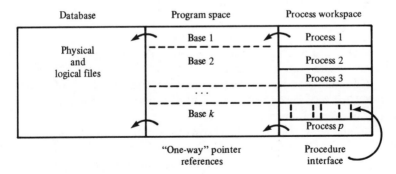

Dashed lines indicate program controlled interfaces
Solid lines are architectural interfaces

Fig. 16.7 Protection boundaries in BLM

must be protected by normal authorization, journalizing and roll-back procedures.

Programs contain two sorts of segment in which storage errors endanger system security. For capabilities (and more particularly for codewords) access authority can be rechecked at time of use by reference to descriptor tables (SCT in PP250, PRL in CAP, segment table in BLM) whose structure can be chosen to achieve complete partitioning. In that sense, responsibility for error containment is removed from the capability structure and placed on the descriptor tables, which are presumed to be smaller and to have correspondingly smaller chance of producing errors. In practice, one might achieve the same effect by physical partitioning of memories in a multicomputer system. In nearly all systems, however, there is a need to share segments between partitions, either for communication of data, I–O, or to save duplication of application programs. It then becomes more difficult to make absolute claims about error propagation. An alternative approach is to reinforce the normal parity checks on memory by redundant coding of capabilities or descriptors. In PP250, for example, a one-word checksum is maintained with each two-word entry in SCT. One can never assert complete immunity from memory failure, but there is nothing to prevent the probability of error, and resulting costs, being reduced to the same level as on a conventionally paged machine.

The second type of segment that requires attention is that representing a control module. The main dangers are from chance generation of the small number of tag-forming functions or references to special registers. Here the BLM took advantage of control abstraction and relied on the fact that code could not be overwritten by normal means. In more conventional design a privileged control state would be associated with the few system routines using such functions. Alternatively, they could be pushed down into microcode. In either case the problem is transformed into one of deciding when to enter privileged state (capability option, descriptor control bits, Fig. 15.2) and of protecting the associated mechanisms. Control segments also contain the base indices used in constructing access-list elements. Memory failure in a base index would give illegal (unauthorized) access to the current base. Here again, redundant coding can be used to reduce the probability of undetected error, but for very secure access it might be preferred to remove the locus of control to a separate base.

It should be stressed that the above discussion is aimed at defense against hardware errors. It offers no protection against errors in microprogram or privileged code. On the assumption that the hardware and microprogram is working correctly and that the "system base" is correctly initialized the security of programs and integrity of abstraction mechanisms can be guaranteed.

After so much laundering the formation of an address in the process workspace might be compared with the arrival of Tamino at the Temple of Wisdom. From that point onwards, malfunction of the addressing circuits could enable a process to overwrite any portion of main memory. There is no directly comparable situation in conventional architecture, in which addresses are formed only transiently by reference to datum registers, segment or page tables (nevertheless, BLM users complained that they "couldn't store addresses", forgetting that they didn't have addresses to store on other systems). The closest comparison is with the contents of microregisters, scratchpad, control or cache memories in the underlying micromachine, for which the same considerations apply: what happens if a bit is "lost"? What are the chances of losing a bit? Risk assessment must be based on specific designs rather than on general architectural features.

Writing addresses into program space certainly increases the risk of corruption unless extra precautions are taken, and some designers would argue that the advantage gained is not worthwhile. The sort of additional checks that could be applied are to retain the segment *id* in the address (as seen in VCS, p. 118), re-checking accessibility when the address is loaded into a microregister; to retain pointers in codeword form in the registers; or to enforce the constraint that addresses are private to processes, so that corruption of an address will not spread to other processes. We shall see in Chapter 18 how such ideas work in practice.

Undoubtedly the major source of difficulty in a tagged architecture results when addresses are thought of as *direct* representations of reference variables as used in high-level languages. Then the language requires that addresses shall be stored in program space, often as parts of mixed segments whose structure must be dynamically indicated by the use of tag bits. In such situations provision has to be made for tagging every word in memory and for carrying tags into auxiliary storage. An important practical distinction can be drawn between such systems (which include IBM System/38) and those in which reference variables are mapped into spaces provided by the microsystem, for which the problems are not so acute (see Fig. 6.5, p. 119).

It will be seen from Fig. 16.7 and from the preceding discussion that the two sets of boundaries between bases and between procedures are not sharply regulated by the BLM architecture. To do so would entail a loss of efficiency which, on balance, does not appear to be justified. Application programs can enforce what discipline is implied by the security policy.

The reader might still be asking what use all this is to computer manager or maker. At the consumers' end we can distinguish between direct and indirect costs. The direct costs are most likely to be reduced if there is substantial effort in program or system development and maintenance; or if the workload is very variable in character, involving dynamic adjustment to changing situations. Protection and abstraction mechanisms are often presented as tools for complex system programming; equivalently, they are the means of solving less complex problems with less experienced staff. Indirectly, the effect of tagged architecture on the quality and reliability of manufactured software can be profound. To give one example, the process workspace on the BLM was about 4 Kbytes per process, and the encapsulation overhead on procedures was less than 100 bytes: applied to our earlier transaction processing example (Fig. 14.1) that means that the partitions between phases can be precisely and economically matched at the architectural level. An alternative approach, based on virtual machine architecture, has been known to require over 50 Kbytes for each process partition, and to be unable to provide flexible partitioning between procedures. Such comparisons imply a complete change of approach to TP problem solution.

The issues faced by the computer maker are as follows. A refined protection mechanism reduces the cost of developing and maintaining software and enhances response to dynamically changing application environments (such as TP or operating system). To be effective the mechanism must not incur extra cost or degrade performance: if those conditions are only met in a narrow band of the performance spectrum it is easy to predict panic measures at the extreme ends, losing the strategic advantage of range architecture and absorbing unnecessarily large fractions of research and development effort.

Once a commitment is made to abstraction, self-application within the system brings further benefits: for example in file management, abstraction of the instruction code, or distribution of function. Those benefits are lost if not taken in the earliest stages of system design. The final package depends, of course, on the style of the manufacturer. In the next chapter we examine a system which, in the language of car sales, might be called "loaded". The final chapters describe an economy model exploiting the same principles.

16.5 FURTHER READING

In the end, the BLM was not used, even in part, as a product (the original model was scrapped in 1970 but emulated on the E1 emulator).

The aims of the BLM project are described in SCA68 and again in ILI69. The origins of the design and some details of machine and system functions are given in ILI72a. The ideas are, however, much more easily presented in the terms that have evolved with the growth of interest in reducing software development and maintenance costs. (At the time of BLM design, for example, we had very little feeling of what to expect from the use of tag-dependent functions or from system support for abstract objects.)

The use of tags is discussed in more general terms in FEU73 and again in

MYE78. Tags probably owe their existence to the support by the US Atomic Energy Commission in the 1950s of the MERLIN computer at Brookhaven National Laboratory and MANIAC at Los Alamos. The original idea was to identify data points which might, for example, represent boundaries of irregular geometries in iteration schemes. The arithmetic or control functions were set to "trap" and take special action on certain tag combinations. Later, a similar idea was incorporated in "word marks" used to signal the boundaries of fields in character machines such as IBM 1401. The Rice University computer started as a copy of MANIAC, but the tag concept was developed further in the direction of general support for "program objects" such as code and data segments and descriptors, and for dynamic storage allocation. The first commercial use of tags was made in 1961 by the Burroughs corporation in support of segmentation on the B 5000. They have continued to feature largely in successors to the B 5000.

17 IBM SYSTEM/38

It is widely recognized that many of the norms of computer design owe their acceptance to the technical and marketing skills of IBM. The transitions from tape to disk auxiliary storage, from assemblers to compilers, from nothing-in-particular to range-defined architecture were all cued by product announcements from IBM. In each case the underlying technology had been explored in more than one laboratory, but commercial users could barely articulate the demand that was about to be satisfied, and those responsible for product development were required to have an uncommon grasp of strategic issues affecting the industry. An exact parallel can be drawn in the case of capability machines. The announcement in 1978 of IBM System/38 is therefore potentially one of the most important developments in computer design of the past decade.

It will be clear from preceding discussion that, once the idea of controlled pointer formation has been accepted, there are many different ways of developing the details and using abstraction in system design. There are corresponding variations in terminology, and because we are about to introduce a new batch of technical terms it might be useful to review the options. Starting from the high-level requirement of manipulating classes of abstract objects (Fig. 17.1) we have seen that the primary distinction is between interpretive (and therefore hardware or microcode assisted) and linguistic (compiler assisted) methods. Neither is sufficient in itself, but in general terms classes with unpredictable membership or rapidly changing attributes, which would include program space itself and many of the objects encountered in system programming, require hardware support. For the latter, the key requirement is to establish precise domains of protection reflecting authority acquired either in the course of *constructing* a program or by *inheritance* during its execution. A protection domain is defined as a set of pointers and

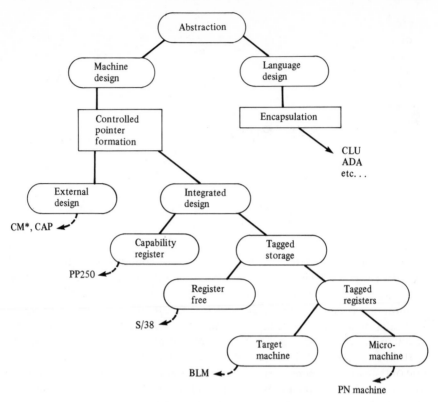

Fig. 17.1 Taxonomy of capability machines

the objects that can be accessed by applying the machine's addressing functions to them. In mechanizing that concept we can distinguish *external* designs
which seek to preserve a conventional program interface, controlled behind
the scenes by a capability addressing unit and supporting microprogram, and
integrated designs in which pointers are visible to programmers. The latter
designs can further be divided into those which preserve the integrity of
pointers by strict partition of program space and those which use self-
identifying tags as necessary. Further classification is based on the level of
machine definition. In System/38 we shall see that the user interface is high-
level, register-free, and that it supports a direct mapping from reference
variables that might occur in high-level languages into pointers as recognized
by the machine architecture. In the BLM, tagged registers were defined at the
user interface and reference variables were translated into index paths relative
to the tree-structured program store. In other respects the BLM was a high-
level machine, but it would be incorrect to assume that a capability machine

has to be defined at a high level, as we shall see in later chapters. The term "Pointer" as used in System/38 closely corresponds to "capability" as used elsewhere, i.e. it includes both general abstract objects and the important subclass of store segments referenced by "codewords" on the BLM.

Orthogonal to the preceding classification, and not shown in Fig. 17.1, is a set of decisions concerned with system partitioning and deferred authorization. In theory, controlled pointer formation is sufficient to establish any required partition of program space, but designers have found cause to subdivide the operating environment in various ways that supplement or override the pointer facility. Somewhat similar mechanisms arise in at least four different contexts:

(1) providing extra security checks in case of machine error;
(2) revoking authority previously granted by program;
(3) simplifying physical resource management;
(4) requiring to make strong assertions about the existence, use or ownership of certain classes of object.

In each case the final authorization is deferred to time of use, when it is verified by reference to appropriate tables. In different machine designs we encounter primary and secondary capabilities, Process Resource Lists, bases, System Capability Table, segment table, and master object tables playing one or more of the above roles. There is no uniformity of terms that makes their purpose clear and, as usual, IBM's entry onto the scene introduces a new crop of terms for concepts that seemed clear enough. Understanding the design therefore entails penetrating the description to the extent of recognizing components seen in other machines, and explaining divergent features. The following subsections retain IBM terms for ease of reference to sources.

17.1 WHAT THE USER SEES

The declared aim of System/38 is to offer on a low-cost system more function and greater ease of use than previously available in the same price range. Downward trends in store costs and increased performance at circuit level provide the basis for such a development, but the essential step towards "ease of use" is to present the machine as one in which a range of objects known to the system and user can be manipulated in a natural and consistent way. The alternative approach, of defining only the arithmetic and control interfaces and then building subsystems, e.g. for batch, interactive, or transaction processing, was recognized as a major source of inconvenience and inefficiency in conventional design. Accordingly, the machine supports a

Table 17.1   System/38 System objects

Type	Use
Access Group	To permit physical grouping
Context	Name-object list, with type
Controller	Abstraction of I−O device controller
Cursor	Address of data space
Data Space	Arrival sequence file of single format records
Data Space Index	Logical ordering of records
Index	General-purpose list accessed by binary radix-tree search
Logical unit	Abstraction of I−O device
Line description	Abstraction of communication network
Process Control Space	Process abstraction
Program	Control module
Queue	Message port (process/I−O)
Space	Data segment up to 2^{24} bytes
User Profile	Authorization list

number of primitive objects (Table 17.1) and the function set includes indivisible commands for operating on objects and their attributes. It is also possible to set up combinations of control fields which cause implicit actions to do with authorization, binding, naming, and checkpointing, and key advantages are attributed to their consistent application throughout the system.

From Table 17.1 it will be seen that conventional storage segments are called Spaces. Access to a Space allows manipulation of binary data, but each word (4 bytes) carries one extra tag bit which is set to indicate that it forms part of a Pointer: a single Pointer occupies 4 words. If any part of a Pointer is overwritten with binary data it reverts to numeric status. The only way of forming a Pointer is by using the machine functions designed for that purpose. Space Pointers can be used as bases for offsets supplied in the program which must, of course, lie within the bounds supplied for the Space. A Pointer contains a Type code and usually subtype and other fields. There are four types of Pointer:

(1) Space Pointers refer to specific bytes in the space associated with a system object (including a Space object). Space Pointers can be modified and used as bases (in the sense of PL/1 BASED data objects).
(2) Data Pointers refer to specific bytes in a Space and provide scalar data object attributes (binary, decimal, etc.).
(3) System Pointers address system objects which identify themselves as

belonging to one of the 14 types given in Table 17.1. A System Pointer also contains an options field which is used to determine access authority (see later).

(4) Instruction Pointers indirectly address instructions in a program.

The system objects form a basic set from which others such as database files, job descriptions and messages can be constructed. For each, a Space Pointer is created referring to the components of the composite object. Responsibility for managing such objects and for many other services is assumed by a SIL known as the Control Program Facility (CPF). Figure 17.2 illustrates how the system objects might be used to form a composite database file reference. The database user never has access to actual physical records, but operates through a Cursor which maps logical records into one or more Data Spaces, using a Data Space Index to determine the logical ordering of records. The Cursor is responsible for applying record locks and reformatting or editing fields as required to meet the logical file specification. To initiate a Read operation the user would present the database file pointer (p in the example) to the database manager (in CPF), which would in turn use Cursor, DSI and Data Space management functions to select, transform, and move the record into a buffer defined by the user. The expansion of access rights that is implied in going from one domain to another is reflected by a change of User Profile, as will be seen later.

A machine function is provided to generate a Program object from a binary representation. System/38 users can only write programs in RPG-III,

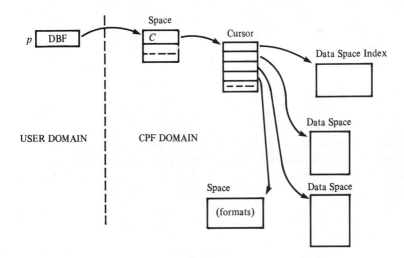

Fig. 17.2 Representing a database file in System/38

Cobol, or Command Language. Language compilers generate an intermediate symbolic representation, similar to assembly language, which is translated to binary form by CPF. The final binary form held in Programs is not accessible: the machine prohibits direct access to encapsulated programs and allows invocation only at the proper entry point.

An unusual feature of the symbolic representation, viewed as a target language, is that data attributes are declared separately from instructions. Instructions refer to operands by name in a Dictionary which gives data type, length, storage class and other attributes. Consequently, as in most high-level languages, there are relatively few arithmetic functions (such as *ADD*), but they are refined by reference to the Dictionary during translation. Data types include Pointers, and a comprehensive set of instructions is provided for pointer manipulation. Besides computation, branching and data manipulation functions, CPF includes programmer, operator and system services, job control, work station, library and data management functions in a unified structure.

Certain operand references that cannot be completely specified during translation are carried into the Program as **unresolved** Pointers. They act as free variables that can be bound to their environment at execution time. There are two forms of late binding. An unresolved System Pointer specifies the name of a system object to be found in a list of Contexts associated with the current process. The Contexts are searched in a pre-defined order to match a given name, type and subtype; if successful, a (resolved) System Pointer is returned. For example, in a language subsystem with various default options there might be two Contexts, one for user-specified actions and one defined by the conventions of the language, and they would be scanned in turn to find an exception-handling procedure. As another example, it might be required to set up a test environment for which selected external conditions could be simulated. Positioning a "test Context" ahead of all others in the search would enable such substitutions to be made without altering the program under test.

The second sort of delayed binding applies to unresolved Data Pointers. Here the machine is caused to search for the corresponding "externally named" and statically allocated data object in some program activated in the current process. A (resolved) Data Pointer is returned. The use of unresolved Data Pointers enables programs to be written to operate on data objects whose attributes have not been determined. A closely related facility allows operation on entries in database files whose attributes differ from those declared in the program: conversion is carried out when necessary by the database access function.

The full object name (32 bytes) must be unique in a Context. The same names can occur in different Contexts, but each of them must refer to a different object. Only system objects are addressed by Contexts, and any given system object can be addressed by at most one Context. A name can be inserted in a Context, optionally, at time of creation; machine functions are provided to rename and reassign references, subject to the above constraints.

Acquisition of a Pointer does not, however, guarantee access to the object to which it refers. Each permanent object (Section 17.2) is owned by a unique User Profile which can retain control of all attempts to access it. The User Profiles represent internally the divisions of responsibility outside the computer. As in other systems the log-in procedure positively identifies the user and establishes a User Profile that will determine rights of access. In a simple environment the need for separate UPs for each interactive workstation user, machine operator, system programmer, maintenance engineer, database security and installation manager can be foreseen. Internally, each can delegate rights to other User Profiles. Whether they cooperate by telling each other their passwords is outside the control of the system. In theory, any attempt to operate on a non-Space object can be referred back to its owner for authorization. In the next subsection we examine how that is done.

An unusual and pervasive feature of System/38 is that the address range available to Pointers is extremely large, so that object *id*s, which are mapped onto segment *id*s, are never re-used in the lifetime of the system. The segment identifier is 40 bits, so that even at the unlikely rate of generating one object per millisecond the segment space would last for over 30 years. Segments can be destroyed, but Pointers might continue to refer to them and would, if used, be detected as meaningless by the addressing mechanism. Pointers are "global" to the system and persist across shut-down and restart operations, and they can occur in the Space component of any object. Such an approach obviously puts a high premium on the ability of the physical storage system to carry tagged data securely in main memory and auxiliary devices. It can be contrasted with other capability-based designs in which the operating environment is more rigidly divided, e.g. into database and program areas, process- or user-specific domains, or in which object indices are recycled by individual class managers. The designer has to balance "ease of use" arguments on both sides against the cost of manipulating and maintaining Pointers.

The remaining machine objects listed in Table 17.1 are easily recognized. An Access Group is a set of objects intended to coexist either in main or auxiliary memory. It is an optimizing tool allowing the user to advise the system of working-set requirements. An Index is a general-purpose table manager that allows data to be entered and retrieved under a given key. It is used by machine procedures for Context, User Profile, database and storage management, and is available to programmers.

From the above outline it will be seen that apart from the treatment of abstraction a lot of "ease of use" is bought by delayed binding techniques: the use of Contexts, of logical files, and of flexible job-management functions all allow the maximum use to be made of program modules without the need to rewrite or even recompile. Such facilities can be seen as valuable byproducts of the control of pointer formation and use.

17.2 AUTHORIZATION

A new object can be created by application of the appropriate function, supplying control parameters and initial values of attributes from the control sequence. The Name of the object can be put into a Context, together with a Pointer to what is, in effect, a segment containing its attributes and control fields (Fig. 17.3). A distinction is drawn between *temporary* and *permanent* objects. Temporary objects are not owned, not secured against system faults,

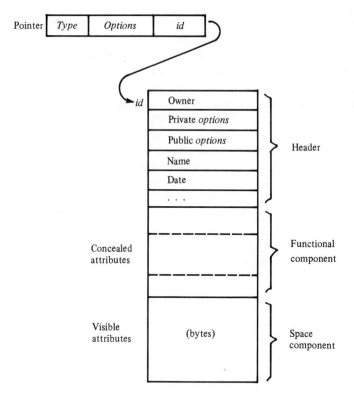

Fig. 17.3   Model of an object in System/38

and are charged to individual processes. They are implicitly destroyed at system restart. Permanent objects are owned by, and charged to, User Profiles and implicitly destroyed when their owner is destroyed. The User Profiles impose a single-rooted tree structure on program space, defined by the ownership relation and maintained by system functions. (In contrast, Pointers in Space objects allow arbitrary structure to be defined.) Control of authorization can be exercised only by reference to User Profiles, hence temporary objects, having no owners, have unrestricted access rights from time of creation.

From Fig. 17.3 it can be seen that in general there are three points of control in the access path: in what we have called the *options* field in the Pointer; in the Header associated with the object; and in the User Profile identified by the *owner* field in the Header. For each object, eight independent options are specified, as shown in Table 17.2, and whether or not the programmer can apply a particular function successfully depends on its type ("update", "access" and so on) and on the setting of the authority bit for that type. Thus, having Access right no.1 allows the program to destroy the object; no.2 permits renaming and delegation of rights to other users, and so on.

The site of access control bits is determined by program. For best performance they should be held in the Pointer, but in doing so the possibility of revoking rights is lost. The act of forming a System Pointer complete with options field containing access rights is under control of Access right no.3 (Table 17.2). Note that for Space Pointers no control over access is exercised, other than bounds check, and that there is no associated "read-only" option.

The "controlling rights" of any permanent object are held in the User Profile which owns it. A subset of rights can be granted either to specific User Profiles or to all: the latter are the **public** rights which are stored in the

Table 17.2   Access rights in System/38

Number	Functions permitted	Usage
1	Existence	Allows destruction of object or transfer of ownership;
2	Management	Allows renaming, delegation of rights;
3	Pointer	Allows delegation of authority to Pointer;
4	Space	Allows formation of Space Pointer;
5	Retrieve	
6	Insert	Manipulation of concealed contents
7	Delete	of object
8	Update	

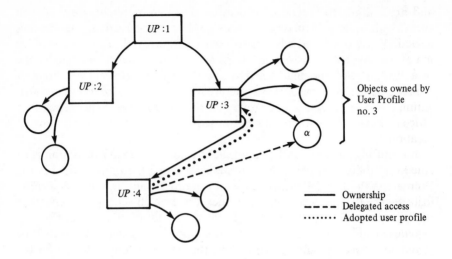

Fig. 17.4   System/38 ownership structure

object header. It is also possible to create a Program with the attribute of "adopting" a User Profile when it is invoked, thereby increasing its access rights. Consider an object such as α in Fig. 17.4, which is owned by UP:3 but for which the Retrieval right has been made public. Then any process running in UP:4, say, which obtains the System Pointer to α can only apply retrieval functions to it. However, if a program is invoked under UP:4 which adopts UP:3 then it acquires the "rights of ownership". The adopted User Profile can, optionally, be propagated to subsequent program invocations.

The authority to use system objects available to a process at any instant is thus the union of (1) authority stored in the Pointer, (2) public authority, (3) private authority deriving from ownership and delegation, and (4) authority granted to User Profiles that are adopted by programs invoked by the process. Logically, the order of checking these sources makes no difference. Therefore the fastest checks and those most likely to succeed are made first.

Apart from object management, User Profiles are also the sources of authority for many machine functions such as those for creating and changing User Profiles, initiating and controlling processes, installation management, dumping and reloading back-up copies of objects or their attributes on a selective basis and, last but by no means least, an "all object" authority which confers feudal powers.

17.3 PROCESS ACTIVITY

All activity in System/38, including I – O operations, follows from the initiation of processes. A process is represented by a data structure which includes (1) a Process Control Space containing protected data such as Program Pointers and register values associated with procedure activation; (2) a Pointer defining the current locus of control; (3) two Space objects for allocating static and automatic storage classes; and (4) a User Profile which is the basis for authorizing access to permanent objects. Initially, a process is isolated from all others, and its capacity for influencing the outside world is determined by the Contexts under which it operates. Conversely, the ability of other processes to access temporary data internal to the process is governed by its own policy in handing out Pointers.

When two or more processes attempt to retrieve, update or control the existence of the same object concurrently, implicit controls are provided to prevent inconsistency. A program can place a **lock** on any object. Associated with such an object is a list of processes that have applied locks and the mode of access required (update, multiple read, or other discipline: there are five types of lock). A process exception will occur if an attempt is made to use a locked object in a conflicting way; to avoid that exception it must lock the object, thereby joining the queue to use it. When a process is forced to wait in a queue, a wait time limit value is specified which prevents indefinite hang-up. Software is responsible for detecting or avoiding deadlocks. Machine instructions use special internal locking protocols to assure deadlock avoidance on indivisible operations.

An alternative method of interprocess communication is through Queue objects. Machine functions are provided to Enqueue and Dequeue messages in a specified Queue. In this context a message is itself a data object (supported by CPF) containing a prefix (giving size and an optional message key) and a text consisting of a byte string. The text may contain Pointers. The size of Queue (maximum number of waiting messages), maximum size of message, whether they can contain Pointers, and the method of servicing are amongst the attributes assigned at time of Queue creation. The method of servicing can be FIFO (first in, first out), LIFO (last in, first out) or by comparison with a key supplied by the Dequeue instruction. A Queue is shared by any number of communicating processes. To receive a message a process must issue a Dequeue instruction (specifying a maximum wait if there is no message available) or listen for an event to be signalled, indicating the arrival of a message.

Turning to in-process structure, we know that one of the requirements of any abstraction mechanism is to be able to alter the access list when control passes from one domain to another. The key elements in System/38 are

Names occurring in Program objects, Contexts, and User Profiles. According to the authorization rules a program cannot construct a reference to another object unless it names it, finds the name in the current Context, and the derived Pointer is either authorized already or, when used, is found to be authorized for the function requested. That convention corresponds to the rule used for constructed access lists in the Basic Language Machine. We saw earlier how authority can be expanded by adopting User Profiles.

Treatment of inherited rights is rather more difficult because it requires both a positive assertion of what is to be available and negation of rights currently enjoyed. In the BLM that control was provided by allowing register values to be stacked (and cleared), and sealing the stack frame on procedure call. There is no corresponding structure on System/38, all data in the automatic and static Spaces associated with a process being unprotected. A faulty procedure could, for example, wipe clean the variables of all incomplete procedure activations in the same process. Space pointers could be formed, saved, and used after the operands referred to had been destroyed. To guard against such errors, many management functions which could logically be called by in-line procedure activation must be invoked by the inter-process message-handling functions, as in CM*/STAROS.

Finally, it should be noted that abstraction as a *user* facility is not supported in System/38. All Pointer functions are designed to support the basic set of system objects and composite objects presented by the Control Program Facility.

17.4 MICROMACHINE SUPPORT

A high-level machine definition deliberately allows freedom in implementation. Nevertheless, the way in which a function is supported (hardware, microprogram, intermediate code) determines its relative speed and the way it is expected to be used. Figure 17.5 outlines the common features of the first versions of System/38 to be announced (Models 3 and 5). It is seen to be a single order-code processor accessing the main memory system through a Virtual Address Translation (VAT) unit. A channel controller shares the VAT, but direct access to main store control is allowed for data transfer.

Main memory is organized as 40-bit words, each consisting of 32 data bits, one tag and 7 error-correcting code bits. Memory size ranges from 512 Kbyte to 2 Mbyte in increments of 256 Kbytes.

Control memory is either 4K or 8K words of 32 bits each. The micro-instruction cycle time is in the range 400–500 ns in Model 3 and 200–300 ns in Model 5. Main store cycle times are 1100 ns and 600 ns respectively.

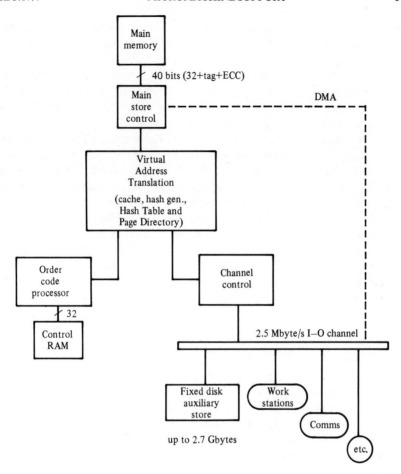

Fig. 17.5   Micromachine schematic diagram for System/38

Microinstructions are vertically coded and control the transfer of micro-register fields in units of 1 or 2 bytes through an ALU with binary and decimal arithmetic capability. The microprogram is organized as a fixed component plus 64-word overlays brought in from main memory by a resident overlay supervisor. Apart from interpreting target instructions resident in main store, microprogram is also responsible for the implicit functions of task management, I–O servicing, Queue and exception handling, and authorization.

Somewhat confusingly, main-store resident programs are also referred to as "microcode", but whether directly obeyed (as overlays) or interpreted is an implementation option. The internal binary code encapsulated in Programs uses a register-based instruction set not far removed from IBM 370 formats, but making use of a distinct set of Pointer registers in place of the base index registers. Clearly, the possibility exists of using a variety of target representations depending on the characteristics of the original source language, but that is not exploited in the design.

Main memory is physically allocated as 128-word (512 data byte) page frames. Segments are identified by a 48-bit virtual address (see diagram) of which 24 bits give the segment *id*, 15 give the page identifier *pid*, and 9 give a byte offset *b*. Segments are classified as small (up to 128 pages) and large (up to 32K pages); in the latter case 256 contiguous small segments are assigned. The number of pages required initially is specified at time of creation. Only the amount required is allocated, but it can later be extended, truncated or destroyed. All pages are allocated disk space, and each page is preceded on disk by header information which includes its virtual address. The encoding of virtual addresses is such that temporary and permanent objects can be distinguished and the system directories can be reconstructed by scanning pages on disk.

24	15	9	
id	*pid*	*b*	S/38 virtual address

Although hardware supports only a 24-bit segment identifier, it is extended by microprogram to 40 bits and the *pid/b* fields are retained in Pointers as 24 bits. In a Space Pointer the virtual address therefore occupies 8 bytes. Address bounds are stored in the Header of the Space object. All Pointer formats are interpreted by microprogram.

Conversion of segment *id* to physical page frame is completed in the VAT unit with the help of three tables. Firstly, a 64-word cache memory is used to catch recently used segments. If not successful a logical combination of *id* and *pid* is used to form an index H which selects a second index h from a Hash Table. The index h is used as the starting point of a search through a Page Directory (Fig. 17.6). The Page Directory contains one element for each main store page frame, so that a 1 Mbyte store would use a 2048-element Page Directory. Each element contains *id* and *pid* of the page currently occupying the corresponding position in main memory. It also contains a link to the next element whose *id/pid* yields the same hash index H, or an "end-of-chain" indicator. If the page required is in main memory it will eventually be found at position f, say, of the Page Directory. The physical address is found by concatenating f with b. The cache memory can then be updated.

The hashing algorithm is implemented in hardware and is intended to

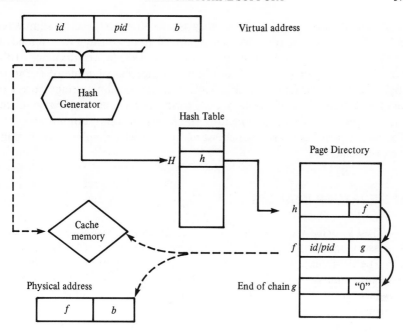

Fig. 17.6   Virtual-address translation in System/38

produce a uniformly distributed set of hash codes H from the expected population of *id/pid*. Typically, the Hash Table is twice the size of Page Directory giving, in theory, an average of 1.25 "probes" to find the correct page. If no match is found a page fault is indicated and the store manager will locate it on disk and transfer it into main store. Microprogram is responsible for updating the Hash Table and Page Directory.

From the above brief description it can be seen that very considerable computing power is brought to bear on abstraction and related facilities in System/38. Referring back to the criteria used to measure other systems (p. 294), it can be seen that the system is foolproof in the sense that one cannot circumvent the control structures to establish illicit structures. It is probably not as foolproof as some would like *within* processes, particularly across procedure boundaries. That will lead to more frequent use of process change than is strictly necessary unless protection can be established at a lower level. As for being "cheap and fast", those are relative terms and it might be argued that in the intended application areas speed is a secondary consideration. The manipulation of 16-byte pointers by microprogram will certainly discourage their use as components of fine structure. We have referred elsewhere to the "inertial effect" of having to change microprogram, scratchpad registers, control tables, cache memory and so on when there is a significant change of control environment. There appear to be considerable overheads of that type in System/38, even in comparison with the performance of the machine instruction set, which might discourage use of some of the more sophisticated abstraction mechanisms. Delayed binding brings speed of adaptation to change of workload, file format, and operating environment, which is probably seen as a more important attribute than computing power. The two requirements are not necessarily in conflict, as will be shown in the next two chapters.

17.5 FURTHER READING

The most informative technical papers are SOL79 and BER80. An interesting discussion of design issues for this class of computers is in RAD76.

The IBM publication (IBM78) contains 29 short papers, but is generally more informative on hardware than software design. Technical documentation has recently appeared (IBM80) and should be consulted for further information on topics mentioned in this chapter.

An IBM research effort in the same area as System/38 is described by Myers (MYE78). An account is given of SWARD, an experimental architecture designed to improve reliability of programs by a combination of techniques:

detection at run time of semantic errors common to many languages;
detection of program logic errors;
containment of errors;
design of an architecture to encourage good programming practices.

In SWARD the primitive data elements are 4-bit tokens, or strings of tokens, and tagging is used at elementary level to control arithmetic interpretation as well as addressing. Variable-length instructions are used, directly reflecting high-level constructs. Thus SWARD combines some of the attributes of DEL codes discussed in Chapters 5 and 6 with abstraction techniques of the BLM and System/38.

At the time of going to press the Intel iAPX 432 computer has been announced, without giving sufficient detail to allow comparison on the terms we have been using. It appears to use tags to support abstraction. Interested readers should peruse the technical description when it becomes available.

18 POINTER-NUMBER MACHINES

On learning that tens of thousands of bytes of microprogram are invested in abstraction functions, and that the critical paths involve hundreds of micro-steps, the designer might choose to take the alternative path towards software reliability. Further enquiry will show that a language such as ADA requires a ¼-Mbyte compiler, together with a filing system able to support library and module specifications in a secure manner. It would be understandable to conclude that abstraction is only for specialists and big spenders. On the contrary, this chapter will present a micromachine design in which the essential requirements of abstraction are achieved with the help of a table of 80 bytes and in which the critical paths are measured in single microsteps. We shall concentrate on *what* is provided and how it achieves its effect, hoping that *why* has been made sufficiently clear in preceding chapters. Study of the example in the final subsection will give a fairly complete picture of the support required.

We have seen that a fundamental design requirement is to make a distinction at register level between pointers and numerical data. Reflecting that distinction, the machine to be described is called a **Pointer-Number** or simply "PN" machine. It should be emphasized that unlike the machines described in previous chapters the PN machine exists only in simulated form at present, and that the claim to simplicity is based on comparison with registers and state transitions observed in existing micromachines. In the PN instruction set the use of both interpretive techniques and planar memory functions is anticipated, so the description draws together many of the ideas developed in Parts 1 and 2. In particular, it is taken as axiomatic that abstraction facilities must be available to the lowest level of program control, i.e. to the micro-program. It is insufficient to use microprogram only to support abstraction at a higher level.

One of the abstraction facilities exploited in the BLM and System/38 is the ability to support a symbolic definition of the architecture. The advantage of using a language (rather than simply tabulating the machine functions) is that coding details need not be frozen, and the construction of the first layer of software (the microsystem in the case of PN machines) is much simplified. How far one can progress in that way is a matter of style, but from some point one would expect most of the program input to be derived from higher-level SILs and problem-oriented languages. In the present instance the PN machine definition is embodied in a language called "P" which, not surprisingly, makes extensive use of the register transfer operations used throughout this text.

A PN machine is designed to support at hardware level the ideas of:

(1) abstraction, i.e. handling classes of objects whose representation is concealed from the user, and enabling users to invent new classes to suit application requirements;
(2) protection, i.e. providing precise control of the information that can be acted upon by a program at any instant;
(3) interpretation of language-oriented target codes as an alternative to compilation;
(4) active memory functions on bit planes; and
(5) distributed program execution, allowing data and control information to be drawn from any PN machine in a closely coupled assembly.

A PN *system* consists of an assembly of PN machines, according to the general model of Fig. 1.2. It follows that a unique combination of features, which includes capabilities, codewords, tagged registers, array registers and distributed program space, has to find expression in P while keeping as close as possible to established practice in other respects.

In this chapter we shall be concerned with a single PN machine. In passing, mention is made of distinct "hosts" or centers of activity within an assembly. Discussion of multiple computer systems is deferred to the next chapter.

Encoding is centered on a particular implementation of a PN machine using 16-bit words, which is sometimes referred to as "microPN" or "μPN". With minor changes it could apply to a machine with longer words, bigger planes and more extensive address space. However, as the main interest at present is in the logical organization of programs and design of software structures, and many simulators have 16-bit registers, the shorter wordlength is used. In any case, the justification for using longer words is not obvious in a multicomputer environment.

18.1 WORKSPACES

The workspace of a programming system is (roughly speaking) the collection of coded information to which users might refer at any instant, though in practice they can never refer to the whole lot at once. Moreover, it is usually required to view different parts of the workspace at different levels of detail, to concentrate on certain operations without concern for the inner workings of others, and to move easily from one aspect to another.

For that reason three distinct workspaces are recognized in the PN system:

(1) *abstract objects*, i.e. various classes of things whose detailed representation is concealed from the user, who sees only selected attributes;
(2) *global segments*, which are of two types: *control*, which contain encoded programs, and *data*, which are further subdivided into *numeric* (binary strings accessed as byte, word or plane) and *pointer* (referring to the abstract and global spaces);
(3) *local workspace*, which includes numeric bit strings and pointers as in (2), though here the pointers can also refer to the local space; in addition, the local space contains *registers* and other task (process) related data.

As one might expect, there is no guarantee that an abstract object exists in the form imagined: a "file" taken from a database provides a typical example, where the extraction of a field from a record might involve scanning the records of a second file in which the first is embedded. (There are naturally some abstract objects that correspond closely to physical reality in the shape of devices, volumes, processors, etc.)

At global level, data representation is made explicit, so that by appropriate indexing one can read and write bytes, planes and words of data. The whereabouts of a segment is not relevant, though it is required to be wholly within the local store of some computer in the system. In that sense the program space is distributed. When necessary, interprocessor messages are sent by the addressing mechanisms. The pointers serve a purpose very similar to that of directories in a file system, structuring the space and providing access paths to further data to anyone who can "reach" the pointers.

A general property of abstract and global objects is that they can be accessed simultaneously but in a controlled way by concurrent tasks in one or more processors. In contrast, local space is strictly partitioned between tasks and, indeed, between processors: it is not possible to address the local space of one processor from another. Consequently, even though two tasks might co-exist in the same store they would communicate at global or abstract level, and would not be affected if they were to be separated by adopting a different task-allocation strategy.

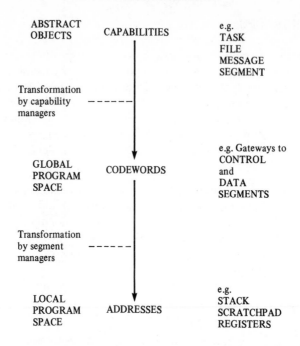

Fig. 18.1   Levels of program space in PN system

To summarize (refer to Fig. 18.1): the abstract space corresponds most closely to user-oriented problem descriptions, in which details are not disclosed but general strategies of solution can be described and the object classes needed to support them can be invented; next comes the global description, in which representation is made explicit but there is still some choice in the siting of data and control; finally, at the local level we are concerned with forming addresses, extracting data into registers, manipulating the registers and writing the results back to (global or local) store. Parallels can be drawn between writing in a conventional high-level language and writing P programs at global level, and between microprogramming and writing P programs at local level. However, we shall see that it is not possible to draw sharp distinctions.

The following paragraphs give further details of each workspace, this time from detailed to abstract.

Local workspaces

A local workspace is uniquely associated with each task. Programmed access to the workspace is gained either via the registers or by naming an element of the **task environment**. We have seen that the local workspace consists of numeric and pointer sequences. A task environment can be regarded as a sparsely populated pointer sequence.

Each element of a pointer sequence is either a (numeric) word or a reference to one of the workspaces, each giving rise to its own form of pointer, i.e.:

Workspace	*Pointer*
Abstract	Capability
Segment	Codeword
Local	Address

In PN machines the type of a variable is assigned dynamically — it can change as the result of an assignment — so it is carried in coded form, associated with the value of the variable to form a 32-bit composite element. Although we have seen the need for only four primary types it is convenient to practice to divide them into sixteen, distinguished by a 4-bit tag value as shown in Table 18.1.

The tagged formats completely describe the values a scalar variable can take. A "pointer" or "mixed" sequence consists of a string of such values placed consecutively in store, while a "pointer segment" comprises elements with tags 0–7 only (i.e. global values). For the most part it is unnecessary to be aware of detailed formats, and certainly any dangerous misuse will be detected by hardware; in general, a user program can easily "untag" a value and examine its component fields, but cannot construct a tagged value without system help.

Each task makes use of two sets of registers: scalar and array.

There are eight general-purpose scalar registers. Each contains a tagged element of the form just described. At any instant the registers determine exactly which parts of the workspace can be referenced directly and, as calculation proceeds, changes in the environment are reflected by changes in the register values. Operators are provided in P for expanding and contracting the program environment in a controlled way, as well as for the usual arithmetic and logical functions.

A further set of eight scalar registers is reserved to each task for language and system use, as follows:

2 for parameter passing;
3 for expression evaluation; and
3 for task status, stack pointers, etc.

The user will be indirectly aware of these registers from various facilities of the input language.

Table 18.1   Tagged elements in micro PN

...GLOBAL values
...ARITHMETIC

	4	4	8	16
... Tag 0: 16-bit numeric	0	*high*		*i*
... Tag 1: Entry pointer	1	*h*	*g*	*i*
... Tag 2: Indexable capability	2	*h*	*c*	*i*
... Tag 3: Indexable codeword	3	*h*	*g*	*i*

... NON-ARITHMETIC

	4	4	8	16
... Tag 4: System capability	4	*h*	*c*	*i*
... Tag 5: Control pointer	5	*h*	*g*	*i*
... Tag 6: Capability	6	*h*	*c*	*i*
... Tag 7: Codeword	7	*h*	*g*	*i*

...LOCAL values, i.e. addresses
... READ−WRITE permission

	4	12	16
... Tag 8: Byte sequence	8	*n*	*f*
... Tag 9: Word sequence	9	*n*	*f*
... Tag 10: Plane sequence	10	*n*	*p*
... Tag 11: Mixed sequence	11	*n*	*f*

... READ−only

	4	12	16
... Tag 12: Byte sequence	12	*n*	*f*
... Tag 13: Word sequence	13	*n*	*f*
... Tag 14: Plane sequence	14	*n*	*p*
... Tag 15: Mixed sequence	15	*n*	*f*

where:

	c	is a capability class identifier
	f	is the first byte location of a sequence in local store
	g	is a gate index
	h	is a host (processor) identifier
	high	is a "soft" flag associated with integers (12 bits)
	i	is a numeric value or index
	n	is the *limit* of the addressed sequence
and	p	is the first plane location of a sequence in local store

A stack is associated with each task. It consists of a number of *stack frames* used for temporary register storage (*save, unsave* statements) in a strictly last-in − first-out order. The current stack frame is sealed and a new one started at each procedure call; on return, the current stack frame is discarded and that defined at the time of call is reinstated.

Finally, there are three array registers, each capable of holding a word plane of 256 bits (in microPN), i.e. 16 words of 16 bits. Array register use is specialized as follows:

A-register: a mask used only to control "array store" instructions;
B-register: is the array accumulator;
C-register: is the "array carry" plane, used only in bit-serial arithmetic.

Operators are provided in P for planar arithmetic and logic, and for data transfer between plane and scalar elements.

The scalar and array registers, task environment and stack constitute the "status vector" private to an individual task. Within any processor the local workspace is precisely the region of store accessible from the task status vectors defined in that processor. The entire local workspace of the PN system is simply the sum of local workspaces in each processor.

Global segments

The global workspace consists of control and data segments.

Control segments are derived directly from control modules (source programs) by the P compiler. Their internal structure is not disclosed. Once formed, a control segment can be used without change in any appropriate environment. It must be accessed according to the rules outlined below for data segments, though for the most part control segments are invariant and can be obeyed simultaneously by several tasks without special provision for synchronization. The properties of control segments reflect those of control modules discussed in Section 18.3.

Global data segments are of two types: *numeric* and *pointer*. Numeric segments start life as plane sequences (and are therefore multiples of 32 bytes in microPN) but can be remapped as words or bytes in the course of use. Pointer segments are defined as sequences of tagged values and cannot be viewed in any other way. In microPN no segment may exceed 4096 bytes: larger structures can be built using arrays of pointers.

When a segment is created a segment *capability* containing a unique index is associated with it and returned to the user. From that instant the segment is in abstract workplace. Access must be requested explicitly, and if successful a segment *codeword* containing host and gate indices is returned. The segment is regarded as materialized into global space. Thereafter, using the codeword as pointer, store operations can be performed in the usual way. When no longer in use, the gate must be released explicitly (referring to the segment codeword). When the segment is no longer needed it can be deleted, this time by applying the *Release* function to the capability.

The distinction between "existence" and "accessibility" is most important. It can best be illustrated by an example using some of the system functions (*x* and *y* are scalar registers).

$x = Num(7)$;	Creates a new segment of 7 planes and returns its capability to x, e.g.

4	8	16	18109

tag 4, host 8, class 16 (data segment) and unique identifier 18109.

$y = Access(x,9)$;	Allows update access to x as a word sequence, returning a codeword to y, e.g.

3	8	74	111

tag 3, host 8, gate 74, index 111 (the index gives the largest valid index for the codeword).

y & 0;	Sets index $= 0$.
$y+9 =$. 25;	Assigns the value 25 to the tenth element of y.
$Release(y)$;	Stops access via gate 74 in host 8.
$Release(x)$	Prevents further codewords being generated, waits for all relevant codewords to be released, then deletes the segment.

Note that several access paths may be open at the same time from one or more tasks, using different gate indices; in general only one update path is allowed at a time. Tasks may be queued by the *Access* function, either waiting for *Release* or waiting for a new gate index. Tasks may be synchronized using *Access* and *Release* or by using explicit control functions such as *Wait* and *Signal*.

Note that the index portion of a codeword must select an element within the segment, the first having index zero. Store operations fail if the index is out of bounds. The index can be modified by arithmetic and logical operations, using an integer (tag 0) second operand as in "$y + 9$" above.

It is sometimes required to "freeze" a codeword to point to a particular element. A P operator (*protect*) is provided which, applied to a codeword, returns the same value with tag 7. That has the effect of disabling arithmetic, the other operations being unchanged.

Abstract objects

A capability identifies an object of a particular class and, in some cases, proscribes the operations that can be applied to it. The integrity of the class depends on the fact that such pointers can only be created under strictly controlled conditions. The capability can be copied and stored, passed as a parameter, etc, without restriction and without effect until a second capability (or pointer) swims into the environment: that of the "class manager segment" that provides the characteristic functions of that class, typically some form of "create", "read/write attribute" and "delete".

Capabilities are widely used in PN system management and are distinguished (tag 4) from "user" classes. The latter are further subdivided into "indexable" and "non-indexable" forms (tags 2, 6 respectively) in the same way as codewords. The interpretation of the index is entirely "soft". The host index normally specifies a processor with ultimate responsibility for the object, e.g. containing its manager and associated tables. Execution of management functions may be entirely "in-task" or by queueing requests on management tasks. The system capabilities are given by Table 18.2.

Table 18.2 PN System capabilities (Tag 4)

	Class	Index
Null	0	(assigned by user)
Control segment	1	segment *id*
Pointer segment	2	segment *id*
Base	3	base *id* and options
Task	4	task *id* and options
File	5	file *id* and options
Host	6	host *id* and options
CFC	7	capability class and options
Function error	8	error code
Numeric segment	$\geqslant 16$	segment *id*

The use of classes 0–5 is conventional. Function error codes are generated by system functions and certain machine functions.

The "CFC" or "capability-forming capability" does just that on behalf of management functions. If a new type of object has to be invented, the system will supply a CFC whose low-order index byte denotes a new capability class. That capability, together with an index field, can then be used to create a user capability. For example,

$x = Mkcfc();$	Returns to x the CFC of a new class, e.g.

4	2	7	39

tag 4, host 2, CFC index 39

$y = Mkcap(x,27)$	Returns to y the capability for "object 27" in the new class:

2	39	27

We shall see later that it is for the user defining the new class to provide entry points to all the management functions and to check that a valid capability is being presented at all times — which can be done simply by breaking up the argument and looking at its parts. It is also vital to ensure the safety of the magic CFC (the one and only means of creating a capability of that class). Application of *Release* to a CFC removes all objects of that class from the system. If the CFC is lost the class can only die out by natural wastage or some more drastic system measures.

Finally, the rôle of bases in defining workspace should be noted. A **base** is a sparsely populated pointer segment that provides the global and abstract environment of one or more tasks. Just as the task vectors determine the content of local space, the bases define the extent of global and abstract space: a segment or object that cannot be reached, directly or indirectly, from some base or task ceases to exist, whatever the intentions of the programmer.

18.2 MICROPN: SCHEMATIC

The main components of microPN are as shown in Fig. 18.2. The register file (*X*) is a fast store containing 16 32-bit general purpose registers, accessible as 16-bit words. Most internal machine operations can be completed in two cycles of the ALU, typically processing the "high" portion of the operands first, which includes checking their tags, followed by their "low" halves. The ALU carries out elementary logic, arithmetic, and shift operations on numeric words, and the special manipulations required in controlled address formation.

The control unit plays a conventional role in sequencing instructions. It contains the control pointer and condition codes. Less frequently used control fields are found in registers $X3-X5$, i.e. stack base, context (current base and task indices), current stack frame and current control segment.

The local memory controller (LMC) serves requests for data and instruction access within the processor and external requests arriving via the global memory controller (GMC). The operations carried out by the memory include normal fetch and store of byte, word, plane and mixed (tagged) data and the functions arising from its role as an active memory array: PN instructions operate either on *X*-registers via the ALU or on bit planes in memory.

In a tagged machine the instruction set is designed to carry out normal arithmetic and logical functions on numeric data and to provide separate operations, notably "modify" and "limit", for manipulating pointers. In devising a function set comparable with vertical microinstructions in com-

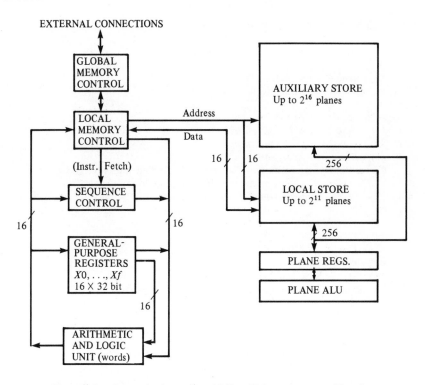

EXTERNAL CONNECTIONS

Fig. 18.2 General schematic of MicroPN processor and local memory

plexity the tag interpretation implicit in the Basic Language Machine is much reduced. The distinction between different types of numeric data has gone, and automatic dereferencing to obtain an operand of the required type no longer applies. The addressing rules have been relaxed to allow easier address calculation in the global space. However, the essential protection mechanisms have been retained.

Hardware registers are addressed directly by PN instructions. Indexing and indirection are not used, because of their complexity, so that access paths have to be built up from explicit modification and loading commands. The distinction between local and global pointers is not concealed because to do so here would raise the question again during program execution, with consequent delay. In a typical application the user's declared data sets would be held in global space while problem state information, temporary results, parameters, context pointers, etc., would be addressed locally.

In microPN the instructions are uniformly 16-bit words with four 4-bit subfields (designated *fvxy*). The primary code *f* gives rise to eight function

Table 18.3 MicroPN Instruction Formats

PN FORMATS

Instruction fields f v x y each of four bits
PC (program counter) points to next instruction

$f=0$ *go unconditional to PC + vxy signed*
$f=1$ *form data pointer in X0 referring to PC+vxy*
$f=2$ *Xv = xy signed; set conditions*
$f=3$ *if v go to cptr+xy signed*
        Condition codes: Bits $v = ccct$ where c selects a status bit and t
                           specifies the value for branching.
$f=4$ $Y = fv(X)$ Register transfer operations
        40   $Y = X$ 44 $Y = -X$
        41   $Y = X$ *word*   45 $Y/t x$
        42   $Y/h X$ 46 $Y = X$ *protect*
        43   $Y = X$ *high*   47 $Y = X$ *byte*
$f=5$ Register X and literal y, setting conditions
        ---------------- Result to Xx ----------------   ---------------- Result to $X0$ ----------------
        50 $X \geqslant y$ 54 $X + y$ 58 $X \geqslant y$ 5c $X + y$
        51 $X \ll y$ 55 $X - y$ 59 $X \ll y$ 5d $X - y$
        52 X *mask* y 56 $X'y$ 5a X *mask* y 5e $X'y$
        53 X *mask* $- y$ 57 $X^{\wedge}y$ 5b X *mask* $- y$ 5f $x^{\wedge}y$
$f=6$ $fv(X,Y)$ or $fv(X,y)$ memory operations
        60 $Y = X.$ 64 *unsave X*   68 $X=PC.;PC'1$ 6c *ARRAY X*
        61 $Y = X.bycol$ 65 *return*   69 $PC + x$ 6d *ARRAY X'*
        62 $X = . Y$ 66 *save X*   6a *sysfn entry* 6e *MOVE:x y*
        63 $X = bycol Y$ 67 *call X*   6b *goto X*   6f —

groups (see Table 18.3) of which four are tag-independent, three restrict the
tag of general-purpose register x and one restricts the tag of both x and y.
The tag limitations are simply expressed in tabular form (see Table 18.4).

Thus a register transfer statement which might be written in P as

$X6 + 3;$

has the encoded form

5	4	6	3

and requires (Table 18.4, Group 5 line 4) the tag of $X6$ to have value 0,1,2 or 3
(Table 18.1). The *tag* is unchanged by the operation; the *high* field of $X6$ is
unchanged, and the result is written to the low half of $X6$. The tag of X is
checked by the same mechanism in function groups 4–7. In the last group,
the tag of Y must be zero. In case of failure, the task is aborted with a
Tagcheck error.

Table 18.3 (cont'd)

$f = 7$ $fv(X, Y)$ Arithmetic and addressing functions setting conditions

---------------- Result to Xx ----------------   ---------------- Result to $X0$ ----------------

70 +	74 %	78 +	7c %
71 −	75 *	79 −	7d *
72 &	76 ′	7a &	7e ′
73 |	77 ˆ	7b |	7f ˆ

$fv = $ 6c,6d: $ARRAY$ and $ARRAY'$ functions on bit plane X selected by y

$y = 0$ add	$y = 4$ mask	$y = 8$ add −	$y = $ c mask −
1 and	5 load	9 and −	d load −
2 or	6 adw	a or −	e adw −
3 equ	7 st	b equ −	f stm

$fv = $ 6e: $MOVE$ control

	N	S	E	W	
PLANE	0	1	2	3	(Values of x,
CYCLIC	4	5	6	7	distance y)

Status bits:	7	6	5	4	3	2	1	0
Value 0:	F	—	—	—	GT	GE	ZE	VA
1:	T	—	—	—	LE	LT	NZ	IA

Tag values   --------------- GLOBAL ---------------   --------------- LOCAL ---------------

	0 integer (a)	4 syscap	8 byte	c byte (r)
(a) arithmetic	1 entry ptr (a)	5 ctrl ptr	9 word	d word (r)
(r) read-only	2 capability (a)	6 capability	a plane	e plane (r)
	3 codeword (a)	7 codeword	b mix	f mix (r)

Tag tests: See Table 18.4 for X tag checks on functions $f = 4. .7$;
when $f = 7$, Y tag must be zero.

The most complex function group is that concerned with storage ($f = 6$). Apart from the normal provisions for store access we should note:

(1) special actions involving stack manipulation, arising from change of protection domain (*save, unsave, return* and subroutine *call*);
(2) control of planar arithmetic and shifts (*ARRAY* and *MOVE* subgroups); and
(3) inter-module references generated by use of codewords, involving Global Memory Control.

It is in these areas that costs not normally associated with microcode are encountered, though only (1) is attributable to abstraction.

In arithmetic, only single-cycle operations on 16-bit integers are defined in microPN (apart from multiply and shift). Unused functions leave room for expansion, though the choice depends on implementation details.

Table 18.4   Tagcheck tables

Tagchecks are performed on the X register in function groups 4−7. The following tables show in hexadecimal form the acceptable tag values for each function variant, i.e. a "1" indicates that the tag value is accepted.

GROUP 4:		X TAG VALUES			FUNCTION
	0123	4567	89ab	cdef	
$v = 0$	f	f	f	f	copy
1	0	0	2	2	word
2	f	0	0	0	set *high* field
3	f	f	f	f	high
4	f	0	0	0	negate
5	f	f	f	f	set *tag* field
6	3	f	f	f	protect
7	0	0	4	4	byte

GROUP 5:

	0123	4567	89ab	cdef	
$v\&7 = 0$	f	0	0	0	rt shift
1	f	0	0	0	lt shift
2	f	0	0	0	mask
3	f	0	0	0	mask −
4	f	0	0	0	add
5	f	0	0	0	subtract
6	0	0	f	f	modify
7	0	0	f	f	limit

GROUP 6:

	0123	4567	89ab	cdef	
$v = 0$	1	1	f	f	fetch
1	1	1	2	2	fetch by column
2	1	1	f	0	store
3	1	1	2	0	store by column
4	f	f	f	f	unsave
5	f	f	f	f	return
6	f	f	f	f	save
7	4	4	0	0	proc. call
8	f	f	f	f	load lit − 16
9	f	0	0	0	switch
a	f	f	f	f	SYS function entry
b	4	4	0	0	goto
c	0	0	2	2	array fns
d	0	0	2	2	array fns, modify
e	f	f	f	f	move B plane
f	—	—	—	—	(unused)

GROUP 7:

$v\&7 =$					
0	f	0	0	0	add
1	f	0	0	0	subtract
2	f	0	0	0	and
3	f	0	0	0	or
4	f	0	0	0	exor
5	f	0	0	0	mult
6	0	0	f	f	modify
7	0	0	f	f	limit

An effect of the protection system is to make it easy to apply "execute-only" options to control segments. Advantage has been taken of that to preserve engineering flexibility and to undertake some security checks during program translation. For example, all register, base, task, label and system function indices are checked by the compiler and written into code sequences knowing that they cannot subsequently be changed. Similarly, privileged function codes can be used without direct control by the programmer so that there is no need for a distinct "system state". There is, of course, a possibility of code being corrupted by store malfunction which, like pointer errors, could lead to wider breakdown. Whether to contain such errors in the code, the pointer, the task, the host, . . . or at some other system boundary depends on the type of availability and reliability that is demanded.

18.3 MICROSYSTEM FUNCTIONS

The PN microsystem supports the following classes of abstract objects: *host, file, segment, base* and *task*. The aim of each abstraction is to disclose as much about each class as the user needs to know in order to operate on it efficiently, concealing attributes that are in any way irrelevant or liable to change. For example, binary instruction formats are concealed in the definition of control modules in order to allow freedom to change the instruction representation. The system abstract objects constitute the resources available for program construction at the lowest design level. To reach the level of facilities normally seen by application or system programmers new classes of objects such as "message" or "queue" would be implemented in terms of those that already exist. From Table 18.1 it can be seen that system resources are distinguished by tag from all others.

Table 18.5 gives a brief list of some PN microsystem functions, including those used in the example that follows. All microsystem functions are accessible without special authorization.

Table 18.5   PN Microsystem functions: summary

Local store allocation

Byte(n)
Word(n) ⎫
Plane(n) ⎬   Return the address of a new sequence of *n*
Mix(n) ⎭   elements of the specified type (accessible only to
current task)

Global store allocation

Num(n) ⎫   Return a capability for a segment of *n* planes or
Ptr(n) ⎭   tagged elements.
Access(c,t)   Request access of type *t* to segment *c*.
P("filename")   Loads a control module from filestore and grants
access immediately, returning the entry pointer.

Base management

Getbase()   Returns new base capability *b*.
Base(b)   Changes base environment to *b*.
Bcopy(x,b)   Moves object *x* from current base to *b*.

Capability management

Mkcfc()   Returns new capability class CFC.
Mkcap(c,n)   Forms capability with index *n* in class *c*.
Null(n)   Returns Null object, index *n*.
Release(x)   Releases object *x*.

Task management

Exit(n)   Terminate task with result *n*.
Fork, Wait,   (Not used here)
Signal.

Access to files

In P programs, file-access functions are used to drive the predefined
file-management function of the host. At present, capability control of file
structure is not exercised. A file capability contains the file *id* used by the
host. Commonly used interpretations are placed on *Create, Open, Close,
Get, Getc, Put, Putc.*

Hosts

For any class of objects there is a choice of performing the management
function locally or by reference to one or more specialized sites. For example,
requests to allocate store segments are often met locally; a less frequently used
resource such as a list of user account numbers may be managed by a single

processor. Although the definition of most programs is independent of which choice is made, it is recognized that explicit control is sometimes necessary. The idea of a host is introduced for that reason. It can be regarded as the abstraction of a processor–memory pair: in most situations it is realized by allocating precisely one host to one p–m pair.

Files

A file provides an abstraction of data stored outside the PN system. There is often a direct mapping from abstract files onto physical devices such as terminals or disks, but the intervention of the file manager allows logical reordering. Only numeric information can be transmitted to and from files, which are outside the protection boundary of the system, i.e. it is impossible to read control segments or pointers directly from file. If a file is structured, then one of the functions of the file manager is to map that structure into PN program space. In the simulated system file access functions are mapped onto those of the host machine.

Control segments

We distinguish between modules and segments, the latter being representations of the former. In the case of data the binary encoding is direct, but for control information there is considerable difference between the *source* control module and the *object* segment that represents it.

A control segment contains encoded instructions and data derived from definitions given in the P programming language. Although many features of the PN machine are abstracted, the segment size, which contributes to working set and channel loading, is not: in microPN implementation the maximum size is 4096 bytes. There is only weak connection between segments and control flow, i.e. change of segment does not imply change of procedure, nor vice versa, the reason being that although one can take advantage of such conventions it is generally undesirable to couple logical control structure to physical store assignment.

The definition of a control module includes a precise specification of the registers it uses, the entry points, and the external connections that may be established with reference to its task environment and base at time of use. The compiler, in conjunction with machine functions, ensures that the bounds so defined are strictly observed. That is the essential requirement of software engineering.

In P programs the connectivity of a module is declared in its heading.

Following the register identifiers are lists (possibly empty) of named resources associated with the current base and task to which reference might be made, as in:

REGS	[*x y z*]	register names
BASE	[*R Q*]	base references
TASK	[ ]	task references
ENTER	[*A B C*]	entry points

which indicates that only three general-purpose registers are used, that connection might be made to the elements named *R* and *Q* in the base, that no connection is made to task-dependent data, and that there are just three points to which control can legitimately be transferred from outside the module. Note (in Table 18.1) that an entry point is represented by a tag 1 pointer which identifies the gate leading to the code.

Once formed, a control segment is ready for execution. There is no requirement to load or consolidate it into a particular program base, task or processor space. The free variables are resolved by dynamic association with the base or task environment, as appropriate. The reason for that design decision is that it gives the greatest flexibility in program construction at a cost which, from experience of similar systems, appears to be small.

The system function *P* ("*filename*") is used to translate a module from file space to program, returning the entry pointer to the module. There is no need to maintain a database relating abstractions to implementations: all type and parameter checking is dynamic.

Secure program structure depends on controlling the connections established between modules. A control segment acts as a building block with a prescribed set of entry points and external connections. A logical property of such a module that is important in establishing protection bounds is that the only resources it can use are those inherited at the point of entry (*A, B* or *C* in the diagram), or those constructed by using external connections (*R* or *Q*), or those that it creates by using one of the resource managers.

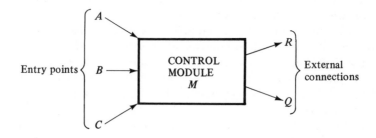

It is theoretically attractive to have precise control over which of the entry points to a module can be used in any context. For example, if M controlled a class of queues and A, B, C allowed users to enqueue, to dequeue and to "delete"a specified queue, it might be desirable to withhold C from all but a limited subset of users. That would mean having distinct capabilities for each entry point and increased overheads in the management of bases. On balance, it is preferable to define only a single entry pointer for the module, corresponding to M, and to enumerate the legitimate indices as $M, M+1$ and $M+2$ corresponding to $A, B,$ and C in the example used above. More precise control can be achieved in a variety of ways: by using separate modules for A and B on one hand and C on the other; by using options in capabilities presented as arguments; or by controlling index formation in a higher-level language.

It can be seen that the only method of constructing access rights during program execution is through the list of free variables (R and Q in the example), and strictly speaking the inclusion of a name in a control module should be subject to formal checks. It would be possible to give a list of authorized names for free variables to each user or group of users, but here again the advantage gained from a strict rule of construction must be balanced against the cost of applying it. The influence of a control module is confined to the bases and tasks in which it is executed. The contents of the bases and tasks depend in turn on how they were formed, and what resources in other bases or in the file system were available to the controlling program.

Data segments

Data segments are divided into numeric and pointer types. As for control segments, there is an overall limit in microPN formats of 4096 bytes, i.e. 2048 words, 128 planes or 1024 tagged elements. Application systems map larger structures onto sets of data segments. It is not possible to access a pointer segment as numeric, or vice versa.

At any instant there may be 0, 1 or more access paths to a given segment, each using a distinct gate index. Their allocation is controlled by system functions in such a way as to facilitate data sharing. Update access is granted to only one task at a time, and having gained access a task is required to release it explicitly on completion of the update operation.

Bases

The role played by bases in program construction has already been mentioned.

They provide the environments in which control modules are executed. Because a control module can be in simultaneous execution with respect to several bases a special form of "sparse" indexing is used, derived from symbolic names for base elements. A base is represented by a pointer segment and therefore consists only of global objects, i.e. integers, codewords, capabilities and control pointers. A "system base" is defined initially. Subsequently new bases can be created, populated and deleted by user programs. The majority of programs execute in a fixed base, though it is possible to move from one to another, e.g. a log-in sequence might start in the system base and move to another once the user has been identified.

Tasks

In many practical situations operations are expressed by the application of procedures that can proceed in parallel. In P code a new task is started by a *Fork* instruction, and subsequent control is exercised explicitly by *Signal* and *Wait* instructions, or implicitly by lockout on segment access. The option of local or remote execution might be decided by the task scheduler on the basis of the location of parameters, e.g. if parameters (necessarily global) belong to host h then a sensible rule might be to execute the task in h.

The state of a task is defined by a task vector of about 15 planes (treated as tagged elements). Some applied systems incorporate their own form of parallelism, so it is particularly important to make the PN task control functions as simple and direct as possible, without implying a "hierarchy" or relating task to program structure in any way.

Capability management

Abstract objects are managed with the help of one or more master object tables (MOTs): the object identifier within a capability is used to select an element in the appropriate MOT which gives either the attributes of the object or an indirect reference to further tables of attributes. The tables used to allot gates to codewords are examples of MOTs of the latter type. Local storage can be seen as an MOT of the former type because the pointer (an address) gives direct access to the attribute (the stored value).

It was noted earlier that an object class can be managed in one host for the entire system, in which case the host in question would contain the entire MOT and management routines; alternatively, control can be distributed to several hosts, each of which has an MOT containing attributes of the objects for which it has responsibility. There is clearly a difference in scale between object classes that can be managed locally, knowing that no pointers to them exist in other hosts, and those that require system-wide store searches. The management of local storage on one hand and global segment tables on the other again provide the best-known examples. However, apart from updating the attributes themselves the objective is the same in each case: to allocate indices (i.e. identifiers) to "new" objects with minimum system overhead. If the object space is ordered, the further complication of having to find sequences of indices arises.

Disregarding the Mad Hatter's approach often adopted in practice, of expecting the system to collapse before the MOT is exhausted, it is necessary to find a method of recycling disused indices, and to apply it often enough to keep the master object tables down to acceptable size. The PN system provides the following support functions for abstraction:

(1) A new class index can be requested, which takes the form of a "capability-forming capability" or CFC.
(2) New objects of a given class can be defined, and they take the form of capabilities with index supplied by the user and class defined by a CFC.
(3) A given capability can be deleted from the system.
(4) A given capability class can be deleted.

The above facilities, together with the interpretation placed on tagged elements in general, are sufficient for the user to define and maintain new object classes in complete security.

Inevitably, the tagged elements must be scanned looking for capabilities as a result of (3) or (4). In a multicomputer system the rate of scanning memory has two important characteristics: (1) it is relatively high, because of the close connection between processors and memories; and (2) it is roughly constant, because additional memory brings with it additional processing power. In the PN design the use of bit-plane operations gives a very high scanning rate in certain recovery operations. Consequently we can consider using capability management strategies with a small population of "free" indices in each class. The strategy used in small systems can be expected to remain effective throughout the performance range. (The contribution of planar functions to index management is discussed in Chapter 13.)

For any machine or system function construed as "failing" there is a choice of aborting the task or returning a recognizably invalid result from system capability class 8. The choice is a practical matter: for example, illegal tags abort the program, whereas address overflow returns an invalid address. If the former option is taken the "result" of a task is itself a class 8 capability. In all cases the encoding of the index field gives the function class and reason for failure. For example, the encoding of the *Mkcap* function, presented with a CFC and index value n, is as follows:

Mkcap(cfc,n):   *if(cfc tag < > 4 or cfc high < > 7)*
                  { "IA" ' 2;   / set IA condition */*
                  return($4003 /h 8 /t 4)}
              else { cfc /h 0;"IA" ' 0;
                  return (n /h cfc /t 2) }

Here, a failure on tagcheck applied to *cfc* results in an invalid condition and a "function error" system capability (code $4003) is returned. Note the use of the privileged operator */t* for setting the tag field. The second argument tag is ignored, only the low-order 16 bits being used to form the capability.

A similar convention can be applied in the user domain, returning a class 0 system capability (*Null()*) to indicate failure. With regard to dynamically programmed type checks, there are three possible courses of action:

(1) to assume all types are correct and expect to fail later (e.g. on tagcheck) if they are not;
(2) to check types and fail gracefully; or
(3) to check types and return a Null result for the caller to deal with.

There are many tactical variations; which to use depends on the level of understanding between caller and callee. It is important not to preempt the decision in system design.

18.4 DATA ABSTRACTION: AN EXAMPLE

One of the requirements of the PN machine is to support the idea of abstraction. We are now in a position to show one way of doing that, which incidentally shows off another feature of the design in the array-handling operations. The chosen example returns to the management of a class of integer sets, as discussed in earlier chapters.

In summary, the functions required are:

make (n)	which creates a set S of at least n integers;
scrap (S)	which deletes a set S;
insert (S,n)	which inserts an element n into a set S;
remove (S,n)	which removes an element n from a set S;
has (S,n)	which indicates whether or not $n \in S$;
similar (S_1, S_2)	which indicates whether S_1 and S_2 contain identical elements, or not.

Because we are dealing with a class of sets, two more functions are required to complete the picture:

initiate (*n*)	which creates a new class of at least *n* sets; and
terminate ( )	which deletes the entire class: not to be confused with scrapping a particular set.

It might be thought that one should be able to define a "class of classes of integer sets", but we draw the line under the eight operations listed above. (The *copy* function is left as an exercise for the reader.)

The objective of data abstraction is to offer precisely the basic operations without revealing how the representation is achieved and, of course, without allowing any possibility of outside interference with the integrity of the data. However, not even a PN machine has infinite resources, so without giving the game away we have asked the user to make some guesses about the capacity of the "space" he wants to use: when initiating a class, to say the maximum number of sets it can contain; when making a set, to state the maximum number of words it can contain. Moreover, we shall arbitrarily assume that no more than 65 535 sets will ever be invented in a particular class instantiation.

Having imposed limitations, we have to say what happens when they are violated. The options are to give up or to return a null value in place of the result expected by the user. Here we shall take the former option, aborting the task with a Null result which will be recognizable from its index as:

$1111	illegal operands;
$2222	attempting to add to a full set;
$3333	more than 65 535 sets created;
$4444	attempting to add to a full class.

A third possibility is to cope by extending the representation, giving meaning to a wider class of operands, etc. In a dynamic system such extensions are not particularly difficult: the main problems are in assessing what sort of deviation to allow.

Mechanization

We shall develop a single control module *INTSET* containing all the management procedures. In programming terms, a set will be denoted by a user capability (tag 6), and its elements by 16-bit words other than $8000 (see below).

There are many ways of representing sets, the best choice depending on size and usage, e.g. the more care taken on insertion the quicker the response to membership enquiries. In this example we shall use very crude algorithms, but exploit the high data-scanning rates of the AMA functions to make for fast operation.

A set representation is rounded up to a whole number of word planes, sufficient for the declared number of elements. The representation uses the largest negative number ($8000) as an "undefined" element: all words are initially set equal to $8000. To insert a new element the first word with value $8000 is overwritten with the new entry, and to remove an element it is over-written with $8000. Searching is carried out a plane at a time, comparing the search argument with 16 values in parallel.

Before designing the module, we have to consider the use of the abstraction: Is it unique to a task? If shared, is it unique to a base? Are the operations on sets amenable to concurrent execution in different tasks? It is possible that different modes of use could be combined without users' knowledge. However, it is assumed here that management functions are executed in-line and without sharing data. The control segment is sharable and might be used simultaneously by several tasks to create different classes of integer sets.

A task-specific representation vector (*SETREP*) is defined, consisting of $n + 4$ mixed elements, where n is the maximum number of sets allowed. The first four elements of *SETREP* define constants and workspace needed by the management functions, viz.:

0:   four workplanes used in the search procedure (*assoc*), viz.:

       0:   argument plane;
       1:   saves the B plane from the AMA;
       2:   a workplane;
       3:   the constant word sequence 0, ... , 15;

1:   the CFC for the class;
2:   the last issued set identifier;
3:   a plane sequence, known as the *id sequence*, containing all currently defined set identifiers.

The reason for the last item is that the object identifiers stored in capabilities, which range from 1 to $ffff$, are mapped internally into indices of *SETREP*. If the object i occurs as the jth element of the *id* sequence its representation is accessed via a plane pointer at position $j + 4$ of the representation vector. The relation of a set capability S to *SETREP* is shown in Fig. 18.3. (In the *id* sequence the "undefined" elements have value zero.)

The *INTSET* control module is given in full in Fig. 18.4. The following notes amplify the annotation on the figure.

①   The convention is adopted of using the first register (*rep*) to refer to the representation vector: its address is found in the task environment. No more than three other registers are required (x, y, z). There is no base reference in *INTSET*, and the only object referred to in the task space is

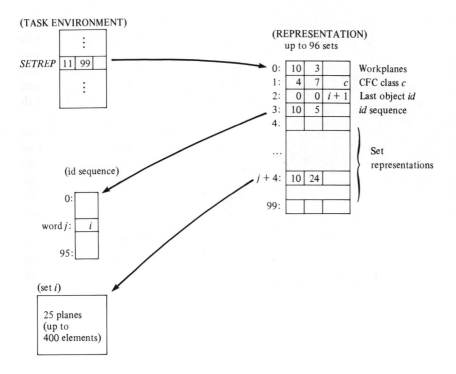

Fig. 18.3 Integer-set representation in PN machine

capability x: | 6 | *c* | *i* |

The figure shows the configuration after executing
... *init* (96); ... *x* = *make* (400); ...

SETREP. The identifier "*SETREP*" maps into a pointer to the task element (see Table A.1).

② The internal procedure *assoc(p,n)* is used to search a plane sequence *p* for an occurrence of a word with value *n*: if found, its index relative to the start of the sequence is returned, with condition *VA*; otherwise the *IA* condition is set. Note that *assoc* ignores the tag of *n* and compares only the least-significant 16 bits.

③ The internal procedure *check(c)* is used to verify that an argument is indeed a capability for the current instance of the class of integer sets.

④ Error terminations all abort the task, which automatically causes *SETREP* to disappear. As an aid to system management the CFC should be released explicitly.

```
        REGS [rep  x  y  z]
        BASE[]  TASK[SETREP]
        ENTER [init make scrap insert remove has similar term]

/* Associate a 16-bit argument (any tag, high ignored)
   with a plane sequence p, returning VA and index of
   matching element if found, else return IA and zero  */

assoc(p,n):    save [x  y  z];
               x = rep.;                  /* workplanes    */
               @ st x'1;                  /* save B reg    */
               x =. n;           /* set up argument plane */
               n = 0;
               do {@ load p;@ equ x;@ st x'2;
                       y= x'2.bycol+0;
                       if NZ goto match;
                       n+1;p'1 } while VA;
               /* Here the plane sequence has been scanned without
                  finding a match */
                   n=0; @ load x'1;x'4      /* unsave B, set IA*/
        exit:  unsave[z  y  x];return(n)
               /* Here find the coordinate of the most significant
                  matching word - remember x'3 points to 0,1,2,..,15 */
        match: x =bycol -y&y;@ load -x;@ or x'3;@ st x;
               n<<4+x. ;@ load x'1; goto exit  /* with VA */

/* Check argument is a valid capability for the class */

check(c):      if(c tag = 6 and c high = rep'1. /h 0)
                     {c = assoc(rep'3.,c); if VA return(c)};
/* Error exits */
illegalarg:    Exit(Null($1111))      toomanysets:  Exit(Null($3333))
setfull:       Exit(Null($2222))      classfull:    Exit(Null($4444))
               ;return

/* Initialize a class of at least n integer sets */

init(n):       save[rep x];n+15 mask -4;     /*    round n up    */
               rep = Mix(n+4); SETREP =. rep; /* representation */
               rep =. Plane(4) ;             /*    workplanes    */
               rep'1 =. Mkcfc();             /*    new    CFC    */
               rep'2 =. 0;                   /* last object id */
               x = Plane(n>>4);rep'3 =. x;   /*   id  sequence   */
               /* Initialize id sequence */
                   do{x =. 0;x'1} while VA;
               /* Initialize index plane used by assoc() */
                   rep.'3 word;              /* points to index plane */
                   x=0; do{rep =. x;x+1;rep'1} while VA;
                   unsave[x rep]; return

/* Terminate class representation */
term():        SETREP =. Null(0);return

/* Create a new integer set */
make(n):       save[rep x y];rep = SETREP.;
               if(n tag <> 0 or n<=0) goto illegalarg;
               n+15>>4 mask 8;                /* round n */
```

Fig. 18.4 Integer set manager

```
                /* Create representation and initialize all "undefined" */
                    x = Plane(n);y=x;do{y =. $8000;y'1} while VA;
                /* Find a new internal set index */
                    y = assoc(rep'3.,0); if IA goto classfull;
                    rep'y'4 =. x;
                    x = rep'2.+1; if ZE goto classfull;
                    rep'2 =. x;
                    rep'3.word'y =. x;
                    n = Mkcap(rep'1.,x) protect;     /* make capability */ (6)
                    unsave[y x rep];
                    return(n)


    /* Delete a set */

    scrap(c):       save[rep];rep = SETREP.;
                    c = check(c);                    /* internal index */
                /* Clear representation and external index */
                    rep'3.word'c =. 0; rep'4'c =. Null(0);
                    unsave[rep];return(0)


    /* Insert a new element */

    insert(c,n):    save[rep x y];rep = SETREP.;                    (7)
                    c = check(c);                    /* internal index */
                    x = rep'c'4.;                    /* representation */
                    assoc(x,n) ; if VA goto insend; /* already there  */
                    y = assoc(x,$8000);              /* find space     */
                    if IA goto setfull;
                    x word'y =. n
            insend: unsave[y x rep]; return(0)


    /* Remove an element */

    remove(c,n):    save[rep x y];rep = SETREP.;
                    c = check(c);                    /* internal index */
                    x = rep'c'4.;                    /* representation */
                    y = assoc(x,n);if IA goto remend;/*   not there   */
                    x word'y =. $8000                /*    remove it   */
            remend: unsave[y x rep]; return(0)


    /* Membership */
    has(c,n):       save[rep];rep = SETREP.;
                    c = check(c);
                    assoc(rep'c'4.,n); unsave[rep];return(0)


    similar(c1,c2): save[rep x];rep = SETREP.;                      (8)
                    c1 = check(c1); c1 = rep'c1'4.;
                    c2 = check(c2); c2 = rep'c2'4.;
                /* Now c1 and c2 point to the set representations;
                   for all x. in c1, find if they are in c2 ... */
                    x = c1 word;do {(x.%$8000);if NZ assoc(c2,x.);
                                    if IA goto simex;x'1} while VA;
                /* ... and conversely */
                    x = c2 word;do {(x.%$8000);if NZ assoc(c1,x.);
                                    if IA goto simex;x'1} while VA;
                    c1'0                 /* sets VA condition */
            simex:  unsave[x rep];return(0)
```

(5) It is possible to re-initialize the class manager several times, each causing previous instances to be terminated. Note that the system manager responsible for capabilities will ensure that all references to a capability class have disappeared before re-issuing the class *id*. Here and elsewhere we have ignored the possibility of the system being unable to deliver a resource (*Mkcfc, Mix, Plane*). Note that the capability-forming capability is retained in *SETREP.* ' 1.

(6) A set capability is returned by *make(n)*: that must be presented to authorize all subsequent operations on the set. To scrap a set, its representation and internal index are deleted.

(7) The argument *n* presented to *insert, remove* and *has* can have any tag: only the least significant 16 bits are used. To restrict the argument to integer values would require:

$$if (n \ tag \ < > \ 0) \ goto \ illegalarg$$

If the "undefined" value $8000 is presented, then no exception is made: *has* (*S*,$8000) returns *VA* if the set is "not full".

(8) For equality, capabilities can be compared without calling *INTSET*:

$$equal \ (S1,S2): \quad if (S1 \ tag \ = \ S2 \ tag$$
$$and \ S1 \ high \ = \ S2 \ high$$
$$and \ S1/h \ 0 \ = \ S2/h \ 0)$$
$$return \ ("I" \ '0) \quad /* \ VA \ */$$
$$else \ return \ ("I" \ '1)/* \ IA \ */$$

For *similar* (*S1,S2*) the *subset* procedure is applied.

Using the set manager

As a demonstration of operations on "sets" we define a procedure *zap* that reads a given file one character at a time and forms a set consisting of the distinct character codes found therein; the lower-case letters will be removed from the set and the remaining characters will then be displayed. (Clearly the same effect could be achieved more economically by a direct indexing method: the technique we have outlined would be used only when the number of distinct arguments was much larger, making a tabular method unsuitable.)

The demonstration module appears in Fig. 18.5. It is assumed that *INTSET* is available as a control module in filestore. The kernel function *P("chap18-4")* returns the entry pointer, which is retained in register *sets*. In order to show some of the inner workings of the set manager we have cheated by allowing the demonstration module to access *SETREP* and display the

```
        REGS [sets file setcap char]
        BASE [output]  TASK[SETREP]
        ENTER [zap]

/* Procedure to open an input file, read all characters
   and note those that occur, to delete lower case letters
   from the list and write the remainder to the output file */

zap(infile,outfile):     file = Open(infile,0);
                         if IA Exit(Null(1));      /* Can't   open  */
                         sets = P("chap18-4");
                         if IA Exit(Null(2));      /* Can't compile */
                         init(16);                 /* Allows 16 sets*/
                         setcap = make(128);       /* Creates a set */
        /* Getc(fc) gets next character from file given by file
           capability fc, returning ZE on END OF FILE */

                         char = Getc(file);
                         while NZ do{insert(setcap,char);char=Getc(file)};
                         Close(file);

                         file = Create(outfile, 0660);
                         if IA Exit(Null(2));     /* Can't create  */
        /* Diagnostic */
                         Put(file,"\nINTSET(a):\tASCII coded characters
                                                  in set:\n\n");
                         print(file,SETREP.'19.word);

        /* Now eliminate lower case */
                         char = "abcdefghijklmnopqrstuvwxyz";
                         do{remove(setcap,char.);char'1}while VA;
        /* Diagnostic */
                         Put(file,"\n...(b) having removed lower case:\n\n");
                         print(file,SETREP.'19.word);

        /* Now write out the remainder */
                         Put(file, "\nThat leaves the characters:\n");
                         char=32; do{has(setcap, char); if VA Putc(file,char);
                                 char+1} while (char<128);
                         Put(file,"\nEnd of demonstration\n");
                         Close(file);scrap(setcap);term();
                         sets=0;file=0;return

/* External connections */
        init: goto(sets)           make: goto(sets+1)
        scrap:goto(sets+2)         insert: goto(sets+3)
        remove:goto(sets+4)        has: goto(sets+5)
        print:goto(output.+6)      term: goto(sets+7)
```

Fig. 18.5 Test module for set manager

INTSET(a):   ASCII coded characters in set:

54	3a	34	2d	38	31	65	72
75	67	69	46	20	2a	2f	a
63	5b	53	47	45	52	9	6e
61	66	6c	64	6f	6d	74	73
30	4f	3d	29	28	77	2c	7a
4e	50	4b	41	42	5d	68	70
7d	7b	5a	79	62	76	6b	36
32	33	22	27	43	78	49	3b
8000	8000	8000	8000	8000	37	35	3c
2b	56	71	6a	39	2e	5c	44
8000	8000	8000	8000	8000	8000	8000	8000
8000	8000	8000	8000	8000	8000	8000	8000
8000	8000	8000	8000	8000	8000	8000	8000
8000	8000	8000	8000	8000	8000	8000	8000
8000	8000	8000	8000	8000	8000	8000	8000
8000	8000	8000	8000	8000	8000	8000	8000

...(b) having removed lower case:

54	3a	34	2d	38	31	8000	8000
8000	8000	8000	46	20	2a	2f	a
8000	5b	53	47	45	52	9	8000
8000	8000	8000	8000	8000	8000	8000	8000
30	4f	3d	29	28	8000	2c	8000
4e	50	4b	41	42	5d	8000	8000
7d	7b	5a	8000	8000	8000	8000	36
32	33	22	27	43	8000	49	3b
8000	8000	8000	8000	8000	37	35	3c
2b	56	8000	8000	39	2e	5c	44
8000	8000	8000	8000	8000	8000	8000	8000
8000	8000	8000	8000	8000	8000	8000	8000
8000	8000	8000	8000	8000	8000	8000	8000
8000	8000	8000	8000	8000	8000	8000	8000
8000	8000	8000	8000	8000	8000	8000	8000

That leaves the characters:
 "'()*+,-./0123456789:;<=ABCDEFGIKNOPRSTVZ[\]{}
End of demonstration

Fig. 18.6 Output from test *zap* (*"chap* 18-5*"*, *"chap* 18-6*"*)

representation (a) after processing the file, and (b) after removing the lower case alphabet. (Note that *assoc(p,n)* returns the largest index of a matching element within a plane, so that the first internal set index is 15, and the representation is at *SETREP.'*19.) The results are shown in Fig. 18.6. In practice, of course, modules other than *INTSET* would not be authorized to access *SETREP*, but even this simple example demonstrates the need to get round the rules in special circumstances.

A change of access list occurs whenever control is transferred to another control module via the external connections. In this example both *output* and *INTSET* are trusted not to tamper with the registers defined at the point of call. In less friendly environments the caller would save and clear the registers before making the control transfer and unsave them afterwards.

19 ABSTRACTION IN SYSTEM DESIGN

When performance and cost are not critical it is possible to treat abstraction as an "optional extra" in system design. That is to say, by using external mechanisms and taking advantage of an already long logical path between micromachine and main memory, or by linguistic means, useful forms of object management can be supported. Both methods are important because, after all, not every application is limited by CPU performance. Arguments based on the overall development time (starting from scratch rather than adding patches) or on circuit trends (trading a factor of two in performance for a time lag of 3–4 years) might also support the "add-on" philosophy. However, if abstraction is required without loss of performance, or if the full benefits of self-application are to be enjoyed, there is no alternative but to adopt the essential mechanisms as cornerstones of design: there is no more important decision at architectural level.

This chapter will illustrate ways in which abstraction mechanisms interact with microsystems and active memory arrays in the context of general-purpose system design. It will be assumed that the reader is conversant with the problems encountered in Chapters 7 and 13. We shall also summarize some of the main conclusions drawn in earlier chapters.

Recalling the multicomputer model (Fig. 1.2), consider in general terms the interactions involved in servicing a user's request to compile and run a program module already in the database of such a system. Four computers are involved in the discussion, their memories are labelled M_a, . . . , M_d in Fig. 19.1. We outline "steps" corresponding to possible user commands.

Step 1 M_a contains a terminal handling task which services the log-in request and generates a user capability which it presents to the authorization manager (Base or User Profile control in BLM or S/38 respectively) in M_b.

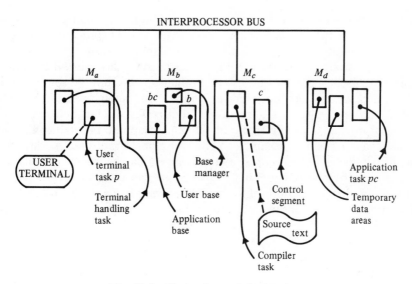

Fig. 19.1   Illustrating user interaction

The corresponding Base capability b is returned. A user terminal task p is started in M_a, based on b.

Step 2 The user accesses the source text file in M_c via b (access to file manager and user directories). A compilation task is started in M_c which results in the control segment C. The codeword for C is added to the base b in M_b.

Step 3 On completing the compilation a new base bc is created in M_b and selected resources, including C, are copied into it from b. Then a task pc is started to execute C in M_d. Note that p can examine the progress of pc from the terminal by sending status requests to the task manager, which are serviced in the host M_d. The user can log out and return later to see what has happened provided the capabilities for bc and pc are retained in b.

Step 4 Results of executing pc can be stored in b by using shared data modules. Resources defined in bc remain until the base is deleted. Temporary data areas created by C are released as soon as pc terminates and the task vector is deleted.

Step 5 The user (or a subsystem acting for the user) deletes bc and logs out.

From the above example we see that when the dynamic behavior of programs is examined in the context of a distributed program store the flow of information must be considered in both the physical and logical senses. As another example, consider the action of updating a filed text, where the terminal receiving the editing commands is attached to one processor and the

auxiliary store containing the text to another. Should the updating information be sent to the file manager, or the file to the terminal processor? Is there
a natural division of the job that allows it to be split between processors, and
can such a strategy extend to multiple texts? How will it work if the same
computer usually contains both the terminal process and the source text?
These and similar questions recur in compilation, database access, and all
other data-processing tasks, and call for the greatest originality in solution.

To provide a specific frame of reference, suppose that the computer
modules are indeed PN machines, and that the global and abstract workspaces
are distributed. In other words, a given segment can be located (wholly) in
the memory of any computer in the system, but can act as source of data or
instructions in the way defined for a single machine in the preceding chapter.
The implied interactions are indicated in Fig. 19.2. Each computer contains
a segment table addressing the segments it contains. The segment capabilities

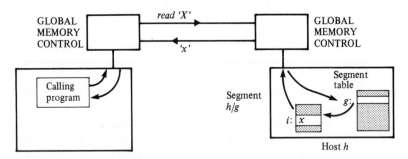

Fig. 19.2   Access to remote global data

and codewords are encoded in such a way that the *host* computer can readily
be identified from the *id* field, for example (see diagram) from a 4-bit host h
and gate g (8 bits). Then a "read" request ($\$60XY$) examines the codeword X
to find the host index h. If this is not in the current processor the entire
codeword is sent to h together with the *read* request. In h, the gate index g is
used by the global memory control to address the segment table and extract
an address which is then modified by i to obtain the datum. The result x is
retrieved and returned to the requesting program. If invalid access is
attempted an indication is given so that the caller can take action.

$$X \quad \boxed{\begin{array}{c|c|c|c} 3 & h & g & i \end{array}} \qquad PN\ codeword$$

It is clear that the information-handling capacity of such an assembly
depends on the bandwidth of the interprocessor bus and the extent to which

retrieval and updating operations can be distributed to points of origin of the data. One cannot be more specific about the bus-sharing algorithm until more is known about program behavior, which depends in turn on software structure.

From past experience, the most flexible program structure provides the best base for optimizing physical data flow. Commitment to rigid store mapping, to the siting of programs, to data and instruction formats, etc., should be minimal, though not to the extent of preventing an applications programmer from exploiting special knowledge of the workload or taking advantage of performance measures. For that reason it seems important to abstract the notion of a "host computer" so that suitably authorized programs can control the allocation of tasks and placement of global data, class managers, etc. An important engineering objective, closely related to abstraction, is to allow graceful transition from one level of working to another without loss of efficiency or security. The distinction between pointers and numbers is the key to managing both the program workspace and its physical representation.

To summarize the overall design objectives of such a computer system: it is intended to reduce software development and maintenance costs and improve reliability by using fine-grain protection mechanisms; to achieve efficient language implementations by compiling and interpretive methods based on a primitive control and arithmetic interface; to improve ease of use by applying abstraction techniques in applications and system support functions; and to minimize design and development costs by replicating a single processor-memory module to achieve the required performance range. Standing slightly to one side are the possibilities of offering planar arithmetic functions for high-speed data manipulation and of adding specialized circuits for floating-point, decimal or emulation functions.

The following subsections attempt to clarify the next level of design decisions.

19.1 PHYSICAL PARTITIONS

In terms of the store hierarchy (Fig. 1.3) our objective is to support the highest performance at the base of the pyramid with minimum investment in main memory, control, scratchpad and registers. In the design of multiprogrammed machines all the above resources are shared and the operating system switches from one activity to another to achieve the required response and resource utilization. In the present context the top three levels (equating control and scratchpad with "local store" in PN systems) are separated into distinct modules. If, in addition, the program space is partitioned by computer module, each program has to be written bearing in mind the physical limitations of individual local memories. The use of other computers to provide "backing storage" in the shape of shared data is simply a restatement in modern terms of the classic overlay problem, which can be solved fairly well in batch processing but not at all well in more dynamic environments.

In many applications it is required that programs quickly adapt to variations in their input or in the computing resources available. For that reason the program space, i.e. the region accessed in response to "read", "write" and "execute" orders, must be dynamically assigned; and to permit memory utilization comparable in efficiency with centralized machines such assignment must be possible across the boundaries of individual computer modules. The possibility of reducing a program's execution time by applying several processors to it in parallel is associated with the same general requirement.

Systems with distributed databases already exist, e.g. as centralized computer systems with intelligent terminals or front-end processors. They can use conventional hardware because the need to understand a reference such as a file name is sufficiently uncommon to be dealt with by interpretive code at machine level. In contrast, distributed program space implies in-line translation of every program address, and therefore hardware assistance at micromachine level. We saw in Chapter 15 how that problem was tackled in CM* (p. 319). We saw also that access times to non-local data were strongly affected by the interpretation carried out in the mapping processors.

The relevance of controlled pointer formation should now be clear. Any system with distributed program space has to answer the same set of questions on every store access:

Q1 Is the pointer valid for the operation requested?
Q2 If valid, is it "local"?
Q3 If local, which physical location is referenced?
Q4 What is the value of the datum?

Q5 If not local, what is the global form of address?
Q6 Where to look for the datum?
Q7 What is its value?

Q8 If not immediately accessible, is it worth waiting or should the program be rescheduled?
Q9 If the address is invalid, how did that happen?

The time taken to answer the questions makes an important contribution to processor speed, or lack of it, and it is probable that delays will result if external mechanisms have to be invoked. As a general rule it should be possible to answer Q1–Q4 without going outside the micromachine. In the

PN machine Q1–Q3 and Q5–Q6 can be answered by inspection of the address or codeword without reference to any tables: in effect the descriptor contents are broadcast into the pointers to give the fastest response.

Another factor contributing to speed is the interval of time between *forming* an address and wanting to *use* the associated datum. One of the advantages of in-program capability mechanisms is that address formation is explicit and can be used to anticipate store access before a read or execute order is issued for the datum. In microPN there are at *most* sixteen elements in store to which reference can be made at any instant. In many situations the answers to all of Q1–Q7 could be produced "in advance" by a sophisticated memory control unit.

The examples of physical store management given in Chapter 13 (p. 270) exploit the properties of pointers in memory control. The essential requirement of micromachines is to present instructions and data at speeds corresponding to microregister transfer times, which (unless CRAY-1 is contemplated) entails organizing two levels of main store. Example 13.1 showed how the entire local workspace could be mapped into fast storage using active memory operations. Example 13.2 suggested an alternative approach, less dependent on AMA support but involving additional circuitry to control loading of register planes. The choice of method therefore depends partly on the availability of planar transfer functions but also on the style of programming adopted. If it is mainly interpretive the local workspace will be compact, intensively used, and easily transported. If a greater proportion of in-line code is generated the workspace will be larger and it may be more practical to map it on demand into a relatively small number of page frames, as in Example 13.2.

19.2 LEVELS OF CONTROL

There is no doubt that the choice of control interfaces determines whether what is theoretically possible is achieved in practically useful form. One cannot expect any control scheme to improve on the performance levels of the circuit components, but the proportion of time that current systems direct their power to visibly useful ends is notoriously low. Amongst the hazards to be negotiated are procedure, process, and protection domain changes, not to mention the possibility of microprogram interpretation. The overall design objective must be to use the appropriate interfaces at any time without constraints on security, resource allocation, programmability or domain switching time.

In practical terms any control scheme is a mixture of "application" code (such as a language subsystem) and resident kernel or "system" code.

Although, as suggested above, each might be executed in the best possible way, there is considerable room for mismatch in moving from one to the other. If the associated cost is high, artificial pressures affect the choice and use of control functions. For example, in the Variable Computer System, which provided for language-oriented microprogram extensions, the round trip from user to system and back took about 50 microinstructions and appreciably lengthened the control path in certain high-level operations. In microPN the same trip takes 10 microinstructions. In general, there are three sources of inefficiency to guard against:

(1) that a change of control state might not be *necessary*;
(2) although necessary it might be too *costly*;
(3) that the implementation of the service function might itself be inefficient.

As an example of (1), recall the examples already encountered in which a change of state is forced simply to enter a new protection domain, e.g. going from target level to micromachine, or forcing a change of process to simulate in-line protection. For (2), think of any all-purpose procedural interface, and for (3) read any fixed, general-purpose high-level machine definition.

The importance of abstraction, as practised on the PN machine, is that it provides security of code at a level corresponding to microprogram. Three ways of realizing the programmers' intentions can be considered:

M1 Translate into a fixed, general-purpose instruction set;
M2 Translate source statements into a language-oriented intermediate code;
M3 Translate into the micromachine instruction set.

The first two methods imply the use of interpreters. Most machines on the market are of type M1, using hardware support at the top end of the performance range. On the basis of space and time M2 is certainly better than M1, but as we saw in Chapter 7 it is open to two objections: it is variable, so less amenable to hardware assistance; and it achieves code compression by formalizing the constructs of the language, with the result that the most general conditions have to be catered for on every function and datum access.

Naturally, when complex formats have to be handled it is best to revert to interpretation, but it is impossible to say in the design stage how best to encode programs for execution. The goal of design is to provide a *choice* in the final product of the actual combination of M1, M2 and M3 to be used. The microPN instruction set offers such a choice. Almost certainly, performance could be enhanced by adding more hardwired functions for arithmetic and emulation purposes; whether that is practical depends on the size of control box that can be manufactured economically.

We have now refined our processor—memory module to one with two levels of storage: the fast buffer or *local* store of (micro)instructions and

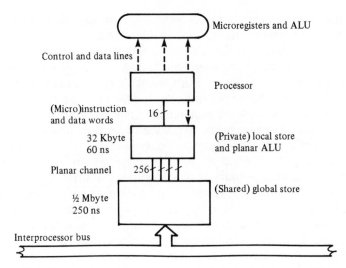

Fig. 19.3 Storage hierarchy in a processor–memory module

data private to the module, and a global store containing sharable information. Some typical sizes and speeds using current technology are shown in Fig. 19.3. The microinstructions correspond to register transfer orders of the processor. Store access operations are assisted by hardware support for global reference. Pointers are distinguished and controlled to achieve protection. The local store replaces control and scratchpad memories as used in existing micromachines. With such an organization it is possible to offer the benefits of interpretation without its systematic disadvantages. What is unclear at present is the performance range achievable by adding modules without saturating the interprocessor bus. The answer depends in part on successfully distributing system- and user-supplied services, and one of the objectives of the microsystem must be to remain flexible in that area.

19.3 SUMMING UP

The state of the art in three areas of computer design has been surveyed in the preceding chapters. Factual information is not much use unless it is related to design goals, and in trying to define objectives there has inevitably been speculation on the likely direction of development. One result of the method of presentation has been to illustrate a new approach to general-purpose computer design, affecting both hardware and software structure. It is unlikely that machines will take exactly the form suggested, but it might be hoped that when divergences do appear it will be possible to give a reason that is meaningful in the terms we have introduced.

Although stress has been placed on "raw" performance it must be in convertible form: we might want to exchange it for enhanced reliability, compatibility or other strategic attributes at short notice and long after the design is frozen. Hence the emphasis on flexibility in control and in storage. The key has been to seek the required effects in an economical and easily understood way. Dependence on hardware or software overkill would have the opposite effect. It might seem paradoxical that at a time of great abundance in circuitry there is such emphasis on economy. It must be remembered, however, that a large proportion of system costs is attributable to training enough people to maintain, enhance, and use the resources available.

The background provided by cost reduction in semiconductor devices needs no elaboration. Computer engineers have always been concerned with reducing the numbers of distinct components and making use of replicated parts whenever possible. The arrival of LSI and its continuing development have not been presented as major events in computer architecture. The conclusion drawn in Part 1 was that although we might see more complex arithmetic devices as semiconductor components there is much less likelihood of standardizing on "control" or "access" mechanisms. Rather than trying to *raise* the architectural level it seemed preferable to dismantle many of the constructs (such as elaborate stack mechanisms, built-in descriptors, high-level procedure interface) that afflict current architectures.

One of the consequences of increased automation in manufacture is that we are forced away from the starting point of a "multi-model range" towards "multicomputer systems" in order to exploit the low cost of replication. Consequently many of the assumptions inherent in computer design need to be re-examined. For example, architectures have tended to become "high level" partly because of the long paths between processors and memory banks in centralized systems. When that path is shortened, what happens to the architecture and the benefits it was intended to confer? An answer is attempted in Part 1.

An important feature of modern circuits is the difficulty of making changes once committed to manufacture. Hence the importance of "getting it right" or at least leaving enough control to "put it right" in the field and at low cost. Here again, the merits of simple hardware with alterable control memory are evident. For the purpose of emulating a well-documented architecture, however, greater use of ROM and hardwired control is predictable.

In terms of "what the user sees" it is clear that one writing in a standard programming language to operate on standard files will see very little direct benefit from some of the advanced facilities we have discussed.

Most of our attention has been to the "user" who is a specialist, e.g. in a language-support system, with access to micromachine and microsystem functions. Where a need is perceived for program modularity, controlled resource sharing, parallelism, protection or error management there are direct advantages in the mechanisms discussed in Part 3. Whether the benefit is taken in lower design and development costs or in providing more function is a matter of choice. The idea that such specialist users are not confined to manufacturers' laboratories will not be universally acceptable. Many suppliers would prefer to increase rather than decrease their responsibility for "system function", as shown in the discussion of IBM System/38.

In the context of system software there are two main sources of improvement, and they reinforce one another: there is often less to do (because of improvements in system-management algorithms, choice of DEL output from compilers, for example), and there are better tools with which to do it. The techniques discussed in Parts 1 and 3 expect the System Implementation Languages to exploit DEL techniques and to benefit from abstraction mechanisms. The choice of structures has far-reaching effects on operating characteristics, but they are very difficult to quantify (perhaps that is why their importance has taken so long to be recognized).

The array architectures discussed in Part 2 have well-publicized applications in such areas as signal processing, large-scale numerical calculation and image enhancement. Just as for scalar computation, it is helpful to separate the "arithmetic" from "data access" or "routing" components. Hitherto, array processors have suffered from having too little data storage and relatively expensive arithmetic units, a situation not unknown 30 years ago on scalar processors but one that is likely to become less critical. The attraction of Active Memory Arrays is in their flexibility in data handling and control. The array functions can be seen as an extension of microprogram, in the same need of protection and support if they are to be used widely.

A related way of looking at planar operations is to note that program stores using 64- or 256-Kbit chips will be large by present standards — perhaps several megabytes on even the smallest machines. As a result, more of the data now held in files will migrate to program space. Operations such as text editing, index searching and sorting will be correspondingly fast provided the processor can keep the memory tidy, which calls for the high data-handling rates of AMA. In Part 2 it is suggested that a substantial part of the cost of an AMA could be recovered from its contribution to store hierarchy and capability management. Although the arithmetic powers of machines such as the DAP are not to be ignored, the view taken here is that within a few years they will be augmented when necessary by arrays of word-organized ALUs, and that the main contribution of bit-organized Active Memory Arrays will lie in their object management and routing function.

19.4 QUESTIONS AND FURTHER READING ON PART 3

1 Suppose you are writing a general-purpose simulation program and would like to make use of a class of push-down stores, accessed strictly on a last-in–first-out basis. Define a set of functions that could be used to create and manipulate such a collection in the manner of a data abstraction. How does what you define differ from a set of procedures that might be written in, say, Algol or Fortran?

2 Compare the implementations of abstraction by linguistic and mechanical means, showing how the push-down stores in Question 1 would be represented in ADA and the Plessey PP250.

3 Take any minicomputer that you are familiar with and outline the operating environments of (a) a user program, and (b) the supervisor program. Describe in detail how they differ and how the locus of control changes from (a) to (b) and back. How are program data shared between the two environments? Are addresses passed to the supervisor as parameters? How does the supervisor check that such addresses are valid references to the user's data?

4 Suppose an addressing system is designed with a number of protection domains $D^{(1)}, \ldots D^{(n)}$, each with its rule $V^{(1)}, \ldots, V^{(n)}$ for validating addresses. In other words if a program address A refers to an area of $D^{(i)}$ then $V^{(i)}(A)$ returns a VA condition, otherwise IA. Now suppose that a procedure $P^{(i)}$ in $D^{(i)}$ wants to communicate A as a parameter to a procedure $P^{(j)}$ in $D^{(j)}$, for which $V^{(j)}(A)$ would return IA. How can $P^{(j)}$ be applied to A without setting the IA condition? Can $V^{(i)}$ be used to supplement $V^{(j)}$? How about validating A on entry to $P^{(j)}$? But suppose $P^{(i)}$ had acquired A from some $P^{(k)}$ (perhaps even $P^{(j)}$) and that $V^{(i)}(A)$ also returns IA? What if A refers to a data structure containing further addresses: how can they be validated? If they are, what if asynchronous procedures run in $D^{(i)}$ and $D^{(j)}$, such that the addresses are changed *after* validation? If $P^{(j)}$ calls $P^{(i)}$ does the validation procedure work in the reverse direction? These questions illustrate some of the very real problems arising from inherited access rights in virtual machines. More than one system has been subverted because they were not dealt with satisfactorily. Make sure you understand the problems that arise, and how they are avoided in machines with controlled pointer formation. If possible, provide examples from machines with which you are familiar.

5 You are probably acquainted with file systems in which the access matrix is represented by a list of "authorized users" for each file. How are such lists created? Where are they kept? What authority is required to access the lists? Suppose you open a file and then someone with the right to change the access list rescinds your right of access: what happens to your program?

6 The situation described in Question 5 is often referred to as *revocation*: the ability of a resource manager to modify the access matrix in such a way as to deny rights previously enjoyed. Show how access to a system object could be revoked in IBM System/38.

7 In the example at the end of Chapter 18, show how to introduce a function *copy(S)* to *INTSET*, which returns the capability of a copy of the given set *S*.

8 It is sometimes required to prevent a certain capability, or class of capabilities, from being transmitted outside the operating environment of a particular procedure, task, or processor. Discuss steps that would be taken in machine design to be able to give such an assurance.

9 Jones and Wulf (JON74) introduce the idea of an *unclassified courier*, i.e. an operating environment through which pointers are transmitted but which is denied all rights of access to the information to which they refer. Consider, for example, a software monitor that wants to find out how often a particular procedure is being called, or a message handler providing a pipeline between asynchronous tasks. How would such a policy be enforced on the BLM and PN machine?

10 In machines such as CAP and CM* the object referred to by an address depends on the contents of windows or capability registers at time of use. Such machines can be contrasted with those using *global* addressing, in which a pointer, once formed, is invariant with respect to the operating environment. The BLM, System/38 and PN machine are all of the latter type. Examine how the adoption of one or other principle of design affects procedure and process interfaces.

11 Describe how the attachment of tags to data elements affects the specification of arithmetic, addressing and control functions of a computer. What restrictions must be placed on tag usage to give precise control over access to data in program space?

12 What advantages or disadvantages follow from applying abstraction mechanisms to file system design? Examine the effects of treating (a) file identifiers, or (b) record pointers as abstract objects.

13 One of the basic design questions concerns longevity: What happens to capabilities when power is switched off? In IBM System/38 permanent system objects are secured on disk for the lifetime of the installation. In the BLM data on file was regarded as outside the protection boundary of the system, and authorization procedures were re-applied on System Restart, so the lifetime of a capability was usually less than 24 hours. Examine how the design of capabilities and class managers is affected by the approach adopted.

14 How would the designs arising in Question 13 be affected by application on a multicomputer system in which individual modules (hosts) could start and stop asynchronously?

15 Geneticists would probably agree with the ADA designers that our constructed rights are really inherited (from the parent, who provides authority to have red hair, etc.), and that our inherited rights are environmental. The imagery intended was of the long-lost uncle, from whom you inherit bits of the family estate, with or without shooting rights. Pursuing that theme, suppose it is system policy to detect and tax all such gifts: what controls would you seek to impose on communication between the parties involved?

16 In Chapter 17 it was seen that IBM System/38 supports a system object known as an Index, which provides a mapping from names onto binary integers. Such facilities are often incorporated into compilers and other software packages as utility procedures. What is the purpose of making a system object do the job? Devise a similar abstraction for the PN machine, using planar operations if possible to speed up the name association. (Restrict names to 32 bytes or less, and use one plane for each name.)

17 You are required to use AMA4 to simulate operations on 256*256 black-and-white TV images. Specify a screen manager that would allow users to create frames, define subframes (windows) and position them. Use abstraction techniques to ensure that the internal representation of the image is not visible to users.

  Examine alternative representations in terms of convenience of programming, performance, and output to the display screen. What functional enhancements would contribute most to overall performance? What would be the effect of moving to AMA6?

18 In a particular language environment it is required to offer a 1 Mbyte address space for numeric and "reference" values. Source programs will be translated into a DEL representation to be interpreted by PN programs. Show how PN pointer and numeric sequences could be used to provide a "paged" address space within a single task. Discuss alternative ways of representing (a) the reference variables, and (b) the qualifiers of the language.

19 In the PN system control segments constitute a permanent class of objects supported by the kernel. The creation and deletion functions are respectively $P()$ and *Release()*. It was pointed out in Chapter 18 that authority to include certain functions and external names is checked at time of creation. The inference is that some authorizations (such as the "list of privileged users") change much less frequently than others (such as the BASE and TASK environments). Examine carefully the implications of such a mode of design. What attributes and additional management functions would be defined for control segments? Consider the proposition that there should be a class of objects known as *name lists*, and that a name list should be given explicitly to P, as in $P(filename, namelist)$, to ensure that the resulting control segment can only attempt connection to BASE and TASK elements that are named in the name list. What management functions would be appropriate to name lists?

20 Part 3 has mainly been concerned with proposals to reduce life-cycle costs of software projects. A breakdown of costs (staff and machine services) might be as follows:

(Functional specification	20%	pre-design)

Coding	15%	
Test and validation	20%	
Modification and enhancement	35%	
Maintenance	20%	
Management	10%	

Describe three attributes of language or machine that would contribute most to reducing costs, and summarize your reasons for saying so.

APPENDICES

1   PROGRAMMING IN P

2   SOLUTIONS TO SELECTED EXERCISES

3   REFERENCES

(From N. Thelwell, *Thelwell Country,* Eyre Methuen (1959))

APPENDIX 1: PROGRAMMING IN P

The notation used in this book is designed to show concisely and exactly what machine operations are used to produce certain effects. When consideration is given to support for "high level" constructs such as program segments, processes, system functions or protection domains we need to be able to express operations on such objects. The result is a language called "P", which should be thought of as a machine-defining notation rather than a general-purpose programming language. The following subsections outline the main features of P, and should be read to supplement the notations introduced in Chapters 1, 9 and 18.

P programs are obeyed with reference to operating environments which are made up from two independent components:

the *base*, which defines resources shared by several concurrent activities; and

the *task*, which defines resources strictly private to a particular control stream.

Amongst the resources are *control segments* which represent *modules* of P source text. Control segments are created by a privileged kernel function which translates modules from the file store into control segments. In common with other resources, control segments can be created and attached to the operating environment at any time, and detached or moved as required to set up new environments.

The following description summarizes the internal structure of control modules. Reference should be made to Table 18.1 (p. 384) for details of elementary data formats.

OUTLINE OF A MODULE

A source text consists of a *heading* followed by one or more *definitions*.

The heading describes the way the module "plugs in" to its context and enables protection bounds to be established. It consists of three parts: register, context and entry-point declarations. For example,

REGS   [*x*   *y*   *z*]
BASE   [*P6*]   *TASK*   [*S*1]
ENTER   [*loca*   *locb*   *locc*   *locd*]

Here the first three general-purpose (scalar) registers are identified as "*x*", "*y*", and "*z*", and it is implied that no other will be touched. The connections "*P6*" and "*S*1" will be established in the context defined at time of use, and again it can be inferred that no other connection will be made directly. Finally, the module can be entered only through one of the four labels "*loca*", . . . , "*locd*", using index values 0, . . . , 3 respectively.

Following the heading, a set of definitions associates constant values (control or data sequence) with identifiers whose scope is limited by the text of the module. The source module is not block-structured: the declarations in the header and in the definitions are effective throughout the text, the only "renaming" facility being in the use of parameters, which is explained below. Apart from the declared identifiers the only built-in definitions are those of kernel functions, which are used by default if a local declaration does not override.

A control sequence is defined by a statement sequence, i.e. a set of statements separated by semicolons (if there are two or more). For example,

loca: $x = locb()$; $z = y$.;
        $if(z \ tag = 4)$ { *Put* (1, " *Table full*\n"); y'1 }

defines *loca* as a sequence of three statements, one of which is compound. Control passes from one statement to the next except as directed by control statements. After executing the last statement control passes to the next sequence in the text, ignoring data definitions, unless explicitly directed elsewhere. Internally, *loca* is represented by a control pointer.

Data definitions introduce constant byte or word sequences (not plane). For example,

datmon: " *J,F,M,A,M,J,J*"

defines *datmon* as a 13-byte string (tag 12, limit 12) using ASCII internal codes. Any graphic character is accepted in the quoted string, together with the following escapes:

\\"	for	"	code	34
\\\\	for	\\	code	92
\n	for	newline	code	10
\t	for	tab	code	9
\b	for	backspace	code	8

Constant sequences can also be defined as in

> *days*:   (31, 59, 90, 120, 151, − 181)

which defines *days* as a word sequence (tag 13, limit 5) with the given values (the element size used is the least required to represent the numbers). An integer value of up to 16 bits can be specified in any of four ways:

decimal:	as above
hexadecimal:	as *$10ff, $e, $6ab2*
octal:	as 0777, 0145, 07071 (i.e. with leading zero)
graphic:	as _*A*, _%, _*$*

In each case the value is right-justified in its field. A preceding minus negates the value arithmetically. Twos complement binary representation is used.

Constant byte or word sequences can also be used in expressions, as in . . .; *Put (f, " Job done\n"); . . .* which would output to file *f* the 9-byte constant in quotes.

The format of P programs is quite free. As a matter of style it is suggested that labels should be aligned to the left-hand margin, using spaces, tabs and new lines to enhance readability. A statement must not be split in the middle of an identifier, integer or operator symbol. Comments are bracketed as in PL/1 and C. Identifiers have up to 32 alphanumeric characters, the first being alphabetic. Upper and lower case are distinguished. It is advisable to avoid possible confusion by not using the P terminal strings in the role of identifiers. Kernel function names follow the convention of an upper-case letter followed by a lower-case string.

Before going into greater detail let us look at an example of a complete module designed to read a character file whose name is supplied as a parameter (*fn*), sort it, and display the result in decimal or hexadecimal form. The following notes refer to the listing in Fig. A.1.

(1) The heading identifies working registers *x, y, z,* an external base connection to *output*, and two entry points *disp* (for decimal display) and *dispx* (for hexadecimal). There is no task-dependent connection to be made.

(2) The *sort* subroutine is presented with the address of the sequence to be sorted (*r*). It is immaterial to *sort* or *swap* whether the elements are bytes or words.

```
                REGS [x   y   z]
                BASE [output]
                TASK[]
                ENTER [disp  dispx]                                    ①


/* Bubble sort subroutine */

/* Sort the sequence r into ascending order
   and return r */

sort(r):        do{ y=0; z=r;                                          ②
                        do{if(z. > z'1.){swap(z,z'1);y¦1};
                        z'1} while(z high > 0)
                } while (y <> 0);
                return(r)

/* Swap bytes addressed by p and q */

swap(p,q):      x = p.; p =. q.;q =. x; return

/* Get file into local store and return its address */

getfile(fn):    if(fn tag & 14 <> 8){Put(2,"No file name given\n");
                                Exit(Null($2222))};
                x = Open(fn,0);
                if IA {Put(2,"File not available\n");                  ③
                                Exit(Null($3333))};
                y = Byte(Size(fn));                                    ④
                Get(x,y);
                Close(x);
                return(y)

/* Sort and display in decimal */

disp(fn):       save[x   y   z];
                table(2,sort(getfile(fn)));
                unsave[z   y   x];
                return($1111)

/* Sort and display in hexadecimal */
dispx(fn):      save[x   y   z];
                hextable(2,sort(getfile(fn)));
                unsave[z   y   x];
                return($1111)

/* EXTERNAL CONNECTIONS */
table:          goto(output.+5)                                       ⑤
hextable:       goto(output.+6)
```

Fig. A.1 Control module to sort and print a byte file

③ *Open, Get, Close, Put* and *Size* are kernel functions providing access to files. The result returned by *Open* is a file capability (see p. 395). The parameter *fn* is checked because it comes "from outside", and if it is not a byte sequence (tag 8 or 12) the task is aborted (*Exit*). Note that internal calls to *sort* and *swap* are not checked explicitly because their types are assured by construction of the module.

④ *Byte* is a kernel function for allocating local workspace, returning the address of a sequence of bytes.

⑤ *output* is a library module which includes procedures for tabulating numerical data (entry points 5, 6). The file identifier "2" used in *Put* (2, . . .) and *table* (2, . . .) refers to the terminal output device.

To use the module it must be translated into a control segment. Its codeword can be stored in any mixed segment for later use. If, for example, it is stored at *sortfile* in a particular base, then calls of the form *sortfile.("testdata")* will display *testdata* results in decimal, and *(sortfile. + 1)("testdata")* will display hexadecimal.

EXPRESSIONS

Expressions are always evaluated from left to right, the first or left-hand term being combined with the next as determined by an infix binary operator. A leading minus sign negates the first term arithmetically. The first term must have tag 0, 1, 2, or 3, but succeeding terms must have tag 0, e.g. it is not possible to combine two codewords arithmetically. Here, as elsewhere, tag conditions are checked at runtime and if not satisfied the program is aborted with a "tagcheck" error.

The value of an expression has the same high-order fields as the first term, only the low-order 16 bits being affected by arithmetic and logical operations (except for $/h$ and $/t$, see below).

The binary operators used in P are + (add), − (subtract), ∗ (integer multiply), % (not-equivalent), & (and), | (or), ≪ (left-shift), ≫ (arithmetic right shift) and *mask*. For shift and mask operations the second term must be literal value less than 16; all other operators allow any expression evaluating to an integer. The effect of *mask* is to clear all but the specified number of low-order bits: for example,

x ≫ 8 *mask* 4

results in the second hexadecimal digit of x, counting from the high-order end. The effective mask is complemented by "*mask* −".

A side-effect of expression evaluation is to set condition codes according to the sign and value of the result. The mnemonics used in conditional statements are:

> ZE NZ LT GT LE GE   for arithmetic tests
> VA IA   for address validation

(No overflow or carry indication is given at present.) Evaluation of a single term does not affect condition codes unless it is a literal or a procedure call, e.g. evaluation of *"x"* does not change condition codes, while *"x + 0"* or *" – 2"* or *"f(x)"* might do so. In negating the first term of an expression condition codes are unchanged.

Each term in an expression is a *datum*, possibly followed by one or more *selectors*. The datum is evaluated according to the rules given in Table A.1.

Table A.1   Interpretation of datum values in P

Datum		Value
integer		binary equivalent of *integer,* tag 0, high 0
(expression)		value of *expression*
"quotes"		address (tag 12) of quoted string
(conset)		address (tag 12 or 13) of integer sequence defined by *conset*
identifier	∈ *REGS*	content of named register
	∈ *BASE*	codeword (tag 7) pointing to base element of given name
	∈ *LABEL*	control pointer to code (tag 5) or address of constant byte or word sequence
	∈ *SYSF*	entry pointer to microsystem function
	∈ *TASK*	address (tag 11, limit 0) of element in current task vector

The binary selectors are ′ (modify) and ˆ (limit). Each requires the first operand to evaluate to an address, the second to give an integer (specified by either a literal, a register or an expression in parentheses). The result is a new address spanning a subset of the original: for example,

> *"0123456"* ˆ 3   gives the address of *"0123"*
> (5,10,15,20) ′2 ˆ 0   gives the address of (15)

In other words, modification advances an address over a specified number of elements and limitation resets the *limit* to a lower (non-negative) value. Only the address is affected: the values remain in store and might be accessed by another path. If the second operand exceeds the limit of the address a system capability (tag 4, class 8) is formed as a result and the Invalid Address condition (*IA*) is set; otherwise, Valid Address (*VA*). It is often useful to terminate a scan of local memory on that test: for example,

$$x = Byte\ (26);\ z = \_A;\ y = x;$$
$$do\ \{y =.\ z;\ z +1;\ y'1\}\ while\ VA$$

Here *Byte*(*n*) is a system function returning the address of *n* new bytes of local store. The effect of the above statements is to leave *x* pointing to the upper-case alphabet, *y* invalid and *z* = *$5b*.

Table A.2   Interpretation of (postfix) selector operators in P

First operand				Operator	Result			
(*any value*)	t	n	f	*high*	0	0	n	
(*any value*)	t	n	f	*tag*	0	0	t	
$t \in address \mid codeword$					Value of first element in string			
$t \in plane\ address \mid codeword$				*.bycol*	Value of first plane read "by column"			
$t \in address \mid codeword \mid capability$				*protect*	Protected pointer			
$t \in word\ address$				*byte*	Equivalent byte address			
$t \in plane\ address$				*word*	Equivalent word address			
$t \in control\ ptr. \mid entry\ ptr.$				(*params*)	Value returned by procedure call			

Unary selector operators are defined as in Table A.2. The effect of *high* is to allow the program to inspect the high-order field of any value, setting the tag to zero; the tag itself is isolated as an integer by *tag*. The "dot" operator performs a store access which may be local or global (see p. 381): it results in the first element of the string pointed to by the first operand. If plane, the result is the logical "and" of the 16 words in the first plane in the string. If the stored element is numeric, tag 0, high 0 is attached to the result; if mixed, it brings its own tag from store. On byte elements the sign is extended to give a 16-bit numeric value. The alternative store fetch operator is ".*bycol*" which applies only to planes: the *i*th bit of the result is the logical "and" of the bits in the *i*th word of the first plane, the sign being "bit 0", e.g. if *p* is a plane address, then "*p.* +0" is *LT* iff all 16 words in the plane are negative, while "*p.bycol* +0" is *LT* iff the first word = -1 (see Chapter 9).

For example (check that you agree with the following valuations):

Assume   s1: "12345"   s2: ($aaaa, $bbbb, $cccc)

TERM	VALUE
s1 *high*	4
s2 *tag*	13
s2'2. *mask* 8	$00cc
s2'(s1'1. − __0).	$cccc
s2'2. *mask* −7	$cc80

The meaning of *protect* is slightly different for addresses and codewords or capabilities. It turns an address into the "read-only" form. It freezes a codeword or capability into "non-arithmetic" form (access rights are determined when the pointer is created). The effect of *byte* is to turn a word address into a byte address for the same numeric string, while *word* turns a plane address into a word address (here again, the unit of access to a global segment is determined when access is granted). To turn a plane address into a byte address you have to go through the word form, e.g. if *p* is a plane address, the second byte in the plane is extracted by *p word byte'* 1.

For example (check that you agree):

Assume s1 and s2 as above and $x = 3$

EXPRESSION	VALUE	CONDITIONS		
s2 *byte* 'x.	$ffbb	*unchanged*		
s1'x. − "0".	4	GT	GE	NZ
s2. & s2'2. ≪4 *mask* 8	$0080	GT	GE	NZ
−s2. % s2'1.	$eeed	LT	LE	NZ

Use of /h and /t. The binary operator */h* is used to set the *high* field of the left-hand side to the low-order 12 bits of the right-hand operand and sets the tag to zero (integer). The tag field can only be set by the operator */t*, which requires system privileges. It sets the tag to a given numeric literal value.

Procedure call

The final selector listed is a set of parameters. The parameters are evaluated and a procedure call to the first operand is obeyed. The value returned by the procedure yields the value of the term.

ASSIGNMENT

We have already encountered the two main forms of assignment: to overwrite a register use " = ", but to overwrite any other position in store we use " = .". In the latter case the left-hand side can be any expression that on evaluation results in a codeword or an unprotected (read−write) address.

Thus "$x = 6$" puts the integer 6 into register x, while "$x = . 6$" requires x to point to a sequence of data values, the first of which is overwritten by 6.

Many register assignments take the form of an updating operation, such as "$x = x + 1$" or "$x = x \ll 1$", i.e. the destination is the same as the first datum on the right-hand side. In such cases the assignment may be abbreviated to "$x + 1$", "$x \ll 1$" etc., the destination being implicit. To avoid that interpretation, put the expression in parentheses: "$(x - 1)$" subtracts 1 from x, sets condition codes, but does *not* store the result.

A store assignment (= .) is valid for any right-hand side. The destination is interpreted as follows:

TYPE OF SEQUENCE ADDRESSED	EFFECT
Byte	Store low-order byte of r.h.s.
Word	Store low-order word of r.h.s.
Plane	Store low-order word of r.h.s. to each word in the plane
Mix	Store tagged (32 bit) value

In general, the value stored by " = ." is recovered by the "dot" selector, except for significant bits lost by truncation. No warning is given of loss of significance.

If the left-hand side is a codeword, the destination is found from the host/gate indices (set by the *Access* function), and the index field is used as a modifier to select a particular element. Provided the index is within range the above interpretation is then applied.

For example, (check that you agree with these store operations; remember that all accesses in P are explicit, no special meaning is given to "left-hand" or "right-hand" occurrences, and dereferencing is not automatic):

Assume s: $(1, -1, \$2222)$
           $b = $ Byte (3)
           $w = $ Word (3)

Then after executing:	the value of y is:
$b = . s' 1.; y = b.;$	-1
$b = . s' 2.; y = b.;$	$\$0022$
$w = . s' 2.; y = w.;$	$\$2222$
$w = . s; y = w.;$	(First byte location of s)
$w\,byte = . s\,tag; w\,byte' 1 = . s\,high; y = w.;$	$\$0d02$

(In these examples the high-order fields of y are set $= 0$)

The remaining assignment operator is " = *bycol*" which applies only to a plane and broadcasts the *i*th bit of the right-hand side to each bit in the *i*th word in the plane, the sign being written to the first word. For illustration of the use of plane assignment, refer to Chapter 9. (The operator " ← ", which is used in describing vector operations in Part 2, does not feature in P.)

CONTROL STATEMENTS

The normal flow of calculation is from one statement to the next in sequence. Explicit changes of direction are indicated by control statements.

The simplest and in many instances the clearest way of directing control is to use *goto*. The only valid destinations are entry points (tag 1) and control pointers (tag 5), and any expression yielding such a result according to the general rules of evaluation is acceptable. However, for syntactic convenience we distinguish between "single identifier", "switch", and "general" forms of destination.

A single identifier used as a destination must be a label or register declared in the current control module, e.g.:

> ...; *goto locj*; ...
> *locj*:   /* *Statements follow* */ ...

or:

> ...; *x = locj*;...; *goto x*; ...

In the second example register *x* is first given the value of a control pointer referring to *locj*, which is later used as a destination.

A switch consists of a bracketed sequence of identifiers followed by a modifying expression which must yield an integer value, e.g.:

> *goto* [*fa fb fc*] ′*y* ≫ 3;

where if the low-order two bits of the modifier have value 0,1 or 2 the destination is taken to be *fa, fb,* or *fc* respectively; otherwise the next statement in sequence is obeyed. Switches are restricted to no more than 16 destinations, each being a label or register identifier. Given a list of *k* destinations, the low-order $\lceil \log_2 k \rceil$ bits of the modifier are used in computing the destination, all other bits being ignored.

The general form of destination is an expression in parentheses, e.g. if *P*6 is a control module attached to the current base, then

> *goto* (*P*6. + 3)

transfers control to the fourth entry point of *P*6 (remember that *P*6 addresses the base and *P*6. obtains an entry pointer, index assumed zero, from the base). The program fails if an out-of-range entry point is used.

The compound control statements *if, while* and *do* make use of condition tests which take the form of condition mnemonics (*GT, LT,* etc.) or more general conditional expressions built up from relations logically combined by *and* and *or*, e.g.

if(x tag < > 4 or f(2) high = 6) return(– 1);

The relational operators are:

=	arithmetic equality
< >	inequality
< =	less than or equal
> =	greater than or equal
<	less than
>	greater than

Conditional expressions are evaluated from left to right, giving precedence to conjunction (*and* terms) and not continuing once the outcome is known (i.e. relation satisfied in disjunction, not satisfied in conjunction), so that in the above example, *f(2) high* would be examined only if *x tag* = 4. The precedence of conditions can be further controlled by using parentheses. (The control statement *where*, used in Part 2 to describe conditional vector assignment, does not feature in P.)

When using condition mnemonics, remember that an arithmetic condition can be set only by using one of the binary arithmetic or logical operators in an expression, or by a procedure call, and that the address condition (*VA, IA*) can be set only by an addressing operator (' or ^) or procedure call.

Interpretation of the compound control statements is as shown by the flow diagrams in Fig. A.2, where "*next*" is taken to be the next statement in sequence unless a *goto* or *return* is obeyed. In each instance "*stat*" can have compound form, i.e. a parenthesized sequence of two or more statements separated by semicolons. Note that *goto* statements can be used freely to break out of a compound statement but one can never jump into the middle, because there are no labels to go to.

PROCEDURE AND MODULE INTERFACING

Procedures are not a "strong" feature of P. Any control or entry pointer can be "called" with different numbers and types of parameters at different points in a program. Except for the parameter registers and the stack frame there is no change of environment on entering the new procedure. More sophisticated interfaces depend on prior agreement about register usage and manipulation on either side of the "call", but the facilities of P are sufficient *if ∘ cond ∘ stat ∘ elstat?*

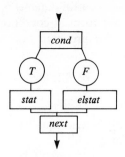

e.g.

> *if NZ x = y−3 else x = 0;* /* *the else clause is optional* */
> *if (x+6>f(y, 2) and z<0 or z tag = 4) goto locj;*

while ∘ cond ∘ do? ∘ stat

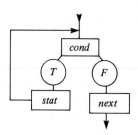

e.g.

> *while VA {x =. y;y+1;x'2};*
> *while (x > 0) {z'x =. 0;x = y;y'1};*
> *while (p <0) do p'1;* /* *The "do" is decorative* */

do ∘ stat ∘ while ∘ cond

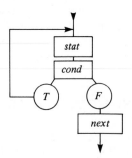

e.g.

> *do {x =. −1;x'1} while VA;* /* *the "do" is essential* */
> *do Put (1, "Help ...\n") while (1 >0);* /* *Goes on for ever* */

Fig. A.2 Flow of control in compound control statements

for calling kernel functions and simple procedures. For most practical purposes a control module can be constructed as a set of procedures following
conventional rules of application.

The syntax of P allows zero, one or two parameters to be declared in a
control sequence: for example,

/* *Procedure to convert an ASCII decimal string to binary* */
$$cdb(x): y = 0; do\{y*10+x. - \_\_0;x'1\} while\ VA; return(y)$$

where x is a formal parameter whose scope extends from the declaration of
cdb to the next procedure declaration or end of program text. Other labelled
sequences may occur in the "body" of *cdb*, but remember that the scope of
labels and registers is the entire module. Control is allowed to jump from one
procedure to another using *goto* (though a warning is given); it is not allowed
to "run on" into a new procedure by the normal sequencing rule. In other
words, procedures must be terminated in the text by *return* or *goto*.

A declared formal parameter acts as, and is in fact, a tagged register: it
can be used both as source of an actual value supplied by the calling sequence
and (as the above example shows) as a working register. If more than two
parameters are needed, then one or both of the formals should be used to
address a sequence in store. Strictly speaking one formal parameter is always
enough: allowing two gives more efficient code in many instances.

If fewer actual than formal parameters are supplied, the parameter value
"drops through" from the calling procedure and returns as a "result", e.g. in
the above example *cdb*() applies *cdb* to the first parameter of the calling procedure, which is returned "invalid" as the result of being used as a working
variable in *cdb*. Such effects are sometimes useful, but their complication
can be avoided simply by using the same number of formal and actual parameters at all times. Supplying more parameters than are needed has no effect,
e.g. *cdb*(x,7) is a valid application of *cdb* with the same effect as *cdb*(x).

Type checking is entirely left to the called procedure, where there are
three possible courses of action:

(1) to assume types are correct and expect to fail on a tagcheck error if they
     are not;
(2) to check tags and "fail gracefully";
(3) to check tags and return an invalid result so that further checking is up to
     the caller.

For *cdb* the second and third actions might be expressed by:

```
cdb(x):    /* x must address a byte string up to 5 chars */
           if( x tag & $b < > 8 or x high > 4)
                  { Put(1, " Failure in cdb\n ");Exit(Null(3)) }
           else /* as before */ ...
```

$cdb(x)$: $if(x \, tag \, \& \, \$b < > 8 \, or \, x \, high > 4)$
            $return(Null(27))$
            $else \, /* \, as \, before \, */ \, \ldots$

where *Null* returns a class 0 system capability which will lead to failure if it is used arithmetically. There are many variations on the above strategies. Which to use depends on the level of understanding between caller and callee.

Unless there is prior agreement on the use of registers a procedure must find its own local workspace, which it does by copying register contents onto the stack and resetting them before returning. For example,

/* *In this example a signed integer n is converted to a character string at*
   the end of the buffer s. Two working registers (x and y) are needed */
$cbd(n,s)$: $save \, [x \quad y] \, ; \, if(n < 0) \, x = -n \, else \, x = n;$
              $y = s \, high;$
              $do \, \{s'y =. \, Rem(x,10) + \_0;y-1;$
              $\quad x = Div(x,10)\} \, while \, NZ;$
/* *Insert minus sign* */ $if(n < 0)\{s'y =. \, \$2d;y-1\};$
              $s'y'1; \, unsave[y \quad x] \, ;return(s)$

Note that *unsave* retrieves values in the reverse order to *save*, though it is not necessary to bring them back all at once or to their original positions.

The single value returned by a procedure is used in expression evaluation in the normal way. Condition codes set in the procedure can be tested on return (see the use of *Div* above).

A procedure call might have the effect of changing register values: we have already seen how a properly designed procedure would preserve working registers unless a side effect were intended. For procedure calls within a module the declared registers are always the same and there should be little difficulty in controlling their use. In cross-module transfers the new registers simply rename the old ones, for example:

/* *Caller* */ $REGS \, [x \quad y \quad z]$
                                  $\downarrow \quad \downarrow$
/* *Callee* */ $REGS \, [p \quad q]$

Here unless the callee calls a module with three or more declared registers the caller need not worry about z, but if he does not trust the callee to look after x and y he must save them before making the call. Similarly, if p and q contain private data the callee should clear them before returning. The above remarks apply to in-task protection; stronger boundaries are placed between tasks as they cannot share registers or indeed any local workspace.

KERNEL FUNCTIONS

It may be assumed that kernel functions produce no unexpected side effects, and return no private data. Kernel functions are summarized in Table 18.5 and defined as required in the text. (The term "kernel function" is used in the same sense as "microsystem function" elsewhere in the text.)

ARRAY STATEMENTS

The array statements (PE functions and plane routing) are described in Chapter 9.

SYNTAX OF CONTROL MODULES

The formal syntax of register transfer statements used in the text is given in Fig. A.3.

Privileged functions (other than /t) and error-management facilities have been excluded. The formal grammar makes use of a number of special *ACTION* and *STRING* recognizers, whose effect is explained in comments, and coding tricks to deal with the special symbols " – " and ":" by defining their internal character codes (*HEXP*).

Page numbers in the list of terminal symbols refer to explanatory text.

```
                REGS-[-ident*-]
                -BASE-[-ident*?-]-TASK-[-ident*?-]-ENTER-[-ident*-]-def*-EOF

addrop:              '    ^
alphnum:STRING  *lud*     /* allows l.case, u.case and decimal */
andrel:              and-rel
arrayop:             move-dirn-int-geom?        pefn-min?-ident-modify?
assign:              =.-expr       =bycol-expr        =-expr
binop:               +   minus   &   ¦   %   /h
bitop:               >>   <<   /t    mask-min?
bopterm:             binop-term       bitop-int
cexpr:               ,-expr
char:   ACTION 4   /* graphic other than space, tab, newline*/
cident:              ,-ident
cint:                ,-min?-int
colon:  HEXP 3a
cond:                VA  IA  ZE  NZ  GE  LT  GT  LE  (-condexp-)
condexp:             conj-orconj*?
conj:                rel-andrel*?
conset:              min?-int-cint*?
datum:               ident    quotes   (-expr-)         (-conset-)
decimal:STRING  *d*
def:                 ident-scope?-colon-sequence
dest:                ident   [-ident*-]-'-expr          (-expr-)
dirn:                W  E  N  S
elstat:              else-stat
EOF:    ACTION 1  /* checks end of file */
expr:                min?-term-bopterm*?
formals:             ident-cident?
geom:                cyclic
hex:    STRING  *hd*     /* allows hexadecimal */
ident:               letter-alphnum
int:                 decimal $-hex   _-char
intid:               int ident  (-expr-)
letter: ACTION 2   /* checks upper or lower case letter */
list:                expr-cexpr*?
min:                 minus
minus:  HEXP 2d
modify:              '-intid?
orconj:              or-conj
pefn:                stm    add   and  or equ  mask  load  adw    st
quotes: ACTION 3                    /* recognizes escapes */
rel:                 expr-relation-expr      (-condexp-)
relation:            <=   >=   <>   <   >   =
result:              (-expr-)
scope:               (-formals?-)
scstat:              ;-stat
selectors:           protect  byte  tag  high  word
                     .bycol   .     addrop-intid   (-list?-)
sequence:            quotes  (-conset-)         stat-scstat*?
stat:                if-cond-stat-elstat?            while-cond-do?-stat
                     do-stat-while-cond             goto-dest
                     @-arrayop                      save-[-ident*-]
                     unsave-[-ident*-]              return-result?
                     {-stat-scstat*?-}      /* compound statement */
                     expr-assign                    expr
term:                int  datum-selectors*?
```

Fig. A.3(i)   Formal syntax of P

		see page
add	planar "add", vertical mode	177
adw	planar "add", horizontal mode	177
and	planar logical "and"	177
BASE	identifies external connections	396,428
byte	postfix address operator	433
cyclic	defines end-around planar edge-connection	180
do	loop control	13,438
E	planar move direction	179
else	conditional control	13,438
ENTER	identifies entry points to module	396,428
equ	planar logical "equivalence"	177
GE	arithmetic condition	11
goto	sequence control	13,436
GT	arithmetic condition	11
high	postfix field selector	175,433
IA	address condition	11
if	conditional control	13,438
LE	arithmetic condition	11
load	planar "load" to *B* register	177
LT	arithmetic condition	11
mask	⌠ planar "load" to *A* register, or	177
	⌡ arithmetic field specifier	12
move	planar "move"	177
N	planar move direction	179
NZ	arithmetic condition	11
or	planar logical "*or*"	177
protect	postfix pointer operator	433,434
REGS	declares registers used in module	11,396,440
return	terminates procedure	13
S	planar move direction	179
save	saves registers in stack frame	181
st	planar "store" *B* register to memory	177
stm	conditional planar "store" under mask *A*	177
tag	postfix field selector	175
TASK	identifies task-specific connections	396,428
unsave	restores registers from stack frame	181
VA	address condition	11
W	planar move direction	177
while	loop control	13,438
word	postfix address operator	175,433
ZE	arithmetic condition	11

Fig. A.3(ii)   Terminal identifiers of P

		see page
$	precedes hexadecimal string	429
%	scalar "not-equivalence"	12
&	scalar "and"	12
'	address modification	432
(		
)		
+	scalar "add"	12
−	scalar "subtract" (unary "negate")	12
.	"fetch" from store	175, 433
.bycol	planar "fetch" by column data lines	176, 433
/h	set register high field	434
/t	set register tag field	434
:		
;	statement separator	
<	relational operator "less than"	
≪	logical left shift	12
< =	relational operator "less than or equal"	
< >	relational operator "not equal"	
=	relational operator "equal" or	
	assign to register	433
= assign to store		175, 433
= bycol	planar assignment by column	176, 436
>	relational operator "greater than"	
> =	relational operator "greater than or equal"	
≫	arithmetic right shift	12
@	precedes array operators	177
[		
]		
^	address limitation	432
—	(underline) precedes graphic symbol	429
		scalar "or"	12

Note the following symbols used in the text which do not feature in P programs:

←	indicates term-by-term vector operations and assignment	155
⌈x⌉	is used to denote the smallest integer not less than x	
where	is used to indicate selective array assignment	162

Fig. A.3(iii) Terminal symbols

APPENDIX 2: SOLUTIONS TO SELECTED EXERCISES

CHAPTER 4 (p. 79)

1 *i*1: (*C*) *t* = *TRUE M* = 12 *I* = *PUSH*
   *i*2: (*A*) *s* = 3 *b* = 4 *ijk* = 0305
   *i*3: (*C*) *t* = *TRUE I* = *RFCT*

Time step:	0	1	2	3	4	5	6
(*A*)	...		*do i*2		*do i*2		*do i*2
(*C*)	...	*do i*1		*do i*3		*do i*3	
control memory	*fetch i*1	*fetch i*2	*fetch i*3	*fetch i*2	*fetch i*3	*fetch i*2	*fetch i*3
top of stack	...		*i*2	*i*2	*i*2	*i*2	*i*2
μ*PC* at	*i*2	*i*3	*i*4	*i*3	*i*4	*i*3	*i*4
end							
R	...	12	12	11	11	10	10

2   (*A*) *ijk* = 0107 *a* = 1 *b* = 2 *M* = 1

3   (*C*) *I* = *CJP t* = *OV M* = *ISOV*
             (*A*) *ijk* = 0523 *a* = 9 *b* = 8 *M* = 5 *d* = 1
             (*C*) *I* = *CJP M* = *END*
ISOV: (*A*) *ijk* = 0403 *a* = 9 *b* = 8
END: (continue)

4   (*C*) *I* = *PUSH M* = 7
             (*A*) *ijk* = 0307 *b* = 4 *s* = 2
             (*C*) *I* = *RFCT*

5   (*A*) *ijk* = 0405 *a* = 1 *b* = 2 *s* = 0 |*R*2 = *R*1 ⫸ 1
             (*A*) *ijk* = 0732 *a* = 2 *y* = 2 *d* = 1 *M* = *$ff*|*SAR* = *R*2;*R*2 = *$ff*
             (*A*) *ijk* = 0541 *d* = 1 *M* = 1 *a* = 1 |(*R*1 & 1)
             (*C*) *w* = 3 *I* = *CJP t* = *NZ M* = *HIBYTE*|Read; test odd/even
/*Low-order byte, sign extend */
             (*A*) *ijk* = 0543 *d* = 3 *b* = 2 *a* = 2 |*R*2 = *SDR* & *$ff*
             (*A*) *ijk* = 0541 *a* = 2 *d* = 1 *M* = *$80* |test sign
             (*C*) *I* = *CJP t* = *ZE M* = *END*
             (*A*) *ijk* = 0573 *d* = 1 *M* = *$ff a* = 2
               b = 2 |(negative)
             (*C*) *I* = *CJP M* = *END*
/*High-order byte, shift down */
HIBYTE: (*A*) *ijk* = 0733 *d* = 3 *b* = 2 |*R*2 = *SDR*
             (*C*) *I* = *PUSH M* = 7
             (*A*) *ijk* = 0305 *b* = 2 *s* = 3 |*R*2 ⫸ 1
             (*C*) *I* = *TWB t* = *FALSE M* = *END*|exit

11 Add $PC'n$. to the accumulator AC

AP: (A) $ijk = 0501\ a = PC\ d = 2\ y = 2$ $SAR = PC'n$
       (C) $w = 3$ $SDR = SAR.$
       (A) $ijk = 0503\ a = AC\ b = AC\ d = 3$ $AC + SDR$
       (C) $I = CJP\ t = NINT\ M = MAINLOOP$

12 $SP - n$

LSP: (A) $ijk = 0513\ a = SP\ b = SP\ d = 2\ M = 1$ $SP - n$
       (A) $ijk = 0121\ a = SP\ b = SB\ M = 1$ $(SP - SB)$
       (C) $I = CJP\ t = LT\ M = STACKVIOL$
       (C) $I = CJP\ t = NINT\ M = MAINLOOP$

13 (a) *Fetch PC'n. to SDR*
     FPC: (A) $ijk = 0501\ a = PC\ d = 2\ y = 2$ $SAR = PC'n$
          (C) $w = 3\ I = CRTN$ $SDR = SAR.$
     (b) Push $PC'n$.
     PPC: (C) $I = CJS\ M = FPC$ $SDR = PC'n.$
         (A) $ijk = 0412\ a = SP\ b = SP\ y = 2$ $SAR = SP; SP1$
         (A) $ijk = 0121\ a = SP\ b = SB\ M = 1$ $(SP - SB)$
         (C) $I = CJP\ t = GE\ M = STACKVIOL$
         (C) $w = 1\ I = CJP\ M = MAINLOOP$

14 Set conditions, assuming PS bits 0 and 1 are zero
    SETCC: (C) $I = CJP\ t = GE\ M = POS$
          (A) $ijk = 0533\ a = PS\ b = PS\ d = 1\ M = 3$ "11"
          (C) $I = CRTN$
     POS: (C) $I = CRTN\ t = NZ$ "00"
         (A) $ijk = 0533\ a = PS\ b = PS\ d = 1\ M = 2$ "10"
         (C) $I = CRTN$

15 if ZE branch backwards n
    BBZE: (A) $ijk = 0541\ a = PS\ d = 1\ M = 2$ $(PS \& 2)$
         (C) $I = CJP\ t = ZE\ M = END$
         (A) $ijk = 0513\ a = PC\ b = PC\ M = 1\ d = 2$ $PC - n$
     END: (C) $I = CJP\ t = NINT\ M = MAINLOOP$

CHAPTER 9 (p. 197)

```
REGS[ wk p q r
x y z]
BASE[] TASK[]
ENTER[ex1a ex1b ex3 ex5 ex7 ex9 ex11 ex13 ex15 ex17 ex19]
```

```
/* User take care! Registers are NOT saved */

/* p is a Boolean plane. Detect(a) at least one zero (b)one one */
ex1a():return(p.+1)
        /* If p is all 1's so is the word p. and therefore
           the ZE condition is returned; otherwise NZ
           indicates the presence of at least one zero */
ex1b():@ load -p;@ st wk; return(wk.+1)
        /* Here NZ indicates that wk contains at least
           one zero, therefore p contains at least one one */

/* p contains at least one zero. Find its coordinates. The
   following procedure will select one of several zeros */
ex3(): x = p.bycol;    /* Read out along columns */
        /* Now x contains one or more zeros indicating
           columns in which zeros occur. To find the leftmost
           zero in x: */
        z=0; x+0; while LT {z+1;x<<1};
        /* Now z contains the index of the first column
           in p containing a zero. For a faster method
           see assoc() in Fig 18.4.  To find the row
           index extract the relevant word: */
        x = p word'z.;
        y=0; while(x mask 1 = 1){y+1;x>>1};
        return(y<<4+z)

/* Eliminate isolated white cells: none of the edge
   elements is isolated because plane geometry is assumed */
ex5(): @ load p;@ move E 1;@ and p;@ move E 1;
        @ and p;@ st wk;
        /* Now each cell in wk contains the logical sum
           of three cells in a row of p */
        @ move N 2;@ and wk;
        @ move S 1;@ and p;@ move W 2;@ and p;
        @ move E 1;
        /* Now B=1 if and only if all eight neighbors
           of the element in p are black */
        @ or p;@ st p;return

/* Word association in horizontal mode */
ex7(): return /* See assoc() in Figure 18-4 */

/* Sum the four neighbors of each element in b */
ex9(a,b):      wk =. 0;@ load wk;@ add wk;     /* clear carry */
```

```
        @ load b;@ move S 1 cyclic;@ st a;
        @ load b;@ move W 1 cyclic;@ add a;
        @ st a;@ load wk;@ add wk;@ st a'1;
        /* Now a,a'1 is the sum of the N and E neighbors */
        @ load a;@ move N 1 cyclic;@ move E 1 cyclic;
        @ add a;@ st a;
        @ load a'1;@ move N 1 cyclic;@ move E 1 cyclic;
        @ add a'1;@ st a'1;
        @ load wk;@ add wk;@ st a'2;
        return

/* a=max(a,b) and b=min(a,b) in each element position */
ex11(a,b):      p=a;q=b;wk=.0;@load -wk;@ add -wk;
        do{@ load p';@ add -q'} while VA;
        /* Now sign of result (ignoring OV) is in B plane :
           for treatment of overflow see Figure 10-8 */
        @ st wk;@ mask wk;
        do{@ load b;@ st wk;
           @ load a;@ stm b';
           @ load wk;@ stm a'} while VA;
        return

/* Scale a down by b, element by element */
ex13(a,b):      x=1;do{@ mask b;scum(a,x);x<<1;b'1} while VA;
        return
/* Scale a by n under mask */
scum(a,n):      save[x];@ load a'(a high);        /* sign plane */
        x = a'n;while VA do{@ load x;@ stm a';x'1};
        do{@ stm a;a'1} while VA;
        unsave[x];return

/* The perfect shuffle is seen to rotate the index bits of
   each element one position left (Chapter 9).  Perfect
   unshuffle must therefore rotate right */
ex15(a):        x=0;do{shuff(a,x);x+1} while (x<7);return

/* Hex pattern */
ex17():wk =. $aaaa;
        @ load p;@ move N 3;@ move E 1;@ mask wk;@ stm p;
        @ move E 1;@ mask -wk;@ stm p;return

/* Isobars, iso(a,b) */
ex19(a,b):      p =. 0;
        do{@ mask -p;maxel(b);wk =. -1;@ load wk;@ stm a;@ stm p;
           (p.+1); if ZE return;
           a'1} while VA; return
/* maxel finds the maximum under a preset mask of 1's in the
   activity plane */
maxel(a):       save[x];x = a high;
        wk =. -1;@ load -wk;@ stm wk;
        do{@ load -a'x;@ stm wk;
           (wk.+1);if NZ @ mask -wk;x-1} while GE;
        unsave[x];return
```

APPENDIX 3: REFERENCES

AGR76   A.K. Agrawala and T.G. Rauscher
Foundations of Microprogramming: Architecture,
Software and Applications
Academic Press, New York
(1976)

ALJ79   M.M. Al-Jarrah and I.S. Torson
"An empirical analysis of Cobol progams"
Software Practice and Experience **9** (5), 341–59
(May 1979)

AMD64   G.M. Amdahl, G.A. Blaauw and F.P. Brooks Jr.
"Architecture of the IBM System/360"
IBM J. Res. Dev. **8**, 87–101
(April 1964)

AMD80   *The Am2900 Family Data Book*
Advanced Micro Devices Inc.
901 Thompson Place, Sunnyvale, CA 94086

AND77   H.C. Andrews and B.R. Hunt
Digital Image Restoration
Prentice-Hall
Englewood Cliffs, NJ 07632
(1977)

AND80   M. Andrews
Principles of Firmware
Engineering in Microprogram Control
Computer Science Press, Potomac, MD
Pitman, London
(1980)

BAR68   G.H. Barnes, R.M. Brown, M. Kato, D.J. Kuck,
D.L. Slotnick and R.A. Stokes
"The ILLIAC IV computer"
IEEE Trans. Comp. **C-17** (8), 746–57
(Aug 1968)
See also BEL71 pp. 320–33

BAR79   I. Barron and R. Curnow
         The Future with Microelectronics
         Open University Press, Milton Keynes
         (1979)

BAT68   K.E. Batcher
         "Sorting networks and their applications"
         Proc. AFIPS Spring JCC, **32**, 307–15
         (1968)

BAT77   K.E. Batcher
         "The multidimensional access memory in STARAN"
         IEEE Trans. Comp. **C-26** (2), 174–7
         (February 1977)

BAT79   K.E. Batcher
         "The massively parallel processor (MPP) system"
         AIAA Computers in Aerospace Conference
         Los Angeles
         (October 1979)

BAT80   K.E. Batcher
         "Design of a Massively Parallel Processor"
         IEEE Trans. Comp. **C-29** (9), 836–40
         (September 1980)

BAU78   G. Baudet and D. Stevenson
         "Optimal sorting algorithms for parallel computers"
         IEEE Trans. Comp. **C-27** (1), 84–7
         (January 1978)

BEL71   C.G. Bell and A. Newell
         Computer Structures: Readings and Examples
         McGraw-Hill, New York
         (1971)

BER76   R. Bernstein
         "Digital image processing of earth observation
         sensor data"
         IBM Res. Dev. **20**(1), 40–57
         (January 1976)

BER80   V. Berstis
         "Security and protection of data in IBM System/38"
         7th Comp. Arch. Conf. Proc.
         La Baule
         (May 1980) pp. 245–52

BER78   R.E. Berry
"Experience with the Pascal P-compiler"
Software Practice and Experience **8** (5), 617–28
(September 1978)

BOU72   G. Boulaye and J. Mermet (eds.)
"Microprogramming"
Proc. Adv. Summer Institute
San Raphael
Hermann, Paris
(1972)

BUR46   A.W. Burks, H.H. Goldstein and J. von Neumann
*Preliminary Discussion on the Logical Design of an Electronic
Computing Instrument*
Report prepared at the Institute for Advanced Study,
Princeton, NJ, for the US Army Ordnance Department.
(June 1946)
See also *Datamation* September 1962, pp. 25–31
        Datamation October 1962, pp. 36–41
or   BEL71 pp. 92–119
or   J. von Neumann: *Collected Works,* **5**, Pergamon Press, New
        York, 1961

BUR73a   *B1700 System Reference Manual*
Burroughs Corporation
Detroit, Michigan
Form no 1057155
(1973)

BUR73b   *B1700 COBOL/RPG S-language*
Burroughs Corporation
Detroit, Michigan
Form no 1058823-015
(1973)

BUR79   *B1870/B1860 Systems Reference Manual*
Burroughs Corporation
Detroit, Michigan 48232
Form no 1090644
(March 1979)

CHE72   T.C. Chen
"Automatic computation of exponentials,
logarithms and square roots"
IBM J. Res. Dev. **16**, 380–8
(July 1972)

CHE77   "Design of high level language oriented processors"
            SIGPLAN Notices **12** (1), 40−51
            (January 1977)

CHU80   Y. Chu (ed.)
            International Workshop on High-Level Computer Architecture
            Department of computer science
            University of Maryland
            (May 1980)

DAP79   *DAP: Introduction to Fortran Programming*
            ICL 2900 series publication TP6755
            Developing DAP Fortran Programs
            ICL 2900 series publication TP6920
            International Computers Limited, London
            (1979)

DAV69   R.L. Davis
            "The ILLIAC IV processing element"
            IEEE Trans. Comp. **C-18** (9), 800−16
            (September 1969)

DEN66   J.B. Dennis and E.C. Van Horn
            "Programming semantics for multiprogrammed computations"
            CACM **9** (3), 143−55
            (March 1966)

DUF73   M.J.B. Duff, T.J. Fountain and G.K. Shaw
            "A cellular logic array for image processing"
            Pattern Recognition **5**, 229−47
            (1973)

DUF74   M.J.B. Duff, D.M. Watson and E.S. Deutsch
            "A parallel computer for array processing"
            IFIP Conf. Proc. North-Holland
            (1974) pp. 94−7

DUF77   M.J.B. Duff
            "Parallel processing techniques"
            in B.G. Batchelor (ed.)
            Pattern Recognition Ideas in Practice
            Plenum
            (1977) pp. 145−74

DUF78   M.J.B. Duff
            "Review of the CLIP image processing system"
            National Computer Conf. Proc.
            (1978) pp. 1055−60

ELS76   J.L. Elshoff
         "A numerical profile of commercial PL/1 programs"
         Software Practice and Experience **6**, 505–25
         (1976)

ECK79   R.H. Eckhouse Jr. and L.R. Morris
         Minicomputer Systems, 2nd edn
         Prentice-Hall
         Englewood Cliffs, NJ 07632
         (1979)

ENG74   D.M. England
         *Capability Concept Mechanism and Structure
         in System 250*
         International workshop on protection in
         operating systems
         IRIA, Rocquencourt
         (August 1974) pp. 63–82

FAB74   R. Fabry
         "Capability-based addressing"
         CACM **17** (7), 403–12
         (July 1974)

FEU73   E.A. Feustel
         "On the advantages of tagged architecture"
         IEEE Trans. Comp. **C-22** (7), 644–56
         (July 1973)

FLA77   P.M. Flanders, D.J. Hunt, S.F. Reddaway and D.Parkinson
         "Efficient high speed computing with the
         Distributed Array Processor"
         *Symposium on High Speed Computer and
         Algorithm Organization*
         University of Illinois
         Academic Press
         (April 1977)

FLA80   P.M. Flanders
         *Musical Bits — a Generalised Method for a
         Class of Data Movements on the DAP*
         Private communication
         (June 1980)

FLY66   M.J. Flynn
         "Very high speed computing systems"
         Proc. IEEE **54**(12), 1901–9
         (December 1966)

FLY77   M.J. Flynn
"The interpretive interface: resources and program
representation in computer organization"
Symposium on High Speed Computer and Algorithm Organization.
University of Illinois
Academic Press
(April 1977)

GON77   R.C. Gonzalez and P. Wintz
Digital Image Processing
Addison-Wesley, Reading, MA
(1977)

GOO75   G. Goos and J. Hartmannis (eds.)
Parallel Processing
Lecture notes in computer science No. 24
Springer-Verlag, Berlin, Heidelberg, New York
(1975)

GRE63   J. Gregory and R. McReynolds
"The SOLOMON computer"
IEEE Trans. Elec. Comp. **EC-12**, 774–81
(December 1963)

HAG80   H. Hagiwara, S. Tomita, S. Oyanagai and K. Shibayama
"A dynamically microprogrammable computer
with low level parallelism"
IEEE Trans. Comp. **C-29** (7), 577–95
(July 1980)

HAL79   E.L. Hall
Computer Image Processing and Recognition
Academic Press, New York
(1979)

HAN78   A.R. Hanson and E.M. Riseman (eds.)
Computer Vision Systems
Academic Press, New York
(1978)

HAS76   A. Hassitt and L.E. Lyon
"An APL emulator for System/370"
IBM Systems J. **15**(4), 358–78
(1976)

HEH77   E.C.R. Hehner
"Information content of programs and operation encoding"
JACM **24** (2), 290–7
(April 1977)

HOE77   L.W. Hoevel and M.J. Flynn
*The Structure of Directly Executed Languages:
a New Theory of Interpretive System Support*
Digital Systems Laboratory
Stanford University
T.N. 130
(March 1977)

HOP53   G.M. Hopper and J. Mauchly
"Influence of programming techniques on the design
of computers"
Proc. IRE **41**, 1250–4
(October 1953)

HUS70   S.S. Husson
Microprogramming: Principles and Practices
Prentice-Hall
Englewood Cliffs, NJ
(1970)

IBM78   *IBM System/38: Technical Developments*
IBM General Systems Division
Publication G580-0237
(December 1978)

IBM80   *IBM System/38: Functional Concepts Manual*
IBM General Systems Division
Publication GA21-9330-0
(June 1980)

ICH79   J.D. Ichbiah *et al.*
"Preliminary ADA reference manual"
SIGPLAN Notices **14** (6) Part A
(June 1979)

ILI69   J.K. Iliffe
"Elements of BLM"
Computer J. **12**, 251–8
(1969)

ILI72a   J.K. Iliffe
Basic Machine Principles 2nd edn.
American Elsevier/Macdonald
(1972)

ILI72b   J.K. Iliffe and J. May
"Design of an emulator for computer
systems research"
in BOU72 281–306

INF79   "Supercomputers: invited papers"
Infotech State of the Art Conference
Maidenhead, Berks
(1979)

JOH78   P.M. Johnson
"An introduction to vector processing"
Computer Design
(February 1978) pp. 89−97

JON75   A. Jones and W.A. Wulf
"Toward the design of a secure system"
Software Practice and Experience 5, 321−36
(1975)

JON80   A.K. Jones and E.F. Gehringer (eds.)
The CM* Multiprocessor Project: A Research Review
Dept. of Computer Science
Carnegie-Mellon University
Report No CMU-CS-80-131
(July 1980)

JOR75   T.L. Jordan
Gaussian Elimination for Dense Systems on STAR and a
New Parallel Algorithm for Diagonally Dominant
Tridiagonal Systems
Los Angeles Scientific Laboratory
Report no. LA-5803
(June 1975)

JUM72   J.R. Jump and D.R. Fritsch
"Microprogrammed arrays"
IEEE Trans. Comp. **C-21**. 974−84
(September 1972)

KAU68   W.H. Kautz, K.N. Levitt and A. Waksman
"Cellular Interconnection arrays"
IEEE Trans. Elec. Comp. **EC-17**, 443−51
(May 1968)

KNU71   D.E. Knuth
"An empirical study of Fortran programs"
Software Practice and Experience 1, 105−33
(1971)

KNU73   D.E. Knuth
The Art of Computer Programming
Vol 3: Sorting and Searching
Addison-Wesley
Reading, Mass.
(1973)

KUC68   D.J.Kuck
"ILLIAC IV software and application programming"
IEEE Trans. Comp. **C-17** (8), 758–78
(August 1968)

KUC77   D.J. Kuck *et al.* (eds.)
"High speed computer and algorithm organization"
University of Illinois Symposium
Academic Press
(1977)

KUC68   D.J.Kuck
The Structure of Computers and Computations,
Vol. 1"
John Wiley
(1978)

LAN76   T. Lang and H.S. Stone
"A shuffle-exchange network with simplified control"
IEEE Trans. Comp. **C-25** (1), 55–65
(January 1976)

LEE61   C.Y. Lee
"An algorithm for path connections and its applications"
IRE Trans. Elec. Comp. **EC-10**, 346–65
(September 1961)

LIS76   B.H. Liskov
"An introduction to CLU"
Laboratory for Computer Science
Massachusetts Institute of Technology
Computation Structures
Group Memo 136
(February 1976)

LIS77   B.H. Liskov, A. Snyder, R. Atkinson and C. Schaffert
"Abstraction mechanisms in CLU"
CACM **20** (8), 564–76
(August 1977)

LIS79   B.H. Liskov *et al.*
CLU Reference Manual
Laboratory for Computer Science
Massachusetts Institute of Technology
Report No MIT/LCS/TR-225
(October 1979)

MAR73   J. Martin
Security, Accuracy and Privacy in Computer Systems
Prentice-Hall, Englewood Cliffs, N.J.
(1973)

MAR80   P. Marks
"Low-level vision using an array processor"
Computer Graphics and Image Processing **14**, 281–92
(1980)

MCC63   B.H. McCormick
"The Illinois pattern recognition computer
— ILLIAC III"
IEEE Trans. Comp. **EC-12** (6), 791–813
(December 1963)

MEG62   J. Meggitt
"Pseudo-division and pseudo-multiplication
processes"
IBM J. Res. Dev. **6**, 210–26
(April 1962)

MIC80   J.R. Mick and J. Brick
Bit-slice Microprocessor Design
McGraw-Hill
(1980)

MYE78   G.J. Myers
Advances in Computer Architecture
John Wiley
New York
(1978)

NAS79   D. Nassimi
"Bitonic sort on a mesh-connected parallel computer"
IEEE Trans. Comp. **C-28** (1),
(January 1979)

NAS80   D. Nassimi and S. Sahni
"An optimal routing algorithm for mesh-connected
parallel computers"
JACM **27** (1), 6–29
(January 1980)

NEE77   R.M. Needham and R.D.H. Walker
"The CAP computer and its protection system"
ACM 6th Symposium on Operating System Principles
(1977)

NEU75   C. Neuhauser
An Emulation Oriented Dynamic Microprogrammable Emulator
Digital Systems Laboratory
Stanford University
Technical Note TN.65

NEU78   P.G. Neumann
           "The use of formal specifications in the design,
           implementation and verification of large
           computer systems"
           see WEG78

OPP65   A.V. Oppenheim and R.W. Schafer
           Digital Signal Processing
           Prentice-Hall
           Englewood Cliffs, NJ
           (1975)

PAT80   D.A. Patterson and C.H. Séquin
           "Design considerations for single-chip
           computers of the future"
           IEEE Trans. Comp. **C-29** (2), 108–16
           (February 1980)

POP79   G.J. Popek and C.S. Kline
           "Encryption and secure computer networks"
           ACM Comp. Surveys **11** (4), 331–56
           (December 1979)

PRA78   W. Pratt
           Digital Image Processing
           John Wiley, New York
           (1978)

RAD76   G. Radin and P.R. Schneider
           *An Architecture for an Extended Machine with
           Protected Addressing*
           IBM Development Laboratories
           Poughkeepsie
           Report TR00.2575
           (May 1976)

RAK69   L.L. Rakocsi
           "The computer-within-a-computer:
           a fourth generation concept"
           Computer Group News **2** (8), 14–20
           (March 1969)

RAK72   L.L. Rakocsi
           "Microprogramming the MLP-900 as a fourth
           generation computer system"
           In BOU72 pp. 329–40
           (1964)

RAU80   T. Rauscher and P. Adams
           "Microprogramming: a tutorial and survey of
           recent developments"
           IEEE Trans. Comp. **C-29** (1), 2–20
           (January 1980)

RED73   S.F. Reddaway
           "DAP — a distributed array processor"
           1st Annual Symposium on Computer Architecture
           Gainesville, FA, pp. 61–65
           (1973)

REY79   D.N. Reynolds and G.G. Henry
           "The IBM System/38"
           Datamation, 141–3
           (August 1979)

RIT74   D. Ritchie and K. Thompson
           "The UNIX time-sharing system"
           CACM **17** (7), 365–75
           (July 1974)
           See also *Bell System Technical Journal*
           57 (6) Part 2 (July–August 1978)

ROB75   S.K. Robinson and I.S. Torsun
           "An empirical analysis of Fortran programs"
           Computer J. **19** (1), 7–62
           (January 1975)

ROS76   A. Rosenfeld and A.C. Kak
           Digital Picture Processing
           Academic Press
           New York
           (1976)

ROS69   R.F. Rosin
           "Contemporary concepts of microprogramming and
           emulation"
           ACM Computing Surveys, **1**, 197–212
           (1969)

ROS72   R.F. Rosin, G. Frieder, R.H. Eckhouse Jr
           "An environment for research in microprogramming
           and emulation"
           CACM **15** (8), 748–60
           (August 1972)

RUB74   F. Rubin
           "The Lee path connection algorithm"
           IEEE Trans. Comp. **C-23**, 907–14
           (September 1974)

RUS78   R.M. Russell
          "The CRAY-1 computer system"
          CACM **21** (1), 63−72
          (January 1978)

SAL73   A.E. Salisbury
          *A Study of General-purpose Microprogrammable
          Computer Architectures*
          Digital Systems Laboratory
          Stanford University
          Technical Report TR.59
          (July 1973)
          See also *Microprogrammable Computer Architectures*
          North-Holland, New York
          (1977)

SAL75a   J.H. Saltzer and M.D. Schroeder
          "The protection of information in computer systems"
          IEEE Proc. **63** (9), 278−308
          (September 1975)

SAL75b   A. Salvadori, J. Gordon and C. Capstick
          "Static profile of Cobol programs"
          ACM SIGPLAN Notices **10** (8), 20−33
          (August 1975)

SAM78   A.H. Sameh and D.J. Kuck
          "On stable parallel linear system solvers"
          JACM **25** (1), 81−91
          (January 1978)

SCA68   G.G. Scarrott and J.K. Iliffe
          "The Basic Language Project"
          IFIP Congress Proceedings 1968
          North-Holland, Amsterdam, pp. 508−13
          (1969)

SLO62   D.L. Slotnick, W.C. Borck and R.C. McReynolds
          "The SOLOMON computer"
          AFIPS Fall JCC Proceedings **22**, 97−107
          (1952)

SOL79   G. Soltis and R.L. Hoffman
          "Design considerations for the IBM System/38"
          Compcon 79 (Spring) *Proceedings*, pp. 132−7
          (1979)

STE75   K. Stevens
          "CFD — Fortran-like language for the ILLIAC IV"
          SIGPLAN Notices, 72−80
          (March 1975)

STO70   H.S. Stone
         "A logic-in-memory computer"
         IEEE Trans. Comp. **C-19** (1), 73–8
         (January 1970)

STO71   H.S. Stone
         "Parallel processing with the perfect shuffle"
         IEEE Trans. Comp. **C-20** (2), 153–61
         (February 1971)

STO73   H.S. Stone
         "An efficient algorithm for a tridiagonal linear
         system"
         JACM **20** (1), 27–38
         (January 1973)
         See also *Parallel Tridiagonal Equation Solvers*
         NASA Technical Memorandum TMX-62, 370
         (April 1974)

STO75   H.S. Stone
         "Introduction to computer architecture"
         Science Research Associates
         Chicago
         (1975)

STO77   R.A. Stokes
         "Burroughs Scientific Processor"
         In KUC77, pp. 85–9

TAN76   A.S. Tanenbaum
         Structured Computer Organization
         Prentice-Hall
         (1976)

THO77   C.D. Thompson and H.T. Kung
         "Sorting on a mesh-connected parallel computer"
         CACM **20** (4), 263–71
         (April 1977)

THO78   C.D. Thompson
         "Generalized connection networks for parallel
         processor interconnection"
         IEEE Trans. Comp. **C-27** (12)
         (December 1978)

THU76   K.J. Thurber
         Large Scale Computer Architecture
         Hayden, NJ
         (1976)

TUC67   "Microprogram control for System/360"
        IBM Systems J. **6** (4), 222–41
        (1967)

TUR75   R. Turn and W. Ware
        "Privacy and security in computer systems"
        American Scientist **63**, 196–203
        (March 75)

UNG58   S.H. Unger
        "A computer oriented towards spatial problems"
        Proc. IRE **46**, 1744–50
        (October 1958)

WAR62   S. Warshall
        "A theorem on Boolean matrices"
        JACM **9** (1), 11–12
        (January 1962)

WEB67   H. Weber
        "A microprogrammed implementation of Euler on
        System/360"
        CACM **10** (9), 549–58
        (September 1967)

WEG78   P. Wegner (ed.)
        Research Directions in Software Technology
        MIT Press
        Cambridge, Mass
        (1978)

WIC73   B.A. Wichman
        Algol-60 Compilation and Assessment
        Academic Press, New York
        (1973)

WIL72   W.T. Wilner
        "Burroughs B1700 memory utilization"
        AFIPS Fall JCC Proc., 579–86
        (1972)

WUL81   W.A. Wulf, M. Shaw. P.N. Hilfinger and L. Flon
        Fundamental Structures of Computer Science
        Addison-Wesley, Reading, Mass
        (1981)

YAM80   M. Yamamoto, R. Nakazaki, M. Yokota and M. Umemura
        "A Cobol machine design and evaluation"
        Int. Workshop on High Level Computer Arch.
        Department of Computer Science
        University of Maryland
        (May 1980)

INDEX

abstract object, 4
  in PN system, 381
abstraction, 300*f*
  compile-time, 302*f*
  example in microPN, 400*f*
  in microprogram, 379
  of program space, 302,
    344
  self-application, 361
access field, in capability, 324
access list, 295*f*, 338
  construction, 296
  inheritance, 296
access matrix, 295
access operators in AMA, 175
access path, 90, 119, 132, 141
  generalized, 95
access rights in IBM
    System/38, 371
access to remote global data,
    412
access via codeword, 385
accumulator register plane in
    AMA, 176
Active Memory Array
    (AMA), 162
active memory functions, 380
active store blocks, 271
activity register plane in
    AMA, 176
ADA, 310*f*, 312, 379
address, 18
address mapping in IBM
    System/38, 376
Advanced Micro Devices
    (AMD), 63
ALGOL, scope rules, 304
ALGOL-68, 336
  statement execution times,
    89
ALU, Am2901, 68*f*
amplification in STAROS,
    319

APL, 37, 96, 118, 126
  as array control language,
    255
archetype, ICL-1900, 51*f*
  PDP-11, 50*f*
architectural level, 197, 418
architecture, objectives of,
    133
area functions in image en-
    hancement, 228*f*
arithmetic, planar, 177*f*
array processor,
    schematic, 145
array registers in PN machine,
    385
assignment, and addressing
    rules, 15*f*
  implicit, 12, 17, 434
  in P, 434
associative access to data,
    118*f*
Atomic Energy Commission,
    362
attributes of typed objects,
    301
authorization, 279, 338
  by capability, 301
  deferred, 365
  in BLM, 346
  in IBM System/38, 370*f*
  of access, 276

Babbage, 19
Backus Normal Form, 9
base, 115
  in BLM, 344
  in PN machine, 388, 397,
    427
Basic Language Machine,
    114, 120, 340*f*
Batcher sort, in AMA, 209
  in DAP Fortran, 258
BCPL language, 142

benchmark testing, 83
binding, dynamic, 279
  in BLM, 356
  in IBM System/38, 368
  in PN system, 396
bit steering, 43
bit-serial algorithms, 203*f*
bitonic sort, 209
branching in pipeline pro-
    cessors, 169
browsing, in file space, 338
  in operating environment,
    350
Burroughs B 1700, 58
Burroughs B 1800, 130
Burroughs B 5000, 90, 362
Burroughs B 6700, 90
  system space, 90
  value call operator, 93
Burroughs COBOL/RPG,
    121

C language, 142
cache, 359
  capability, 336, 342
  in IBM System/38, 376
Cambridge University, CAP
    computer, 334*f*
  microprogramming, 39
CAP computer, 346
capability, 18, 114, 273, 300,
    314*f*, 380
  abstract, 318
  classes in BLM, 344
  data, 318
  entry to code, 322, 335
  expansion, 324
  integer, 330
  machines taxonomy, 364
  management, 277
  management in PN
    machine, 398*f*
  operations in PP250, 326

465

capability (*cont'd*)
  options, 309
  register, 321
  representation, 318
  token, 318
Capability-Forming-Cap-
  ability, *see* CFC
Carnegie-Mellon University,
  316
carry plane in AMA, 176
CDC 6600, 89
CDC 7600, 263
cellular arrays, 171
CFC, in PN machine, 387,
  402
CFD for Illiac IV, 254
chaining in CRAY-1, 154
change of access list, 296
circuit specification, 1
class manager, 301
  in BLM, 351*f*
  in CM*, 319
  in PN machine, 400
  in PP250, 328
CLIP, 236*f*
CLU language, 304*f*
cluster, 304
CM*, 316*f*, 346
Cobol, critical timing path,
  123
  target code, 106*f*, 132
  target language (CTL),
  108, 123
codeword, 18, 117, 273*f*, 344,
  380
column, assignment in AMA,
  176
  output in AMA, 176
compaction of storage, 273
comparison elements for
  sorting, 222
compile time affected by
  microcode, 124
condition codes, 11
constructed access rights, 296,
  396
  in BLM, 346
Context in IBM System/38,
  368
control, ICL DAP, 243
  two-level, 131
control interface, 415*f*
  in SIL, 120
control memory, 7, 40, 359
  in high speed processors,
  142
  in IBM System/38, 375
control module in PN
  machine, 395
control overheads in DAP,
  263*f*
control pointer, 18

Control Program Facility in
  IBM System/38, 367
control segment in PN
  machine, 385, 395
control statements in P, 436
control type in VCS, 117
control unit, AMA, 165
  Am2910, 71*f*
  Illiac IV, 158
correctness, program, 301
cost of active memory, 269
CRAY-1, 151*f*
  performance, 196
crosspoint, 58*f*
CTL, *see* Cobol Target
  Language
cyclic reduction of tridiagonal
  systems, 221

data division in Cobol, 106
data segment in PN machine,
  385
datum in P, 432
DEBUG in Cobol, 108
Debugging in BLM, 356
DEC PDP-11, 24*f*
  address options, 26, 30
  archetype, 50
  in CM*, 317
  instruction usage, 84
decomposition, hierarchical,
  313
  of array problems, 201
  procedural, 312
dedicated language pro-
  cessors, 129
definition in P syntax, 428
delay, in sorting, 207
DELtran, instruction formats,
  102
  operator codes, 104
  target code, 99*f*
descriptor, 18, 91
  in DELtran, 99
  vector, 94
direct control, 42
display registers, 91
distributed database, 412
distributed program, 380, 411,
  412
distributed systems, 5
domain of class manager, 302
dynamic chain, 88

edge-detection in image enhancement, 230
ejection in store managment,
  271
encapsulated data type, 314
encoded control, 42
enhancement, image, 227

entry point to control module,
  396
Euler language, 97
evaluation, of expressions, 12
exchange, of array index bits,
  191, 223
expression evaluation, 85*f*
  in Cobol, 110
  in Fortran, 99
  in P, 431

factored performance tests, 83
failure of machine or system
  functions, 399
fault avoidance, 5
fault tolerance, 5
Fermat number transform,
  254
file, abstraction of, 395
flexibility, microprogram, 127
Floating Point System
  AP-120B, 146*f*
floating point in AMA, 188
format of microPN instructions, 390
Fortran DAP extensions, 254*f*
Fortran EQUIVALENCE,
  350
FORTRAN vectorizing pre-
  processors, 169
Fourier transform in DAP,
  249*f*
frame store, TV image, 242
function units in CRAY-1,
  153

gap-filling in image enhancement, 233
gate in PN machine, 384
geometry in AMA, 179
global memory control in
  PN machine, 388
Global Segment Table, in
  PN system, 412
  in VCS, 117
global segments, 381
Goodyear MPP, 282
grade of interpretation, 31
grammars, formal, 8*f*

Hadamard transform, 254
hashing algorithm in IBM
  System/38, 376
heading in P, 395, 428
heading of program section,
  10
hesitation in peripheral
  transfer, 52
hierarchical decomposition,
  313

hierarchy in AMA store design, 270
of bases, 115
of design, 3
of store, 7, 169, 417
of system organization, 298
histogram, intensity, 230
horizontal data in AMA, 172
horizontal micro-instruction, 44
host in multicomputer system, 380, 394
host, interpretive, 23

I—O support for high speed computation, 170
IBM 1401, 362
IBM 360, 2, 19, 98, 122
instruction usage, 84
Model 50 ALU, 52*f*
range definition, 340
IBM 370 program space, 316
IBM 7090 Gibson mix, 84
IBM System/38, 130, 363*f*, 419
ICL 1900, 32*f*, 98
archetype, 51
supporting language microcode, 123
ICL 1904 microprogram, 47
ICL DAP, 224, 243*f*, 419
ICL E1 emulator, 55, 361
microprogram, 49
registers, 57
Illiac III, 241
Illiac IV, 157*f*
image generation, 236
inactive store blocks, 271
Index in Cobol, 106
index management, 276*f*
index of array elements, 191
index space, 277
indexing, in arrays, 165
Illiac IV, 158
indirect addressing, 27, 341
inheritance of access rights, 296
insertion sort, 214
integer arithmetic in AMA, 185
interconnection of programs, 292
interpretation, aims of, 35*f*
of tags, 349
interpretive systems, 283
inversion of array index bits, 191, 223
iterative reduction of tridiagonal systems, 221

job control, 3
Job Control Language, 341

kernel functions in microPN, 394
kernel of microsystem, 114, 132
Kmap in CM*, 317

language-oriented design, 95
Laplace's equation, 262
large-scale integration, *see* LSI
leakage through protection boundaries, 333
Lee algorithm, 285
limitation in BLM, 350
limitation operator, 432
line functions in image processing, 232*f*
list processing in array, 265
load time affected by SIL, 124
load-and-go compiler, 125
local memory control in PN machine, 388
location number, 18
lock in IBM System/38, 373
logical operations in AMA, 184
loop control statements, 13
LSI, arithmetic devices, 134
effect on array processor design, 268, 283
effect on function boxes, 123
effect on processor design, 13, 131, 158, 418

machine state of VCS, 115
machine states, 10*f*
MANIAC computer, 362
many-body problem, 264
mapping, from file to process space, 337
in CM*, 318
of array data, 201
of digitized images, 225
of hexagonal connections, 226
onto array processor, 166
mask (activity) register plane in AMA, 176
mask for selective PE control, 160
masks, as control elements, 217
for thinning, 234
in DAP, 258
masquerading in PP250, 331
master object table, 277, 357, 398

matrix inversion, 263
in DAP Fortran, 258
matrix multiplication, 218, 263
matrix operations in AMA, 217*f*
maze problem, 285
merge in DAP, 258
merging of array calculations, 202
MERLIN computer, 362
message, in IBM System/38, 323
in STAROS, 320
microcode, embedded, 128
in IBM System/38, 376
use in system, 118
micromachine, 39
in IBM System/38, 374*f*
microorder, 43
microPN, 380*f*
schematic, 389
microprocessor, 5, 63
interpretive control of, 37
revolution, 2
microprogram, abstraction, 379
horizontal, 146
in array processor design, 197
in system, 417
optimized, 133
security problems, 312
tactical use of, 128*f*
microsystem, 283, 343
design, 122
in PN machine, 393*f*
problems, 126*f*
mixed sequence in PN machine, 381
modification, in BLM, 350
operator, 16, 432
modular programming, 294
module in P, 396, 429, 437
multicomputer model, 6, 410

Nanodata QM-1, 43, 55
nanoinstruction, 43
null register value, 347
numeric representations used in P, 429

object of computation, 114
object in IBM System/38, 366
odd-even exchange sort, 207
operating environment, 18, 91
in BLM, 344*f*
in PN machine, 396
in VCS, 116
options in capability, 309, 315, 324

orthogonal instruction set, 103
overlay, in microprogram, 130
in multicomputer system, 132
ownership in IBM System/38, 369

P language, 380
P system function in PN machine, 396
package in ADA, 310
packaging, 292
of systems, 2
paging by SIL, 118*f*
paragraph in Cobol, 106
parallelism in programs, 169
parsing, 85
partition, physical, 413*f*
partitioning, of arrays, 279*f*
of programs, 293
PE schematic, for AMA, 183
for CLIP-3, CLIP-4, 238
for DAP, 247
for Illiac IV, 159
for Goodyear MPP, 282
perfect shuffle, application of, 223
PERFORM, in Cobol, 107
performance/cost compari-sons, 98
performance/cost in Cobol, 113
performance measures in AMA, 194*f*
performance, of active memory, 267
of address mapping in CM*, 319
of array processors, 166*f*
of BLM, 355
of capability cache, 342
of capability operations in PP250, 328
of capability operations in STAROS, 320
of language subsystem, 124*f*
of pilot DAP, 248, 253
of protection mechanism, 298
permutation in array, 222
personal computer, 131
picture coding, digital, 227
pipeline, ALU, 282
arithmetic, 143
in microprogram, 46, 149*f*
pixel, 225
plane pointer, 174
Plessey PP250, 321*f*

pointer formation, 271, 276, 298
Pointer Number machine (PN machine), 379*f*
pointer resolution in IBM System/38, 368
pointer types in IBM System/38, 366
pointer, global, 297
in access list, 297
in PN machine, 381
to system space, 18
used to access store, 16
portability, 169
portable language, 131
postfix addressing operators, 175
predictive store allocation strategies, 272
predictive use of cache, 343
preset control, 43
privacy of workspace, 348
private type in ADA, 310
privilege of code, 298
procedure, control block in CAP, 337
division in Cobol, 106
interface in P, 437
variable in Cobol, 108
process dump in PP250, 325
Process Resource List in CAP, 336
Process State Vector in BLM, 347
Processing Element, *see* PE, 158
projection, in AMA, 218
in DAP, 256
protected procedure in CAP, 335
protection, 380
boundaries, 393, 396
boundaries in BLM, 357
domain, 350
zone, 298
pseudo-multiplication, -divi-sion, 204

qualifier, 18, 94, 132, 278
in COBOL, 110
queue in IBM System/38, 373
quicksort, 214

range, archetype, 57
definition, 6, 127
strategy, 361
recycling, of indices, 278, 399
of intermediate results, 281
of storage, 271
reference to stack, 92

reference variable, 119, 359
register, transfer operations, 11*f*
types, 10
registers in microPN, 383
Release, in PN machine, 385
in VCS, 120
reliability of tagged systems, 357*f*
reordering functions in DAP, 256
residual control, 43
Rice University, 342, 362
rotation, in AMA, 193
of array data, 223
routing, costs in sorting, 212
effect on performance of, 168
in AMA, 163
in Illiac IV, 158
network, 144
planar, 179
subroutines in AMA, 189*f*
row and column selection in DAP, 257
row assignment and output in AMA, 175
run unit in COBOL, 105, 112
run-on effect, 46

save function, 181
scalar registers in PN machine, 383
scope, 302, 304
scratchpad, 7
access by micromachine, 59*f*
in EMMY, 105
on chip, 131
store, 48
searching in AMA, 216
secondary store transfer rates, 170
section in COBOL, 107
security, 37
of microprogram, 128, 133
of microsystem, 127
policy, 312
seeding in image processing, 230
segment, allocation in multi-computer, 132
capability, 314
construction of capability, 332
in ICL DAP, 244
table in access list management, 297
table in store manage-ment, 275
types in BLM, 345
types in PN machine, 385

selector in P, 433
semaphore, 120
sentence in Cobol, 106
sequencer, microprogram, 40
sequencing rule, 13f, 23
sequential machine design, 1
shared access to global seg-
    ments, 381
shift-exchange operation, 191,
    223
shifts in AMA, 190
shuffle of array elements,
    191, 223
shuffled-index sequence, 212
SIL, 99, 112, 341
    design of, 114f
    effect on performance
        measures of, 123
    requirements of, 95f
SIMD computers, 171
simplex method, 265
skewed data mapping, 168
slave store, 342
smoothing in image pro-
    cessing, 229
software engineering, practi-
    cal constraints of, 294,
    308, 333, 354
sorting, 207f
source module in COBOL,
    105, 109
spacing, effect on time of
    operation, 157
splitting of array calculations,
    202
square, bit-serial, 206
square root, bit-serial, 204
stack, frame in PN machine,
    384
    in BLM, 347
    in micromachine, 60
    in microprogram, 71
    in PP250, 326, 333
    in target machine, 88
    in VCS micromachine, 115
    vector, 92
Standard Computer Corpora-
    tion MLP-900, 55
Stanford University, 100
    EMMY, 55, 95f
STARAN, 284
STAROS, 317f
statement in Cobol, 106
static chain, 88
store management, 270f
subroutine interface, 180

subroutine, "parameterless",
    13
subsystem design, 1
summation of array elements
    in DAP, 257
SWARD architecture, 378
switch, 14
    in microprogram, 75
syllable, instruction, 87
synchronization of access to
    segments, 347
synchronized access to data,
    386
syntax of P control modules,
    441
System Capability Table in
    PP250, 324
system capability in PN
    machine, 387
System Implementation Lan-
    guage, see SIL, 83
system mode, interpretive, 32
system objects in IBM
    System/38, 366
system pointers, 117

tag, 318
    on capability, 314
    on data, 93, 106, 175
    user, 119
tag-dependent machine
    instructions, 349f
tagcheck, error, 390
    in microPN, 392, 400
tagged data segments, 118
tagged element, in BLM, 345
    in PN machine, 384
tagged register, 339, 364
tags in sorting, 222
target machine, 23
task, 114
    environment, 381, 383
    in PN machine, 398, 427
template, in DELtran, 99
    process definition in
        PP250, 332
terminal identifiers in P, 443
terminal symbols in P, 444
thinning in image processing,
    232
thresholding, 229
timing of microinstructions,
    44
tracking in image processing,
    232

transaction processing, 3, 292
translation of data in DAP,
    257
tridiagonal systems, 220, 224
    in DAP, 262
type check, in AMA, 175, 181
    in CLU, 305
    in P, 400, 439

Unger, proposal for image
    processor, 241
Univac 1108, 89
universal emulator, 31, 55
University College London,
    236
UNIX, 312
    job mix instruction fre-
        quency, 84
unsave function, 181
user mode, interpretive, 32
User Profile in IBM
    System/38, 369

valid address condition, 433
validity of pointer, 11
Variable Computer System,
    see VCS
variable precision arithmetic,
    55
VCS, access to microsystem,
    416
    checks on accessibility, 359
vector, assignment, 154
    operations in AP-120B,
        149
    processor schematic, 144
vectorizing compilers, 169,
    217
verb frequency in Cobol, 107
vertical data in AMA, 172
vertical microinstruction, 44
virtual address in IBM
    System/38, 376
VLSI, see LSI
von Neumann machine, 19,
    292

Warshall algorithm, 286
where clause in array assign-
    ment, 162, 444
window, in ADA specifica-
    tion, 310
    in CM* address space, 318
workspace in PN system, 381